MEXICANOS

A HISTORY OF MEXICANS IN THE UNITED STATES

MANUEL G. GONZALES

INDIANA UNIVERSITY PRESS · *Bloomington and Indianapolis*

This book is a publication of

Indiana University Press
601 North Morton Street
Bloomington, IN 47404-3797 USA

http://www.indiana.edu/~iupress

Telephone orders 800-842-6796
Fax orders 812-855-7931
Orders by e-mail iuporder@indiana.edu

The paper used in this publication meets the minimum
requirements of American National Standard for Information
Sciences—Permanence of Paper for Printed Library
Materials, ANSI Z39.48-1984.

Manufactured in the United States of America

Library of Congress Cataloging-in-Publication Data

Gonzales, Manuel G.
    Mexicanos : a history of Mexicans in the United States / Manuel G.
    Gonzales.
        p.   cm.
    Includes bibliographical references (p.   ) and index.
    ISBN 0-253-33520-5 (cloth : alk. paper)
    1. Mexican Americans—History.   I. Title.
E184.M5G638   1999
973'.046872—dc21   98-50954

    1   2   3   4   5   04   03   02   01   00   99

To my wife,
CYNTHIA LOUISE MERRILL,

and our daughters,
VANNA ANTONIA AND AMALIA MARTA

CONTENTS

ACKNOWLEDGMENTS

I owe a great deal to my professors of Latin American History at the University of California at Santa Barbara. These esteemed historians include Donald M. Dozer, Philip Wayne Powell, Lawrence Kinnaird, John Francis Bannon, and Jesús Chavarría. I also wish to express my appreciation to Professor Pedro Castillo, who selected me as one of his teaching assistants for the first course on Chicano History taught at UCSB.

The genesis of this book is to be found in a wonderful National Endowment for the Humanities summer seminar in 1986 taught by David J. Weber, "Southwestern America: New Approaches to the Hispanic Past, 1540–1910." I learned a great deal not only from Professor Weber, who encouraged me to resume my studies of the American Southwest, but also from my colleagues in the class: Dieter Berninger, Adrian Bustamante, Gilbert Din, Albert Hurtado, Ricki Janicek, Marta López-Garza, Kirk MacGugan, Hal Rothman, Federico Sánchez, and David Sandoval.

I wish to thank the many individuals who took time out from their own busy schedules to read all or part of my manuscript. They include my colleagues at Diablo Valley College, Patrick Leong, Ed Trujillo, and Ernie Valenzuela; Arnoldo De León of Angelo State University; Carlos Larralde of Golden West College; and David Weber of Southern Methodist University. David Sandoval, Lucero Arellano, and my daughter, Vanna, were also kind enough to read chapters and offer helpful suggestions. Although they expressed widely varying views of Chicano History, often at odds with my own interpretations, all my readers offered constructive criticisms and encouragement. From time to time they forced me to ask hard questions, a valuable service, and on many occasions they saved me from making embarrassing mistakes. Whatever inaccuracies are to be found in my work are clearly my sole responsibility.

Conversations with Olga Arenivár of Los Medanos College and Alex M. Saragoza of the University of California, Berkeley, provided me with greater insight into the Chicano movement and Chicano historiography respectively. I also owe a debt of gratitude to Alvaro Ochoa Serrano and Martín Sánchez Rodríguez, scholars at the Colegio de Michoacán, Zamora, who helped me gain a deeper understanding of Mexican immigration. Thanks, too, to my youngest daughter, Amalia, who asked provocative questions, shared pertinent insights and readings from her classes, and generally provided the valuable perspective that only a college student can contribute.

The staffs of the Chicano Studies libraries of the University of California at both Santa Barbara and Berkeley were extremely accommodating. I am especially indebted to Lillian Castillo-Speed, the head of Berkeley's Chicano Studies Library, who gave me generous counsel and went out of her way to help me find materials. Christine Marín, Curator/Archivist of the Chicano Research Collection at Arizona State University, also provided helpful advice and information. I am grateful as well to Walter Brem and the other librarians of the Bancroft Library at the University of California, Berkeley.

For help with illustrations, I am indebted to archivists Mario Einaudi, Arizona Historical Society; Santiago Hernández, Benson Latin American Collection, University of Texas, Austin; Kelly Hobbs, Fresno City and County Historical Society; and Tom Kreneck, Special Collections and Archives Department, Texas A&M University at Corpus Christi.

The Indiana University Press staff was exceptionally supportive. Robert J. Sloan, senior sponsoring editor; Jeffrey Ankrom, managing editor; and Cindy Ballard, assistant acquisitions editor, deserve special mention. Michael Baker was a superb copy editor. This project could not have been completed without their patience and dedication. It was a privilege to work with this talented group of professionals.

Lastly, I wish to thank my wife and able partner, Cindy Merrill Gonzales, who read the entire manuscript and was my most thorough critic, as well as my closest collaborator. During these many years, I appreciate, more than words can say, her moral support, always unconditional, and especially her unshakable optimism.

MEXICANOS

INTRODUCTION

The systematic study of Mexicans in the United States—popularly known as Chicano History—has its genesis in the turbulent decade spanning the late 1960s and early 1970s, when Mexican-American students at the University of California, inspired by the tenets of Chicanismo, hence calling themselves *Chicanos*, initiated a search for the historical roots of the *movimiento* (movement). These fledgling efforts, found notably in the influential and highly original journal *Aztlán*, soon expanded in scope. Aided by research in other social sciences, Chicano historians soon earned the grudging respect of large segments of the mainstream academic community. During the past thirty years Chicano scholarship has become increasingly sophisticated; indeed, much of this work has been on the cutting edge of research done on race, class, gender, and sexuality.[1]

Given the intellectual climate that spawned the profession, the study of Mexican-American history has been virtually monopolized by scholars who identify themselves with the movimiento. Today the academic discipline continues to be taught almost exclusively within the friendly confines of Chicano Studies departments rather than by History faculties. The ideal Chicano professor has been, and continues to be, the activist-scholar. Unfortunately, this ideological orientation has worked against the complete acceptance of Chicano historians and other Chicano scholars by their colleagues in the academy. Critics charge that research done by Chicanos is tainted. Regrettably, it must be admitted that there is some truth in this assertion. It is difficult, if not impossible, to accomplish the dual objectives ethnic historians have attempted since the sixties: that of giving a faithful account of the past while at the same time instilling ethnic pride in their people.

The tendency to accentuate the positive at the expense of the negative often makes for omissions and other distortions. For example, Chicano historiography has focused almost completely on heroes when describing the Mexican community; but most people, of whatever ethnic background, are not heroes, at least not most of the time. Moreover, I would argue, even *vendidos* ("sellouts") have a history. Anglos have been portrayed as equally one-dimensional; they are the greedy oppressors. Unfortunately, this "good guys–versus–bad guys" approach, as the historian Alex M. Saragoza has pointed out, was still in the ascendancy as the decade of the nineties opened.[2]

The dilemmas inherent in the traditional Chicano Studies approach to Mexican-American history have not escaped thoughtful Chicano historians, who, as social scientists, are dedicated to the search for objectivity. The kind of independence of mind that refused to accept the "internal colony" model as the official interpretation of Chicano Studies in the 1970s is still very much alive today.[3] The result in recent years has been a trend toward more nuanced interpretations, despite denunciations and charges of backsliding from the old sixties militants who continue to dominate ethnic studies departments.

It has been said that every generation rewrites its history. Certainly, present-day concerns influence the way we look at the past. I share the belief of many Chicano colleagues that given the dynamic changes that have taken place within the Mexican-American community during the past few years, the time is ripe for a fresh reassessment of the Chicano experience in our nation's past. During the last thirty years a significant body of literature relating to this experience—although nowhere near what has been written on African Americans or even native Americans—has developed in all the social sciences, much of it produced by Chicano scholars themselves, both male and female. The volume of this literature, as well as the growing interest in Chicanos due to recent demographic gains, justifies a new attempt at synthesis, the objective of this modest effort.

Though the field is relatively new, there are a number of good general studies which have addressed the subject from a historical perspective. The pioneering survey of Mexican-American history was Carey McWilliams's *North from Mexico*, which appeared in 1949.[4] All subsequent efforts to treat the subject owe a great deal to McWilliams, who approached his subject with intelligence and sympathy, and whose work, in many respects, remains unsurpassed. I am amazed at the book's continuing relevance every time I have occasion to use it. Most Chicano historians share my positive assessment.[5] The strength of *North from Mexico* was not only the painstaking research it reflects, but also the originality of its insights. Reissued in 1968, with a new Introduction by the author, the textbook dominated the field for years, both because of its inherent strengths and the dearth of other works on the subject.[6]

McWilliams ended his narrative in the mid-1940s. As time went by, this deficiency became more and more pronounced. A major attempt to bring McWilliams up to date was *The Chicanos: A History of Mexican Americans* by Matt S. Meier and Feliciano Rivera, historians from the University of Santa Clara and

California State University at San Jose respectively, who published their work in 1972.[7] As the title indicates, this volume tried to present a balanced and noncontroversial history of Mexicans in this country during a period of tremendous turmoil within ethnic communities. The book was very timely. It fulfilled a pressing need as Mexican Americans everywhere developed a passionate interest in their roots, among the most important by-products of the cultural regeneration engendered by the emerging Chicano movement. Although the authors relied heavily on the original research of McWilliams, as almost everyone else did before the 1970s, their book was an admirable attempt to synthesize the expanding literature on the subject. A revised and updated edition of this work, retitled *Mexican Americans/American Mexicans: From Conquistadores to Chicanos*, appeared in 1993.

The first real effort to provide fresh insights on Mexican-American history since McWilliams was *Occupied America: The Chicano's Struggle toward Liberation* by Rodolfo Acuña, also published in 1972.[8] His survey represented a major breakthrough. Trained in Latin American History, Acuña received his Ph.D. from the University of Southern California in 1968, before being appointed Professor of History at California State University at Northridge. During this period, Acuña was heavily influenced by the Chicano movement. A participant himself, he represented a new breed of scholar emerging at this time: Chicanos eager to write their own history from a minority perspective. Acuña offered a radical alternative—a "counterhegemonic work," as he would label it—to the moderate views of Meier and Rivera. The book was eagerly embraced during the seventies, especially in southwestern universities where Chicano Studies courses began to proliferate, and this work made Acuña "by far the most influential [Chicano] intellectual of the period."[9] He emphasized conflict and racial strife in his narrative, a point of view which appealed to young militants much more than the middle-of-the-road perspective of older Mexican-American and Anglo writers. Whether his philosophical orientation was an improvement on *The Chicanos* or not is open to debate, but no one would deny that Acuña uncovered a wealth of new material, especially for the period after World War II, and that his grasp of contemporary events was, and remains, unparalleled. Moreover, revised editions of his book (1981 and 1988), retitled *Occupied America: A History of Chicanos*, are commendable in their effort to describe the Chicano experience beyond the Southwest and to incorporate more material on Chicanas, the women of the ethnic community.

The Acuña book, however, was not without its critics.[10] They pointed out that the writing was often amateurish, the treatment of the subject uneven. An overreliance on statistics in the text—material that for the most part should have been relegated to footnotes—made it hard to see the forest for the trees. The work had no bibliographies, a deficiency not addressed in subsequent editions. The author's concern for labor history was laudable, but he spent entirely too much time on a long litany of strikes (almost all of them failures) in an attempt to disprove "the myth of Mexican docility." Acuña had little to say about the period before the Mexican-American War, an oversight which makes it impossible to understand many important aspects of Chicano life after 1848.

But the main flaws were those that continue to characterize Professor Acuña's work today, a narrow focus and a lack of balance. Purportedly a history of Chicanos, *Occupied America* was actually a history of Chicano-Anglo relations; or, more specifically, as the original title suggested, a history of Anglo oppression of *La Raza* (literally, "The Race," another designation for the Mexican-origin population in the United States). Mexicans in this country, we are told, have been subjected to an endless series of abuses by racist Anglos from the mid-nineteenth century to the present. While Acuña assures us that Chicanos have resisted in every way possible, his negative assessment of their socioeconomic status today would indicate that the forces of evil have ultimately triumphed, a point of view he graphically illustrates in his latest book, *Anything but Mexican: Chicanos in Contemporary Los Angeles* (1996). Thus, Acuña represents the chief exponent of the school of Chicano historians who advocate a "good guys–versus–bad guys" approach to the study of Chicano history. Not surprisingly, when Dr. Acuña's bid for a position in the Chicano Studies department of the University of California at Santa Barbara was denied in 1991, UC officials justified their decision by claiming that his scholarship was "more political and passionate than objective and substantive."[11]

In both revised editions of *Occupied America*, the author moderated his views. But the lack of objectivity remains the central problem. In his second edition, Acuña readily admitted that his book was written "to expose past injustices in order to correct present inequities and prevent future ones."[12] Ultimately, he had a broader vision. His third edition, according to the cultural historian Richard García, "is a cry for a return to the spirit of the 1960s in order to re-establish the unity, the action, and the community of that period," a noble but quixotic effort by "the last Rousseauian romantic," an intellectual who has lost touch with the times.[13] This failure on his part is unfortunate because Rodolfo Acuña, author of more than a dozen books, deserves more credit for his historical investigations than he has received by colleagues outside the field of Chicano Studies.

Essentially, what is wrong with Rodolfo Acuña's perspective is that the Chicano—a term he and others use interchangeably with Mexican American—is reduced to a victim, albeit a struggling victim. This feature is most apparent in the first edition of the book, where Acuña popularized the internal colonial model, "the quintessential victimization framework," according to Professor Saragoza.[14] No Chicano historian today would deny that oppression has been severe—Professor Acuña has chronicled this register of crimes and misfortunes so thoroughly that it is beyond dispute—but to dwell on this one aspect is to tell only part of the story. There are still many vital questions to be probed. What about the role of women? The dynamics of the Chicano family? The relationship between Mexican immigrants and native-born Chicanos? The victimization approach, furthermore, misrepresents the status of Chicanos, historically and at present. Yes, there are severe problems in Chicano communities today, as Acuña avers, but what about the achievements? A veritable cultural renaissance has occurred among Chicanos during the past thirty years. Acuña tends to neglect this and other positive aspects of the Chicano experience. Historians need to approach their subject in the context of objectivity.

Fortunately, a start in this direction has already been made. Beginning in the early 1980s, some Chicano historians started to recognize the complexity of their history and to take issue with some, though not all, of the major premises of the nationalistic approach championed by Rodolfo Acuña.[15] These scholars—the most insightful and prolific historians have been Arnoldo De León, Mario T. García, Juan Gómez-Quiñones, and Richard Griswold del Castillo—have subjected the Chicano past to greater scrutiny than ever before, constructing a picture of Chicanos—and Chicanas—that bears little resemblance to the monolithic victim portrayed in the 1970s.[16] We are discovering that there has always been great diversity in Mexican-American communities, distinctions created by geography, race, gender, class, and other factors. One result has been a proliferation of studies on aspects of Chicano history that were neglected previously. These new studies and others currently under way will make it more difficult to generalize about Chicanos over time, but they will present a truer-to-life portrait of what the Mexican experience has been in this country. In my study, I hope to synthesize the fruits of this recent scholarship, most of it hidden away in the pages of historical journals rather than in books, and thus largely inaccessible to the nonprofessional.

Although not a complete survey of the subject, one other study deserves special mention. In 1973, David J. Weber, then a young history professor at California State University at San Diego, published an excellent introduction to Chicano history, *Foreigners in Their Native Land: Historical Roots of the Mexican Americans*.[17] Ostensibly an anthology of documents, this work was actually a brief and insightful synopsis of Mexican-American history during the nineteenth century. Although generally in agreement with the radical interpretations of Acuña and other contemporary Chicano scholars—Juan Gómez-Quiñones and Luis Leobardo Arroyo lauded his book as "an innovative and significant contribution to Chicano history"[18]—Weber placed the history in a broader context and, as is typical of his work, maintained a high academic standard. His volume is important because despite his youth, Weber, already a respected scholar, gave much-needed credibility to the emerging field of Chicano history. He also provided a model of excellence which many Chicano historians have attempted to emulate. Having written his introduction to Mexican-American history, Weber chose not to pursue this scholarly path, insisting that their history should best be left to minority scholars themselves. Focusing instead on the Spanish Borderlands, he is widely considered the leading authority in this field of study.

The five authors above have built a firm foundation. Virtually every course in Chicano History uses one of their books as the course text. All of them have made valuable contributions, which I have incorporated into my own work. I owe a debt of gratitude to all of them.

Although I have never been an activist and by temperament am inclined to avoid affiliation with any group, I consider myself a Chicano historian; that is, I experienced the movimiento and I was influenced by it in a positive way. While I sometimes take Chicano/a colleagues to task, my criticisms have more to do with differences of interpretation than with fundamental principles. I should also make it clear at the outset that my academic training has made me more sensitive to class than to race. I was influenced by Marxism as a college student at UC Santa Barbara, like many other Chicano/a scholars who received their training in the 1960s and 1970s. Although I still accept many Marxist tenets—that people are moved primarily by self-interest is undeniable, in my view—this perspective is a secondary rather than a primary theme in my work.

What I hope to accomplish is a concise and balanced account of the history of Mexicans in the United States, including background information beginning in the sixteenth century. I propose to incorporate the latest findings on the subject, paying particular attention to the work found in professional journals of history and related disciplines. Throughout, my major emphasis will be on narrative history—which concerns itself with who did what when—but when dealing with interpretations, I will attempt to maintain objectivity and let the chips fall where they may. While realizing the impossibility of writing a value-free study, I still maintain faith in what one Chicano historian has labeled "the so-called ideal of objectivity."[19] I am convinced that every people has a valid and interesting history, and Mexican Americans are no exception. Our story needs no embellishments. I will describe our triumphs as well as our trials and tribulations.

Since I am sometimes critical of what have become mainstream interpretations in Chicano Studies departments during the past thirty years, many of my Chicano colleagues will find my work excessively conservative. This perception may not only have something to do with the generation gap but also with the fact that my academic training in Modern European and Latin American History has encouraged me to look at Chicano History with a certain sense of detachment. However, being an outsider has its advantages. Moreover, I believe that there is room in the field for moderate as well as radical interpretations. In fact, I have discovered that there is a good deal of diversity among Chicano historians, a trend that will become more rather than less pronounced as time goes by.

Most of all, I have tried in this history to provide a balanced view of the Mexican experience. One example is my belief that the Indian and the Spanish heritage are equally important in explaining the rise of Mexican culture, the matrix of Chicano culture. The accepted position among most Chicano scholars today—as the Columbus debate made clear recently—is to glorify Indian contributions and to denigrate those of the Spaniards. This perspective reflects the anti-imperialistic sentiments that spawned the radical movements of the 1960s, when Chicano/a Studies were born. This view is also a reaction to an older generation of scholars, mainly Latin Americanists, who made exaggerated claims for the Spaniards in their attempt to demolish the Black Legend, the portrayal of Spaniards as inherently evil. Psychologically, I have always identified myself as an Indian and tend to sympathize with "underdogs," but in the Indian-versus-Spaniard debate it seems to me that the pendulum has swung too far in the other direction. As Carlos Fuentes, Mexico's leading novelist, has pointed out, the Spaniards brought great gifts to the Americas—first and foremost the language—as well as great evils. Strong people do not go around apologizing for their roots.

My work may also displease some Chicana scholars, who will point out that women do not receive nearly the attention they deserve in my narrative. This is a valid criticism. In fact, this is a glaring deficiency in the entire field of Ethnic Studies, though valiant efforts are being made to correct it, notably by Chicanas themselves.[20] However, I would point out once again that my work is a synthesis of studies in the field (I make no pretense of doing original research myself); and, as noted above, Chicanos have not given their sisters as much attention as they warrant. Moreover, with few exceptions, it was only in the 1980s that Chicanas began to study their own history. One of the problems is the small numbers of women scholars in the field. "Of the hundreds of historians across the United States," according to my colleague Angelina F. Veyna, "there are only about 20 women today who personally identify as Chicana historians."[21] I would guess that at present there are less than a dozen published book-length studies by Chicana historians.[22] In other words, the history is there, but it remains largely untold.

Finally, a word on terminology is in order. Based on interviews conducted in 1989–1990, the Latino National Political Survey (LNPS), the first nationally representative sample to provide solid empirical evidence about how Latinos see themselves, concluded that the most popular self-referent among people of Mexican background in the United States was *Mexican*. According to Rodolfo O. de la Garza, a respected political scientist at the University of Texas and one of the authors of the study, 62 percent of people of Mexican heritage born in this country preferred this term, as did 86 percent of the immigrant population.[23] In light of these surprising findings, many Chicano scholars have abandoned the term *Chicano* for the term *Mexican* in their writings, a practice that I too will employ, especially since I plan to investigate newcomers as well as the native-born. When there is a need to distinguish between native-born and immigrants, I will use *Mexican Americans* for the former and *Mexicanos* (and/or *Mexicanas*) for the latter. To avoid confusion, the term *Chicanos* (and/or *Chicanas*) will be employed to specify members of the Mexican community who, during the 1960s and subsequently, endorsed the major tenets of Chicanismo; that is, Mexican Americans who, as the journalist Rubén Salazar defined them, had a non-Anglo image of themselves. Although Chicano historians generally dislike the term *Hispanics*—mainly because they feel that it stresses the European legacy to the complete exclusion of indigenous roots—I will use the term, which is commonly used by others, interchangeably with the preferred *Latinos* (and/or *Latinas*) when referring to Americans of Latin American descent; that is, all Spanish-speaking people in the United States, exclusive of Spaniards and their descendants. *Tejanos*, *Californios*, and *Hispanos* (and/or their feminine forms) will designate native-born Spanish-speaking inhabitants of Texas, California, and New Mexico respectively.

SPANIARDS AND NATIVE AMERICANS

PREHISTORY–1521

1

Mexican American is a term devoid of meaning before 1848. The number of Mexicans residing in the United States before the Mexican Cession was negligible. Yet it would be a mistake to begin this history with the Treaty of Guadalupe Hidalgo, for the roots of Mexican-American history are buried in the distant past. In order to understand the people and their culture it is necessary to go back at least to the sixteenth century. Like most other Latin Americans, Mexicans are predominantly *mestizos*; that is, they are products of race mixture. When Spaniards invaded the New World in the 1500s and initiated contact with Amerindians in Mexico, the genesis of the Mexican community in the United States began.

After a period of political and economic stagnation in the fourteenth century, the Renaissance, centered primarily in Italy, witnessed not only a tremendous expansion of Europe's intellectual and artistic horizons but also an enormous widening of its geographical limits. The Age of Exploration represents the first major expansion of the Europeans, who subsequently came to dominate much of the globe, thanks primarily to their superior technological development. Inspired by God, Gold, and Glory, Europeans pushed their frontiers in all directions, with their most significant acquisition being the New World. America was named after an Italian explorer, Amerigo Vespucci, but in the forefront of the process of discovery and conquest were the Spaniards, the chief beneficiaries of this initial wave of Western imperialistic activity.

THE SPANIARDS

Who were the Spaniards and why were they so successful? Like other Europeans, Spaniards are a product of a multiplicity of cultures. Spanish history can be traced back to the Upper Paleolithic period (35,000 B.C.–10,000 B.C.), when primitive people dwelling in the Iberian Peninsula began to leave evidence of an emerging culture. Cave paintings, like those discovered in the 1890s in Altamira, near the northern port of Santander, illustrate the amazing creativity of these early inhabitants. These ancient pictures, mostly abstract depictions of animal life, have led modern scholars to designate the Upper Paleolithic the Cradle of Art.

The following millennia are shrouded in mystery but the Iberian Peninsula, a natural bridge between two continents, must have attracted a variety of people. Among them were Iberians, "dwellers along the Ebro River," as they came to be called by the Greeks; Basques, whose origins are still much debated; Celts, who dominated the region in the period 900 B.C.–650 B.C.; Phoenicians, contemporaries of the Celts, who established colonies from their base in the eastern Mediterranean; and Greeks, who came at around 600 B.C. to settle the coastal areas.

Undoubtedly, however, the most influential of the ancient peoples to arrive were the Romans.[1] Victors against Carthage, a Phoenician colony in modern-day Tunis, Roman legions acquired Hispania (their name for Spain) as a prize in 202 B.C., at the end of the Second Punic War. The Celt-Iberians put up a mighty resistance but in the end Rome's famed legions prevailed. Though exploited as colonials, the natives received valuable concessions from the Romans. Some of them went on to win fame and fortune within the Empire. Seneca, the brilliant Stoic philosopher, and Hadrian, one of Rome's most powerful Caesars, were from Hispania. The cultural contributions Rome bestowed far outweighed the material riches it extorted from its conquered subjects. Rome imposed its laws, one of its finest achievements. It contributed Latin, which eventually gave rise to Castilian Spanish, a language so beautiful that reading it is still an emotional experience, as well as Catalán and Gallego. Rome also brought a belief system, Christianity, made the official religion of the Empire in the fourth century and a force second to none in shaping the emerging national character of the people.

Increasingly beset by political and economic problems, the Roman Empire weakened after the third century of the Christian era; and, overrun by Germanic tribes who administered the *coup de grâce*, the western half collapsed by the fifth century. Vandals now controlled North Africa, Franks reigned supreme in France, and even Italy found itself occupied, first by Ostrogoths, later by Lombards. The Visigoths, following other northern tribes, settled in Spain, establishing their capital in Toledo. However, Germanic influence proved to be short-lived.

"Spain," its detractors are fond of saying, echoing a statement originally attributed to Alexandre Dumas, "begins at the Pyrenees." In fact, the impact of African culture has been profound on the Spanish psyche, something Spaniards were unwilling to concede until recently. Taking their cue from the philosopher

Miguel de Unamuno, Spanish intellectuals in the early part of the twentieth century began to reassess the role of the Moors in their history. Now most Spaniards find the Moorish legacy a source of considerable pride. The historian Américo Castro felt that Spanish history began with the arrival of the Moors in 711, when Tarik ibn Zizad led seven thousand Berber troops, recent converts to Islam, on a religious crusade across the Strait of Gibraltar. The campaign was a huge success; the peninsula was overrun at breakneck speed. The Moors (Berber and Arab Moslems) penetrated into western Europe as far north as modern-day Poitiers; where, with their religious zeal waning and their lines of communication overextended, they were finally stopped by Germanic Franks under Charles Martel. Retreating across the Pyrenees, Moslems began to consolidate their conquest of the Iberian Peninsula, the western frontier of a vast empire. Islamic Spain came to be known as al-Andalus.

As Europe declined during its Middle Ages, the mantle of civilization shifted to the East—to Constantinople, the center of the Byzantine Empire, and to the Islamic World beyond. Moslem strength reached its zenith in the eighth century, when Islamic ships gained control of the Mediterranean, putting the Byzantines on the defensive. The caliphate was transferred from Damascus to Baghdad, in modern Iraq, in 750; and during the next few decades wealth from throughout the far-flung empire poured into that magnificent city, fueling an enormous upsurge of intellectual activity. Thereafter, the Islamic world itself began to weaken, mainly because of internal problems. In the year 1000 there were three caliphates instead of one, as Baghdad was now rivaled by Cairo and Córdoba. By this time, Moorish Spain, completely independent of Baghdad, had created a brilliant culture.

Moors occupied the Iberian Peninsula for over 750 years. During this period their influence came to permeate every aspect of life, especially in the south, in today's Andalusía, where they established their major cities, including Sevilla, Córdoba, and Granada. During their heyday in the tenth, eleventh, and twelfth centuries, they developed a civilization that was the envy of their northern neighbors. Moorish scholars not only helped to preserve the classical heritage of the West, but they also made significant contributions of their own, notably in the arts, literature, mathematics, and philosophy. The most original Moorish man of letters was Averroës (1126–1198), an authority on Aristotle and a powerful influence on Christian thinkers during the late Middle Ages.

The culture of al-Andalus was also enhanced by Jewish scholars. The diaspora into Iberia, which began as early as the second century A.D., had produced a flourishing Jewish community in Moorish Spain; which, though open to exotic elements, largely maintained its own traditions, a freedom conceded by Tarik and his successors. The Jews prospered. They established academies in Barcelona,

Córdoba, Granada, and Toledo. They translated the Talmud into Arabic. Their men of letters were renowned throughout the realm. Undoubtedly the most celebrated of these Sephardic thinkers, possibly the greatest philosopher Spain has ever produced, was Maimonides (1135–1204), who lived in Córdoba, like his contemporary, Averroës.

While the Moors enjoyed a happy coexistence with the Jews—at least until 1146, when a fanatical Islamic sect from Morocco, the Almohades, introduced religious intolerance—their relationship with the rest of the conquered population was far more complicated. From time to time the two peoples, colonizers and colonized, got along reasonably well; trade took place and intermarriage occurred. Some Christians, called *mozárabes*, assimilated Moslem culture. These amiable relations, however, were the exception rather than the rule. For the most part, there was animosity on both sides. From the very beginning of Moslem colonization, a small enclave of resistance emerged in Asturias, in the mountainous northwestern corner of the peninsula. Under the leadership of the legendary Pelayo, this liberation movement, called the *Reconquista* (Reconquest) by Spanish historians, was modest at first. But by the thirteenth century, when Christian successes—notably the famous victory by King Alfonso VIII of Castilla at Las Navas de Tolosa in 1212—forced the Moors to take refuge in Granada and its surrounding area, it had become a mass movement.

By now, too, religion had come to play a vital role in Spanish life. Every campaign against the Moors was a holy crusade. Although the Age of the Christian Crusades is generally assumed to have begun in 1095, when Pope Urban II launched the first crusade against the Saracens in an effort to regain the holy city of Jerusalem, Spanish knights by this time had a long tradition of warring against their Islamic adversaries under the banner of Santiago (Saint James), their patron saint. As in Ireland after the Protestant Reformation, religion in Spain came to be wedded to nationalism. The result was a very militant form of Catholicism. The Spaniards' fanatical devotion to their faith, reflected later in the Holy Office of the Inquisition (1480–1812) and in the zeal with which they proselytized Amerindians, is rooted in these early crusades.

The Moors had a far-reaching impact on Iberian culture, on agriculture, music, and language; but none was more influential than the profound religiosity that they wove into the fabric of life of the Spanish people. "Spain is perhaps the most avidly Roman Catholic country in Europe," it is generally agreed, "both in the sense of its official affiliation with the church in Rome and to the degree that the culture is permeated and uniquely colored by it."[2]

The marriage of Ferdinand of Aragón and Isabella of Castilla in 1469 paved the way for the final stage of the Reconquest. *Los Reyes Católicos* (The Catholic Kings), as they styled themselves, were deeply religious. However, both monarchs were equally absorbed with achieving political ends, especially Ferdinand, who was later used as a model by Machiavelli. In early January 1492, Granada, the last Islamic stronghold, was taken through force of arms and the Moors were expelled from the country. Jewish expulsion followed a few months later. The unification of Spain was now complete.

The religious zeal that had resulted in the campaigns against *judíos* (Jews) and *moros* (Moors) was soon transferred overseas. In 1492 a New World was discovered with millions of potential converts and Spain was anxious to propagate the faith. The Spaniards were ideally situated to play this pioneering role not only because of their early creation of a unified national dynastic state but also because of their geographical position. Jutting out into the Atlantic, the Iberian Peninsula would be the launching pad for the early voyages of exploration.

It was the Portuguese, Spain's Iberian neighbors, who took the lead at the outset. Up to the twelfth century, Portugal was part of León, one of several provinces which emerged from the lands reclaimed from the Moors. During these years there developed a distinct Portuguese sense of nationalism as well as a separate language. By the end of the twelfth century, a robust dynastic state was competing with those in other parts of the peninsula. The most famous of the Braganzas, the ruling family, was the son of King Joao I, Henrique, better known as Prince Henry the Navigator (1394–1460), who is credited with initiating Portugal's interest in overseas exploration and settlement. This fascination was primarily economic in nature. At first, the Portuguese sought to monopolize trade with West Africa, which was rich in gold reserves. Eventually, as is well known, they became obsessed with the quest for an all-water route to *Las Indias* (The Indies), a vague geographical area that consisted of Southeast Asia and its offshore islands, the source of the coveted spices which had enriched Indians, Arabs, and especially Italians. The fantastic profits made by the *veneziani* (Venetians) and *genovesi* (Genoans) go a long way in explaining the Italian Renaissance. By the mid-fifteenth century, Portuguese mariners trained at Sagres, a maritime academy established by Prince Henry on Portugal's southernmost cape, were venturing out into the Atlantic. Having some knowledge of Africa's contours, apparently based on Phoenician sources, the Portuguese felt that by sailing south they could get around the continent, thus arriving on the Indian Ocean, the gateway to the vast riches of the Orient.

During the course of these epic fifteenth-century voyages, the Portuguese discovered and laid claim to several valuable islands, the Azores and the Madeiras being the most attractive to mainland entrepreneurs. They also initiated the slave trade in West Africa, the pernicious traffic in human beings which yielded fantastic financial profits to Europeans until its demise in the nineteenth century. A long series of arduous expeditions culminated in 1488 when Bartholomeu Dias rounded the Cape of Good Hope. Ten years later, in what is arguably the greatest maritime voyage of the Age of Exploration, Vasco da Gama reached Calicut in India, thus inaugurating Portugal's short-lived golden age. In fact, this voyage brought about a momentous transformation in the balance of power. In the aftermath of da Gama's successful mission, the world's major theater of commercial activity was rapidly transferred from the Mediterranean Sea to the Atlantic Ocean, an economic shift signaling the decline of Italy, and ultimately its cultural hegemony, and the rise of Western Europe. The primary beneficiary of this imperious change, however, was not Portugal but rather its larger and more powerful neighbor, Spain.

One of the supreme ironies in history is that the most famous figure in Spanish history should be an Italian. The Genovese Cristoforo Colombo (1451–1506) was a native of a nation with a proud and glorious past but one rapidly eclipsed during his lifetime by his adopted homeland. Though ironic, Columbus's role is not surprising. The Renaissance was a cosmopolitan period when nationalism was only just emerging—in many parts of Europe, regional allegiances continue to predominate over national sentiments to this day—and movement between nations, while limited by technological and financial impediments, was relatively easy. At a time when maritime skills were highly valued, Italian mariners, the best in Europe at the time, found their services much in demand, and they displayed little temerity in hiring out to foreign employers. Giovanni Caboto, who sailed for the English under the name John Cabot, and Giovanni da Verrazano, a contemporary and one of France's leading explorers, are good examples. Columbus himself seemed to have few qualms about living in Spain and serving its rulers.

The details of Columbus's life are vague but its general outlines are clear enough. The son of a wool weaver, Cristoforo spent his youth learning the skills of seamanship, and by his early twenties he was already making regular trips throughout the Mediterranean aboard Italian vessels. Eventually, in 1479, he wound up in Lisbon, where he married Felipa Perestrello e Moniz, daughter of an Italian mariner and a member of one of Portugal's oldest families. They settled down in Porto Santo, a small island, part of the Madeira Archipelago, where Columbus went into the chart business.

This livelihood was but a means to an end—Columbus dreamed of tapping the enormous wealth of the Spice Islands, known as the Moluccas to the Portuguese. He was aware of Portuguese expeditions moving south along the African coast, but he came to believe that the fabled lands, rich in silks, spices, and gems, could best be reached sailing westward. He initiated a series of petitions in an effort to win financial backing to prove his theories. Upon the death of his wife in 1485, he left for Spain. After an initial rebuke, followed by many trials and tribulations, he convinced Queen Isabella, apparently won over by his charm and bulldog determination, to back the risky enterprise.

The *Niña*, the *Pinta*, and the *Santa María* left the port of Palos de la Frontera on 3 August 1492. Taking on supplies at the Canary Islands, the tiny ships then struggled across the Atlantic. Having miscalculated drastically, the admiral was forced to alter his ship log to bolster the flagging morale of his men. On 12 October, his crew on the verge of mutiny, Columbus sighted land. He had arrived somewhere in the Bahamas. Sailing southwestward, the expedition came upon Cuba and Española, islands which would later be used as a springboard for exploration in every direction. Columbus returned to Spain with a small number of natives and just enough gold to convince his patrons of his success; and incidentally, as Alistair Cooke aptly notes, to initiate "the longest, most determined, and most brutal gold rush in history."[3]

The Admiral of the Ocean Sea made three subsequent voyages to the New World. Although these expeditions were largely disappointing, since they earned him little fame or fortune, Columbus believed he had reached Asia, a misconception he apparently maintained to his death on 20 May 1506.

It is not easy to assess Columbus's role in history. In the past, most historians have agreed with the eminent biographer Samuel Eliot Morison, who saw in Columbus not only a great mariner but also the most remarkable figure of his age. Today, however, the Italian explorer is perceived less favorably.[4] Given the current loss of faith in Carlyle's Great Man Theory of History, scholars are less impressed by elites than they used to be. More importantly, however, Columbus is currently associated with European imperialism, a discredited and much-maligned phenomenon of the postcolonial world. Critics, especially in societies where multiculturalism has become increasingly popular, charge that Columbus saw Indians as inferior and treated them accordingly. His legacy was not confined to the exploitation of peoples; he is also vilified for initiating the European assault on the virgin environment. Kirkpatrick Sale in his popular 1990 work *The Conquest of Paradise: Christopher Columbus and the Columbian Legacy* argues trenchantly for this revisionist interpretation.

While Columbus was guilty of ethnocentrism and exploitation of peoples and resources, he was typical of his age. While the period of the Renaissance and Reformation was an epoch of almost unprecedented artistic and intellectual achievement, it was also an age of barbarism and intolerance. "It was . . . a time much given to terror, war, pestilence, famine, slavery and religious persecution, most emphatically not one to encourage gentleness or ecological concern."[5] While Europeans took advantage of native Americans, it is also true that they victimized each other. Nor were the native peoples morally superior. "The innocence of the indigenous Americans," John Noble Wilford reminds us, "was more imagined than real. To one degree or another, they knew warfare, brutality, slavery, human sacrifice, and cannibalism."[6] Certainly, there was nothing peculiarly European about exploitation; the Age of Columbus would not be the first time that the strong would take advantage of the weak, nor would it be the last. Finally, it can be argued, if Columbus was no better than his contemporaries, he was certainly no worse. While this era is sometimes called the Age of Titans, few of these so-called titans were noted for their saintly qualities, certainly not Machiavelli, nor even Luther. These individuals suffice to remind us that greatness is not defined by moral character but by influence. Perhaps the best assessment of the much-maligned explorer is given by the Oxford historian Felipe Fernández-Armesto: "The real Columbus was a mixture of virtues and vices like the rest of us, not conspicuously good or just, but generally well-intentioned, who grappled credit-ably with intractable problems."[7]

THE AMERINDIANS

Although Europeans often saw the Americas as "virgin" territory, at the time of contact, according to current estimates, the two continents were occupied by almost one hundred million inhabitants. Under the mistaken assumption that he had reached Las Indias, Columbus referred to the people as *Indios*, and the term *Indians* came to be applied to them. Today, however, many tribal Americans prefer the term *native Americans* (*Indian* and *native American* will be used interchange-ably in this work). From the very beginning, there was enormous heterogeneity among the native peoples of the Americas; indeed, as the historian Wilcomb E. Washburn has pointed out, there was probably more diversity among native Americans than there was among the various European ethnic groups who came to colonize the area.[8] This diversity belies a common origin.

The question of Indian origins is still the leading question of New World archaeology. While it can be stated categorically that native Americans did not evolve from lower forms of animal life independently in the New World—the genesis of human beings apparently occurred in east central Africa some three to five million years ago—there is much speculation as to their migration. One famous theory, endorsed by the Church of Jesus Christ of Latter Day Saints as well as a few non-Mormon scholars, is that all or most Indians are descended from people who migrated from the eastern Mediterranean basin. The most promi-nent hypothesis, however, has its origins in 1589 when a Spanish Jesuit, José de Acosta (c. 1539–1600), guessed that native Americans were descended from Asian peoples, a notion based on physical characteristics.[9]

The rise of modern science has tended to substantiate this latter theory, now called the Bering Strait Hypothesis, though in a much more sophisticated form. According to this view, the first nomads entered the Americas via an ice or land bridge connecting modern-day Siberia and Alaska sometime between 50,000 B.C. and the end of the last Ice Age around 10,000 B.C. Today this body of water is the Bering Strait (hence the designation of the theory), named after Vitus Bering (1680–1741), a Danish navigator who sailed through it during the eighteenth century. The consensus of informed opinion is that the first immigrants were a small band of hunters and gatherers who came in search of large game animals in about 30,000 B.C. They were probably *Homo sapiens sapiens*, that is, anatomically they were identical to humans living today, though scholars are not in agreement here. It appears there were several incoming waves of nomadic hunters, with the Eskimos representing the last large-scale migration, sometime shortly before the time of Jesus Christ. Penetrating south along the slopes of the Rockies, these nomads eventually diffused in all directions over the course of several millennia, finally arriving at the southern tip of the Americas sometime around 8,000 B.C. This theory of Mongolian origin and north-to-south migration is supported by the artifact record, as well as specialized studies of blood types, dental records, and linguistic analysis.

When Europeans first encountered them, native Americans were found throughout the Western Hemisphere. However, they were not living uniformly throughout the two continents. Clearly, there was a tendency by these early immigrants to avoid less attractive areas, tropical rain forests and deserts, and to seek healthier environments—preferably in moderate zones, or, when forced into the tropics, in highland areas. When Europeans arrived in the Americas, there were two large centers of population concentration: the Andean altiplano and Mesoamerica.

While the tribal peoples of South America are fascinating, this area is not essential in explaining the roots of the people of Mexico and their communities in the United States. It is the tribes of Mesoamerica that provide the key to an understanding of the Mexicans' Indian legacy.[10] The heavy population density of Mesoamerica reflected the advent of agriculture. The transition from a nomadic to a sedentary society seems to have occurred first in the highlands of south central Mexico. Certainly it was there, according to studies made by the Canadian anthropologist Richard S. MacNeish in the Tehuacán Valley in the state of Puebla, that corn (or maize), the basis of all Mesoamerican civilizations, was initially cultivated in around 5,000 B.C. From this source, the cultivation of maize spread both north and south. By the time Europeans arrived in the Americas, corn had been introduced into the Southwest and throughout the eastern part of North America via the Mississippi Valley. Amerindians cultivated a variety of crops, including beans, squash, tomatoes, avocados, potatoes, and pumpkins, but it was corn that made possible the rise of cities, the urban revolution which inaugurates the rise of civilization.

The first of the pre-Columbian civilizations of the Americas developed in the lowlands of southern Vera Cruz and Tabasco, near the shores of the Caribbean Sea, not far from the cradle of agriculture on the central plateau. Discovered in the late 1930s, by the American archaeologist Matthew W. Stirling, the ruins of these first cities, San Lorenzo and La Venta being the most impressive, have been dated as early as 1200 B.C. Built by a people who came to be called the Olmecs, after a later tribe of the same name, these first urban clusters were actually ceremonial centers rather than full-fledged cities.

The artifact record permits scholars to reconstruct a general outline of Olmec life. The economic mainstay of this advanced society, of all pre-Columbian civilizations, was agriculture. In addition to corn, farmers cultivated squashes, peppers, and tomatoes. However, there was also some manufacturing and considerable commerce. Having abandoned a nomadic lifestyle, the Olmecs, like other peoples in similar circumstances, began to develop a stratified society. At the top were priests, who exerted political power, which they shared with the nobility. Since warfare was common—the rise of civilization increases the amount of strife in society wherever it occurs—the nobles were a warrior aristocracy. Merchants and artisans constituted a small percentage of the population, but they exerted an influence far greater than their modest numbers might indicate, as there is evidence of an extensive trading network. The majority of the people, the commoners, were peasants. They lived on the outskirts of the ceremonial centers and in the surrounding countryside. At the bottom of the social pecking order were undoubtedly slaves, probably war captives from other tribes and Olmec citizens who forfeited their freedom because of mounting debts.

The relative affluence of Olmec society permitted the rise of a complex and advanced culture. A rudimentary hieroglyphic writing system (not yet deciphered) evolved, perhaps—as in Mesopotamia and other early civilizations—an innovation introduced by merchants to facilitate financial transactions. A calendar permitted farmers to keep track of time. Another remarkable element of Olmec culture was art. Some experts have argued that the Olmecs superseded all pre-Columbian peoples in this regard. Their most prominent artistic creations were massive monolithic stone heads. Made of basalt, most stand about eight feet high. Evidence of a high degree of sophistication, these beautiful colossal heads may reflect an African influence. (Undoubtedly, as New World archaeology progresses, scholars will discover that there were many transoceanic contacts between the Americas and other continents, including Africa, only 1,500 miles from the Brazilian coast.) The most vital aspect of Olmec culture was religion, which influenced every aspect of life. The Olmecs believed in a variety of deities (polytheism). These gods were highly revered; and there is good reason to believe that they exacted, through their priests, continual sacrifices, including human sacrifices, one of the outstanding characteristics of virtually all Mesoamerican civilizations. In general, these civilizations displayed amazing similarities, which suggests that they had a common heritage, probably the Olmecs.

Olmec civilization came to an end shortly before the Christian Era for reasons yet to be explained; but in the epoch between A.D. 300 and A.D. 900, the classical period of New World civilization, there was an extraordinary flowering of culture in Mexico. During this golden age, a number of civilizations rose to prominence. One centered on Monte Albán, an elaborate ceremonial citadel discovered in the 1930s in the southern Mexican state of Oaxaca. Built by the Zapotecs, the city, high atop an artificially flattened hill, was the focal point of an extensive empire that was influenced by both Olmecs and Mayas. Dominated by a powerful priesthood, Monte Albán flourished until the ninth century. Occupied thereafter by Mixtecs, a neighboring tribe to the west, the city was eventually abandoned; and, overgrown with jungle, it soon sank into oblivion.

In the Valley of Mexico, site of present-day Mexico City, the classical period witnessed the rise and fall of another mighty urban society, Teotihuacán, "the place of the gods," as the Aztecs later called it. With a population which may have reached 200,000 at its zenith in A.D. 600, it represents the largest metropolis in Mesoamerica up to that time. Its hub was the ceremonial center dominated by two gigantic monuments, the Pyramid of the Sun—its base larger than that of the Pyramid of Cheops in Egypt's Giza Valley—and the smaller Pyramid of the Moon. Dedicated to commerce, Teotihuacanos (it is not known what they called themselves) extended their economic influence over most of southern Mexico before their sudden and mysterious destruction around A.D. 750.

The greatest civilization of the classical period, indeed the most advanced of all New World societies, was the Mayan. Beginning at about A.D. 300, a major cultural awakening took place in the inhospitable rainforests of Belize, Honduras, El Salvador, Guatemala, and neighboring parts of Mexico, where the Mayas established their first city-states. Tikal, located in the Petén district of Guatemala, was the largest of these. Thought at first to be ceremonial centers like those of the Olmecs, with the population always dispersed in the surrounding area, it now appears that some Mayan sites were true cities. Cultural heirs of the Olmecs, the Mayas carried their inheritance far beyond their predecessors. Given their primitive technology, the advances made in the intellectual realm are astonishing. At their height in the eighth century, the Mayas tracked stars, developed the concept of the zero, and had the ability to perform simple brain operations. Their astronomers traced the path of Venus with an error of only fourteen seconds a year. They created the only true writing system in the Americas (about a third of their hieroglyphics have been deciphered) and an elaborate calendar which was more accurate than that used in Europe before the Gregorian calendar of the late sixteenth century. Their art and architecture, well represented in Mexico City's renowned National Museum of Anthropology (completed in 1964), are among their most cherished accomplishments.

While they excelled in arts and sciences, the ancient Mayas—like the Greeks in the Old World—were unable to overcome their political differences. Divided into city-states controlled by warrior-kings, among the most celebrated being Pacal of Palenque, Shield Jaguar of Yaxchilan, and Yax-Pac of Copán, they proved incapable of creating a true empire. Warfare was endemic among them. Since the 1960s, scholars have discovered that human sacrifice was at least as characteristic of their society as it was of the Aztecs. Wars may account for the decline of urban life at about 900, when they mysteriously abandoned their cities in the southern highlands and migrated to the Yucatán Peninsula, which had been a peripheral area before. The archaeologist Sir Eric Thompson attributed the decline to peasant uprisings. Most scholars today, though, emphasize ecological problems, notably soil exhaustion.

Yucatán witnessed the rise of new centers, including Chichén Itzá, Uxmal, and Mayapán. The northern migration revitalized their culture during the next few centuries, but the Mayans never regained their former eminence. The final decline began after the mid-thirteenth century. When the Spanish encountered the Mayas in the sixteenth century, they were a mere shadow of their old selves, their days of glory practically forgotten by now. During the postclassic period, from 900 to the Spanish Conquest, there were few intellectual and scientific advances.

Physical evidence discovered at cities in Yucatán, especially Chichén Itzá, indicates that during this postclassic era the Mayas were influenced profoundly by some alien culture, possibly that of the Toltecs. Scholars know that this warlike tribe entered central Mexico from the northern arid steppes sometime around the tenth century. Establishing their capital at Tula—north of Teotihuacán, an abandoned city by that time—in the modern state of Hidalgo, the Toltecs assimilated the superior culture of the tribes of the Valley of Mexico, whom they came to dominate as they adopted an aggressive expansionist policy. Perhaps it was the opposition of these tribes which eventually forced the Toltecs to forsake Tula in the twelfth century and descend from the highlands to the shores of the Caribbean. They bequeathed a number of impressive aspects of their culture to the people they subjugated, among them their chief deity, the benign Quetzalcóatl. Often depicted as a plumed serpent, this god would be incorporated into the religious beliefs of both Mayas and Aztecs.

Like the Toltecs, the Aztecs trace their origins to the northern deserts of

Mexico—a term derived from *México*, which is what they called themselves—though the site of their mythical homeland, Aztlán, continues to be the object of intense speculation. Náhuatl speakers, both tribes emerged from the Chichimecs ("the dog people"), a generic name for the wild tribes of the North. The Aztecs appeared in the Valley of Mexico, which they called Anáhuac, sometime in the early thirteenth century. Despised by stronger and more advanced tribes, they were forced to continue a nomadic existence in search of a homeland for many years. According to ancient prophecies, the sight of an eagle perched on a cactus plant with a serpent in its mouth would signal the spot where they were to stop, build a capital, and inaugurate their quest for hegemony. Apparently this event came to pass in 1325—scholars are able to decipher their calendar, which differs significantly from that of the Mayas—for in that year they began to build Tenochtitlán (present Mexico City) in the midst of Lake Texcoco.

Having constructed their capital, the Aztecs embarked on a series of military campaigns which resulted in the creation of a vast empire at a phenomenal speed. By the end of the fifteenth century, a Triple Alliance, consisting of Tlacopan, Texcoco, and Tenochtitlán, had been forged, but the Aztecs were first among equals. When the Spaniards entered their expanding domain in 1519, they encountered a militaristic and theocratic kingdom of more than six million inhabitants stretching throughout southern Mexico. A desire for war captives, dictated by a mystical religion which demanded continuous human sacrifice, seemed to motivate these conquests. The most bloodthirsty of their deities was Huitzilopochtli, their war god. Not all sacrificial victims were war captives; occasionally, their own citizens were offered up to the gods. "There is no indication of voluntarism among victims," Inga Clendinnen notes, "although some appear to have acquiesced in their fate."[11] Like the Romans, whom they resemble in many ways, Aztecs were master builders as well as valiant warriors. An extensive system of highways helped consolidate their power. Trade became as pivotal as warfare in spreading Aztec culture. What they contributed to their vassals was not insignificant.

Given the massive destruction wrought by the conquest, there are few surviving Aztec relics, but the written records of the *conquistadores* indicate awesome achievements. Tenochtitlán itself, the greatest of New World cities, with a population of some 400,000 by 1519, is testimony to their genius. According to its conquerors, it resembled Venice, a city acknowledged by these veterans of military campaigns throughout the Mediterranean world and beyond as the most beautiful in Europe. Only Naples and Constantinople could rival Tenochtitlán in grandeur. Rising magically from the depths of a blue lake, its center traversed by canals and crowned by brightly colored temple-pyramids, the city must have seemed a veritable heaven on earth to its conquerors. Influenced by the Mayas—

via Teotihuacanos and Toltecs—Aztec culture never quite achieved the level of sophistication of the older civilization. But it should be pointed out that this culture, centered on the Valley of Mexico, was still in the process of developing when the Spaniards arrived. How far the Méxicas could have advanced had their society not been suddenly and completely demolished by external forces is a question that is as intriguing as it is futile.

THE CONQUEST OF MEXICO

The conqueror of the Aztecs was Hernán Cortés (1485–1547), the archetypal conquistador. Cortés was born to a relatively well-to-do family of minor nobility in Medellín, in the western Spanish province of Extremadura. At the age of thirteen, he was sent off to the University of Salamanca (established in 1243), then the ranking university on the peninsula, but he found academic life less than inspiring. Having dropped out of school, Cortés soon determined that his future was overseas. His career was not unique; like young sons of England's noble families of a later date, many ambitious members of the Spanish aristocracy sought fame and fortune in the expanding empire. The young Spaniard arrived in Española in 1504 at the age of nineteen. He took up farming until 1511, when he distinguished himself in the conquest of Cuba, where he had a series of adventures before settling down in Santiago, the island capital. An able administrator, he became a man of some political prominence, even serving as mayor.

Meanwhile, rumors began to circulate of a vast inland empire on the mainland where natives were surrounded by incredible riches. When Diego Velásquez, governor of the island, decided to send an expedition to investigate, Cortés, with his immense energy and charisma, became the logical choice of a leader. The small fleet, consisting of eleven ships and about six hundred men, sailed for Yucatán on 18 February 1519. Following the coast northward, the ships landed several days later at a site Cortés christened La Villa Rica de la Vera Cruz, near present-day Vera Cruz. By now Cortés and Velásquez had had a falling out, and the crew was divided in its allegiance. Such personal animosities and intrigues would be characteristic of Spain's emissaries to the New World throughout this early period. Legend has it that the enterprising Cortés exposed his enemies by scuttling all but two ships, much to everyone's dismay, then promised that those who chose to do so might return to Cuba aboard one of the surviving vessels. However, upon taking the vote, the wily captain destroyed the promised craft, leaving no avenue of escape. The story may be apocryphal, but the fact remains that though he was roundly criticized then and later, Cortés was not only calculating, he was also fearless and single-minded in pursuit of his objectives. After this episode, there would be no turning back. Leaving some of their comrades to defend their beach-head, 450 men marched off to meet their fate.

Good fortune smiled on the expedition from the very beginning. An Indian slave girl, Malintzin Tenepal (1502?–1527?), whom the Spanish named Doña Marina—later called La Malinche—was a peace offering given to them by a tribe of Tabascans. A speaker of Náhuatl, Doña Marina would serve as their faithful guide on the arduous journey. She proved to be invaluable; it was mainly because of her help that the Spaniards were able to survive a series of pitched battles against tribes friendly and unfriendly with the México. Almost three months after they started, the soldiers of fortune arrived at the Valley of Anáhuac, situated atop Mexico's central plateau, some 7,000 feet above sea level.

Moctezuma II Xocoyotzin had been emperor of the Aztec nation since 1502. Like Cortés, he would be a main player in the drama that would unfold in the next few months—surely one of the most incredible adventures in the annals of human history. Unlike the Spanish captain, he would prove unequal to the task. Mexican nationalists have not been kind to Moctezuma, who proved weak and vacillating under pressure; and yet, in retrospect, it is hard not to feel a certain empathy for the vanquished leader. His priests had prophesied that one day the god Quetzalcóatl, bearded and light-skinned, would return from the East, where he had disappeared in exile sometime in the dim past (a legend inherited from the Toltecs). It is one of the remarkable coincidences in history that Cortés and his army appeared precisely at the time Quetzalcóatl was supposed to return. Impressed by their timely appearance, Moctezuma came to believe that the strangers might be gods, a suspicion fortified by the Spaniards' apparent invincibility.

Adopting an excessively cautious stance, the curious priest-king permitted the Spaniards, less than four hundred in number, to march into Tenochtitlán on 8 November 1519. With only token resistance, Moctezuma wasted one of his most precious advantages, the city's magnificent strategic position in the middle of Lake Texcoco. Once inside the city, Cortés played his cards flawlessly, first gaining Moctezuma's trust and then gradually turning the gullible emperor into a prisoner in his own palace. Using him as a hostage, the Spaniards, whose numbers fluctuated in the next few months as they reestablished contact with Cuba, extorted from the native peoples vast amounts of gold and silver, treasures brought in from all corners of the empire.

Eventually, the México rebelled. Disillusioned with their impotent and resigned leader, an obvious pawn in the hands of their enemies, they staged a demonstration in which Moctezuma was fatally injured, leaving Cortés and his men to face the prospect of imminent destruction. In dire straits, they took a desperate gamble: under cover of darkness in the early hours of 1 July 1520, *la noche triste* (the sad night), they attempted to sneak out of the city, their horses' hooves muffled, and their pockets stuffed with loot. A fierce battle ensued. Fighting in total darkness and badly outnumbered, the Spanish faced formidable odds. Many of them, some 450 troops, perished in the bloody battle. Cortés himself barely avoided capture. At daybreak, the survivors, weak from exhaustion, gathered themselves on the mountains high above the Aztec capital, where, according to legend, Cortés, discouraged and mourning the losses suffered, wept under an ahuehuete tree. Bernal Díaz del Castillo, one of the survivors and the leading chronicler of the epic undertaking, reports that the Spaniards, their numbers reduced to about four hundred men, staggered back to Tlaxcala, whose inhabitants proved to be faithful allies in this hour of extreme need.

Several months later, fortified by Tlaxcalans and other friendly natives, the irrepressible captain returned to gain his revenge. His objective was Tenochtitlán itself. Using Indian labor, the Spaniards constructed thirteen ships to be used in an amphibious attack on the Aztec stronghold. Weakened by disease and hunger, after a three-month siege, its inhabitants braced for the final assault. Mexican resistance was tenacious, but in the end, supported by native auxiliaries, the undaunted Spaniards prevailed. The fateful day was 13 August 1521. Surrounded by their enemies, the end in sight, many warriors preferred suicide to ignoble defeat, as they hurled themselves from atop the pyramids. Twenty thousand defenders died in the final campaign. Those who survived, including their heroic leader Cuauhtémoc, had nowhere to go, for during the last assault their homes had been systematically leveled and their temples dismantled stone by stone. Mopping-up operations would take many years, the southern jungles providing the most resistance. Still, given the vertical nature of the empire, where all authority—in theory, at least—emanated from the center, the conquest was virtually achieved with the destruction of the Aztec capital.

The victory, given the disparity in numbers between Europeans and Amerindians, especially in view of how quickly it was accomplished, seems improbable. Less than one thousand Spaniards made the final assault on Tenochtitlán. They faced an empire reputedly numbering in the millions. Nor should it be forgotten that the Aztecs were the finest and most successful warriors ever known in the Americas. However, European advantages were numerous. Horses were among the most telling of these. Though the horse had originated in the Americas, it had been extinct for thousands of years. Aztecs were much in awe of these spirited animals. Cortés, appreciating the possibilities, was quick to take advantage, sending in his cavalry to wreak havoc among his opponents at every opportunity. And the Spanish were marvelous riders; they were so adapt at horsemanship that the Méxica, according to their own accounts, initially thought that horse and rider were one single animal. Mastiffs, too, were effective weapons given that their victims had no experience with large and ferocious dogs.

Indian allies, some 200,000 of them, were also valuable. William Hickling Prescott, whose nineteenth-century account of the Mexican Conquest is a literary masterpiece, was exaggerating only slightly when he concluded that the conquest was essentially an Indian victory.[12] At first, the Spaniards probably saw the empire as a monolithic whole. Almost immediately, however, it became clear that there were deep-seated divisions among their adversaries. In fact, most tribes had been subjugated by force and were ruled through terror. Particularly repugnant to the vassal states was the demand for human tribute, slaves to be sacrificed to the gods. A hatred of the Aztec ensured that many tribes, notably the Tlaxcalans, who had maintained their independence under the most trying circumstances, would conclude that the Spaniards were the lesser of evils; hence, the disparity between the two armies was less one-sided than one would expect.

Disease was another factor that favored the Spaniards. In 1520 an epidemic raged throughout the empire killing tens of thousands of inhabitants; a demographic revolution had been initiated, one that would ultimately reduce the Indian population by 90 percent. "Clearly," the University of Chicago historian William H. McNeill reasons, "if smallpox had not come when it did, the Spanish victory could not have been achieved in Mexico."[13] Native Americans had virtually no immunity to European diseases, which indicates that though there may well have been numerous transoceanic contacts with other parts of the world prior to the appearance of the conquistadores, these contacts involved only modest transfers of population. It seems clear that even before the battles began, morale was flagging among the México, a marked contrast to the robust energy and confidence displayed by their adversaries.

Finally, the difference in technology, in the opinion of the British historian Hugh Thomas, was perhaps the most important single factor in explaining the Spanish triumph.[14] In possession of cannon, crossbows, harquebuses, and steel armor, the Spaniards were more than a match for native troops using primitive weapons. During the next four centuries, Europeans would be helped immeasurably by their superior technology. Only when this material advantage was lost did European hegemony in the world erode.

The physical destruction of Tenochtitlán was decided by the conquistadores but most of it was carried out by their native allies, who hardly needed encouragement. The vehemence that other Indians displayed in seeking revenge serves to remind us that the Aztecs were widely despised by their neighbors. México priests and warriors, after all, had committed terrible atrocities. Their contemporaries seemed to fear them more than respect them. And yet the destruction of this civilization inspires sadness. It is perfectly understandable that Bernal Díaz del Castillo should be filled with remorse when recounting the final fall of Tenochtitlán.

The Aztecs' cultural accomplishments were extraordinary, and many aspects of their lives were admirable and worthy of emulation. Most importantly, the Aztecs and the other Indians of Mexico, civilized or not, have left an imposing legacy to the emerging nation. Octavio Paz (1914–1998), arguably the best interpreter of the Mexican national character, puts it best: "Not only the popular religion of Mexico but the Mexicans' entire life is steeped in Indian culture—the family, love, friendship, attitudes toward one's father and mother, popular legends, the forms of civility and life in common, the vision of death and sex, work and festivity."[15] Because the Indian legacy was especially strong among the lower classes, who represent the overwhelming majority of Mexican immigrants into the United States, it is hard to disagree with the renowned native American scholar Jack D. Forbes, who claims that Mexican Americans are the largest Indian tribe in this country.[16]

Today both Mexicans and Mexican Americans exalt their Indian roots (*indigenismo*) while denying or condemning their Spanish past. This is a vast change in perspective from the early twentieth century, when the exact opposite was the case. It is currently in vogue to condemn the Spaniards for their past transgressions, especially their ill-treatment of Amerindians, whether it was Columbus (never mind that he was an Italian by birth) in the Caribbean, Cortés in Mexico, or Junípero Serra in California.

Of course, this was the central argument employed by its enemies in the past—when France, England, and the Netherlands attempted to discredit Spain by charging that its people were uniquely cruel and avaricious, what Spanish historians call *la leyenda negra* (The Black Legend). Historically, however, Spain's first and most damaging critic was a Spaniard himself, the sixteenth-century Dominican, Bartolomé de Las Casas (1474–1566), so perhaps it should not be surprising that at present Spain's most animated critics come from within the Hispanic community.[17] That the Spanish were religious fanatics, given the zeal engendered by centuries of crusades against the Moors, is undeniable. On the other hand, in its attitude toward native Americans (as well as Africans) and, more importantly, its treatment of them, Spain rates as more humane than most of its detractors, as Mexican writer Carlos Fuentes has pointed out.[18]

Like Las Casas, many segments of Spanish society, notably the monarchy and the clergy, saw Indians as *Hijos de Dios* (Sons of God); and although the treatment of native peoples was characterized by extreme exploitation, it is also true that genocide was rarely practiced. Indeed, marriage between Indians and whites was sanctioned and even encouraged. Cortés himself—who is buried in Mexico, according to the terms of his will—set the precedent when he took La Malinche as his mistress. The mestizaje that came to characterize society in New Spain, including its northern frontier, has no meaningful parallel in the United States before the twentieth century, for economic as well as religious and historical reasons.

Moreover, whether its sins were great or small, undeniably Spain left a profound and lasting imprint on the peoples of the Americas, not just in the matter of race but on every aspect of their life. This is certainly the case with religion and language, the most basic elements of a people's culture. The fact remains that although Protestantism has made major inroads in recent years, Latin America, with its enormous population, is about to become the leading Catholic area on the globe. Then, there is the language. The Chilean poet Pablo Neruda once exclaimed: "What a great language I have, it's a fine language we inherited from the fierce Conquistadors. . . . Wherever they went, they razed the land. . . . But words fell like pebbles out of the boots of the barbarians, out of their beards, their helmets, their horseshoes, luminous words that were left glittering here . . . our language. They carried off the gold and left us the gold. . . . They carried everything off and left us everything. . . . They left us the words."[19] Mexico today has the largest Catholic as well as the largest Spanish-speaking population in the world; in significant ways it has become more Spanish than Spain itself.

Mexicans in the United States have a rich heritage. Their culture is the product of a wide variety of influences. The most recent of these is that of the dominant Anglo society: albeit slower than with most immigrant groups, assimilation inevitably—though often reluctantly—is taking place. A community of humble means, Mexicans also have much in common with other people who occupy the lowest socioeconomic levels, what the anthropologist Oscar Lewis termed the "culture of poverty." Catholicism continues to be another key factor shaping Mexican-American life. However, the Spanish and Indian elements which fused after the collapse of Tenochtitlán in 1521 are what give the culture its distinguishing characteristics. It was at this crucial juncture that the foundation was laid for the emergence of a unique people whose fascinating history is only now coming to light. Perhaps this is what Richard Rodríguez, the celebrated though controversial Mexican-American writer, has in mind when he concludes: "My life began, it did not end, in the sixteenth century."[20]

THE SPANISH FRONTIER

1521–1821

On 12 July 1893, Frederick Jackson Turner (1861–1932), a young professor from Wisconsin, gave a scholarly presentation entitled "The Significance of
the Frontier in American History" at the annual convention of the American Historical Association in Chicago. The most influential work ever written by an American historian, this seminal essay proposed that the key to understanding the
American people was to be found in their frontier experience, or, as he put it, "the
existence of an area of free land, its continuous recession, and the advance of
American settlement westward, explain American development."[1] A product of
three hundred years of westward movement into an environment with immense
resources but few people (exactly the opposite of Europe), the national character
came to be characterized by a strong work ethic, rugged individualism, and an
unflagging optimism. Yet the most profound legacy of this adventure into the
wilderness was democracy. While he discovered many other character traits—not
all of them flattering—it was Turner's description of Americans as paladins of
democracy that left a lasting impression; by the time of his death in 1932, the idea
that "democracy was born on the frontier" had been elevated to an article of faith
among his countrymen. A brilliant analysis of the American past, the Turner thesis soon became the dominant interpretation of the United States and what the
nation stood for.

Today Turner's views remain popular, and rightfully so, but they are no
longer universally endorsed. Among the most severe critics of the Frontier thesis
in recent years have been Chicano historians, who tend to emphasize the racism
and oppression that accompanied the westward movement. These scholars also
question, as others have done in the past, the notion that the American national
character can be explained exclusively by the westward movement of English-
speaking people. Chicanos point out that the Spanish also left a meaningful legacy

in the United States. This influence, mostly found in the Southwest, has generally been neglected by textbooks on American history. Moreover, as the Jesuit historian John Francis Bannon, one of the few scholars dedicated to studying the Spanish Borderlands, has justly observed, "A study of the Spanish frontier, the Borderlands, will show that the Anglo-American experience, magnificent and thrilling though it was, actually was not quite as unique as it is sometimes pictured and chauvinistically thought to be. The Anglo-American frontier can be better understood and more properly evaluated by process of comparison."[2]

SPANISH EXPLORATION OF THE FAR NORTH

After the conquest of the Aztecs and the destruction of their capital, the Spaniards fanned out in all directions in search of God, Gold, and Glory, the same quest which had brought them to the New World in the first place. In the forefront of this march was Hernán Cortés himself, who led an expedition westward to the sea that bears his name. Although the land of the Chichimecas to the north was at first neglected, before too long, conquistadores began to venture into that mysterious region as well, the northern frontier of the Viceroyalty of New Spain (Nueva España), the name Spaniards christened present-day Mexico.

The first Europeans in the Far North, however, were not motivated by God, Gold, or Glory; Alvar Núñez Cabeza de Vaca (1490?–1557?) and his men arrived purely by chance. While sailing to New Spain from Florida, which had first been explored by Juan Ponce de León in 1513, a Spanish expedition consisting of several rafts was caught in a tropical storm in 1528 and most of the men perished. Some crew members managed to reach the shores of Texas (named after a local Caddo Indian tribe). Before too long, only four men were left: Cabeza de Vaca, a native of Andalucía; two other Spaniards, Andrés Dorantes and Alonso del Castillo; and Estevánico, a Moor. These strangers, the first whites and the first black to enter what is now the American Southwest, were objects of curiosity and awe. Their survival among the various tribes they encountered must be accredited to the extraordinary ability of their self-appointed leader, Cabeza de Vaca. Possessing a rudimentary knowledge of herbs, the resourceful Spaniard was able to pass himself off as a medicine man. Thanks to his creative ability, the small party survived, sometimes as slaves, sometimes as free men, meandering throughout the Far North for several years hoping to find their way back to the cities of central Mexico. Finally, in 1536, the motley group, more Indian than white in appearance by now, was rescued by a Spanish expedition in the wilderness northwest of Mexico City, the viceregal capital.

The men had had incredible adventures. They told tales of exotic peoples and strange flora and fauna. As often happens in similar circumstances, the stories were embellished as they circulated among listeners eager to validate their own aspirations. In time, rumors had it that Cabeza de Vaca had actually sighted the famed Seven Cities of Antilia (later called the Seven Cities of Cíbola), legendary towns adorned with gold. The rumors stimulated a fascination with the lands beyond the northern frontier, and in 1539, fray Marcos de Niza, a Franciscan, was sent north to investigate. His reports were encouraging. In fact, the friar reported seeing the fabulous cities. Soon three major expeditions were underway in an effort to find the coveted wealth.

In retrospect, it seems odd that the conquistadores, cold and calculating in many respects, could be so gullible during the Age of Exploration. On the flimsiest of evidence they were ready to risk life and limb in a quixotic quest for beautiful women, unimaginable wealth, and even eternal life. Of course, they failed to find the Amazonian beauties of the fictitious island of California; the gold-laden lake where El Dorado, the Indian chief who was covered in gold from head to toe, took his annual bath; and the fabled Fountain of Youth, not to mentioned a multitude of other mirages. But it should be remembered that the medieval mindset, with its preoccupation with the magical and the supernatural, characterized Western society during the Renaissance and persisted well past the Scientific Revolution in many corners of Europe. And Europeans *had* made one amazing discovery after another since the time of Marco Polo. "Moreover," the historian David J. Weber adds, "Hernán Cortés and Francisco Pizarro had proved the existence of great kingdoms and extraordinary wealth.[3]

The first Spanish thrust into the north took place along the Caribbean shores of North America. In May 1539, the governor of Cuba, Hernando Méndez de Soto y Gutiérrez Cardeñosa, set out to explore Florida with about six hundred colonists. Venturing far and wide, the expedition eventually came upon the Mississippi River—possibly the first white men to cast their eyes upon this wonder—before reaching present-day Arkansas. In search of wealth, Soto lost his life in a futile effort to find it. He died of a fever on 21 May 1542. The survivors of the ill-fated expedition eventually made their way back to New Spain late in the following year.

As the Spanish explored the American Southeast, they also stretched across the continent to the American Southwest.[4] The second attempt to uncover the alleged riches of the North was led by Francisco Vásquez de Coronado (1510–1554), the most famous of the early Spanish explorers of North America.[5] The scion of a wealthy and respected family from Salamanca, Vásquez de Coronado arrived in the New World as a young man of twenty-five. He quickly established himself as the leading political presence on the northern frontier after his appointment in 1538 to the governorship of Nueva Galicia, the coastal province lying northwest of Mexico City. Shortly thereafter he was selected by Viceroy

Antonio de Mendoza to head an expedition which would resume the search for the Seven Cities where fray Marcos de Niza had left off.

In February 1540, Vásquez de Coronado set out from Compostela, in Nueva Galicia, leading an expedition that numbered over one thousand men, including some eight hundred Indians and several women. The route he selected was similar to that taken by the friar, north along the western coast of the mainland, through the Sonoran desert, and into the area now known as Arizona. The expedition gradually made its way into present-day New Mexico where the explorers encountered the Zuñi. Farther east, they came across other Pueblo tribes along the Rio Grande, or the Río Bravo del Norte, as it would come to be known. At this time, there were roughly forty thousand Pueblo Indians living in some ninety towns. Failing to find the Golden Cities—Cíbola turned out to be the villages of the Zuñi—but convinced by natives that farther to the north there existed an equally wealthy kingdom, the Gran Quivira, the conquistadores pushed on. Crossing what is today the Texas Panhandle, Vásquez de Coronado went as far as modern-day Kansas, where he arrived in early 1542. At this point, Vásquez de Coronado realized he had been misled by his Indian guide, who was promptly tortured and executed. Abandoning the venture, the disillusioned explorer returned in disgrace to Nueva Galicia in the early summer, having squandered a fortune.

The return of Vásquez de Coronado coincided with the beginning of the third major attempt to expand New Spain's northern borders, this time along the Pacific Coast. The protagonist of this effort was Juan Rodríguez Cabrillo, a native of Andalucía, not a Portuguese, as is often claimed. He was the first white man credited with seeing the present-day state of California, designated Alta California at that time to distinguish it from the land to the south, Baja California. Cabrillo sailed from the port of Navidad up the west coast of New Spain in the summer of 1542. After exploring San Diego Bay, sighted on 28 September, the expedition proceeded north along the coast as far as the islands off the Santa Barbara coast. There, Cabrillo suffered a leg injury, which proved fatal. He died on 3 January 1543 and was buried in an unmarked grave, probably on one of the channel islands. Undaunted, the expedition continued up the coast as far as present-day southern Oregon, before returning to Navidad. Survivors reported that the lands they had visited were heavily populated and had a multitude of natural resources, not the least of which was the balmy Mediterranean climate so reminiscent of Spain itself. But there was no gold. Moreover, the voyage north, against the strong Japanese current, made travel to Alta California exceedingly difficult. Consequently, it would be another sixty years before the Spaniards attempted another foray into the seductive coastal lands beyond Baja California.

The failure of the conquistadores to find the Golden Cities discouraged further efforts to explore the Far North elsewhere for almost a half century. In addition, there were many obstacles to expansion in that direction, among them arid terrain, vast distances, and the increasing hostility displayed by native inhabitants. The gravest impediment, however, was the apparent absence of precious minerals. Moreover, in the mid-1540s, rich silver lodes were found immediately northwest of Mexico City, in Zacatecas, and soon after in nearby San Luis Potosí and Durango. Prospectors now poured into this region, most of which became the province of Nueva Vizcaya in the 1560s. The line of settlement remained nearly static until the early 1580s, when two expeditions ventured into New Mexico: the first led by the Franciscan Agustín Rodríguez and the soldier Francisco Chamuscada, and the second by a wealthy entrepreneur, Antonio de Espejo. Neither party encountered much success and colonization of the area was delayed for another decade.

SETTLEMENT OF NEW MEXICO

The *entrada* (incursion) that led to permanent settlement of New Mexico occurred in the 1590s, not because the mines of the interior were exhausted, nor because of the declining labor force given the catastrophic impact of European diseases, but rather because of the threats, real and imagined, posed by European interlopers in the northern region. Having been explored previously, it was only now that the lands slated to become the American Southwest in the distant future were occupied by Spanish *pobladores* (settlers).

The most immediate challenge seemed to come from the English. While England had been quick to capitalize on the discovery of the New World, efforts to follow up on these early voyages of exploration had been put on hold by the religious and political problems associated with the Reformation. As the Elizabethan Compromise gradually took shape, English ships were encouraged to venture far and wide in an effort to expand the Crown's influence. The most successful of Queen Elizabeth's sea captains was Francis Drake, who circumnavigated the globe in 1577–1580. During the course of this risky adventure, the bold Englishman initiated a series of raids on Spanish ships and even had the audacity to attack the leading city in South America, Lima. The Spanish feared Drake because of the menace he posed to their shipping, but there were larger issues as well. They suspected that Drake's visit to California in the summer of 1579 would pave the way for further explorations along the Pacific Coast and perhaps to the discovery of the fabled Strait of Anián (the Northwest Passage), a waterway connecting the Atlantic and Pacific oceans which European explorers continued to seek for the next two centuries. At any rate, a British presence in the north would jeopardize Spanish expansion there, and possibly even New Spain itself, with its lucrative mining interests.

The formidable task of establishing the northern colonies, a thousand miles beyond the established frontier, fell on the shoulders of Juan de Oñate y Salazar (1549?–1628?), a truly outstanding frontiersman in Mexican history.[6] Oñate grew up in Zacatecas, where his Basque father made a fortune in mining and became one of the most prominent silver barons in the province of Nueva Galicia. Following in his father's footsteps, Juan de Oñate devoted many years to public service on the frontier, earning a reputation for valor in fighting Chichimeca tribes. Rich and daring, he seemed the logical choice to initiate Spanish settlement of the Far North. The expedition, recruited over a period of several years and numbering about 130 soldiers, some accompanied by wives and children, finally commenced on 26 January 1598. Oñate entered New Mexico in early May and a few weeks later founded San Juan de los Caballeros on the upper Rio Grande as his headquarters.

A string of settlements, usually adjacent to Indian pueblos along the river, soon appeared. Among them was San Gabriel del Yunque, which became the provincial capital for a short time (now an archaeological ruin). Oñate's men were assigned *encomiendas* on the surrounding area; that is, they were given the right to exploit the labor of the native inhabitants of the land in return for protecting and civilizing them. Appointed governor of the territory, Oñate served until 1607, when he resigned and left for Mexico City to face charges of mismanagement. He never returned to New Mexico, but the Spanish consolidated their hold by increasing the number of settlements along the river. The most important of these towns would be the Villa Real de Santa Fe, founded by Pedro de Peralta, Oñate's successor, in 1609 or 1610 (the records are unclear), the oldest state capital in the United States. The pattern of settlement, like many developments in the Spanish frontier, would be dictated by the native American population. The colonists settled among the Pueblos because the indigenous people represented potential Christian converts and a much-needed labor force.

When the Spanish entered New Mexico at the end of the sixteenth century, there were two competing lifestyles among the Indian tribes, sedentary and nomadic. The former were represented by agriculturalists who resided in *pueblos* (towns). Apparently descendants of the Anasazi—or "the ancient ones," whose advanced culture centered on the Four Corners region, where modern-day Utah, Colorado, New Mexico, and Arizona come together—these tribes had immigrated south sometime after A.D. 1000. Some settled in the desert, among them the Hopi, the Zuñi, and the Acoma (the Western Pueblos); the majority (the Eastern Pueblos) resided in a series of towns along the Rio Grande, where irrigation was much easier. In either case, their lifestyle was dependent on the production of corn, which had been cultivated locally since about 1000 B.C., when it had been introduced from central Mexico.

Nomadic tribes were recent arrivals into the region. They had preceded the Spanish by only a few centuries, perhaps even a few decades. Enemies of the sedentary tribes, these wanderers made their living by preying on their relatively affluent neighbors, as well as hunting and gathering. Arriving via the Great Plains, the nomadic tribes maintained some traditions associated with native peoples of that cultural province. Like the Pueblos, the nomads were divided into a number of distinct tribes. Among the most powerful were the Apache, the Navajo, and, somewhat later, the Comanche. During most of the year, the sparse resources of an arid environment necessitated the division of these nomadic tribes into smaller bands. The Jicarilla, the Mescalero, and the Chiricahua, for instance, were all bands of the Apache that would later inspire terror among the pobladores. Small in numbers, the roving tribes were more of a nuisance than a bona fide threat to both Pueblos and Spaniards until the introduction of the horse, which dramatically changed Indian life. Especially after the beginning of the eighteenth century, the nomads, and in particular the Apache, came to dictate the way of life that grew to be characteristic of the present states of northern Mexico and the American Southwest.

In recent years, much has been written about the treatment of the native American by the Spanish, but the subject remains controversial. Practically the only point on which there is general consensus is that it is difficult to generalize about the relationship between the two peoples on the northern frontier. There was a sizable discrepancy between attitudes and treatment, particularly on the part of the Spanish. Moreover, neither group was homogenous. There were vast differences among both settlers and tribal peoples. For their part, the sedentary tribes differed markedly from the nomads, and in turn there were crucial distinctions among the agriculturalists themselves. The Zuñi, the Hopi, and the Pueblos of the Rio Grande Valley were separated by language, customs, and traditions. Every tribe took for granted its superiority over its neighbor. Thus, generalizations about Indians, even when limited to the heart of the Southwest, are difficult at best. The same is true for the Spanish intruders. Colonists, missionaries, and soldiers were rarely in agreement on matters pertaining to native communities. Attitudes and behavior also changed from time to time, depending on many factors—political, social, and economic. Consequently, although it is desirable to trace general patterns of behavior, it is also necessary to understand that there were always significant crosscurrents.

The Spaniards' attitude toward Indians of the Far North, regardless of their cultural level, was similar to their view of the natives of the interior of New Spain: they saw them as inferior beings. In this respect, Spaniards were hardly unique. Like other Europeans, they were guilty of ethnocentrism. Ignorance breeds contempt, and the Spanish saw many things they did not understand. Being tolerant is a relatively modern ideal; few Europeans saw toleration as a virtue until the Age of the Enlightenment.

Yet among the European nations expanding their frontiers, the Spanish position is a subtle variation on the general theme. These differences are explained by a unique historical experience, notably Spain's long contact with the Moors. Inspired by centuries of crusading zeal, the Spanish people of the sixteenth century had developed a religious faith bordering on fanaticism, a fervor illustrated by the popularity of the Spanish Inquisition. During the course of the 1500s, this enthusiasm was fanned by the wars of the Reformation. Under the great Hapsburg ruler of the Holy Roman Empire, Emperor Charles V (King Carlos I in Spain), the Spanish prided themselves on being the paladins of Catholicism. This missionary mindset, this blinding zeal, created a rationale for the many atrocities Indians were subjected to throughout Spain's American possessions.

A prime example is Acoma. The famous Sky City in western New Mexico had been initially sighted by Vásquez de Coronado's men. More than fifty years later, the Spaniards returned to the area and attempted to establish contact with the mesa dwellers; but in 1598, a party sent out by Oñate was ambushed by the inhabitants of the pueblo, and as a result the irate governor chose to make an example of the recalcitrant natives. Acoma was conquered after a brief but violent siege and revenge was swift. Five hundred men and three hundred women and children were massacred in cold blood; some five hundred women and children and eighty men were taken alive, tried, and found guilty of treachery. All those over the age of twelve were condemned to twenty years of slavery, the men over twenty-one had one foot cut off as an additional penalty, and the children were distributed among the priests and soldiers to be used as slave labor.

On the other hand, the influence of the Moorish crusades also had a positive impact on race relations in the Americas. Given the lofty achievements of their civilization, Moors could hardly be seen as racially inferior. Unlike many other Europeans, then, the Spanish did not automatically equate dark skin with innate inferiority. While many Europeans, especially the English, came to regard Indians as "savages," practically indistinguishable from wild animals, among the Spanish the notion developed that Indians were Hijos de Dios; which is to say, though they were ignorant, like children they were still human beings with souls and intelligence, hence potentially equal to Spaniards. This concession allowed the massive mestizaje which came to characterize Hispanic America—a phenomenon not found on the English frontier to any appreciable extent, Pocahontas notwithstanding. Yet the absence of Spanish women and the propensity of conquerors to ravage native women should not be minimized as other significant factors resulting in a merging of the two peoples.

Her critics, both now and in the past, have been unwilling or unable to appreciate the complexity of Spain's Indian policy. In fact, the Spanish attitude toward the Indian was highly ambivalent. Consequently, there were broad inconsistencies in the management of native Americans. Spain treated Indians both better and worse than other imperial powers of the Age of Expansion. Indeed, given human nature, what is remarkable is not so much that the Spanish exploited the Indians but that a significant element within Hispanic society was willing to ameliorate their plight.

All segments of Spanish colonial society exploited the Indians, but the Church tried to also give them something in return: civilization—which to most clergymen meant Catholicism, first and foremost, and then Spanish, "the language of God." So convinced were the missionaries in the righteousness of their cause that many were willing to risk martyrdom to spread the holy faith. Fray Agustín Rodríguez and two Franciscan colleagues lost their lives in 1581–1582 at the hands of the Pueblos. More fortunate was fray Juan Ramírez, still another Franciscan, who arrived in Acoma some thirty years after it had been crushed by Oñate's men, and converted its entire population with nothing more than a crucifix. From a historical perspective, the power of religious faith, especially during the Age of the Reformation, should not be underestimated.

Wherever the Spanish went, they set up missions, perhaps the most characteristic of their institutions on the frontier.[7] Missionary work was entrusted to the regular clergy, whose job it was to convert and Hispanicize the neophytes during a lengthy process of instruction. Following conversion, the native peoples would be turned over to the secular, or diocesan, clergy. Needless to say, as in the Old World, competition between regular and secular clergy continued, with the former only grudgingly giving way to the latter.

The two most active monastic orders on the Spanish frontier were the Franciscans and the Jesuits, though other monks, notably the Dominicans, were employed by the Crown from time to time. The first missionaries in New Spain were the Franciscans, the Order of Friars Minor, who quickly came to monopolize religious instruction in major Mexican cities and sought to maintain that hegemony on the northern frontier.

It was the Franciscans who accompanied Juan de Oñate into New Mexico. They were entrusted with the apostolic mission of administering to the spiritual needs of the numerous Pueblo settlements in the region. This province extended along the Rio Grande from El Paso del Norte (Ciudad Juárez today), where a mission, Nuestra Señora de Guadalupe de los Mansos del Paso del Norte, was founded on 8 December 1659, to the Upper Rio Grande Valley and as far north as the Spanish could expand their influence.

.The *presidio* (garrison) was the other major institution which appeared on the Spanish frontier. As in other European frontiers, the function of the fort was to provide protection against foreign interlopers and to pacify native populations. Unlike other frontiersmen, soldiers were generally not enthusiastic about immigrating into the inhospitable periphery; they were sent there by the Crown, oftentimes with their families, and were expected to endure long enlistments. Once their tenures of service were up, soldier-settlers were enticed to remain on the frontier by generous land grants supplied by the king or his designees.

Crowded into small settlements and surrounded by a hostile population who saw them as a force of occupation, Spanish citizens, both colonists and soldiers, developed close ties with one another. Indeed *presidiales* (presidial troops), as mentioned earlier, were also settlers. The sense of community was strengthened by the limited availability of marriage partners. Perhaps the most compelling factor in solidifying the community, however, was the common perception of the Indian. Both colonists and soldiers grew to fear and hate the Apache and other warlike tribes. Occasionally, relations improved as trade became mutually profitable or alliances against common enemies made cooperation desirable. Late in the colonial period, for example, a flourishing trade was carried out with the Comanches, who supplied pobladores with Indian slaves. In general, though, conflict characterized the relation between the two groups.

The Spanish attitude toward the neighboring Pueblo peoples was much different than toward *indios bárbaros* (wild Indians). Converts to Christianity and providers of cheap labor, the Pueblos were naturally seen in a more positive light. Fearful of the Apache and other hostile tribes, the Pueblos, for their part, were often willing to cooperate with whites. Indeed, some interracial marriages occurred, though most were outside of the aegis of the Church in this early period.

Nevertheless, the prevailing view of the Pueblos among both soldiers and colonists was that they were inferior peoples, a convenient attitude which justified colonial exploitation. As settlement expanded, a rift developed between the missionaries and the rest of the Spanish community, as happened throughout the empire. The clergy attempted to ameliorate the worst abuses of the native people, while the Spanish citizenry, intent on extracting as much work as possible, called for a laissez-faire policy toward the conquered. Ironically, however, it was the friars themselves who ultimately drove Indians to the breaking point. Although a prolonged drought and increased labor demands by pobladores played a role, it was the missionaries' unrelenting and heavy-handed efforts to undermine traditional religious beliefs which did most to alienate their wards.

The result was the great Pueblo Revolt of 1680.[8] Led by the medicine man Popé, from the town of San Juan, Pueblo villagers along the Upper Rio Grande Valley staged a massive uprising on 10 August of that year. Caught by complete surprise, the colonists, who numbered no more than 2,800 at that time, were no match for their incensed foes, who received help from some of the nomadic tribes.

Almost four hundred settlers were killed, as were most of the thirty-three Franciscans serving the province. Spanish villages of the Upper Rio Grande Valley were quickly abandoned as their panicked inhabitants fled south, to the Franciscan mission at Paso del Norte. For one of the few times in recorded history, a European overseas frontier was actually forced to retreat in the face of popular resistance. It took a decade before the Spaniards were able to gather sufficient reinforcements from central New Spain to reestablish their dominance.

The task of reconquering the lost lands was entrusted to an energetic and capable military commander, Diego de Vargas Zapata y Luján Ponce de León, who was appointed governor of the province of New Mexico in 1688. It took four years before all the preparations were made. Santa Fe was recaptured on 16 September 1692, signaling the beginning of the reconquest. A protracted campaign ensued, during which the governor gained the ascendancy as much by diplomacy as by military prowess. By mid-1694, that victory was assured, though mopping-up operations would drag on for years. Spaniards had now made significant inroads in disrupting the traditional life of the native inhabitants, as reflected in the fact that Pueblo Indian auxiliaries actually played a major role in the campaigns against their brothers.

Resolved not to risk another debacle of the kind suffered in 1680, Spanish administration was tightened. More importantly, reforms, like the abolition of the encomienda, were instituted. The worst abuses were also soon abolished, paving the way for pacification of the area. The missionaries, who gradually lost their influence during the following years, were as conciliatory as was the government. While the exploitation of the natives was not ended altogether—indeed many natives found themselves reduced to peonage—relations between the Spaniards and Pueblos would improve markedly during the eighteenth century.

The Spanish not only rebuilt their old towns but they also began to expand into outlying areas. Among the many new settlements were Santa Cruz de la Cañada, Albuquerque, and Bernalillo (where De Vargas died of a fever in 1704). While it may seem that this expansionist policy was ill advised given their scant numbers and the strength displayed recently by their native adversaries, a more crucial consideration was weighing on the conquerors, the prospect of foreign invasion. By now, the French appeared to pose a far greater threat to the Spaniards than the English ever had. Colonization of Texas became imperative.

SETTLEMENT OF THE NORTHERN FRONTIER BEYOND NEW MEXICO

René-Robert Cavelier, sieur de La Salle, made his epic voyage down the Mississippi to the Gulf of Mexico in 1682. He claimed the vast interior of North

America—which he named Louisiana after his monarch, Louis XIV—for the French. His intention was to set up a vast network of trading posts, where valuable furs would be collected from the Indians and taken down the Mississippi to a French city which would be constructed on the delta. La Salle failed to realize this grandiose scheme; he was killed in Texas by mutineers in 1687. But the prospect of a peltry empire centered on the lower Mississippi continued to fascinate his countrymen for many decades to come.

The Spanish, meanwhile, were not oblivious to these heady visions. In fact, they tended to exaggerate the threat posed by the French on their periphery. In the late 1680s, determined to forestall French encroachment there, the Spanish Crown dispatched several expeditions into Texas, which was officially designated a frontier province in 1691. This initial attempt at colonization failed because of serious manpower shortages and Indian resistance.

French persistence, however, forced the Spaniards to refocus their energies on east Texas, and in June 1716, this area was reoccupied by an expedition under the command of Capt. Domingo Ramón. A presidio at Los Adaes and several missions were set up on the eastern periphery, but the most pivotal settlements were established at an intermediate location between these isolated communities and the Rio Grande. Here, on the San Antonio River, an expedition led by Martín de Alarcón founded a mission, San Antonio de Valero, and presidio, San Antonio de Béxar, in 1718. Significantly, this very year the French constructed New Orleans, meant to be the great entrepôt La Salle envisioned. On the San Antonio River, a civilian population joined the missionaries and soldier-settlers in 1731, when the town of San Fernando de Béxar was founded by fifty-five immigrant families from the Canary Islands. These white families were destined to dominate the economic and political life of San Antonio, which became the provincial capital in 1770. However, as the historian Jesús F. de la Teja has shown, the presidiales were numerous and influential enough that the *Isleños* never established a complete monopoly.[9]

Near San Antonio, a number of smaller outposts were constructed during this period, notably La Bahía (Goliad) farther down the San Antonio River in 1721. Other small settlements, among them Laredo, were built along the Lower Rio Grande Valley in the 1740s by pobladores under the command of José de Escandón. Still another wave of immigrants arrived during the economic crisis that gripped the vicekingdom in the mid-1780s.

However, the Texas frontier remained relatively depopulated during the eighteenth century. By 1800, there were only about 3,500 *Tejanos* in the neglected province. The French threat never really took on the dimensions anticipated, and in 1763, this preoccupation disappeared altogether with the Spanish acquisition of Louisiana. The lack of sedentary tribes to provide needed labor to the region also proved to be a major obstacle to effective colonization, as did the hostility of the nomadic tribes. It was the Comanche, above all others, who stymied Spanish designs on the northeast frontier. Immigrating into the southern plains from the Rockies in the early 1700s, the Comanche soon displaced the Apache as the Spaniards' chief adversaries on the Texas grasslands. During this period, they were acquiring the horse and mastering its use as a military weapon. Monopolizing this knowledge, they soon dominated neighboring tribes, establishing their reputation in the process as Lords of the Southern Plains. Spanish settlers were nearly as defenseless against the Comanche as other Indians were. Horses gave the tribe an influence disproportionate to its modest numbers. Under these circumstances, it is clear why presidios and missions maintained a precarious existence in Texas throughout the colonial period.

Meanwhile, the northwestern frontier of New Spain was also moving forward, in fits and starts. Like Texas, present-day Arizona witnessed the entry of the Spanish in the late seventeenth century. Compared to the eastern thrust along the Caribbean, movement up the western corridor of mainland Mexico, between the Gulf of California and the Sierra Madre Occidental—and neighboring Baja California—owed more to religious considerations than to imperial concerns.

Migration north along the Sea of Cortés was initiated early. By the mid-1500s, the province of Nueva Galicia, extending beyond Culiacán (founded in 1531) in Sinaloa, was reasonably well established. In the following decades, expansion proceeded slowly. The failure of Vásquez de Coronado to find treasure was a factor. So was the manpower shortage in the Sinaloa region; settlers preferred the mining areas opening up farther inland, in Nueva Vizcaya (Durango and Chihuahua). The prospects for expansion changed dramatically, however, in 1591, when the Jesuits were given permission to set up missions on the northwestern frontier.

The Black Robes arrived in New Spain in 1572 anxious to do missionary work on the frontier. Since their services were required in the densely populated core area and the Franciscans had established a monopoly on the periphery, they were forced to postpone their plans for a generation. Their chance came once the Crown, stirred to action by news of Drake's foray into California and the prospect of foreign settlement there, decided that Spanish movement toward the northwest was imperative. Beneficiaries of this imperial concern—Franciscan friars were already overextended—the Jesuits were only too glad to take advantage of the opportunity to pursue their own goals of propagating the true faith. No sooner had they received permission to carry out their new assignment, a product of years of intense lobbying, than they dispatched late in 1591 two missionaries to the Sinaloa frontier, Gonzalo de Tapia and Martín Pérez.

Dedicated and hardworking, Jesuit priests were indomitable in their proselytizing campaign. Their persistence became proverbial and their efforts were generally crowned with success. During the course of the seventeenth century, they made steady progress moving up the western corridor. Traveling in pairs, they established missions among the Yaquis, Opatas, and the numerous other tribes of Sinaloa and Sonora. Already by 1620, fifty-five individual missions had been founded.

Although there were many Jesuit fathers who served with distinction, one man stands out among the rest, Eusebio Francisco Kino (1645?–1711), who was among the most remarkable explorers anywhere in the Americas. An Italian by birth, Father Kino was born in the Tyrolese town of Segno. Drawn to the Church at an early age and anxious to escape life in a small provincial hamlet, he opted for the Society of Jesus, the most dynamic order of the day. In Bavaria, he received the best education available and then embarked for the New World.

Kino was one of the first foreigners given permission by the Spanish Crown to enter New Spain. He served briefly in Baja California, where a plan to found missionary centers proved abortive, before arriving in 1687 on the expanding Sonora frontier, where he spent the rest of his life. Practically single-handedly, Kino pushed the mission into the Pimería Alta, today's northern Sonora and southern Arizona. Then the northernmost fringe of the province of Sonora, he entered a land inhabited not only by the Pimas but also the Pápago (or "Tohono O'odham"), the Sobaípuri, and a variety of Yuman peoples. From his headquarters at the mission of Nuestra Señora de los Dolores, in the middle of the Pimería Alta, he disseminated the faith in all directions. During his lifetime Father Kino was responsible for the construction of twenty-four missions from northern Sinaloa to southern Arizona, a truly remarkable record of achievement. If, as one scholar has observed, "Sonora represented one of the most successful mission endeavors of the Jesuit order in the New World, possibly on a par with its organization in Paraguay, established about the same time," much of the credit certainly belongs to the Padre on Horseback.[10] But Father Kino's historical reputation is based only partly on his prodigious proselytizing efforts. He also had a keen interest in science, and he put this fascination to good use conducting experiments in his missions which resulted in improved crops and livestock. His real passion, though, was geography, and his many explorations led to the first accurate maps of the Spanish northwest. Perhaps his most notable accomplishment, in this regard, was his discovery that Baja California was a peninsula rather than an island, a long-held suspicion that he confirmed once and for all, thus rekindling interest in a land route to Alta California.

Eusebio Kino is known as the Father of Arizona. In fact, at least fourteen of his expeditions were made into the area that today constitutes the state of Arizona, where on several occasions, he went as far as the Gila River, the northernmost limit of effective Spanish settlement during the colonial period. Eventually, he established three missions there, with the most successful being San Xavier del Bac in 1700. The last years of his life were spent consolidating this northern frontier; and when he died, he chose to be buried there, at Magdalena, a mission just a few miles south of today's Arizona-Sonora border.

During the twenty years after the death of Father Kino, missionary activity along the Arizona frontier waned, in part because of increased pressure from indios bárbaros, the Apache and the Seri being the most aggressive, and in part because of the lack of sufficient numbers of missionaries available for duty. While the Indian threat did not abate at all, after about 1730 fresh recruits were able to breathe new life into the proselytizing effort. A number of abandoned missions were reactivated, among them Tumacácori and San Xavier del Bac. The efforts of one priest in particular deserve mention, the Bavarian Jacobo Sedelmayr, who carried on the tradition of Father Kino by combining both intense missionary work and geographic exploration. The conversion of the Pápagos during the early eighteenth century is accredited more to him than any other individual. His explorations took him north beyond the Gila River in 1744 and did much to increase Spanish knowledge of the area.

These missionary efforts were only partially successful. The northern frontier erupted again in 1751, when the Pimas rose up in rebellion. Some one hundred frontiersmen, mostly miners and soldiers, lost their lives. It took several months before the revolt was quelled, but the Arizona-Sonora frontier remained unstable throughout the second half of the eighteenth century.

Encouraged by Kino, missionary efforts were initiated in Baja California in 1697 by his friend and colleague, Father Juan María de Salvatierra, another Italian Jesuit.[11] Despite the paucity of its native population and meager natural resources, greatly inferior to those of Sonora, Jesuits were intent on expanding their influence to the peninsula just as they had previously done eastward, across the Sierra Madre Occidental and on into Chihuahua. The Crown was not adverse to the project. In fact, since its discovery in 1533, Baja California had tempted viceregal authorities; but efforts at colonization, beginning with Cortés in the 1530s and continuing to the time of Kino, had been half-hearted, and hence unsuccessful.

Despite its limited resources, Baja California continued to be enticing. It was the gateway to Alta California, which held immense promise. The Spanish conquest of the Philippines in the 1560s paved the way for a lucrative trade route between the islands and New Spain. Laden with eastern luxury goods, Manila galleons, following the swift Japanese current, made their annual trip along the coast of California to the Mexican port of Acapulco. Vulnerable to pirate raids and in need of supply stations, the Pacific convoys gave California a new significance: a potential base of operations against pirates and better access to supplies.

The search for suitable harbors resulted in two authorized expeditions along the California coast. The first took place in 1595, when Sebastián Rodríguez Cermeño, sailing from the Philippines, led his men down the coast from Cape Mendocino. The second occurred in 1602–1603, when Sebastián Vizcaíno explored the coast north from Mexico and brought back glowing reports of a harbor he named Monterey. Neither expedition, however, found the Bay of San Francisco, and nothing short of this kind of discovery would convince the Spanish Crown to invest its limited resources in the risky venture of settling an area so remote and difficult to access.

From the time of Vizcaíno, the Jesuits clamored for the opportunity to set up missions along the well-populated coast of Alta California. Baja California would be a stepping stone in that direction. So enthused were they about the prospect of a string of missions extending the entire length of the California coast that by the end of the seventeenth century, they were willing to finance the venture themselves, through the Pious Fund of the Californias that they established for this purpose. Spared the cost of the enterprise, with nothing to lose and everything to gain, the Crown could do no less than give its approval.

During the late eighteenth century, the only northern frontier to make significant progress was along the coast of Baja California. In other areas, movement was barely perceptible. In Texas, for example, the removal of the French threat dampened enthusiasm for the continued occupation of that region. Nor did the Spanish acquisition of Louisiana in 1763, following the Seven Years' War, improve the situation. Although the peltry trade should have been a natural magnet, drawing Spanish frontiersmen into the recently acquired area, the vastness of Louisiana and the scarcity of available manpower kept Spain from taking advantage of these new opportunities.

Another obstacle impeding movement into the Far North was again the hostility of the Indians. The 1751 Pima revolt reflects the tenuous nature of the conversions among neophytes. The most persistent problems, however, came from the nomadic Indians. In the early 1700s, Spanish settlements in the upper Rio Grande, as well as the neighboring Pueblo villages, began to be assailed by Utes from the northwest and Comanches from the eastern plains. In Texas, the Comanches, moving south, grew so bold that on several occasions, particularly in the 1770s, the province faced the real possibility of having to be abandoned. Equally troublesome were the Apache, who preferred to raid the isolated cattle ranches and mining communities of Chihuahua and Coahuila, but who roamed throughout the northern frontier from Sonora to Texas. Having acquired horses from the Spanish in the 1600s and European weapons from the French, the English, and later the Americans, Apaches were now able to inspire terror far and wide. They were particularly menacing in the Upper Rio Grande Valley. As the historian Marc Simmons has illustrated, during the eighteenth century, despite the ancient Iberian municipal tradition, New Mexican pobladores began to leave the villages to live close to their crops, a pattern of settlement which made them increasingly vulnerable to attack.[12]

The general instability of the frontier encouraged a major administrative reorganization of the northern half of New Spain in the late eighteenth century. The Bourbons—who had succeeded the Hapsburgs to the Spanish throne in 1701—were avid reformers, and they now sought to impose reforms overseas. José de Gálvez (1720–1787), a special agent of the Crown, a *visitador-general* (inspector general), was dispatched from Spain in 1765 to evaluate the situation, develop a plan of action, and carry it out. Practical results were finally achieved in 1776, with the creation of a new administrative structure, the Comandancia General of the Interior Provinces, which united the Californias, Sonora, Sinaloa, Nueva Vizcaya, New Mexico, Coahuila, and Texas. Under a *commandante-general* (inspector in chief), these provinces were expected to perform their administrative functions more efficiently and combat the Indian problem more effectively. Intended primarily to create a more centralized empire, the Bourbon reforms, of which administrative reorganization was only one part, helped to stimulate progressive changes on the frontier after the 1770s. An expansion of the livestock industry, an increase in trade, and a population explosion were among the most wide-ranging consequences. It would seem that despite the prevailing view today, these changes, as the sociologist Thomas D. Hall argues, "collectively lend credence to the claim that the last years of Spanish control of the Southwest were years of prosperity."[13]

At about this time, the decision was made to also colonize Alta California, the brainchild of the visitador himself. The traditional explanation for this expansion is that the Spanish sought to forestall Russian entry into this frontier, and indeed these intruders were one factor taken into consideration, but the decision was made primarily to enhance Gálvez's reputation: by bringing vitality to a moribund frontier, he would ingratiate himself to the Crown and advance his career. The decision was encouraged by the Church, which would be the chief beneficiary of the plan. As it ultimately turned out, and despite Gálvez's intentions, Alta California would become a missionary colony; the soldiers who accompanied the monks would merely serve to ensure their safety.

The entrada into Alta California was carried out by Franciscans, not by their rivals, the Jesuits, who had run afoul of the Crown and had been officially expelled from the Empire by Carlos III in 1767. One of Gálvez's charges, during his lengthy *visita* (1765–1771) in New Spain, was to carry out this edict. The Jesuit missions in the northwest were then entrusted to the mendicant order. The friars in Baja California were designated by Gálvez to make the push north, with the ultimate destination being Monterey, which Vizcaíno had extravagantly praised so many years before. Two men were put in charge of the "Sacred Expedition," as Gálvez called it: Gaspar de Portolá y de Rovira (1718–1786) and Junípero Serra (1713–1784).

Captain Portolá had served many years on the frontier, where he had earned the reputation of a loyal and able servant of the Crown. Governor of Baja California, he was the natural choice to lead the expedition into Alta California. His job was to escort the friars across the wilderness and then return south once the missions were established, leaving his subordinate, Lieut. Pedro Fages, in charge of presidial troops.

The giant in the enterprise, however, would be Father Serra. Born in Petra, a small village on the island of Majorca, he joined the Franciscans and became a professor of theology at the local university. In his mid-thirties, he decided to abandon the classroom to pursue a missionary career in New Spain. He served first on the northeastern frontier, in Nuevo Santander. When the Baja California missions were transferred to his order, Father Serra was dispatched to Loreto as father-president, the head of the entire mission system on the peninsula. On the northern trek to Alta California he was accompanied by one of his former students, fray Juan Crespí, who became his chief aide.

The drive north consisted of two overland parties, assisted by three ships. The first party left Velicatá, Baja California's northernmost mission, on 24 March 1769, and arrived in San Diego on 14 May 1769; and the second party, headed by Serra and Portolá, followed a few weeks later. The difficulties of travel are abundantly illustrated by the mortality rate: most of the three hundred or so men on the expedition died before arriving at their destination.

Undaunted, Serra commenced his work in Alta California with the founding of its first mission, San Diego de Alcalá, on 16 July 1769. Eventually, twenty-one institutions were erected (the first nine by Serra). The last and northernmost mission, Sonoma's San Francisco Solano, was built in 1823, two years after the end of Spanish rule in Mexico.

The mission system came to dominate life in Alta California during the remaining decades of the Spanish era, at a time when it had been eclipsed by the presidio in other stretches of the frontier and had apparently outlived its usefulness, according to many anti-clerical critics. The mission consisted not only of the church buildings themselves but also of thousands of surrounding acres which were meant to sustain the padres and their Indian wards.

The native peoples, of course, were the raison d'etre of the entire missionary system. Essentially, Alta California was settled because of the enormous numbers of potential converts to be found in the area. According to the foremost authority on the subject, Sherburne F. Cook, these numbers exceeded 300,000 in 1769, probably the greatest concentration of native Americans anywhere in North America. Fortunately for the Spanish, most of the Indians lived along the coast, where there were abundant resources for hunting and gathering as well as fishing. The missions established along this narrow strip were easy to link, both via the ocean and overland along the *camino real* (king's highway). While the tribes in the interior, beyond the coastal range, were never brought under effective control, those on the coast, in sharp contrast, were coerced into a life of virtual slavery with surprising ease, even considering the enormous disparity in technology between natives and immigrants.

In the absence of strong resistance, which surfaced only sporadically at the outset, Franciscans were able to produce results that surprised officials in Mexico City. The number of conversions was relatively modest under Serra, but under his successor, fray Fermín de Lasuén, who served as father-president from 1785 to 1803, the number of converts came to exceed fifty thousand. Neophytes were taught agriculture and stock raising, as well as a variety of crafts. However, the positive achievements of the missions were outweighed by the deadly toll taken by Euroasiatic diseases, as was true throughout the frontier, and perhaps even more severely, as scholars Robert H. Jackson and Edward Castillo argue, by the debilitating effects of slavery.[14] The Indian population along the coast declined from about 60,000 in 1769 to about 35,000 in 1800.

Alongside the mission, as in other parts of the Far North, was the presidio. The first garrison was erected in San Diego in 1769 by Captain Portolá, who was also responsible for the second presidio, in Monterey in 1770. He returned to Baja California, according to plan, that very year, leaving Lieutenant Fages in charge.

From the very beginning, problems developed between missionaries and military men. Serra and Fages, in particular, did not get along at all. The clash went beyond personalities. The most substantial point of contention had to do with decisions about where and when missions would be built. Serra wanted to extend the mission system with all due haste; Fages disagreed, arguing that his troops had insufficient strength to ensure the safety of isolated missionaries. In addition, it was not clear who had precedence, religious or civilian authorities.

As vexing as the question of authority, supplies and manpower were a concern in the first few years. It was discovered almost immediately that the missions could not be supplied adequately from the south. Not only was Baja California barren, but movement north, either by land or sea, was slow and dangerous. The only alternative was to open a trail between Alta California and the Arizona settlements of northern Sonora. This arduous task was entrusted to one of the most extraordinary and fascinating of Spain's frontiersmen, Juan Bautista de Anza (1735–1788). Captain of the presidio at Tubac (founded in 1753, in the aftermath of the Pima Rebellion), he led a party of some thirty-five men across the Colorado River and over the southern California desert to Mission San Gabriel, where he arrived on 22 March 1774. Anza was accompanied by fray Francisco Garcés, worthy heir to Kino and Sedelmayr on the Sonora frontier. Anza continued on to Monterey before making his return trip to Tubac. In 1775–1776, he made a second trip to California, this time bringing a company of 240, most of them settlers. Led by Lieut. José Joaquín Moraga, members of this second Anza expedition were responsible for founding the outpost of San Francisco on 17 September 1776. Anza himself returned to Arizona, the region which continued to supply Alta California during the next few years.

In July 1781, however, this trade ended abruptly. An uprising of Yuma Indians who lived along the trail resulted in the massacre of 104 people, including Father Garcés. This grisly episode discredited the route, and as a result, the Spanish population of Alta California grew very slowly in the next few years. In 1800, there were only about 1,200 non-Indians in the area.

MAJOR TRENDS

The settlement of the coastal region of Alta California at the end of the eighteenth century brought to an end the era of Spanish expansion in the north. During the last half century of the colonial period, Spanish exploration continued in many directions, including the Pacific coast as far as Yakutat Bay, Alaska, but the limit of effective settlement had been established. As one surveys these northern colonies during the last decades of the Spanish frontier, an interesting pattern emerges. Essentially, the Far North consisted of three finger-like projections extending into North America. On the Pacific Coast were the California missions; two towns of any significance, San José and Los Angeles; and four presidios, located in San Diego, Santa Barbara, Monterey, and San Francisco. In the center were the New Mexican settlements of the Upper Rio Grande, the most heavily populated area on the frontier, with forty thousand inhabitants in 1821, a quarter of them Pueblo Indians. Santa Fe continued to be the capital and leading city, but nearby Albuquerque (founded in 1706) and Paso del Norte, far to the south, were also key towns along the Chihuahua trail that linked this pivotal province with the Mexican interior. In Texas, the third colonial extension, there were scattered settlements here and there, including some in east Texas, but the only city of any consequence was San Antonio.

Between the finger-like projections, the frontier was virtually uninhabited by non-Indians, except in northern Sonora, where a garrison was established in Tucson in 1776 and continued a precarious existence on the edge of the *Gran Apachería*, the land of the Apaches. These areas of settlement were isolated from one another, as well as from northern Mexican towns and the chief population centers on the central plateau. Several attempts were made to link the three sparsely colonized areas but with little success. The abortive 1776 effort by Franciscans Silvestre Vélez de Escalante and Francisco Atanasio Domínguez to establish a trail between New Mexico and California, via present-day Utah, was only the most notable of many such ventures. As a consequence, distinct ways of life developed in the various pockets of settlements on the northern rim of New Spain. And yet, for all their diversity, there were many commonalties among these Hispanic communities.

Frontier society by about 1800 was significantly different than that which evolved in the Mexican interior during the course of the eighteenth century. The main difference was that the societies of New Mexico, Texas, Arizona, and California were relatively open compared to the hierarchical structures that had crystallized in the great population centers of New Spain toward the end of the colonial period.

As in other parts of the Hispanic world, the family in the core area of New Spain stood at the center of existence. Family life was remarkably stable throughout the Spanish period, regardless of social class. The Hispanic family generally consisted of a husband, his wife, several children, and assorted relatives. The husband was the patriarch who, in theory at least, made the most important decisions, a consequence of his status as the breadwinner of the family. His wife controlled the household, raising the children and performing most of the domestic chores. For their part, the children were taught to respect and help their parents. Boys, if they were lucky, received the rudiments of an education; girls were trained in domestic skills. Marriages were often arranged, especially among the most affluent, and occurred at an early age; women tended to marry when they reached the age of puberty.

On the frontier, this pattern generally prevailed as well, but local conditions necessitated significant modifications. For example, in this peripheral setting, life was much more precarious than in the interior. The social historian Alicia Vidaurreta Tjarks, author of several valuable demographic studies on the Far North, is clear on this point: "Life was shorter in the borderlands; permanent warfare against the Indians, the fight for subsistence in a hostile environment, a deficient and limited diet, and, above all, epidemic diseases like smallpox and *matlazahuatl* fever, which specially ravaged Texas (as most of New Spain) during the years 1785–1786, resulted in the loss of many lives, particularly among the infant population."[15]

Frontier life was hard for both men and women, as well as their children. Mothers often died while giving birth. Indian depredations, however, took an even greater toll on their husbands. The number of widows was always high on the frontier. This was true even after the Spanish period. In Abiquiú, for example, in 1845, 91 out of a total of 338 households (almost 27 percent) were headed by widows. The normal life expectancy, for both men and women, was about forty.

One major difference between established society and frontier society was the relatively greater freedom in the latter available to women. That so many women were widowed was one factor, but the absence of a clear-cut division of labor on the frontier was perhaps more telling. Women often worked outside of the home. *Curanderas* (medicine women) and *parteras* (midwives) were not uncommon. In fact, there were times when women were expected to help men defend the community against Indian raids. The women of New Mexico were especially "liberated," an observation made by many astonished outsiders at the end of the Spanish period and throughout the Mexican period. Unlike their American counterparts, Hispano women were allowed to smoke, drink, and gamble, which often led American observers to conclude that these ladies were lascivious and immoral. In point of fact, these privileges were manifestations of more significant freedoms afforded women in Hispanic society. They were at liberty to run businesses, divorce their husbands, own property, and sue in court. These rights were largely theoretical in central New Spain, but they were exercised on a regular basis by the women of colonial New Mexico. The historian Albert Hurtado feels that women in Hispanic California followed a more traditional pattern.[16] It is likely, though, that New Mexico was the rule rather than the exception on the northern frontier.

If gender roles were blurred on the frontier, the same appears to be the case with social classes. Mexican society was highly stratified by the eighteenth century, but society was relatively fluid on the frontier. For one thing, the caste system appears to have totally broken down by 1800. Ethnic boundaries, says the historian Adrian Bustamante, "became blurred, causing the system to become muddled and largely ineffective."[17] No longer was there a tight correlation between color and class, though a preoccupation with racial status continued to be evident in official documents all through the Spanish period. Another reason for the greater social mobility was the scarcity of labor, which was even more chronic on the periphery than in the heartland. Under such circumstances, the acquisition of land was relatively easy. Regardless of the specific frontier area, most pobladores were landowners.

The trend toward greater democratization increased because the extremes of wealth and poverty found in the established communities of New Spain were largely absent on the frontier. Even though there was a tendency to separate society into those who were better off and those who were not, to label them *ricos* (rich) and *pobres* (poor) respectively, at this point in time, is misleading. The lifestyles of the elite and the rest of the population were similar, if not identical, throughout the northern rim of New Spain; both struggled to make a living in the hard frontier environment. This holds true even in New Mexico, where some scholars see the establishment of an "aristocracy" during the colonial period.[18]

The relatively modest socioeconomic status of the elite is well illustrated by the Chicano historian Antonio José Ríos-Bustamante in a valuable study of Albuquerque based on an analysis of the 1790 census, the most complete census undertaken during the entire Spanish period. In a town population of 1,155, seven individuals listed their occupation as rancher, the most lucrative and prestigious category; and, significantly, only twelve individuals identified themselves as servants, the lowest occupation on the town's social and economic scale.[19] Even taking into consideration that most servants were children, and thus were missing from the record, it is clear that the elite, itself quite small, was hardly leading a life of leisure. Don Vicente Armijo, for example, one of the seven ranchers—and one of only four men in town to bear the honorary title of "Don"—had four servants, possibly the most of anyone.

Moreover, in New Mexico and throughout the frontier, members of the upper and lower class were often related by marriage and by *compadrazgo* (coparenthood), which ameliorated the relations between the two segments of society. Perhaps most influential in binding the community, however, was that Hispanic peoples, whether they were white or mixed-bloods—what the Spanish called *castas*—shared a common culture as *gente de razón*, literally "people of reason"; something that was not true of, and distinguished them from, Indians, who were known as *gente sin razón*, "people without reason."

Frontier society was similar throughout the Far North despite some local differences from place to place. Other commonalties existed as well. In particular, during the closing years of the Spanish period, frontier life was dominated by the Indian problem, mestizaje, and American contact.

As previously mentioned, during the course of the eighteenth century the Indian threat to frontier settlements escalated precipitously. Frontier communities faced a multitude of problems, but by the 1770s, none more pressing than the Indian Question. The nomadic Indians committed depredations seemingly at will—often provoked by Spanish atrocities, including rapes and kidnappings. The provinces, left to their own meager resources, were unable to curb the violence. Many policies were attempted, ranging from extermination to bribery. But in the absence of an overall plan coordinating local and national efforts, the shortage of men and money, and the ability of the mounted warriors to move from one province to another in no time at all, pobladores were left completely to the mercy of indios bárbaros. Often entire towns were abandoned, putting the frontier economy in disarray. However, by the turn of the century, the situation, if not completely resolved, improved considerably, and relative security was restored.

This amelioration was a result of an Indian policy which had been formulated several years before. In 1777, Teodoro de Croix was made commandante-general of the Internal Provinces. Making alliances with some of the warlike tribes against other indios bárbaros, often hereditary enemies, he experienced modest success in pacifying the frontier. In the early 1780s, however, the viceroy himself, Bernardo de Gálvez, nephew of José de Gálvez, formulated a more effective plan of action. Rather than adopting a purely defensive and reactive policy against Apaches and other indios bárbaros or relying completely on tenuous alliances, he determined to aggressively subjugate them by invading their strongholds. Exterminating recalcitrants in the process, and requiring that the vanquished tribes settle down near presidios, he sought to undermine their traditional lifestyle, hence forcing them to rely on their conquerors for survival. Essentially, their cooperation, in this last phase, would be ensured through bribery. The ambitious plan was put into operation, and it worked remarkably well in pacifying the frontier. Employing both carrot and stick, Bernardo de Gálvez's successors enjoyed considerable success during the next few years. In fact, the Far North was reasonably secure for a lengthy period which came to an end only in 1810, when the outbreak of the Mexican war for independence necessitated removal of troops from the frontier and encouraged nomadic Indians to again resume hostilities. Yet, in some areas like Arizona the truce held into the 1820s.

A second striking theme during the Spanish period, one that also relates to Indian-settler relations, is race mixture. It is clear that mestizaje was initiated as soon as colonists arrived in the Far North. There is a good deal of disagreement among scholars, however, as to the extent that this process was carried out. Since Indian-Mexican unions could be illicit as well as Church-sanctioned, it is difficult to arrive at a conclusive answer. The written records of the times, of which the most relevant are census and church records, are not much help either. The authorities, both clergymen and servants of the state, were very conscious of race, and in their documents they often alluded to it. However, as many students have pointed out—Manuel Servín, Alicia Tjarks, Antonio José Ríos-Bustamante, and David Weber, among others—*español* (a term indicating that the person in question was white), the most common designation for the non-Indian population on the frontier, was a highly unreliable measure of race since it was often applied to castas, people of mixed blood. Many pobladores would identify themselves or others by this designation as long as they weren't obviously Indian or African. While the use of this term reflected the anti-Indian prejudices of Hispanic society, it was also employed to denote that the individual had adopted a European lifestyle;

that is, the term was often used as a cultural rather than a racial category. Given the difficulties in studying race mixture, any conclusions made at present must be tentative at best. This is one area that needs more study by Chicano and Borderlands historians.

The first settlers to arrive in New Mexico with Juan de Oñate were mostly white. Race mixture in central Mexico, where the pobladores initiated their expedition, was very gradual—as late as the first decades of the nineteenth century, the majority of New Spain's inhabitants were still Indians—and it follows that the same would have been true during the sixteenth century. According to the geographer Richard L. Nostrand, "Of the 210 documented soldier-settlers going to New Mexico in 1598 and 1600, a majority in each year were born in Spain (110), followed by New Spain (55), Portugal and elsewhere (13), and unable to locate (15), or not given (17)."[20] Once in the Upper Rio Grande Valley, pobladores built their settlements away from Pueblo villages, a separation that was encouraged by the Indians themselves as well as the Franciscans, who sought to protect their charges.

But miscegenation began immediately.[21] In New Mexico, and throughout the frontier, especially in the states that constitute northern Mexico today, Spanish frontiersmen were accompanied by significant numbers of Mexican Indians. Tlascalans (or Tlascaltecos), Tarascans, and Opatas were well represented among these Indian settlers. During the colonial period, these tribes gradually lost their separate identity. Undoubtedly, some of them married Pueblos, but many of them must have married Europeans. Moreover, the settlers occasionally married into local Indian society; Pueblos, after all, were accorded full citizenship rights, including the right to marry into the gente de razón. Missionary efforts to segregate the two communities were not always successful. A 1749 census indicates that 570 Indians resided in Santa Fe and another 200 were to be found in Albuquerque. The opportunity for miscegenation, it seems, was readily available.

Finally, among Hispanic colonists, much of the miscegenation was with *genízaros*, generally defined as captives and slaves of nomadic tribes who had been ransomed by the Spanish government, though, as Frances León Swadesh, a specialist on the Spanish-Ute frontier, has shown, Pueblo Indians were also represented in this group in significant numbers.[22] Estimates of the genízaro population by 1776 range as high as one-third of the entire population of the province. Some of these detribalized Indians were allowed to go off to the edge of the frontier to build their own settlements—San Tomás de Abiquiú being the best-known example—as buffers against the Plains Indians. The majority became servants in Spanish households, where they gradually blended in with their masters. Mestizaje, then, was the rule rather than the exception. By the end of the eighteenth century, according to a 1776 census of New Mexico, the majority of its inhabitants were designated as mestizos.[23]

Racial blending may have occurred more rapidly in the Texas area, where the non-Indian inhabitants were predominantly of mixed origins by the end of the Spanish period. Race mixture had little to do with the indigenous population in Texas. Most tribes were nomadic and warlike, making marriage with the colonizers unlikely. However, the great bulk of the immigration to Texas during the period before 1821 already consisted of mestizos, mostly from the northern Mexican states of Coahuila, Nuevo León, and Nuevo Santander. As the historian Andrés Tijerina has pointed out, "Most of the Mexican settlers and soldiers who inhabited the communities and presidios of Texas had come from staging areas in northern Mexico where racial mixing had been prevalent."[24] It is important to note that even more than in New Mexico, the genetic pool was impacted by Africans. Blacks and mulattoes were among the immigrants entering Texas from Louisiana to the east, as well as from Nuevo León and Coahuila to the south. The Isleños, who insisted on marrying within their own community, preserved their European bloodlines longer than other Tejanos, but even they had become thoroughly integrated into the emerging melting pot by the end of the Spanish period.

In Sonora, which included Arizona, the situation was similar to Texas in that many of the native tribes were nomads. Where there were sedentary tribes, the Jesuits succeeded in congregating the neophytes into missions. Missionization, of course, did not encourage race mixture. The mission fathers, who were more or less celibate themselves, discouraged Indian contact with whites, who were thought to have a corrupting influence. They also sought to protect their wards from labor exploitation, miners being the chief threats.

Most of the newcomers to the Sonora frontier, be they ranchers, miners, or soldiers, tended to be mestizos. "Practically all those who wish to be considered Spaniards are people of mixed blood," Ignaz Pfefferkorn, a Jesuit priest who served eleven years in Sonora before his expulsion in 1767, later recalled.[25] Nevertheless, in 1821 the one place on the frontier where a large white population remained well represented was Sonora, where in the late eighteenth century—particularly after 1770 when the Apaches were placated and economic opportunities improved—colonists entered directly from Spain in significant numbers. Another group, the priests, were white, though it is unlikely that they would have had a significant impact on the genetic pool.

Settled in the late eighteenth century, when mestizaje was well established in central Mexico, particularly among the lower classes, Alta California was colonized by people who were much different racially from those who had accompanied Oñate on his entrada into New Mexico. As Manuel Servín, one of the first

Chicano historians to study the Borderlands, pointed out, the overwhelming majority of men who entered California with Portolá and Serra, were either Indians or mixed-bloods; only eight Spaniards spent any time at all in the province.[26] Moreover, two-thirds of the men who settled San Francisco and San José in 1776–1778 were Indians or castas. And of the twenty-three colonists, mostly from Sinaloa and Sonora, who founded the town of Los Angeles in 1781, only two were white.[27] The great majority of troops who came into California in the late eighteenth century were of mixed blood, and the same was probably true of enlisted men throughout the frontier.

Though interethnic marriages were allowed and occasionally even encouraged, for the most part settler-soldiers in California were strictly forbidden from dealing with neophytes by the Franciscans, so interethnic marriages were rare on the northwestern frontier. The incidence of rape, as soldiers took advantage of Indian women, may have been relatively common, as the historian Antonia I. Castañeda asserts.[28] However, it must be remembered, children that resulted from these attacks were generally killed by the tribe. The evidence, then, suggests that unlike mestizaje in New Mexico, the mixture of people in Alta California occurred with Indians from the Mexican interior rather than local indigenous populations.

It is safe to conclude that by the end of the Spanish colonial period, substantial racial mixture via a variety of means had occurred on the northern frontier. Certainly, there was more mingling of the races there than in central Mexico, despite the larger pool of native peoples in the south. Undoubtedly, most "Spaniards" on the frontier in 1821 were mestizos rather than white. Many, perhaps most, of the new arrivals were already mestizos. Once on the frontier, unions, legal and illicit, between so-called Spaniards and Indians were not uncommon, especially in New Mexico, where colonization had a long history and both soldier-settlers and Pueblo Indians were well represented numerically.

One ethnic peculiarity of the New Mexican frontier, incidentally, was the apparent presence of significant numbers of Jews among the settlers. The expulsion in 1492 had resulted in a number of Jewish conversions to Catholicism in Spain, but many *conversos* or *marranos*, as Jewish converts were called, continued to practice their ancient faith clandestinely. The New World provided "crypto-Jews" the opportunity to escape the close scrutiny of the Inquisition, an institution that was much weaker overseas—pagans, after all, were not subject to the Holy Office—and some of them migrated to New Spain. The northern frontier was appealing, since there they could best preserve their cultural and religious traditions, though always surreptitiously. Many Mexicans in the United States today are products of this Sephardic background. According to Frances Hernández, Professor of English and Comparative Languages at the University of Texas at El

Paso, there may be some fifteen hundred families in the Southwest who "have retained an unbroken chain of Jewish matrilineal descent."[29]

The third and final theme dominating the last years of the Spanish frontier is the advent of the *norteamericano*, the American. Though Spain's mercantilist philosophy had theoretically precluded the entry of foreigners into its possessions, the system was very loose in reality, and there was never a time when foreigners were completely absent from New Spain. This was even truer of the Far North, which like any frontier environment was hard to regulate. Moreover, unable to satisfy the material needs of its frontiersmen, Spain found that its outposts on the periphery were often anxious to carry on contraband trade with outsiders. Frenchmen, in particular, seem to have penetrated into the northern rim with some regularity in the eighteenth century, even before the incorporation of Louisiana into the Spanish Empire in 1763. In fact, visitors arrived from all over the globe and for many reasons. Americans were the last but, given their imminent hegemony in the area, the most significant of these interlopers.

By the time of their independence from England, recognized by the Treaty of Paris in 1783, Americans were beginning to develop an interest in expanding their influence to the Pacific, the gateway to the wealth of the Far East. In the 1790s, Yankee ships began to visit the California coast, where they carried on illicit trade. The first of these ships arrived in 1796. The most famous of the visitors was Capt. William Shaler, who saw California in 1803 and published a glowing description of the province two years later. While singing the praises of the land and its resources, he was less complimentary of its Spanish residents, suggesting that their lethargy made progress impossible. Only American energy and diligence, he insinuated, could develop the vast potential of California—one of the first expositions of a sentiment later labeled Manifest Destiny.

Meanwhile, on the Texas borderland, the influx of norteamericanos reached alarming proportions after the Louisiana Purchase of 1803. Already by that date, there were a number of Americans who had settled in Texas legally, many coming in from Louisiana, where the Spanish had actually encouraged Yankee settlement before the territory had been returned to the French in 1800. The cotton gin, invented in 1793, had revitalized the cotton economy in the American South, and new lands were opening up for planters along the Gulf Coast. It was only a matter of time before the United States and Spain would have trouble along their common border, where the new boundary line was in dispute. Problems were precipitated by American citizens, who recognized that the Blackland soils of the eastern parts of Texas, with their many rivers emptying into the Gulf of Mexico, were ideal for both agriculture and ranching. A series of unsuccessful Yankee filibustering expeditions into east Texas, where Spanish control was precarious at best, were staged in the next few years. American land hunger and its own difficulties in enticing settlers into Texas alarmed the Crown. Spanish fears were allayed in 1819, however, when the governments of Spain and the United States agreed on a precise border in the Adams-Onís Treaty.

American contact in New Mexico was less worrisome because the number of Yankee sightings there was so small. The few Americans who straggled into Santa Fe and surrounding villages after 1805 were solitary fur trappers and traders who seemed content to exchange goods. Consequently, Americans met with a mixed reception. Completely dependent on Mexican merchants to the south for their imports, and thus subject to exorbitant prices, New Mexicans sometimes welcomed Yankee mountain men, who sold them pelts at reasonable prices. At other times, outsiders were expelled unceremoniously. One American whose presence was highly unwelcome was Zebulon Montgomery Pike, who suspiciously wandered into Santa Fe in early 1807. He pleaded that he had been sent by the American government to find the headwaters of the Arkansas and Red rivers but had lost his way, which may have been the case. It was suspected, though, that he was on a military reconnaissance mission to probe Spanish defenses in preparation for an invasion. Interrogated and sent to Chihuahua City, he and his men were released later that year.

At the time of the Pike episode, Spanish authorities in Mexico City were slowly coming to the realization that the fledgling nation to the northeast posed a legitimate threat to their northern possessions. But when the day came that the confrontation proved inevitable, Spain would be but a memory on the borderlands.

The Spanish and American frontiers share many similarities, but the differences are more significant.[30] For one thing, religion had a much greater impact on the northern rim of New Spain. The most characteristic institution on this frontier was the mission, which played a relatively minor role in the westward movement.

The attitude toward the Indian, it follows, was also distinct. Few Anglo-American frontiersmen saw Indians as human beings, a view that was common in the Far North. Whether treatment of the native peoples was more humane, is a hotly debated question. The Spanish exploited the Indians heavily, at times instituting slavery. Occasionally, too, they adopted a policy of extermination against the most intractable of the nomadic tribes. On the other hand, miscegenation was widespread, both a cause and a reflection of their more positive attitude toward indigenous peoples. On balance, Indians on the expanding frontier of the United States were probably treated worse than among their counterparts to the south. While genocide may be too strong a term to use here, ultimately, the choice given native Americans on the Anglo-American frontier was life on a reservation or death.

Finally, while the Spanish frontier was never as authoritarian as imperial theory would suggest and the Anglo-American frontier was never as democratic as Frederick Jackson Turner would have us believe, the fact remains that there was a sizable gap in the mindset that emerged in both areas. Individual initiative was more characteristic of the movement west; northern expansion of New Spain was largely a product of government policy and frontier life was heavily regulated.

In the last analysis, though, it may be unfair to compare Spanish frontiersmen with American frontiersmen; perhaps it would be more profitable to compare life in the Far North with life in the Mexican interior. Only then can we truly appreciate the strengths of the men and women who established a firm foundation for the Indo-Hispanic culture which continues to thrive in the United States.

THE MEXICAN FAR NORTH

1821–1848

3

The Mexican period of Southwest History was very brief, lasting from 1821, when Mexico achieved its independence from Spain, to 1848, when the fledgling republic lost its northern territories to the United States with the signing of the Treaty of Guadalupe Hidalgo. The most fateful trend in the Far North during this period was the continuing influx, in ever increasing numbers, of norteamericanos. Beset with a multitude of difficulties, which it shared with other emerging Latin American nations after the demise of the Spanish Empire in the New World, Mexico was unable to devote sufficient attention to its northern border regions. The chief problem, as it had been for Spain, was the inability to populate an enormous area over which it never established effective control. The advent of the United States, a nation with seemingly unlimited resources and a burgeoning population, a people, moreover, brimming with a confidence that bordered on arrogance, could mean only trouble for their southern neighbors. What Mexico needed desperately in the first decades of its existence as an independent nation was a long period of peace, but it was its misfortune to find itself sharing a common border with the Colossus of the North.

MEXICAN INDEPENDENCE

The collapse of Spain's empire had a host of causes. External factors included the influence of the European Enlightenment, which undermined the old order, as well as the examples of revolution in both North America, where the English colonists proclaimed their independence in 1776, and in France, where a decade of unrest was initiated in 1789. As has justly been observed, the Latin American upheavals that followed were part of an Atlantic phenomenon during a period that the noted American historian Robert R. Palmer has termed the Age of the Democratic Revolution.

More important still were internal considerations in Spanish America itself. While economic and political problems were ubiquitous, as was true in both France and the thirteen colonies, social inequalities seem to have played a larger role than in the other two areas. The Latin American revolutions were instigated by *criollos* (creoles), people of Spanish ancestry born in the Americas. Creole discontent during the colonial era was caused by the virtual monopoly exerted by Spanish-born citizens over the administrative hierarchies of both the colonial Church and State. Called *peninsulares* or *gachupines*, these Europeans dominated economic and political life, effectively shutting out American-born residents from positions of power. By the last decades of the colonial period, resentment against the privileged elite was widespread, but while neither Indians nor mestizos, much less blacks, were in a position to challenge the social order, the creoles came to believe that because of their education and wealth, they were destined to replace their fathers, or at least share the positions atop the socioeconomic pyramid. At the same time, they had no real sympathy with the lower classes, a common American origin notwithstanding, and the last thing they wanted was a race war and the destruction of the social order. While the Latin American revolts may have resulted in enhancing social and political democracy, this ideal was almost completely unanticipated by the emerging creole malcontents.

The occasion for the Latin American revolutions was the conquest of Spain by the French during the Napoleonic wars. When Napoleon invaded Spain in 1808 and replaced King Ferdinand VII with his own brother, Joseph Bonaparte, the people rose up in rebellion. This upsurge of Spanish patriotism proved to be the beginning of the end for Napoleon and his dreams of French hegemony in Europe, but the resulting chaos on the Iberian peninsula also had dire repercussions for Spain in the New World. By 1825, its American empire would be in complete shambles.

In New Spain, as in other parts of the empire, creoles were in the forefront of the revolutionary surge. Although a member of this class, the hero of Mexican independence was a very unlikely insurrectionary—the Catholic clergyman Miguel Hidalgo y Costilla. Born in Guanajuato and educated in Valladolid (now Morelia), Hidalgo was ordained a priest in 1778. His unorthodox religious beliefs and liberal lifestyle soon got him in trouble with his superiors. In 1803, the fifty-year-old priest was exiled to Dolores (now Dolores Hidalgo), a small village near his hometown. By now, he had come to embrace a host of revolutionary doctrines. These included the beliefs in Mexican independence and, even more radical, the equality of all people, including Indians, who constituted more than half of the colony's six million inhabitants. The revolution was launched on 16 September 1810, when the courageous priest delivered his famous "Grito de Dolores" (Cry of Dolores): "Long live our Lady of Guadalupe! Death to bad government! Death to the gachupines!" This historic day, the *Diez y Seis de Septiembre*, is now celebrated as Mexican Independence Day.

Marching on a circuitous route toward Mexico City, the revolutionary army grew enormously, which accounted for its early successes. Unfortunately, indiscriminate looting and killing quickly alienated the propertied classes, and the criollos, the natural leaders of the independence movement in other parts of Latin America, drew back in horror before the daunting prospects of social revolution. Having lost creole support, Father Hidalgo's peasant armies proved no match for well-trained and disciplined Spanish soldiers. The backlash was unusually ferocious. Hidalgo himself suffered a martyr's death in 1811. A fellow priest, José María Morelos y Pavón, a mestizo, tried to keep the revolutionary impetus alive, but his capture and execution in 1815 appeared to be the death knell of the movement.

Events in Spain, however, conspired to keep discontent smoldering in New Spain, ultimately bringing about independence—ironically, under the banner of conservatism. In 1812, with victory against Napoleon's army of occupation in sight, the Cortes, the Spanish legislative assembly, drafted a liberal document establishing a constitutional monarchy. But after his restoration, Ferdinand VII reneged on his promise to abide by its terms; and the Constitution of 1812 was repealed, causing a deep rift between the king and his people. Discontent mounted, especially in the army, where liberal sympathies were particularly strong. Late in 1820, Spanish troops at Cádiz, about to embark for the Americas where they were needed against rebel armies, revolted against the Bourbon monarchy. Under the leadership of Col. Rafael Riego, the malcontents demanded the restoration of the 1812 Constitution. Eventually, the Riego uprising would prove abortive, as the major powers—the Concert of Europe—intervened to put an end to this threat to the established order. But in the meanwhile, conservative elements in New Spain, panicked at the prospect of living under an "atheistic" regime, determined to break with the mother country. They found their champion in a creole army officer, Agustín de Iturbide, who declared independence in late 1821 and soon proclaimed himself emperor of the new nation.

Unlike liberation movements in other Latin American colonies, then, national independence in Mexico occurred under the aegis of conservatism rather than liberalism. However, conservative ascendancy was ephemeral. Iturbide's abuse of power served to discredit his political philosophy, as well as the Empire; and in February of 1823, he was deposed by his liberal adversaries, who now established a republican form of government patterned on that of the United States.

The following decades were to be turbulent ones in Mexican history. It was only with the greatest of difficulties that Mexico would maintain its sovereignty.

In the Far North, the change from Spanish to Mexican rule occurred with little violence. During the civil war itself, the pobladores of the northern frontier remained largely unconcerned about the issues being contested by royalists and patriots. Only in Texas was there any genuine enthusiasm for independence, as witnessed by popular though abortive revolts led by Juan Bautista de las Casas in early 1811 and Bernardo Gutiérrez de Lara in 1812–1813. But given the modest size of the local populations and the vast distances from the major theaters of action, the impact exerted by Texan rebels on the periphery was negligible. By and large, the residents of the northern rim remained spectators during the tumultuous decade of revolution.

Still, it was not long before the repercussions of the struggle were felt by *fronterizos*, Mexican borderlanders. The most momentous consequence in the Far North was the resurgence of the Indian threat. The need to combat the rebels forced the Spanish Crown to transfer many of its presidial troops from peripheral areas to the capital and the surrounding areas, centers of Mexican resistance. The abandonment of its northern garrisons encouraged local tribes, especially the various Apache bands, to resume their raids on the unfortunate pobladores, now left to their own meager resources. The revolutionary wars almost completely ruined the nation's mining industry. Devoid of its major source of revenue, independent Mexico was less able than the Spanish Crown to provide military protection on the frontier. The deterioration of the presidial system, more than any other factor, accounts for the revival of the Indian threat after decades of relative calm. The alliances the Spanish government had forged with the Comanche, Ute, Navajo, and Jicarilla Apache crumbled in the 1820s. Still another cause of disruption was the influence of American traders, who provided the natives guns and a market for goods, which encouraged raids on southern settlements. "Few historians," notes a prominent borderlands scholar, "...have understood the extent to which American expansion upset the delicate balance between independent Indian peoples and pobladores in Mexico's Far North, from Texas to California."[1] Indian problems would plague the region throughout the period of Mexican rule.

Another major trend during the Mexican period was Anglo immigration. The weakness of the Mexican government, together with the land hunger that characterized America's westward movement, ensured that the steady stream of Yankees during the last years of Spanish colonial rule would only swell after 1821. Ultimately, the norteamericano proved to be a threat even more menacing than the Indian.

The pobladores of northern Mexico faced a set of common problems, but it should not be assumed that life on the frontier was homogeneous. Then, as now, there were meaningful distinctions between the residents of California, New Mexico, Arizona, and Texas—as a quick survey of the political, economic, and social life of these areas will illustrate.

CALIFORNIA

Far removed from the center of Mexican political life, California took no direct part whatsoever in the events that resulted in Mexican independence. The majority of Californios, some 3,200 people by 1821, had no special feelings about independence one way or the other, and they quickly resigned themselves to the new order. Among the small upper class, however, opinions were sharply divided. News of Mexico's independence was received with genuine satisfaction by some members of the military, among them several young officers representing the region's emerging rancho aristocracy. Disappointed over the lack of support Spain had provided the California provinces, they felt that change could only be for the better. The Franciscans, on the other hand, virtually all of them peninsulares, were hostile to the revolution, especially after the collapse of Iturbide's empire and the apparent triumph of liberalism, a "godless" ideology, with the adoption of the Constitution of 1824. Given the long tradition in Spanish history of a union of throne and altar, the intransigence of the clergy was not unexpected.

The political life of the Mexican Republic during its first decades would be extremely chaotic. Well into the second half of the nineteenth century, a virtual civil war was waged between liberals, who opposed strong central authority and stressed civil liberties, and conservatives, who found an antidote to the country's many ills in a powerful central authority, a solution favored by the authoritarian tradition of the colonial period. Because the advocates of the two philosophical positions were unable to impose their wills on their opponents, a power vacuum was created which paved the way for the rise of the infamous Gen. Antonio López de Santa Anna (1794–1876), an opportunist who came to dominate Mexican politics to mid-century.

Political life in Alta California at this time was also confused. But in the province the struggles had little to do with ideology; virtually all Californios, save the clergy, were resentful of central authority and advocated federalism and liberalism. Ideologically united, the leading families nonetheless engaged in chronic infighting. Insurrections, almost always bloodless, became a regular feature of political life. Californios fought among themselves, as well as the governors Mexico City would periodically try to impose on them. Usually these factions divided along geographical lines, with the southerners, *abajeños*, opposed to the northerners, *arribeños*. Among the most prominent representatives of the former were José Antonio Carrillo, Pío Pico, and Juan Bandini; of the latter, Juan Bautista

Alvarado, Mariano Guadalupe Vallejo, and José Castro. At stake were the governorship and political control of the province.

Beyond their suspicion of Mexico City—particularly after 1834, when the centralists, under Santa Anna, gained control of the national government—the other sentiment that united the liberals of the province was their hostility to the Church. Anti-clericalism was a central tenet of nineteenth-century liberalism. Moreover, the clergy had further alienated liberals, both at the provincial and the national level, by their vociferous and virtually unanimous support of the Crown. The result was the confiscation of ecclesiastical property, the secularization of the California missions, in 1834–1845.

Ideology was stressed at the time by proponents of secularization and was undoubtedly a consideration prompting the legislation. It is likely, however, that economic motives were at least as weighty in explaining the land seizure as were high-minded ideas, as the results of secularization amply demonstrate. Franciscan missions controlled the best land in the province, some 14 million acres along the fertile and accessible coast from San Diego to Cape Mendocino. Rancheros resented this monopoly—as they had throughout the Far North—although their complaints were generally veiled in protests about the mistreatment of the indigenous mission population.

Secularization, however, did little to alleviate the plight of the "poor" Indian. Under the legislation, half of the mission lands were to go to the neophytes who had previously worked them, and the other half to the government. In fact, virtually all lands fell into the hands of some two hundred families who would subsequently dominate the economic and political life of the province. Through a variety of means, some legal, some illegal, virtually all in violation of the spirit if not the letter of the law, the hapless natives were divested of their inheritance. As for the half that was intended for the public domain, provincial governors soon redistributed these holdings, in the form of generous grants meted out to family, friends, and political allies. During the Mexican period, about five hundred private rancho land grants were made, compared to about twenty during the Spanish period. Secularization of the missions made possible the rise of the rancho aristocracy commonly associated with the Halcyon Days of Early California.

By the 1840s, with the gradual disappearance of the missions, the California economy came to be dominated by ranches. These large landed estates were virtually self-sufficient. A great assortment of crops were grown, including corn, potatoes, tomatoes, wheat, oranges, lemons, and grapes. More valuable than the agricultural products, though, was livestock. Horses multiplied rapidly; herds were so vast that they were often permitted to run wild without any supervision whatsoever. Cattle were even more plentiful, and more lucrative, for they were the source of hides and tallow (used for soap and candles). By the 1840s, foreign vessels regularly visited coastal ports to exchange manufactured goods for these commodities. The cattle industry and the commerce it fostered were rapidly transforming life in Alta California on the eve of the Mexican-American War. "In no small way," the political sociologist Tomás Almaguer observes, "the magnitude of the early economic trade carried out between California and New England maritime interests was to help lay the foundation for its later political incorporation into the United States and formal integration as a semiperipheral and then core zone of the capitalist world-economy."[2] While commercial capitalism was in its infancy, signs of affluence, a recent phenomenon, were everywhere.

The chief beneficiaries of this new-found wealth were the rancheros, popularly known today as the "Spanish Dons." Whether born in Spain, Mexico, or California, members of this pastoral elite were predominantly white. At the top of provincial society, they and their families constituted less than 10 percent of the colony's population. Many of them ex-soldiers, most were recipients of generous land grants between 1821 and 1848. A few had acquired lands under the Spanish Crown. Their families were usually large, reflecting the relatively healthy and affluent lifestyle that had evolved in the province.

As in other Hispanic societies, the husband and father had an inordinate amount of power. Women, however, maintained a surprisingly lofty position. Not only was the upper-class woman held on a pedestal, but she also wielded real authority. She had legal rights which were withheld from Anglo women of the time. It is significant that practically all Anglo accounts of life in California during this period comment, mostly in a derisive fashion, about this independence.[3] Among privileges accorded women was the right to own land. Doña Juana Pacheco, for example, widow of Miguel Pacheco and mother of twelve children, received a grant of 17,734 acres in what is now central Contra Costa County in 1834. There were many kinds of grants and altogether some seven hundred were recorded before the American takeover, of which fifty-five (nearly 13 percent) were awarded to women.

José de la Guerra y Noriega (1779–1858) and Mariano Guadalupe Vallejo (1808–1890) were perhaps the best examples of the rancho oligarchy during this period. Born in the Spanish town of Novales, Capt. De la Guerra joined the military in New Spain. Eventually, he was sent to Santa Barbara, where he served as the fifth commandant of the local presidio from 1815 to 1842 and functioned as treasurer for the Franciscan mission system before its demise. At one time, he owned six ranches, totaling over 300,000 acres, on which he ran more than 50,000 head of cattle. He was also the leading merchant in the pueblo.

Vallejo was born in Monterey, where he was educated with Juan Alvarado, a nephew, and José Castro, a cousin. He became a soldier, like his father before him, and was appointed commandant of the San Francisco presidio in 1831. Four years later, Colonel Vallejo was sent into the area north of San Francisco Bay to establish a defensive outpost at Sonoma against the Russians and to pacify the local Indians. Like Captain De la Guerra, he benefited handsomely from the secularization of the mission system; eventually, Vallejo became the largest landholder in the province.

Below the elite and larger in numbers were non-Indians, mainly mestizos, who constituted something of a middle class. Some were soldiers; others were craftsmen. A few even made their living as vaqueros, an occupation highly regarded in this pastoral society. Like the majority of the upper class, these mestizos were illiterate. Disparaged as lazy by Yankee visitors, who were appalled at the number of fiestas in this Catholic society, mestizos worked long hours the rest of the time, especially vaqueros, who performed hard physical labor, often under dangerous circumstances.

Indians remained at the bottom of Californio society. By the 1840s, their mortality rate had leveled off, but conditions had not otherwise improved noticeably. In many cases, their situation may have deteriorated, as these native peoples were now at the mercy of ranchers who were intent on extracting as much labor from them as possible. The paternalistic Franciscans, on the other hand, had felt an obligation to provide for their spiritual welfare.[4] The status of native peoples during this period approximated that of serfdom, but the extent of their exploitation is hard to gauge since the descriptions of their plight were generally written by outsiders intent on finding atrocities which would justify foreign intervention. At any rate, the treatment of the neophytes would worsen after the United States' acquisition of the province.[5]

Beyond the coastal range were indios bárbaros. Before secularization, they continually fomented rebellion among the mission Indians and provided a haven for runaways. After secularization, their numbers swelled as many dispossessed neophytes had nowhere else to go but the inner valleys. Throughout the Mexican period, the interior tribes posed a major threat to coastal settlements, to a considerable extent a reaction to Mexican raiding parties. Mistreatment of indigenous people on the northern frontier was worst in California, it has been argued, probably because of the military weakness of its native inhabitants compared to those of other regions.[6]

NEW MEXICO

Like California, New Mexico experienced major changes during the Mexican period. Generally speaking, historians tend to see New Mexicans as very conservative people; and, given their isolation, this description seems quite appropriate. But between 1821 and 1846, life in New Mexico was altered almost as much as in the maritime province.

Politically, however, little changed for New Mexicans immediately after national independence; it was still difficult to maintain contact with Mexico City, 1,600 miles away, so the people of the territory continued to go their own way with minimal interference. Under normal circumstances, this neglect might have been acceptable. Unfortunately, the renewed Indian offensive of Apaches and Navajos required increased military aid from Mexico City when none was available. The beleaguered settlers continually petitioned the central government for military reinforcements throughout the 1820s and the early 1830s, but to no avail. New Mexican discontent only worsened after the mid-1830s, with the rise to power of the centralists in Mexico City.

Unable to help New Mexico solve its Indian problems but intent on reining in the independent-minded pobladores of the Upper Rio Grande, the central government imposed an unpopular governor, Albino Pérez, who arrived in Santa Fe in May 1835. Perceived as unsympathetic to local concerns, Governor Pérez soon incurred the wrath of the local citizenry. His attempt to impose Santa Anna's centralist constitution of 1836 proved to be the last straw.

In August 1837, a rebellion broke out among the Pueblos and Hispanic settlers living in the area north of Santa Fe. Led by a genízaro, José Gonzales, the insurrectionists went on a rampage, killing the governor and sixteen other officials. The propertied classes of New Mexico, who had initially sustained the malcontents, turned against them when the violence got out of hand. Their champion was Manuel Armijo (1792–1853), ex-governor of the province. Himself an early partisan of the rebellion, he now became its most implacable foe. Armijo's execution of Gonzales, on 27 January 1838, brought the rebellion to an abrupt halt and earned him the gratitude of the region's leading citizens. Subsequently, serving as governor on two other occasions, Armijo would come to dominate New Mexican politics during the remainder of the Mexican period.

Given the arid nature of the land, sheep rather than cattle became the mainstay of the New Mexican economy. In climate and terrain, the area resembled the central plateau of Spain, so it was only natural that Spaniards would foster an industry that had been so profitable in the Old Country. The largest sheep ranches were established in the Rio Grande Valley south of Santa Fe, the provincial capital, in the Río Abajo area centered on Albuquerque. The highland areas north of the capital, the Río Arriba, home of two-thirds of the population, could sustain only small holdings. Consequently, families there did not achieve the wealth and prominence of the southerners.

In both regions, settlers tended to reside close to the Rio Grande, which was indispensable for irrigation. Forced to be self-sufficient, rancheros relied heavily on agriculture. Corn, the ancient staple, continued to be popular; but peppers, potatoes, and a variety of European crops were also cultivated.

Manufacturing was negligible. Discouraged by the mercantilist policies of the colonial era, as well as meager local resources, industry was practiced only on a small scale, forcing New Mexicans to depend on the large cities of central Mexico for the great bulk of their necessities other than food. These commodities were transported on mules across the Chihuahua Trail, which emanated from the population centers of the interior and wound its way through a number of northern frontier settlements before entering New Mexico via El Paso del Norte. As the name of the route indicates, the most important of these settlements was Chihuahua, the chief city of the province of Nueva Vizcaya. Chihuahua merchants monopolized the trail trade. While the basis of their wealth was often the rich mines of the surrounding area and the cattle industry it fostered, by the end of the Spanish period, the Chihuahua elite made their largest profits by pursuing mercantile endeavors. In order to purchase manufactured goods, *Hispanos*, Spanish-speaking residents of New Mexico, paid exorbitant prices to southern merchants, which grew to be a major source of discontent. Yet, as in California, the Mexican period brought dramatic economic changes to New Mexico, and the most portentous of these was in the field of commerce.

The year of Mexican independence, 1821, witnessed the appearance in New Mexico of William Becknell. A trader from Missouri, Becknell hoped to initiate trade with New Spain. Unaware of Mexican independence, the American entrepreneur took a calculated risk that he would receive a warm welcome in Santa Fe. His gamble paid off handsomely. Not only did he blaze the Santa Fe Trail, one of the most famous arteries of transportation and commerce in the annals of the American West, but he also reaped a handsome profit.

In time, trade along the Santa Fe Trail brought huge dividends to norteamericanos who followed Becknell, but it had even greater consequences for the inhabitants of New Mexico. The increase in the volume of trade with the Yankees helped break the Chihuahua monopoly. Hispanos now had access to cheaper and more abundant merchandise and the Mexican entrepreneurs could not compete. Moreover, Americans were willing to pay top dollar, in the form of manufactured goods, for mules, furs, blankets, and other commodities that nuevomexicanos produced.

Life in New Mexico became more convenient and comfortable. As in California, the chief beneficiaries of this affluence were large landholding families. They were eventually able to accumulate enough capital to enter into mercantile ventures themselves, ultimately competing very successfully against both Yankee and Mexican traders. In fact, as David A. Sandoval has noted, during the course of the next twenty years, New Mexican families like the Pereas, Chávezes, and Armijos gradually came to dominate trade on both the Santa Fe and the Chihuahua trails, now a single artery linking Mexico and the United States, mainly because of their enviable position as middlemen.[7] Commerce also opened up in other directions. In 1829–1830, Antonio Armijo, apparently a distant relative of Governor Armijo, blazed a trail, via southern Utah, between Abiquiú, New Mexico, and San Bernardino, California. The Old Spanish Trail, as it came to be called, created a vast market for Hispano sheepmen and was well traveled by the time of the Mexican-American War. As on the Pacific Coast, the Mexican period witnessed the advent of an affluent elite, widening the gap between rich and poor.

From 1821 to 1846, New Mexican society was experiencing unusual ferment, compared to the tradition-bound society of colonial days. At the top were the ricos, a small number of families, centered in Albuquerque and the surrounding area, who monopolized the pastoral and mercantile life of the province. Perhaps the most powerful was the Armijo family, whose best-known representative was Manuel Armijo, the dominant political figure of the times.

Governor Armijo, who was as much a businessman as he was a politician, is one of the most colorful and controversial figures in New Mexican history. American traders, who were asked to pay heavy duties for conducting business in the province, painted an unflattering portrait of him as a ruthless tyrant, and his own people saw him as a coward who refused to defend New Mexico against American invaders in 1846. Virtually all contemporaries agreed that he was venial and corrupt. No doubt, Armijo had many personal foibles; but, as Janet Lecompte, a sympathetic biographer, has argued, he was also a hardworking and dedicated public servant who tried to preserve New Mexico autonomy vis-à-vis both American interests and Mexican central authority.

Beneath the elite were the pobres. Since they resided in the same areas, and in isolation from the rest of Mexican society, they were usually related to the ricos, a situation tending to mute class antagonisms. Like the upper class, pobres were predominantly mestizos. In rural areas, they worked as sheepherders and peasant farmers. In the towns, they performed menial labor, together with genízaros, who occupied a lower social status.

At the bottom of New Mexican society were Pueblos—about nine thousand strong, exclusive of the Hopi, in 1821. While some lived among "whites," working as servants or day laborers, sometimes as virtual slaves, most Indians were permitted to reside in their own towns. Among the largest of these villages—about twenty in number—were Taos, San Ildefonso, and Santa Clara. Encouraged to adopt Catholicism, most indigenous people came to practice a syncretic religion heavily influenced by indigenous beliefs. Some Pueblos rejected Christianity altogether.

ARIZONA

Arizona fared poorly throughout the Mexican period. On the northern rim of Sonora, the pobladores of the Santa Cruz Valley looked to the south—Arizpe, the district capital, in particular—for military and economic support. There were only two settlements of any consequence in the valley, both of them presidios: Tubac, just above today's United States-Mexican border, and Tucson, a few miles farther north. On the edge of the Apachería, both settlements suffered terribly throughout the entire period as Apaches resumed their raids on Sonoran ranches, terrorizing both pobladores and sedentary tribes like Pimas and Pápagos, who relied on the presidios for protection. So intense was the pressure exerted by Apaches that the mission of San Xavier del Bac had to be abandoned temporarily in 1829, and the presidio at Tubac disappeared altogether in 1848. Indeed, throughout the Mexican period, the Santa Cruz Valley, like the rest of Sonora, suffered a steady decline of its fronterizo population.

TEXAS

In Texas—after 1824 a part of the State of Coahuila y Tejas—pobladores were not much better off than in northern Sonora. The Spanish-speaking population was confined principally to San Antonio and La Bahía. Their numbers had dropped precipitously at the end of the Spanish period. The first years of Mexican independence, coming on the heels of the Adams-Onís Treaty, encouraged Tejanos to believe that some progress might be made under the new government. This optimism did not last long. The Indian menace resurfaced immediately, as it did throughout the northern fringe of the new republic. Clearly, the Mexican government was no more able to encourage emigration from the interior nor pacify the Comanches than the Spanish Crown before it. Even San Antonio, a town of some 1,500 citizens in 1821, was vulnerable to Comanche attack. High expectations quickly gave way to bitter disappointment.

THE CLASH OF CULTURES

The central government was also discredited, in time, by its inadequate response to another pressing problem: the renewed pressure of Anglo immigration in east Texas. American interest in the rich agricultural lands of the Texas plains goes back to the beginning of the nineteenth century, when American filibusters, "the 'illegal aliens' of their day," as Patricia Nelson Limerick calls them, began to make forays into Spanish territory.[8] The Adams-Onís Treaty of 1819 seemed to put an end to this threat, but the independence of Mexico two years later brought renewed interest in Texas by American frontiersmen. As early as 1821, the Iturbide government, having gained a false sense of security as a result of the recently signed treaty, determined that rather than following the traditional policy of impeding foreign immigration, it might be wiser to encourage and regulate the entry of American settlers. Unlike Mexican citizens, after all, Yankees were eager to come into Texas. Government policy, which continued after the fall of Iturbide's empire, was to recruit norteamericanos to enter Texas. By using American agents, called *empresarios*, to entice their conationals, Mexican officials hoped to populate the vast expanse of Texas once and for all and transform it into a productive part of the republic.

The most famous agent was Stephen F. Austin (1793–1836). His father, Moses, a Missouri mine operator, had successfully petitioned for an empresario license from Spanish authorities in 1821, shortly before his death. The son inherited the undertaking. After renegotiating with Mexican officials, young Austin was eventually permitted to bring in some three hundred families, who were given approximately five thousand acres apiece along the Brazos River on the condition that they abide by Mexican laws, learn to speak Spanish, and renounce Protestantism in favor of Catholicism. Stephen Austin himself was given a generous grant for his services and the right to collect duties from his recruits. By the mid-1820s, the colony, centered around a town named in his honor, San Felipe de Austin, was thriving. Other Anglo grants were nearly as successful.

As a consequence, thousands of Americans started to enter Texas, many without bothering to obtain Mexican authorization. By 1830, Anglos outnumbered Mexicans 25,000 to 4,000. Tejanos grew alarmed. Not only were they being overwhelmed, but many of the newcomers, it seemed, had no intention of assimilating into Mexican society. A cultural conflict grew increasingly apparent. Anglos and Mexicans were separated by vast linguistic, religious, and political differences. The most crucial element of this cultural gap, however, had to do with race.

Arnoldo De León, the foremost Chicano expert on Texas history, has demonstrated conclusively that the racial animosity of Texans toward Mexicans was well rooted in the period before 1836.[9] The color issue was predictable since "three-quarters of the Anglos in Texas were southerners who were committed to slavery."[10] The central government in Mexico City was slow to appreciate the magnitude of the problem. However, a series of laws were finally enacted in 1830–1832 to ameliorate the situation. Anglo immigration into Texas was forbidden. At the same time, Mexican families were encouraged to colonize the area. In addition, economic ties between Anglos in Texas and the United States were discouraged through a tough tariff policy. The Mexican response was a case of too little, too late. The laws served only to antagonize Anglo-Texans.

Anglo immigration into Mexico in the 1820s was not confined to Texas; Yankees began to penetrate into the republic all along its northern rim. Everywhere the primary motivation was the prospect of economic gain. The potential wealth of the region was obvious to outsiders well before this period, but it was only with the ouster of the Spaniards and the relaxing of immigration and commercial regulations that Yankees were given an opportunity to enter the territory legally.

Americans arriving in New Mexico during the Mexican period came primarily to trap beaver, to engage in the trail trade, or to do both. By the second decade of the nineteenth century, the fur trade, which had been introduced into North America by the French, was centered on the Rocky Mountains, where American and British mountain men competed to gain economic domination. It was at this time that traders and trappers began to make their appearance in New Mexico. Eventually, some of these mountain men elected to settle in the province and set up mercantile establishments. Taos became their chief center of operations. Among the most successful of the Taos traders were Ewing Young and Kit Carson. Like Carson, who married into the Jaramillo family, most of these foreign-born merchants were reasonably well integrated into Hispano society. According to the historian Rebecca McDowell Craver, fifteen of the twenty-two Americans in Taos in 1841 were married to or lived with Mexican women.[11]

The volume of trade in New Mexico increased dramatically with the opening of the Santa Fe Trail. At first, Missouri merchants were content to conduct their business in New Mexico on a seasonal basis, but before long they saw the opportunity to reap huge profits by setting up permanent mercantile establishments in or near New Mexico. The best known of these early outposts was the "fort" established in 1833 by the Bent brothers, William and Charles, along the Arkansas River.

In California, the influx of Americans occurred in three waves before the mid-1840s.[12] These have been labeled the maritime interest, the trapping interest, and the pioneering interest. The first of these consisted of Americans and other foreigners who arrived, mostly after 1821, to participate in the hide-and-tallow trade. Yankees were the most active participants in this lucrative enterprise. After coming around Cape Horn from New England, their clipper ships spent the next few months sailing from one California port to another, exchanging American goods for hides and tallow. They returned home by retracing their initial route. The entire trip lasted two and sometimes three years. The most famous of these voyages was described in 1840 by Richard Henry Dana in *Two Years before the Mast*, an account of his experiences aboard trading vessels along the California coast in 1834 and 1835.

While most seamen only visited the maritime province, a few decided to make their homes there. More typically, though, it was company agents stationed in the port towns of Santa Barbara and Monterey who established residence among the Californios. These individuals married into upper-class society, assimilated the dominant culture, learning Spanish and sometimes practicing Catholicism, and acquired large land grants. The prime example of these outsiders who flourished in California by "going native" was Abel Stearns, who arrived in the province in 1829 and settled down in the Los Angeles area. Stearns married into the family of Juan Bandini, one of the most prominent residents of San Diego, and eventually the likeable and well-connected immigrant became the largest land-owner in the southern part of the province.

After the mid-twenties, another wave of foreigners arrived—the fabled mountain men. Mostly Americans, these newcomers came looking for peltry. Unlike the maritime interest, trappers followed overland trails; and once in California, they confined themselves to the interior valleys, thus sustaining little or no contact with the Hispanic population on the coast. The first of the mountain men to reach the province was also the most celebrated, Jedediah Strong Smith (1799?–1831), who entered the Great Central Valley via the Mojave Desert in 1826. Other well-known trappers who visited the province were James Ohio Pattie, Joseph Reddeford Walker, and James Beckwourth.

By the mid-1840s, on the eve of the Mexican-American War, the largest stream of immigrants began to penetrate the area. These were farmers who followed overland trails blazed by the mountain men and who sought fertile land on the coast. Most of the early emigrants succumbed to "Oregon fever" and headed for the Willamette Valley. In 1841, however, the Bidwell-Bartleson train chose to take a southwesterly route from the Snake River, across the Nevada desert, and into California, thus beginning a mass migration of pioneers that would continue throughout the nineteenth century. Most California-bound immigrants were agriculturalists who came from the Midwest with their families looking for land in the Great Valley. Among them was the infamous party led by John and Jacob Donner which was stranded in the Sierras in the winter of 1846–1847.

THE TEXAS REVOLT

By the early 1830s, given their superior numbers and the increasing antagonism they felt toward both the Mexican government and the Mexican people, Anglo settlers in Texas were rapidly enlisting in the movement favoring independence. All that was needed was a leader and an excuse. The leader appeared in the person of Samuel Houston (1793–1863). So much hagiographic nonsense has been written about Houston by admiring Texas historians that it is almost impossible to separate fact from fiction. Nevertheless, it is clear that he was an extraordinary person with enormous charisma. Born in Virginia of Scots-Irish stock, Houston moved to Tennessee with his family when he was still a boy. Fiercely independent, he ran off into the wilderness while a teenager and lived with the Cherokees, who adopted him into the tribe. He developed an admiration for native Americans that he would always maintain, a rarity on the frontier. Returning home after an absence of three years, Houston served in the military under Andrew Jackson, won a seat in Congress in 1823, as a delegate from Tennessee, and became governor of the state four years later. Resigning political office in 1829, he first entered Texas in 1832, and settled there permanently three years later. Although some historians have speculated that he was dispatched to Texas by Jackson, who became president in 1829, to engineer an American takeover, there is no concrete evidence to sustain this interpretation. But the fact remains that from the very beginning, he became the leader of the Texas faction which called for immediate independence from Mexico, in opposition to Austin and his followers, who wanted a more conciliatory policy.

The occasion for independence arose in 1835, a year after the federalist government in Mexico City was defeated by Santa Anna and the centralists. The new government was determined to squash movements for local autonomy throughout the country, now deeply fragmented politically. Their efforts to divest the Texans of recent political gains were so arbitrary that the centralists succeeded in alienating even the Mexican residents of Texas, most of whom would remain neutral in the coming conflict. Austin and Houston now closed ranks. In 1835, the Texans initiated their rebellion against the Mexican government.

The most famous battle of the conflict occurred on 6 March 1836, when General Santa Anna and his army of some five thousand men attacked the rebel stronghold at the Alamo, an old Franciscan mission in San Antonio, killing 187 defenders.[13] Among the dead were James Bowie, Davy Crockett, and Col. William B. Travis, the commander of the garrison. While every Texas schoolchild recognizes these names as heroes of Texas independence, few people know that eight martyrs at the Alamo were Mexicans: Juan Abamillo, Juan Antonio Badillo, Carlos Espalier, Gregorio Esparza, Antonio Fuentes, Galba Fuqua, José Toribio Losoya, and Andrés Nava. In fact, many Tejanos actively supported the cause of Texas, some fighting bravely to achieve independence. First and foremost were José Antonio Navarro (1795–1871) and Juan Seguín (1806–1890), members of prominent San Antonio families. Whether these men were heroes or traitors is a question that divides Chicano historians today. What is certain is that anti-Mexican feeling became so vehement during the conflict and its aftermath that the Mexican contribution at the Alamo was virtually annihilated from public memory.

The Mexican victory, however, was short-lived. One month after the Alamo, Santa Anna and his troops were surprised by Houston's army at the Battle of San Jacinto. The Mexicans suffered some six hundred deaths, the rebels lost eight men. The capture of Santa Anna, Mexico's president, virtually ended the conflict. Although the vanquished *caudillo* signed the Treaty of Velasco under duress and the Mexican Senate refused to ratify the pact, the country was in such complete disarray that there was nothing the government could do to repair the damage.

During the next decade, Texas existed as an independent nation. Texans asked for immediate admission into the American republic upon winning their freedom from Mexico, but the petition was denied by Congress. The United States feared alienating its southern neighbor, which threatened to go to war over Texas annexation. However, there was a more sensitive question to consider. A balance of slave and free states had been achieved, and Texas's admission would jeopardize the precarious truce between the two sections of the country. During the next nine years, the Lone Star Republic was beset with a multitude of problems, not the least of which was mending fences with its neighbor to the south and placating its own Mexican population.

Under the Lone Star Republic, Tejanos found themselves treated as foreigners in their own land, a process well documented by Arnoldo De León. The negative stereotype which had haunted them before—they were said to be lazy and vicious by nature—was reinforced and used as justification for the seizure of their lands. Despised and abused, many Mexicans fled south beyond the Nueces River, now a disputed boundary with Mexico. Some crossed the Rio Grande, where they found greater security. One of these disillusioned exiles was Juan Seguín himself, who discovered that neither his prominence in the community nor his distinguished service to the independence movement had spared him from the hatred and envy of Anglos intent on ridding Texas of all vestiges of Mexican influence. Border raids by disgruntled expatriates and common bandits alike served only to reinforce the Anglo notion that all Mexicans were criminals and must be dealt with accordingly. Tejanos who paid the heaviest price were generally those who refused to leave their homes. Racial violence was widespread during the entire period, but while blacks and Indians suffered horrible abuses, Mexicans endured the worst treatment.

The loss of Texas was a bitter pill for the proud Mexicans, and the treatment of Tejanos by the Lone Star Republic only added insult to injury. As for Anglos in Texas, their recent success encouraged expansionist sentiments, which Mexico's obvious weakness did nothing to curb. In 1841, the Texans made an attempt to invade New Mexico. They were repelled by their aroused enemies. Governor Armijo claimed full credit for the victory, but it was the Texans' own incompetence that doomed the enterprise to failure from the very beginning. Tensions increased steadily between the two nations thereafter; it seemed only a matter of time before hostilities would resume.

THE MEXICAN WAR

Expansionist sentiments by the 1840s were hardly confined to Texans. By this time, many Americans, particularly on the western frontier, were intent on territorial gains, by force if necessary. Their immediate objectives were the Oregon territory, soon to be acquired from the British, and Texas, the gateway to California. The strength of these bellicose sentiments can be gauged by the election of James K. Polk to the presidency in 1844. An unabashed advocate of expansion, Polk was swept into office on the promise that he would "reoccupy" Oregon and "reannex" Texas.

The election was interpreted as a mandate. In fact, one of the last acts of the ousted Tyler administration was to annex the Lone Star Republic in early 1845. So powerful was the desire to gain Texas, a prelude to the acquisition of California, that Americans were willing to jeopardize the uneasy truce between North and South over the slavery question. From across the border came a howl of protest. Mexican nationalists had suspected that the United States was behind the Texas revolt, and now these suspicions appeared to be confirmed. Incensed, some of the younger members of the Mexican Congress called for war.

Despite the impassioned reaction, Polk initiated efforts to purchase California from the Mexican government in the autumn of 1845, which speaks volumes for the president's insensitivity. So incredible were these obtuse efforts that one must question whether he was acting in good faith. Naturally, his agent John Slidell was refused an audience in Mexico City. Given the anti-American mood of their people, Mexican diplomats understood that any compromise with the United States at this time was tantamount to political suicide.

It was at this point that Polk determined to use war as an instrument of diplomacy. After all, once the Mexicans had refused to negotiate, there was absolutely no other way to acquire California; the Mexican claim was well established, and the maritime province was adequately populated by Mexican citizens. The American president concluded that the ends justified the means; but, adroit Machiavellian that he was, Polk also realized that he had to appear to be acting in self-defense. Only then would Americans be willing to make the sacrifices that an armed conflict required. Moreover, the country's strong Puritan legacy required a "just" war. How to get the Mexicans to initiate hostilities—this was the practical problem that Polk faced. He found the solution in the boundary dispute that the United States had inherited with the annexation of Texas.[14]

When Texans achieved their independence, they argued that the common border between their territory and Mexico was the Rio Grande. The Mexican government countered by pointing out that the province of Texas had been separated historically from the rest of the country by the Nueces River, 150 miles north of the Rio Grande. What was at stake was not only the entire Lower Rio Grande Valley, but the eastern half of New Mexico as well. When Texas entered the Union, the issue was still pending. The American claim was shaky. So convinced were the Mexicans of their position, that they were willing to submit the question to international arbitration. The United States had no intention of permitting the British to mediate the dispute.

At this point, Polk decided to take a gamble. In the last days of March 1846, he instructed Gen. Zachary Taylor to occupy the disputed territory. Once fired upon by the Mexicans, Polk could go to the Senate, in good conscience, asking for a declaration of war. Preparing his war message, the president awaited the outcome.

But the Mexicans vacillated, and Polk grew nervous. Finally, on 23 April 1846, the Mexicans declared war on the United States. Polk's ploy had worked, but for the moment he was ignorant of the war declaration. Intent on acquiring California, he convinced himself that the British had the same designs. He felt he needed to act quickly before his imagined adversaries had a chance to react. Early in May, determined that delay would be too risky, he made up his mind to seek a war declaration, with or without Mexican cooperation. Fortunately for him, he now received word that Mexican troops had attacked Taylor on 25 April. On 11 May, President Polk went before the Senate, where he delivered his famous speech declaring that "Mexico has passed the boundary of the United States, has invaded our territory, and shed American blood on American soil." "The message," the historians Michael C. Meyer and William L. Sherman have concluded, "was remarkable for its distortion and provocative to the absurd."[15] Some Americans were skeptical. Young Abe Lincoln, then a member of Congress, had serious reservations about whether the disputed territory was indeed American property. Nonetheless, the U.S. declaration of war was passed overwhelmingly—the House of Representatives voted 174 to 14, and the Senate voted 40 to 2—and so was initiated one of the most popular and successful wars in American history.

The Mexican War basically consisted of three campaigns, all of them American offensives against opponents who were divided and outmanned. The most consequential thrust was initiated by General Taylor, who led his troops into northern Mexico. His objective was Mexico City. His adversaries put up a stubborn resistance—ultimately, the war would claim fifty thousand Mexican lives. Several tough engagements were fought in the north, before the path to the capital opened up. The last stage of the victorious campaign was a seaborne invasion of Vera Cruz, led by Gen. Winfield Scott, who then marched on the capital, tracing the route that Cortés had followed centuries before. On 13 September 1847, Scott's marines entered the Halls of Montezuma, and the war was over, for all intents and purposes.

In the meantime, the American Army of the West, under Col. Stephen Watts Kearny, marched over the Santa Fe Trail and entered the New Mexican capital in August 1846. The initial takeover was relatively uneventful. While many of his advisors were prepared to defend the province, Manuel Armijo, still governor, went through the motions of preparing a defense, before fleeing south into Durango at the last moment. It is rumored that this ignoble retreat was prompted by a bribe provided by James W. Magoffin, an American trader who had been active on the Santa Fe and Chihuahua trails for years. Devoid of leadership, New Mexicans resigned themselves to their fate. In some quarters, notably among Anglo traders, there was even genuine enthusiasm for U.S. occupation.

Kearny did his best to pacify the native population. He then headed for California in late September 1846, leaving a small garrison in Santa Fe. His soldiers' mistreatment of local residents, however, combined with the New Mexicans' hatred of Anglo and Hispano collaborators, resulted in a brief but bloody uprising. Centered on Taos, the revolt erupted in January 1847. Before it was over, insurgents had slaughtered several prominent New Mexicans, including newly appointed governor Charles Bent. As in the 1837 rebellion, though, the rebels, mainly Pueblo Indians, came to be perceived as a threat by the privileged classes, and the uprising was quelled by the local elite. The Taos revolt makes it clear that the notion of a bloodless conquest of New Mexico, perpetrated by a number of U.S. historians, was a complete myth. In fact, nearly three hundred Mexicans and more than thirty Americans were killed before order was restored.

The war in California seems to have broken out independently of events in Texas. Attractive not only because of its splendid resources, particularly its fine harbors, but also because of its value as an entrepôt for the China trade, California represented the primary objective of American foreign policy at mid-century. Stymied in his efforts to purchase the Pacific province, Polk was determined to use the Texas border dispute as an excuse for a war that would win him the coveted prize. However, other avenues toward this end were pursued concurrently by the wily statesman. His primary agents in these schemes were Thomas O. Larkin and John C. Frémont.

Larkin, a Massachusetts Yankee who arrived in California in 1832, was one of the most prominent members of the maritime interest. He acquired large properties, but he did not marry into local society. Nor did he assimilate the native lifestyle, though he made friends with many influential Californios. Refusing to burn his bridges behind him, he was a logical choice to be American consul in the province, an appointment he won in 1844. A firm advocate of U.S. expansion, Larkin yearned for the day when California would enter the American sphere of influence. On 17 October 1845, he was given the opportunity to further American designs when the U.S. government sent a secret dispatch appointing him "confidential agent in California." James Buchanan, Polk's secretary of state, instructed him to convince prominent Californios, his friends and colleagues, that it would be in their best interests if the province were to secede from the Mexican union. They were not informed, however, of the next step after secession—absorption into the United States. Larkin's efforts were fruitless. While Californio oligarchs did meet in Santa Barbara on 15 June 1846 to debate the issue of secession, the contentious delegates were unable to come to any agreement.

Capt. John C. Frémont, the self-styled "Pathfinder of the West," was a member of the American military and a man of enormous ambition. He, too, became an agent for Polk, who felt that the officer might achieve through force what the consul hoped to accomplish through persuasion. Toward this end, Frémont and a party of sixty-two armed men, appeared in California in December 1845, ostensibly on a "scientific" expedition. A few weeks later, the party advanced into the Salinas Valley, practically on the doorstep of Monterey, the provincial capital. Confronted by José Castro, the military commandant of the area, who no doubt was perplexed by the Americans' interest in the province's flora and fauna, Frémont was asked to leave the territory. Offended by the commandant's brusque manner, Frémont threatened violence—apparently it did not occur to him that he was in a foreign country—before grudgingly agreeing to leave California for the Oregon territory. Frémont and his men then headed north, where they met with American mountain men. The result of this parley was the Bear Flag Revolt. The insurrection broke out on 10 June 1846, and culminated four days later, when William B. Ide and his men arrested Mariano Vallejo in Sonoma. Frémont, who had been riding toward the Oregon border when he heard the news, quickly returned to Sonoma to assume command of the small army of irregulars. The Americans advanced south along the coast, eventually entering Monterey, which had been taken in the first days of July by marines belonging to Comdr. John D. Sloat's Pacific squadron. During the following weeks, the combined American forces captured the Mexican coastal settlements; and, with the occupation of Los Angeles in mid-August, the conquest appeared to be complete.

Disgruntled Californios, led by Capt. José María Flores, made one last desperate effort to reverse the momentum. On 6 December, at the Battle of San Pascual, an Indian village near San Diego, Mexican lancers under Andrés Pico inflicted a surprising defeat on Kearny's troops, recently arrived from New Mexico. But victory was ephemeral; within a matter of weeks, resistance was broken, and the insurgents were forced to recognize the loss of California in the Treaty of Cahuenga, signed on 13 January 1847.

Even before American troops had marched into Mexico City, President Polk dispatched Nicolas P. Trist to the Mexican capital to negotiate the peace treaty. While negotiations were being conducted, American war aims suddenly escalated. Mexico lay prostrate. Many senators now wondered why the entire country might not be annexed. Some suggested that all of Central America was ripe for the taking. There were even those who advocated American hegemony all the way to the tip of South America. Oblivious to these arguments, Trist negotiated a pact, signed on 2 February 1848, which most of his countrymen found excessively lenient. Polk himself was outraged at Trist's failure to respond to the new situation. But, in the end, unwilling to prolong acrimonious debates, the president accepted the Treaty of Guadalupe Hidalgo—named after the Mexico City suburb where it was negotiated. The agreement was ratified by the U.S. Senate on 10 March 1848.

The territorial settlement imposed by the treaty shocked and incensed the defeated people. Many Mexicans, among them Benito Juárez, preferred to go on fighting rather than accept the dictated peace. Mexico not only had to surrender the vast lands of California and New Mexico, but it was forced to recognize the humiliating loss of Texas. Altogether, it lost 947,570 square miles of land, almost half of its national territory, though less than 1 percent of its population. "The Treaty of Guadalupe Hidalgo," Juan Gómez-Quiñones, speaking for virtually all Chicano scholars, opines, "is one of the harshest treaties between countries of the last two centuries with regard to territorial acquisition."[16] Mexicans in the conquered territory were given the alternative of packing up and moving south into Mexican territory—an option that only about 2,000 of the 100,000 eligible candidates chose—or remaining in what had become the American Southwest. Mexicans in the conquered territory were guaranteed "all the rights of citizens of the United States" including "free enjoyment of their liberty and property," according to Article IX. Irate nationalists were hardly placated by a payment of $15 million to the vanquished nation by the American government, which also agreed to assume Mexican debts to U.S. citizens to the tune of some $3 million—compensation for territorial losses which the proud Mexicans saw as blood money.

And so ended one of the sorriest chapters of the American epic. Until very recently, in the aftermath of Vietnam, American historians have been reticent to deal with this embarrassing episode. When the war was mentioned at all, it was the Mexicans who were saddled with the responsibility.[17] Such, for example, is the interpretation offered by the most celebrated American study of the inglorious conflict, Justin H. Smith's *The War with Mexico* (1919), a two-volume work which offers this odd conclusion in explaining the role of Mexico:

> Her treatment of Texans and Americans violated the laws of justice and humanity, and—since there was no tribunal to punish her—laid upon the United States, both as its nearest neighbor and as an injured community, the duty of retribution. In almost every way possible, indeed, she forced us to take a stand. She would neither reason nor hearken to reason, would not understand, would not negotiate. Compensation for the loss of territory, in excess of its value to her, she knew she could have. Peace and harmony with this country she knew might be hers. But prejudice, vanity, passion and wretched politics inclined her toward war; her overrated military advantages, her expectations of European aid, the unpreparedness of the United States, and in particular the supposed inferiority of Taylor and his army encouraged her; and she deliberately launched the attack so long threatened.[18]

Making this judgment seems about as rational as arguing that World War II was a product of Polish aggression against Nazi Germany. While the case for Mexican aggression may not be quite as outrageous, it is clear that Smith's conclusion is baseless. Admittedly, there was a good deal of hawkish posturing in Mexico on the eve of the conflict, but there is no conceivable reason why the Mexicans might want to fight the United States . . . unless they actually strove for dismemberment. The gaping discrepancy in casualty figures between the two armies, once the battles began, amply illustrates what both Americans and Mexicans knew before—Mexico was woefully inadequate to the task of competing against the United States, a nation that Alexis de Tocqueville was already touting as a superpower by the 1830s.

President Polk must shoulder much of the responsibility for the war with Mexico. Admittedly, the smoking gun has never been found, but a survey of the president's actions suggests that his most plausible goal was an armed conflict. What was suspected by many of his contemporaries, who labeled the conflict "Mr. Polk's War," is often conceded today by students of diplomacy. His political enemies in 1846 accused Polk of being the instrument of a conspiracy of southern slaveholders who sought to extend the Peculiar Institution westward—like fellow Tennesseans Andrew Jackson and Sam Houston, Polk was a slaveholder. While this interpretation may be suspect today, the presumption of Polk's bellicose intentions rings true. Not that he ever admitted it. His conduct, he insisted, was motivated by the need to protect American sovereignty, and most U.S. historians have taken him at his word.

Polk's credibility is suspect, to say the least. His duplicity throughout is well documented. His fondness for secret diplomacy went as far as recruiting Santa Anna's help on the eve of the war, when the unprincipled but ambitious caudillo was in Cuban exile. American diplomats have traditionally appealed to high principles . . . and behaved like everyone else. Such was the case with President Polk, who talked of honor and duty, and who declared at the beginning of the war that he was not interested in annexations of territory. What Polk did in 1846, when he instigated a war and blamed the Mexicans, was no different than what Bismarck and Cavour would do in Europe during the next few years. The American president was a pioneer in the use of *Realpolitik*.

Ultimately, however, Polk was not the determining factor. The clash of arms would have erupted with or without him. In fact, the war very nearly broke out in 1842, before Polk began his machinations. In that year, Comdr. Thomas ap Catesby Jones, the commander of the American Pacific squadron, heard a rumor that war had been declared. He had nothing specific to go on, but he headed straight for California. He launched an attack on its capital, Monterey, before occupying the port on 20 October—only to discover, much to his embarrassment, that there was no state of war. He had been misinformed. Although his superiors disavowed his actions, Jones escaped with only temporary suspension from naval service. He was not even reprimanded. This pathetic episode illustrates not only the commodore's incredible audacity; more significantly, it indicates that war was in the air, and that practically everyone in the United States knew who the adversary would be and what was at stake. Jones simply jumped the gun.

The Mexican War has been attributed to the American belief in "Manifest Destiny," a term coined by John O'Sullivan, an American journalist, once hostilities had begun, and best defined by Walt Whitman, the Poet of Democracy, as "the great mission of peopling the New World with a noble race."[19] Of course, there was no mission, nor was there even a belief. The lofty concept was a rationalization for baser motives. The armed conflict occurred for many reasons, but mostly because Americans wanted war, or rather what war would provide. The naked truth remains that Mexico had what its northern neighbor craved—land.

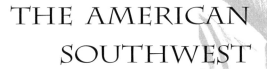

THE AMERICAN
SOUTHWEST
1848–1900

4

Until recently, Chicano historians have tended to neglect the second half of the nineteenth century. When they began their work in the late 1960s, this period was generally viewed as a hiatus between two much more promising epochs: the age of Mexican sovereignty before and the decades of massive Mexican immigration afterwards. It was the latter period, the twentieth century, which tended to dominate historical interest. One reason was that Chicano scholars are generally descended from twentieth-century immigrants and identify very little, if at all, with the so-called Spanish Dons. Moreover, many of them pride themselves on being scholar-activists; consequently, they believe that it is imperative not simply to describe what happened in the past, but to change it, an orientation that naturally leads to a preoccupation with more contemporary issues. Still another reason for the neglect of this period was the abject condition of the Mexican population in the Southwest before 1900. Small and powerless, they were despised and oppressed by mainstream society. It is a sad and depressing story, but one that needs to be told nonetheless. Adversity, after all, left a lasting impression among Mexicans; many attitudes today are products of the trials and tribulations endured at the time. Happily, by the late 1970s, Chicano scholars had come to appreciate this perspective, and today it is recognized that the period was a crucible on which the modern Mexican American has been forged.[1]

GRINGOS AND GREASERS

Anti-Mexican attitudes during the second half of the nineteenth century were ubiquitous throughout the Southwest, as many historians have noted. These sentiments arose for a variety of reasons. Perhaps the most obvious was the legacy of bitterness left by the recent war of conquest. While the fighting had not lasted very long, deep animosities created during the conflict persisted on both sides for many years. Subjugated by their enemies, Mexicans adopted an attitude that is perfectly understandable. The response of the conquerors is more complicated. As in other American wars, enemies were portrayed as evil and unworthy of respect.

This perception of Mexicans was accentuated in the immediate postwar period by the success of Spanish-speaking immigrants in the gold mines of California. Envious of their good fortune, some Anglo Americans inflamed public opinion against these "greasers" as a means of expelling their competitors from the mother lode country. The conflict over land ownership, which inevitably arose after the military campaigns, would likewise encourage the portrayal of Mexicans as a foreign and unfriendly element.

Religious prejudice was another source of anti-Mexican feeling. Vehement anti-Catholicism had been characteristic of England since the sixteenth century, a legacy that remained relatively dormant in its American possessions given the insignificant size of the Catholic population. Nor was there much concern with Catholicism in the new republic during its first decades of existence. The massive influx of Irish Catholics in the mid-nineteenth century, however, rekindled Anglo fears of popery, concerns that were not assuaged in the least when in the midst of the Mexican War several hundred Irish Catholics serving in the American army deserted to the Mexican side. (Led by Capt. John Riley, the Saint Patrick's Brigade performed valiantly, and today the *San Patricios* are honored as heroes in Mexico.) Both Irish and Mexican Catholics came to be seen as lazy, irresponsible, and priest-ridden minorities, largely incapable of assimilation.

Finally, there was the crucial element of race. The folklorist Arthur L. Campa is correct in his assessment when he states: "Cultural, political, and religious differences tended to polarize Mexicans and Anglo-Americans, but the most persistent reason for the prejudice felt by Americans was that Mexicans were dark-skinned people. Despite the rhetoric used to rationalize prejudice in the Southwest, the lack of acceptance of darker skins by most Europeans is by and large the most obvious."[2] The second half of the nineteenth century witnessed the rapid growth of racism throughout the Western world, and the United States was no exception. In the American West, where whites encountered people of color in large numbers, racism was widespread among the emigrants. It was primarily racial factors that led to the intense xenophobia experienced by the Chinese in California, prompting the enactment of the 1882 Chinese Exclusion Act, the first instance of an entire ethnic group being barred from entering the country. While racial attitudes toward Mexicans were never quite as hostile as toward Asians—

most Mexicans, after all, had some trace of European blood—these prejudices were sufficiently powerful to justify their confinement to the most menial positions in the emerging capitalist economy of the Southwest.

The sociologist Tomás Almaguer feels that fellow Chicano scholars have tended to overestimate the amount of racism experienced by their forebears in the nineteenth century, arguing that Mexicans, in fact, received meaningful legal protection, notably in the Treaty of Guadalupe Hidalgo, not accorded other racial minorities in the West.[3] While Professor Almaguer has correctly pinpointed a deficiency among many colleagues, who tend to stress race to the exclusion of gender and class considerations, he underestimates the amount of racial prejudice encountered by the Spanish-speaking population. Legal protection was often the theory rather than the practice. Moreover, it is dangerous to generalize based on the experiences of Mexicans in California, as Almaguer does; if we look at Texas, admittedly the most extreme example, the preeminence of race as the basis for anti-Mexican prejudice and discrimination is perfectly clear.

In fact, relations between Mexicans and Anglos, the most important theme in Chicano history during the second half of the nineteenth century, were complex, far more complex than Chicano scholars realized when they began to examine this relationship in the 1970s. Although there was much hostility between the two ethnic groups, this was not uniformly the case. Some Mexicans, especially among the old elite, adjusted better to the new regime than did others. For their part, some members of the Anglo community rose above the common prejudices of the time. A few—Arnoldo De León refers to them as "our gringo *amigos*"—even formed bonds of friendship with Mexicans.[4] Interethnic marriages were surprisingly common in some areas. Moreover, the passage of time brought changes in attitudes. Finally, there were substantial differences that manifested themselves geographically. Consequently, the best way of understanding the complexity of Anglo-Mexican relations is by surveying the major areas of Mexican settlement, one at a time.

CALIFORNIA

The most complete and insightful study of Mexican-Anglo relations in the Golden State during the aftermath of the war of conquest was written in 1966 by the historian Leonard Pitt, who established the main areas of inquiry that Chicano scholars would later pursue. In his *The Decline of the Californios*, the author makes it clear that the status of the Spanish-speaking population in California rapidly deteriorated after the Mexican-American War. While the relations between the two ethnic communities were bound to be difficult in the aftermath of the war, they were exacerbated immediately by the gold rush.

On 24 January 1848, a little over a week before the Mexicans signed the Treaty of Guadalupe Hidalgo, gold was discovered at Coloma, on the south fork of the American River. The discovery was made by James Wilson Marshall, a Scottish carpenter employed by John Augustus Sutter, while in the process of constructing a sawmill. The two men attempted to suppress news of the discovery, but it was not long before it became common knowledge. During the course of 1848, miners began to penetrate the Sierra foothills from far and wide. By the following year, the trickle became a flood as over 100,000 argonauts poured into the recently acquired territory. Among the most successful of the early miners were Latin Americans who arrived from the Andean highlands of South America and the Sonora region of northern Mexico, both areas with rich mining traditions. Their success, however, was due only in part to their skill; geography dictated that Hispanic miners would reach the gold fields long before most of their competitors, including the huge wave of prospectors arriving from the eastern United States.

Envy and racism, as well as the desire to eliminate economic competition— perhaps the key consideration—soon resulted in the attempt to drive Spanish-speaking peoples, all of them indiscriminately lumped under the offensive category of "greasers," from the gold fields. Violence, never far beneath the surface in frontier society, was soon directed against Mexicans, both native-born and immigrants, as well as toward other people of color. Though they were not as oppressed as native Americans, who were subjected to genocide as their lands were invaded, or Asians, who encountered intense hostility from the time of their initial entry into the Golden State in 1851, the Mexican population nevertheless suffered many indignities.

Their situation was made even more precarious thanks to the widespread use of vigilante law. The rise of vigilantes was predictable given the lawlessness occasioned by the overwhelming temptations of easy profits, together with the absence of state police agencies. While few would argue that anarchy was a better alternative, vigilantism, with all its deficiencies—the burden of proof was on the accused, the punishment rarely fit the crime, and witnesses were often intimidated—proved to be a poor substitute for regular law enforcement. Its failure was most evident when the accused were minorities, given the intensity of racist sentiments at this time.

The outstanding example, one of many, of the oppression of Mexicans at the hands of vigilantes was the infamous case of Juanita. In the summer of 1851, Juanita—her real name was apparently Josefa Segovia—a young Mexican who may have been a woman of easy virtue, killed an Anglo miner who was attempting to break into her cabin in Downieville, a small mining town in the mother lode country. She pleaded self-defense; his friends charged murder. Haled before

a makeshift court consisting of the dead man's friends, Juanita was judged guilty
of murder and sentenced to death. She was hanged on 5 July 1851, the first
woman lynched in the state of California. Had Juanita been an Anglo, even if
found guilty, she would not have been executed, so exalted was the status of a
white woman in western mining camps. It is difficult to avoid the conclusion that
race was the determining factor: Juanita was a "greaser," her unforgivable sin.
Such was also the case with Chipita Rodríguez from San Patricio, who was lynched
in Texas in 1863, under almost identical circumstances.

The law was used in other ways to the detriment of minorities. Mining
codes which excluded Mexicans, as well as the Chinese, from the diggings were
enacted in camp after camp. Discrimination was not confined to the local citizenry. In 1850, the California legislature, reflecting the pervasive anti-foreign sentiments of the fledgling state's population, enacted the Foreign Miners' License
Tax requiring that miners who were not U.S. citizens pay a tax of twenty dollars a
month for the privilege of mining American gold. The tax was not levied on Europeans; only Hispanics and Asians were required to pay. As with the local mining
codes, then, it was clear that discrimination had as much to do with race as with
eliminating economic competition. The twenty-dollar fee was exorbitant, and the
enforcement of the law was subject to much abuse. By the time the act was repealed in 1851, its goal was largely accomplished: over two-thirds of the fifteen
thousand Mexican miners in Calaveras, Tuolumne, and Mariposa counties—the
"southern mines," which they had dominated—were driven away, most returning
to their homes south of the border. Among the victims were many Californios,
whose rights were denied in violation of the Treaty of Guadalupe Hidalgo.

The failure of the pact to protect the state's Mexican population was even
more clamorous in regard to the question of land ownership. The land question
was precipitated by discouraged miners who began to occupy Spanish and Mexican land grants in the Great Central Valley by 1850. Discovering vast tracts of
fertile land, apparently unoccupied, squatters did not hesitate to avail themselves
of the opportunity to become property owners. The grantees, including a number
of prominent Anglos like Sutter and Frémont, as well as the Mexican majority,
resisted encroachment. Faced with superior numbers, however, they were soon
overwhelmed. Both sides, ranchers and squatters, appealed to the federal government to validate their claims. After a series of investigations, the Federal Congress
responded with the Land Act of 1851, which provided that individuals granted
land in California by the Spanish and Mexican governments must produce documents to that effect. A board of three commissioners, sitting mostly in San Francisco, would make the final decision, subject to appeal in the court system.
Essentially, this piece of legislation placed the burden of proof on the grantee, not
the government, a notable exception to the American legal tradition. In the case

of Mexican claimants, it was also a clear violation of both the spirit and the letter of the Treaty of Guadalupe Hidalgo.

Mexican rancheros faced many difficulties in proving ownership. Deeds were required to be extremely specific in terms of boundary lines, but given the vast tracts of land and the relatively small numbers of gente de razón in the province before 1848, as well as the cost involved, neither Spanish nor Mexican authorities had found it necessary to be very precise. Moreover, the overwhelming numbers of Spanish-speaking grantees knew no English and were largely ignorant of Anglo-American legal principles, both serious drawbacks in presenting their case to the American board. Invariably, Mexican landholders were forced to rely on Anglo lawyers, with predictable results.

On paper, it does not seem that Mexican rancheros fared too badly. Three-quarters of the claims submitted to the land commission, which heard cases from 1852 to 1856, were confirmed—some nine million acres of prime land, most of it along the coast. However, these statistics tell only part of the story. Litigation was long and costly, especially when an appeal was involved (the average time of appeal was seventeen years). Consequently, the rancheros, who were land rich but money poor, wound up surrendering large portions of their domain in attorneys' fees. Furthermore, Mexican claimants, most of them unable to monitor their English-speaking lawyers very effectively, were bound to be less successful than Anglo colleagues in retaining their holdings. Eventually, after the validation of titles, immense amounts of land were lost through outright fraud.

In the northern part of the state, which was steadily overrun by Anglo newcomers even before the completion of the transcontinental railroad in 1869, the loss of land by Mexicans was unusually rapid. While there were exceptions—Mariano Vallejo managed to preserve extensive holdings around Sonoma despite the loss of most of his property—Californios in the north retained little economic power by the late 1850s. In the south, the land base was preserved a little longer in the absence of massive Anglo immigration. Indeed, the expanding mining frontier stimulated demand for beef and resulted in high meat prices, which enabled southern rancheros to pay their debts and protect their holdings.

The halcyon days of Old California, however, were numbered. The droughts of 1862–1864 were the beginning of the end for southern rancheros. A depression ensued, which was only made worse during the nationwide panic of 1873. The cattle industry never fully recovered from this setback. Heavily in debt, landholders had a hard time fending off creditors. The crowning blow came in the 1880s, when a massive land boom promoted by the railroads brought thousands of newcomers from the East. Mexicans were reduced to a tiny minority. Most ended up performing menial labor, notably in construction and the nascent citrus industry. "Contrary to past misconceptions," Antonio Ríos-Bustamante notes, "these economic conditions applied to most of the native-born Californios, as well as to more recent immigrants. . . . With few exceptions, the native-born and more recent immigrants merged into a common community."[5]

The process was not uniform throughout the southland, as the historian Albert Camarillo has well illustrated.[6] The displacement of the Hispanic population occurred most readily in the Los Angeles basin, where the town of Los Angeles was transformed almost overnight. During the 1860s, Anglos came to outnumber Mexicans; and by 1880, only about one-fifth of a town population of more than eleven thousand was Hispanic. In Santa Barbara, on the other hand, Mexicans maintained their numerical majority until the last decades of the century, a state of affairs which permitted the local Hispanic elite—which looked to the de la Guerra family—to preserve political influence far longer than was the case elsewhere. By the turn of the century, the town had witnessed dramatic changes, though it never totally lost its Hispanic flavor.

The quarter century following the Mexican-American War and the gold rush witnessed the nadir of Mexican-Anglo relations in California. The ill-treatment of their people has been documented thoroughly by Chicano historians. Many injustices were inflicted on the Hispanic population, of which the loss of land was only the most spectacular example. The attitude of the dominant society toward the dispossessed added insult to injury. Not all Anglos entering the state despised Mexicans as an inferior race, but genuine compassion and respect were rarely extended to the defeated people.

Naturally, the vast majority of Mexicans came to resent the arrogance they encountered. One consequence was the rise of lawlessness, which often took the form of banditry. Lawlessness was not uniquely characteristic of the oppressed Mexican population; it was rampant on the frontier, especially during this period. Indeed, some historians have seen a lack of respect for the law as an American tradition. Still, the fact remains that there were many more Mexican bandits in the 1850s and 1860s than their relatively small numbers would warrant. Some came from the ranks of prominent families, including the Castros, Sepúlvedas, and Vallejos. During the decade preceding the U.S. Civil War, roughly 20 percent of San Quentin's inmate population was Spanish-speaking. This phenomenon has prompted most Chicano scholars to conclude that "social banditry," a concept made popular by the British historian Eric Hobsbawm, is perfectly applicable to what was occurring in California, and throughout the Southwest, during these troubled times.

Briefly, this theoretical model suggests that brigands, individuals or groups, are frequently members of conquered minorities who have been victimized by exploitation, often accompanied by racism, and that their oppressed status is the source of their criminality. This model has its limitations when applied to nineteenth-century Mexicans in the United States. After all, there were many Anglo bandits in the American West at this time. Moreover, banditry was also popular in Mexico, even before the European intervention of the 1860s. Still, social banditry remains the best way of explaining the spontaneous and widespread incidence of lawlessness in the beleaguered community.

The first, and most famous, of the Mexican bandits was the legendary Joaquín Murietta, who apparently initiated his criminal career after Anglo miners invaded his mining claim in the Sierras, raped his wife Rosita, killed his brother, and left Joaquín himself for dead. Bent on revenge, the youth began a series of depredations which took him all over the state. In the process, he terrorized Anglos and was given shelter by the Mexican community, who protected him as one of their own. Joaquín and his lieutenant, Three-Fingered Jack, the story goes, were finally killed in 1853 by a posse led by Capt. Harry Love, who collected a handsome reward from the California state legislature.

Now firmly a part of California folklore, Murietta has been accepted as a historical figure by a number of scholars, the historian Manuel Rojas being the most recent.[7] It is likely, however, as Leonard Pitt has ably demonstrated, that the tale is more myth than reality. Harry Love was real enough, and so was the reward, but there was no Robin Hood of the El Dorado. After extensive research, Pitt found that there were several Mexican banditti operating in California in the early 1850s who happened to have the first name of Joaquín. As criminal activity grew, mass hysteria ensued; soon they merged into one single individual, who eventually was transformed into the romantic hero.

There was no one Joaquín Murietta, but the conditions that fostered the rise of rebels like Murietta were real enough. The very existence of the myth is a testimony to this fact. The legend, which the Mexican community helped preserve, served a psychic need: it provided the marginalized Mexican population with a much-needed symbol of resistance against oppression, a function the myth continues to perform today.

Those in need of real live heroes should not despair, for though Joaquín Murietta may not have actually lived, there were other Mexican bandits whose lives resembled those of the legendary figure and whose existence is beyond dispute. Tiburcio Vásquez, the last of the famous bandidos in California, is a case in point. Born in Monterey on 11 August 1835, Vásquez was the son of an Indian mother and a Mexican father. In the early 1850s, the youth was wrongly accused of being an accomplice to the murder of an Anglo lawman and forced to flee for his life. In 1857, he was tried for horse stealing and sentenced to San Quentin. Freed, he was back in the state penitentiary a few years later, this time serving a sentence for robbery. Upon his last release from prison, Vásquez organized a gang of outlaws who operated with reckless abandon in central and northern California. Occasionally, they ventured as far as the southern part of the state. It was on one of these forays that the increasingly bold gang leader, now with a generous reward on his head and facing a murder charge, was finally apprehended for the last time, betrayed by one of his confederates. Reportedly, he was visited by thousands of visitors while awaiting trial at the Santa Clara county jail in San José. Most of them, according to newspapers, were women eager to catch a glimpse of the infamous Tiburcio. Charged with a murder committed during an 1873 robbery attempt, Vásquez was found guilty and sentenced to death. He was hanged on 19 March 1875, leaving an ambivalent legacy. While most Anglo contemporaries saw him as a vicious and unrepentant criminal, the Mexican community identified with and protected Tiburcio Vásquez.

The fascination by Chicano historians with Mexican bandits has obscured the fact that accommodation by the conquered Mexican population was much more common than resistance. Generally speaking, the higher the socioeconomic status, the greater the propensity to accept entry into Anglo society. This tendency was most pronounced among the Hispanic elite, a trend reflected in the rate of marriage between members of their class and Anglos.[8] Mariano Vallejo, for example, had eight children who married Yankees, as did three of his sisters.

Clearly, many of the unions which occurred were intended to strengthen political and economic ties. The marriages of their daughters were usually arranged by the patriarchs of upper-class families. Undoubtedly, too, the desire to "whiten" their line was a consideration among the elite, who attempted to distance themselves from lower-class mestizos. As rancheros lost their privileged status, these interethnic marriages became less common, a clear indication that Anglos were now firmly in control, although the influx of more desirable Anglo women into the state was another weighty factor.

The degree to which upper-class Mexicans embraced American institutions and customs varied from family to family. Generalization in this area is almost impossible. Some families, among them those of Santiago Argüello, Juan Bandini, Miguel de Pedrorena, and Antonio M. Pico, were eager to ally themselves with their counterparts in the Anglo community, though none of them were as successful as Vallejo in accomplishing their goal. Most prominent Californios, however, were reluctant to abandon their native traditions altogether, especially those who felt the sting of Anglo injustice. Many were resentful of their more accommodating neighbors. Mariano Vallejo, more than any other individual, was the object of their scorn; "I have seen men of pure blood, famous in provincial history, leave the room at the name of Vallejo," observed the historian Charles Howard Shinn in 1890.[9]

Pablo de la Guerra (1819–1874), on the other hand, was a ranchero who made his peace with Anglos, but on his own terms, a position that won him the admiration and respect not only of the majority of the old elite but of the masses as well. Before the American takeover, Pablo de la Guerra, like his father José, had been a steadfast opponent of Yankee annexation, despite the fact that two of his brothers-in-law were Americans. Indeed, during the U.S. invasion of California in 1846, de la Guerra joined the armed resistance, and consequently spent time in prison. Once the conflict ended, though, Don Pablo realized that the clock could not be turned back. He pragmatically accepted the new order, creating a political machine that controlled Santa Barbara for several decades, thus ensuring that his family patrimony stayed reasonably intact. Like a number of the old elite, he also fought to protect the rights of his people, of all ranks in society.

The contrast between Vallejo and de la Guerra in their response to Americanization serves to remind us that the elite reacted as individuals rather than a cohesive class. To dismiss these men as vendidos, pure and simple, as a number of Chicano historians have done in recent years—"The Navarros, the Seguíns, the Vallejos," Rodolfo Acuña declares categorically, "were a bunch of *cabrones* ["bastards"] that sold out their own people"[10]—is certainly to find a pattern where none exists, as well as to fail to appreciate the tough choices embattled rancheros throughout the territory were forced to make.

As for the Mexican masses, those who had never had a privileged position in Californio society, their reaction to Americanization was also complex. Landless, most Mexicans had little to lose in the way of material possessions after the conquest, so there was scant incentive to establish relations with Anglos. In fact, they had few alternatives: despised as racially inferior, they were unable to compete with Anglos on the same level, even had they wanted to. On the other hand, resistance was also impractical, given their modest numbers—some fifteen thousand people during most of the late nineteenth century—and the massive influx of Yankees into the state beginning immediately after the conquest. Moreover, while they felt oppression, they had always suffered indignities, the fate of poor people in all societies of privilege. For the most part, the great majority of Mexicans, both native-born and new immigrants, resigned themselves to Yankee domination. They gained a measure of security by forming ethnic enclaves, both in cities (*barrios*) and in rural areas (*colonias*), and adapted other strategies for survival that might be available to them. In many cases, especially in rural areas, it is possible that Mexican families continued to eke out an existence at the turn of the century very much as they had before, barely impacted by Anglo society.

ARIZONA

The signing of the Treaty of Guadalupe Hidalgo in 1848 left the Mexican population of Arizona, which resided exclusively south of the Gila River, under

Mexican sovereignty. Almost immediately, though, there was strong pressure in the United States to extend the international boundary farther south. By now it was evident that a railroad line would be needed to connect Texas with California, and it was determined that the most feasible route would run through the Mesilla Valley and south of the Gila. An agent, James Gadsden, was sent into Mexico to negotiate a new boundary in 1853. Badly in need of money, the Mexican government of Santa Anna, now at the end of his long and undistinguished career, agreed to sell the Americans thirty thousand square miles of land for some $10 million. On 30 December 1853, Santa Anna signed the Treaty of Mesilla, as the Mexicans called it. Ratified by the U.S. Senate in the spring of 1854, the agreement went into effect immediately.

The Gadsden Purchase created the present-day border between Mexico and Arizona (as well as southern New Mexico), thus incorporating the isolated and impoverished Mexican settlements of Sonora's northern rim into the United States. Administratively, Arizona was made part of the Territory of New Mexico until 1863, when it would be established as an independent territory; but economically and culturally, it maintained close ties to the Mexican communities of Sonora for several decades. Arizona Mexicans were largely confined to Tucson, an outpost of some five hundred inhabitants. Most *Tucsonenses* regretted the change of flags, but in some quarters there was genuine enthusiasm for American annexation.

On the periphery of the Mexican nation, the pobladores of Arizona had been chronically neglected by Mexico City, and even the recent conflict against the United States had failed to arouse any real sense of nationalism among the forgotten frontier communities. At mid-century, moreover, the resurgence of the Apache threat, begun during the late 1820s and accelerating during the recent international conflict, was at full force, prompting the settlers of the Santa Cruz Valley to look to the United States and its military might for the protection that Mexico had been unable to provide.

There were few Anglos in southern Arizona at mid-century. A desert area plagued by Indian problems, the region never enticed foreigners during the Mexican period the way other northern frontier provinces had. The first Anglos to enter were mountain men during the Mexican period, followed by a handful of soldiers who occupied Tucson during the war. But by 1854, most Anglos in the area were argonauts on their way to the California mines who chose to settle down locally for a variety of reasons. During the height of the gold rush, Texas cattle had been driven through the territory to California, where the hungry miners were willing to pay top dollar. Some cowboys settled down in Tucson, becoming either merchants or stockmen; but most of the newcomers eked out a living in local silver mines, a hazardous and largely unprofitable enterprise given Apache resurgence.

During the first years under American sovereignty, antagonism between Anglos and Mexicans was considerable, a residue of the recent clash of arms. Race was also an issue, especially among the Texans. Still, by 1860, when Anglos numbered 168 in a town population of 925, there was ample evidence of bicultural cooperation. Interethnic marriages were both a cause and effect of this improvement. Among recent arrivals who married Mexicanas were A. P. K. Safford, Sam Hughes, Hiram Stevens, and William S. Oury, all of them prominent members of Arizona's political and economic elite during the next few years.

Ultimately, the relations grew to be quite close; in fact, nowhere in the Southwest did Anglos and Mexicans get along as well before 1880 as in southern Arizona, a sanguine legacy still in evidence in the Old Pueblo today. Demographics undoubtedly played a role. The disparity in numbers dictated that Anglos had to accommodate to the dominant Hispanic-Indian culture in order to pursue their livelihood. But perhaps the strongest incentive for interethnic cooperation was the common enemy, the Western Apache. Hatred of the indios bárbaros was pervasive. Indeed, even the Pápagos and Pimas, sedentary Indians in the region, were willing to make peace with the townspeople when faced with the prospect of Apache depredations, which intensified after the Civil War. The depth of this animosity was demonstrated most graphically in April 1871, when more than one hundred Aravaipa Apache, practically all of them women and children, were slaughtered in a surprise attack at Camp Grant by a combined force, led by William Oury and Jesús María Elías, of Tucson's Anglo and Mexican citizens and their Pápago allies.

A small Anglo population also ensured that Mexicans would continue to play a vital role in the regional economy prior to the arrival of the Southern Pacific Railroad, which reached Tucson on 20 March 1880. During this early period of territorial history, ranching reemerged and silver mining, centered on the Santa Rita Range to the south, revived; but both enterprises made little progress as long as the Apache were on the warpath. The most lucrative economic endeavor in the 1860s and 1870s was long-distance freighting. The isolated settlements of northern Mexico and the American Southwest were in desperate need of food and other commodities. The expansion of U.S. military posts also favored entrepreneurial activity. Freighters were willing to respond to the demand given the prospects of immense profits, especially when they set up their own mercantile establishments.

Tucson was ideally situated to service both the pueblos of Sonora, many of them, like Arispe and Alamos, becoming wealthy thanks to the rich silver mines nearby, and the New Mexican settlements along the Rio Grande, notably the new town of Mesilla, which had access to Yankee goods from the East. Tucson blossomed during the 1870s. By the end of the decade, its population exceeded eight thousand. At this time, the Old Pueblo was widely acknowledged as the leading commercial entrepôt between El Paso and Los Angeles.

Among the most active of the freighter-merchants were members of the Aguirre family. The patriarch of this remarkable clan was Pedro Aguirre, a Chihuahua rancher and businessman who immigrated to New Mexico in 1852. Four of his sons subsequently became active traders on the Santa Fe–Chihuahua trails. Eventually, after Don Pedro's death, the family transferred its center of operations to Tucson, where they continued to expand their freighting and mercantile activities, while also acquiring vast ranches.

The most respected of the Arizona traders, however, was Estévan Ochoa (1831–1888). Like the Aguirres, he too was a *Chihuahuense* who profited from the Santa Fe–Chihuahua trail trade. At the age of twenty-eight, he established a store at Mesilla, which he ran in partnership with Pedro Aguirre, Jr. In 1859, Ochoa found a new partner in Pinckney Randolph Tully. Tully, Ochoa and Company, headquartered in Tucson, came to be the most successful freighting firm operating in southern Arizona and northern Sonora. Its operations extended as far east as Kansas. Retail stores were established in Tucson and surrounding towns. Mining and sheep raising were other enterprises that contributed to Ochoa's growing fortune.

A major benefactor, Estévan Ochoa encouraged educational and other civic pursuits. He was also active politically. Elected to the territorial legislature on three occasions, as a representative for Tucson, his crowning political achievement was his election as town mayor in 1875, the only Hispanic to hold this position during Arizona's territorial period (1863–1912). The arrival of the locomotive brought the collapse of his freighting empire and cost him his fortune, but it did not diminish Don Estévan's immense popularity with his fellow citizens, Anglo as well as Mexican.

The advent of the railroad signaled the end of an era in Arizona in many ways. Not only did the railroad reorient the major commercial routes east and west, instead of north and south, thus effectively ending the lucrative freighting connection with Sonora, but it also stimulated the rise of a powerful copper mining boom in southern Arizona in the 1870s and 1880s which required enormous amounts of capital. The advent of corporate capitalism spelled disaster for the Mexican entrepreneurs of Tucson.

As the economic power of the Hispanic elite waned, Anglos realized there was less to gain by cultivating their friendship. The elimination of the Apache threat—which occurred a few short years before Gerónimo's capture in 1886—

had the same effect. But the most telling factor in the erosion of interethnic harmony was the huge influx of newcomers from the East made possible by the railroad and attracted by the expanding mining frontier. Despite continuing immigration from Sonora, the Mexican population of the territory was being overwhelmed by Easterners, who had few ties to the local native population and were less tolerant of cultural diversity than their predecessors had been. As Anglos headed for outlying mining areas, Tucson lost population during the 1880s, the result of an economic stagnation which grew increasingly worse before hitting rock bottom during the nationwide depression of 1893. Economic troubles fanned interethnic strife. The easy relations which had existed in the 1860s and 1870s between the two communities in Tucson waned as Mexicans and Anglos drifted apart.

The deterioration of the relations between Anglos and Mexicans and the ill-treatment of the latter were observed with mounting apprehension by the Hispanic elite. Among their number were individuals who stepped forward at this crucial juncture to provide much-needed leadership for the beleaguered Mexican populace. The most active of these community spokesmen were two recent immigrants from Sonora, Mariano G. Samaniego (1844–1907) and Carlos I. Velasco (1837–1914).

Samaniego and his mother, a recent widow, immigrated in the early 1850s from Sonora, then in the midst of escalating turmoil caused by Apache depredations, to Mesilla, on the Chihuahua Trail. The family opened up a mercantile establishment, which apparently prospered, for young Mariano was sent off to study in Missouri, graduating from Saint Louis University in 1862. Upon his return to New Mexico, Samaniego took up long-distance freighting, supplying American army posts along the Mexican border. His marriage into the Aguirre family gained him powerful business allies, and in 1869, he transferred the seat of his freighting operations to Tucson. Though he was forced to abandon freighting with the coming of the railroad in 1880, he successfully made a transition to cattle ranching, mining, and stage coach transport, thus escaping the fate of his friend Estévan Ochoa.

Like Ochoa, Mariano Samaniego was fascinated by politics, an involvement that began as soon as he arrived in Tucson and lasted for some thirty years, during which time he held a variety of offices in city, county, and territorial government. The civic-minded leader was also a member of the University of Arizona's first board of regents in 1886, president of the Arizona Pioneers' Historical Society on several occasions, and one of the chief supporters of the local Catholic Church.

Throughout his career, Samaniego sought to protect the rights of fellow Mexicans, a concern that dominated his public career after the 1880s, when the strength of nativist sentiments began to alarm the Mexican community. He organized the Spanish-speaking masses and encouraged their participation in electoral politics. Waging a tireless campaign to combat negative Mexican stereotypes, he defended the rights of his people to retain their own culture, doing everything possible to promote traditional customs and practices, including Mexican patriotic holidays and fiestas. He also sought to ameliorate the deteriorating economic conditions in the fledgling Mexican barrios by promoting the organization of mutual-aid associations. By the 1890s, Don Mariano was the acknowledged *patrón* (boss) of Tucson's Mexican community.

Samaniego's electoral successes were supported by Carlos Velasco, editor of the local Spanish-language newspaper. Like many Sonorans of the time, Velasco had moved north to escape political turmoil at home. Political instability, which had been endemic in Mexico since independence, had worsened after the crushing defeat of 1848. The struggle between liberals and conservatives continued unresolved, adding to the nation's ills. Mexico's weakness again invited intervention. As a consequence, during the American Civil War, Napoleon III, anxious to expand French influence wherever possible, was able to impose a puppet government on the Mexicans in the person of Archduke Maximilian of Austria. The ouster of the French army and the execution of the Austrian emperor by Mexican patriots, led by Benito Juárez, paved the way for a liberal victory in 1867 at the expense of the conservatives, who had collaborated with the Austrian ruler and his French benefactors. But the triumph of liberalism did not come easily. Political problems continued to plague Mexico well into the *Porfiriato*, the era of Porfirio Díaz (1876–1911), who was able to fully impose his authority only by the 1880s.

In Sonora, the triumph of liberalism meant the rise of Ignacio Pesqueira, who prevailed over his political rival Manuel María Gándara during the late 1860s. Immediately thereafter, however, Sonoran liberals began to fight among themselves, as was generally the case throughout the country. It was only when General Díaz consolidated his power at the national level that he was able to put an end to chronic violence on the northwestern frontier.

In the meantime, Arizona became a haven for Sonorans, of all political factions, who found themselves in disfavor at home. Generally, they came seeking temporary asylum, intent on returning to their homeland when the violence abated or when their particular champion gained the upper hand. Consequently, Sonoran immigration into Arizona, which peaked in the 1870s, consisted not only of impoverished masses seeking economic opportunities in the mines, but also middle-class émigrés like Velasco.

A member of the Sonoran elite, Carlos Velasco was trained as a lawyer in Hermosillo but soon developed a passion for liberal politics and aligned himself with General Pesqueira. This affiliation gained him a number of key political posts. But in 1865, when the *pesqueiristas* were routed by their opponents, the supporters of Maximilian, Velasco was forced into northern exile, eventually taking up residence in Tucson. Velasco returned to his home in 1870, after Pesqueira reestablished his control in Sonora, and during the next few years he occupied a number of influential offices, including state legislator. The Pesqueira dictatorship, however, grew increasingly unpopular, and when the government was overthrown in 1877, Velasco returned to Arizona, this time permanently.

Velasco had had some journalistic experience in Sonora, and in the Old Pueblo, he quickly perceived the need for a Spanish-language newspaper that would cater to the territory's growing Mexican population. He initiated publication of *El Fronterizo* in 1878, an enterprise that would continue to 1914, an amazingly long life for a frontier newspaper, especially one written in Spanish. Though he never ran for political office, choosing to retain his Mexican citizenship, Carlos Velasco, like Samaniego, became one of the leading citizens of Tucson. More than his compatriot, who needed Anglo votes, Velasco concentrated his efforts on behalf of Spanish-speaking residents of the city. His major influence was exerted through his newspaper, which he used to educate his audience to the leading Mexican intellectual currents of the time and to promote the culture of the Old Country. Don Carlos was not alone in this endeavor; Spanish-language newspapers in the Southwest were first published in the 1850s, with more than 130 established by the turn of the century. Velasco and other editors, sometimes in spite of themselves, played a pivotal role in promoting a bicultural community, a trend that became more pronounced in the twentieth century.

The need to protect the Mexican community became crucial in the early 1890s in the face of a growing tide of anti-Mexican sentiment sparked by the economic depression of the times. In 1894, the American Protective Association, the leading nativist organization in the country, made its appearance in Tucson. The Hispanic elite was mobilized into action by Velasco, ably supported by Samaniego. The result was the creation of the Alianza Hispano-Americana, which was founded on 14 January 1894, by some forty distinguished members of the Spanish-speaking community. These included native-born citizens as well as immigrants. A *mutualista* (mutual-aid society), the Alianza was set up primarily to protect the threatened rights of Mexicans in the Territory of Arizona. A brainchild of the elite, the organization cut across class lines, incorporating workers as well as businessmen. So successful was the association that lodges were soon established in the major population centers of the Territory and beyond. Eventually, it became the first Mexican association to achieve national prominence. By the late 1930s, the height of its influence, the Alianza had over seventeen thousand members in the United States and Mexico.

The Alianza was not the first mutualista formed by Mexicans; these fraternal associations began to appear in the Southwest in the 1870s. Ultimately, mutual-aid societies were formed wherever Mexican communities were established, both in and out of the Southwest. Their significance is best expressed by the political scientist Mario Barrera: "It is no exaggeration to say that after the family, the mutualistas were the most important social organization among Chicanos from the late nineteenth century to the 1930s."[11] Typically, they came to be named after distinguished Mexican patriots, like Benito Juárez or Ignacio Zaragoza, the Texas-born general who defeated the French at Puebla on 5 May 1862 (the *Cinco de Mayo* commemorates this famous victory). The functions of these associations were varied. In the words of a respected Chicano historian:

> Mutual aid societies met the material needs of their members with emergency loans and other forms of financial assistance, job-seeking services, and death and illness insurance. They also offered their members leadership experiences in civic affairs, sponsored other institutions like newspapers and private schools, provided their communities with popular community events for entertainment and socializing, and offered public forums that addressed the important issues of the day. Mutualista organizations thus gave their members and communities a sense of belonging and refuge from an often alien and inhospitable environment. The community, in turn, accorded the members and especially the officers the highly respected status of responsible, civic-minded individuals. A lesser-known characteristic of mutualistas is that they served as a major point of organizational unity that spawned local and regional political struggles.[12]

As Chicano scholars have pointed out, the rise of these mutualistas clearly illustrates that many Mexicanos refused to resign themselves to an animal existence in a hostile environment. Indeed, Mexican men and women initiated and sustained a variety of associations—mutualistas were among the most effective of them—to better their lives. They were not the docile and apathetic population that many Anglo accounts of the time would have us believe.

NEW MEXICO

In New Mexico, the Hispanic population during the second half of the nineteenth century was better able to preserve its heritage than in other parts of the Southwest. The reasons were largely demographic. The Upper Rio Grande Valley had always been the most densely populated area of the northern Hispanic frontier before 1848—there were some sixty thousand Mexican citizens in New Mexico at the time of American occupation—and the relatively sparse Anglo immigration into the Territory during the next decades, given its geographic isolation, meant that Hispanos would retain their numerical dominance until about the time of World War II.

It is customary to refer to the native Spanish-speaking population of New

Mexico by the term *Hispanos* in historical accounts (a practice that will be employed in this narrative), but in the nineteenth century, nuevomexicanos referred to themselves as *Mexicans*. Despite the indiscriminate use of the term, however, *Mexicans* in the late nineteenth century were hardly a homogeneous population. There were a variety of factors that tended to divide them, not the least of which was social standing.

During the Mexican period, as we saw, the growing affluence of the region, due primarily to expanding trade, began to create a significant gulf between those families who were able to accumulate some wealth and the majority of the community, those who were not. By the time of the American occupation, Hispano society, as the anthropologist Nancie L. González indicates, tended to break down into two fairly rigid classes: ricos and pobres.[13] The rapid expansion of stock raising, both cattle and sheep, after the Civil War, would continue to accentuate the class dichotomy.

Hispanos did not live in total isolation, of course, especially during this period. Both native Americans and Anglo Americans occupied the Territory and developed a series of complex relationships with the Spanish-speaking communities which has been only partially understood. Both exerted a decided impact on Hispanos that can still be felt today.

When the United States acquired New Mexico, it also gained some forty thousand native Americans. Indian society was no more monolithic than that of their Hispanic neighbors. As before, the native population of New Mexico was divided between the nomadic plains tribes and the sedentary Pueblos. By the time of the American occupation, Mexicans had long since established a modus vivendi with the latter. Pueblo land grants were meted out by the Spanish Crown, and during the Mexican period, they continued to be honored. Moreover, Pueblos were accorded full rights of citizenship, something that was not true under American rule. Hispanic paternalistic policies met with moderate success; Spanish and Mexican influences permeated both Eastern and Western Pueblos (with the exception of the Zuñi and the Hopi). The Pueblos also had an impact, though more subtle, on their conquerors. The two cultures were bridged by natives who abandoned their traditional lifestyle and adopted Hispanic values and customs, as well as by interethnic marriages. Both peoples were united, too, in their opposition to the warlike plains Indians, their common enemies.

After the occupation, however, the relations between Pueblos and their Hispanic neighbors were often strained, in part because of Mexican encroachment on tribal lands. Resentment on both sides would persist into the twentieth century.[14] Pueblo hostility was perfectly understandable given the Hispanic invasion of their lands and persistent efforts to erode their traditional culture. On the Mexican side, there was resentment because Pueblo communities were protected by the federal government after the occupation, at a time when Hispanics were forced to fight a losing battle while trying to preserve their grants. Then, too, there was the hatred of indios bárbaros, which was bound to impact Mexican attitudes toward all native Americans.

Hispanos were less ambivalent about their relationship with indios bárbaros. Generally speaking, they were as intent on wiping out the warlike tribes as were their Anglo counterparts.[15] Surrounding the tiny Hispanic settlements of the Upper Rio Grande, these tribes included the Utes and Navajo to the northwest, the Jicarilla Apache to the north, the Comanche to the east, the Mescalero Apache to the south, and the Chiricahua and Western Apache to the southwest. When the Americans acquired New Mexico, its embattled Spanish-speaking inhabitants were in the midst of a fratricidal campaign with most of these tribes.

The Comanche were a notable exception. They continued to honor their truce with nuevomexicanos throughout the nineteenth century, and generally maintained good relations with *Comancheros* (Hispano traders), mostly members of the lower classes, who supplied them with essential goods. The Utes, a major source of Indian slaves, sometimes cooperated, as well.

The renewed aggression of the plains peoples at mid-century was a product not only of the weakness of the Mexican government but also the expansion of the Hispanic population into new areas previously considered Indian country. In the 1820s, the Estancia Valley was settled; in the 1830s, Las Vegas and Mora were occupied; and in the 1840s, the Mesilla Valley, just north of El Paso, witnessed an influx of settlers, mostly Mexican immigrants from the south. Expansion continued after the American occupation, as Hispanos migrated from their ancient strongholds in the Upper Rio Grande Valley, motivated by land hunger and a desire to preserve their traditional lifestyle from encroaching American influences. The main thrust was to the north, via the Chama Valley, into the San Luis Valley of southern Colorado in the 1850s and the San Juan basin in the 1870s. This northward movement is described in lavish detail by Frances León Swadesh, who notes "that the pattern of Hispanic community development in northern New Mexico has been one of multiplying, not enlarging, single units."[16] Concurrently, the rich grasslands of eastern New Mexico were attracting Mexican sheepmen, who ventured as far as the Oklahoma and Texas panhandles. The most adventuresome of these Hispanos was Casimero Romero, who led his *pastores* (shepherds) into the Canadian River Valley.

Under the terms of the Treaty of Guadalupe Hidalgo, the United States pledged to pacify the Indians in the newly acquired territory, and after some halting steps in this direction in the 1850s, the American cavalry began to effectively subjugate the nomads during the Civil War, when both the Mescaleros and the Navajo were forced to the Bosque Redondo reservation at Fort Sumner in eastern

New Mexico. Although local residents were discouraged from participating in these military campaigns, settlers continued to form citizen militias to go against their old nemesis, motivated in part by the desire to acquire Indian slaves.

The most famous Hispano Indian fighter was Manuel Antonio Chaves (1818–1889), a nephew of Manuel Armijo. Chaves hated indios bárbaros with a passion—in his old age, he recalled that he had lost more than two hundred relatives to Indian depredations—and he was not above committing atrocities at their expense.[17] On 22 September 1861, for example, soldiers under his command were instructed to fire on a group of Navajo during a minor dispute; a dozen women and children were shot down in cold blood.[18] Admittedly, Chaves was an extreme case, but his attitudes toward hostile natives differed only in degree from those of other pobladores. The same sentiments that resulted in the Camp Grant massacre in Arizona were typical of the frontiersmen of the Rio Grande Valley.

Only a few Anglos settled in the Upper Rio Grande Valley immediately after the Mexican-American War. Of those who did, a number married into Hispano families. Cross-cultural marriages muted ethnic hostility. Unlike Arizona during the immediate postwar period, then, there was relatively little strife between the two societies. Interethnic marriages would continue to be popular even after the Civil War. Darlis Miller has noted that by 1870, these marriages were widespread in the Mesilla Valley: in Las Cruces, 90 percent of married Anglo men were married to Hispanas; in Mesilla, 83 percent; and in Doña Ana, 78 percent.[19]

American sovereignty did expand commercial possibilities in New Mexico, which enticed Anglo entrepreneurs, but these were probably outnumbered by immigrants from Mexico, especially to the Mesilla Valley. The chief beneficiaries of enhanced business opportunities, however, were the local oligarchs. Undoubtedly, many of the ricos had been reluctant to see the change of flags, but fears were quickly allayed as economic opportunities expanded and the Indian menace faded.

Among rico families who prospered from increased commerce were the Chávezes, Armijos, Pereas, and Oteros. Continuing to invest heavily in the trail trade, they were able to establish impressive mercantile establishments up and down the Rio Grande Valley, along the trail linking them to both Missouri and Chihuahua.

The expanding mining frontier and the establishment of military posts in the Southwest accentuated the importance of freighting and merchandising, which favored those families with business experience. Moreover, many of these entrepreneurs, having accumulated sufficient capital, were now able to get involved in land speculation, buying up town lots as well as ranches, large and small. While speculation had always been popular on the Anglo frontier, in the American Southwest it seems to have dated from the Mexican period, when American investors introduced this profitable business. Soon, some Hispanos were competing on an equal footing with the newcomers. Among the most successful of the nuevomexicanos in the field were José Serafín Ramírez and Juan Estévan Pino. More fortunate still was Donaciano Vigil, who made such a fortune on real estate that he abandoned a highly successful political career in the mid-1850s.

Hispanic women played a notable role in the commercial expansion, a contribution which has not been recognized until recently. Perhaps the most famous woman in New Mexico during the nineteenth century was Gertrudes Barceló, known as La Tules, who ran a gambling casino in Santa Fe and made a fortune, which she increased by investing in the Missouri trade.[20] By the time of her death in 1853, she was one of the wealthiest citizens of the territorial capital. Female entrepreneurs were active in virtually all trail stops in New Mexico. In Socorro, for example, Frances García was the proprietress of a lumberyard, and Rufina Vigil de Abeyta served as a director of the Socorro County Bank.

Some women who ran businesses were widows, who made up a high percentage of the population during the middle third of the century, when Indian warfare took a terrible toll. A good example is Doña María Gregoria Rodela de Amador, who arrived in the Mesilla Valley from El Paso in 1846 with her three children.[21] In the 1850s, she established a mercantile store in Las Cruces that formed the basis for the vast merchandising enterprises of her son, Martín Amador. The Amadors, among the first families of Las Cruces, were linked with many of the most prominent families of northern Mexico, notably the Terrazas-Creel clan of Chihuahua.

As prosperity increased in New Mexico, its inhabitants chafed under the territorial status they had been accorded in 1850. Given their overwhelming numbers and potential political clout, Hispanos were anxious to achieve statehood. Congress, fearful of the dubious allegiance of the conquered population, was reticent to go along. But doubts about New Mexican loyalty to the Union were unfounded, as the Civil War demonstrated.

The outbreak of the war in 1861 found New Mexicans divided. Confederate sentiment was confined mostly to the Mesilla Valley, where many Anglo immigrants were Southerners. Led by Lieut. Col. John R. Baylor, a Confederate force invaded the Mesilla Valley in 1861, routing the small Union garrisons in the area and setting up a temporary government in the town of Mesilla. A small Rebel force was sent in 1862 to Tucson, which was occupied briefly. The main thrust, however, was up the Rio Grande Valley. The leader of this expedition, Gen. Henry H. Sibley, was led to believe that the influential rico elite, fearing that the abolition of slavery would imperil the institution of peonage which had taken root in the large estates in the Albuquerque area, would cast their lot with the Confederacy. Some rico families, including that of Miguel A. Otero, *were* swayed by this argument. However, the majority of Hispanos had no stake in peonage. Moreover, New Mexicans detested Texans, an antipathy that antedated the Texan invasion of 1841, and most of Sibley's troops came from the Lone Star State. Finally, the vast majority of Hispanos believed in the Union. The failure to gauge the strength of this sentiment proved to be the decisive factor in upsetting Sibley's plans.

The campaign began well enough, as the invading force encountered little effective resistance, even in Albuquerque and Santa Fe, which were occupied without too much trouble. Spurred on by these easy victories, the Confederate army marched on Fort Union, not far from Santa Fe. Unfortunately for the Rebels, pro-Union Colorado Volunteers, led by Maj. John M. Chivington, arrived just in time, and by taking a shortcut through the Sangre de Cristo Range, they were able to surprise their foes at the Battle of Glorieta Pass on 27 and 28 March 1862. This pivotal battle sealed the fate of the Confederacy in New Mexico. The remains of the Rebel army beat a hasty retreat back to Texas.

The hero of Glorieta was Manuel Antonio Chaves, who had led the Coloradans through the Sangre de Cristos. This was his finest hour. Even his dubious record as an Indian fighter has failed to tarnish the reputation of the Little Lion of the Southwest.[22]

The aftermath of the Civil War witnessed an influx of Anglo immigrants into New Mexico, many of them ex-soldiers. The arrival of the railroad in 1880 brought even more settlers. Many newcomers headed for the mines on the periphery, but some settled in the heart of what the geographer Richard L. Nostrand calls the "Hispano Homeland."[23] Anglos who entered this area were especially drawn to Albuquerque—at the junction of the Atchison, Topeka, and Santa Fe and the Atlantic and Pacific railroads—which became the Territory's leading industrial center by the turn of the century and its biggest city ten years later. For some Hispanic residents, this development proved to be beneficial; however, for the majority it turned out to be more of a bane than a blessing.

Huge profits continued to be made on the trail trade by rico families, permitting further expansion of land holdings, particularly in the eastern portion of the Territory. Much of the land was devoted to stock raising, which had become extremely profitable after the American takeover because of the opening up of eastern markets. While cattle raising remained important, it failed to keep pace with sheep raising, which peaked in 1880, when New Mexicans owned four million sheep. Under the *partido* system, which governed the industry, the sheep were divided among small herders (the *partidarios*), who received a share of the yield; but it was the large rancher who reaped the major benefits.

While large landholders prospered, owners of small and medium-sized holdings floundered, a process that had begun even before 1848. Evidence now indicates that even during the Mexican period, overgrazing had created serious problems for ranchers of the Upper Rio Grande Valley. Their troubles were compounded after the American occupation, when "the land grant business became the territory's major industry."[24] Oftentimes, as in California, they were unable to clear land titles. Taxes took their toll. Ignorant of business procedures, some grantees found themselves swindled out of their inheritance, often by their own people. Dispossession occurred much slower than in California but had equally devastating results. Ultimately, more than 80 percent of the grant holders lost their lands.

Legal chicanery was most pronounced after the Civil War, when the Territory came under the political domination of a group of unscrupulous lawyers and businessmen who have been labeled the Santa Fe ring. Led by Thomas Benton Catron and Stephen B. Elkins, this Republican political machine was able to maintain its power from the end of the Civil War into the 1890s, the most corrupt period in the history of American politics. Based in the territorial capital, the ring was active throughout New Mexico, especially in Taos, Colfax, Lincoln, and Grant Counties. It included upper-class Mexicans, whose support was solicited vigorously because of the voting strength of the Hispanic community (the territorial legislature was predominantly Hispanic prior to 1886). Although the ring eventually fell apart as it lost its political clout, its members reaped economic benefits galore. Catron, himself a lawyer, amassed two million acres in property and was part owner of four million more. His greatest coup was the acquisition in 1883 of the Tierra Amarilla Grant near the Colorado border, which amounted to nearly 600,000 acres. Political rings arose in California, Arizona, and Texas after the Civil War, but none were as successful as the Catron machine.

This postwar period saw the breakdown of law and order throughout the Territory. Violence was most pronounced in the eastern grasslands, where Texas cattlemen began to establish their ascendancy in the 1870s and 1880s. During these decades, they drove Hispanic stockmen from areas settled only a few years before. Oftentimes, the violence took the form of range wars between Texas cattlemen and Hispanic sheepmen. Perhaps the best example is to be found in the Lincoln County wars of 1869–1881, in which race was only one aspect of a complex and confusing series of events involving a multitude of issues. San Miguel County and the San Luis Valley were other areas which experienced extraordinary racial violence. At times, the bloodshed was due only in part to ethnic animosities, which appears to be the case in the deaths of two prominent rico political leaders: Francisco Chávez, a Democrat killed in 1892, and Col. J. Francisco Chaves, a Republican assassinated twelve years later.

As in California, though later than in the Golden State, New Mexico witnessed the rise of Mexican bandits. Among the most notorious were Mariano Leiba of Bernalillo and Vicente Silva of Las Vegas. Although these bandits might not qualify as defenders of the Mexican community, there is no question that the

Gorras Blancas (White Caps) fall into this category. A secret Hispano organization operating in the northeastern section of New Mexico—their stronghold was San Miguel County—in the late 1880s and early 1890s, the Gorras were established to protect Mexicans from Anglo encroachment of their lands. They engaged in a variety of acts of defiance, including cutting fences and burning buildings. Despite their extreme methods, they were supported by some of the most prominent members of the community, among them the influential editor of *La Voz del Pueblo*, Félix Martínez, a resident of Las Vegas.

Hispanos tried to protect their culture as well as their livelihood, particularly through the agency of the Penitente Brotherhood, which was specifically dedicated to preserving traditional religious practices. The chronic shortage of priests in New Mexico during the Spanish period resulted in the formation of a number of *cofradías* or *confraternidades*, lay brotherhoods, that helped to fill the spiritual vacuum. The most celebrated of these grassroots associations was La Confraternidad de Nuestro Padre Jesús Nazareno (The Confraternity of Our Father, Jesus the Nazarene), usually referred to as the Penitentes.[25] The organization's origins are obscure, some scholars tracing them to sixteenth-century Spain. According to fray Angélico Chávez, however, the Penitentes arose sometime in the late eighteenth century, introduced from the Mexican interior, and before too long the society dominated the villages of northern New Mexico.[26]

In the meantime, the Church continued to be hampered by the chronic shortage of clergymen. Moreover, the few priests in the Territory set less than a shining example. Concubinage was common among men of the cloth. Even Padre Antonio José Martínez, possibly the leading Hispano intellectual of his age, as well as the most respected cleric among his contemporaries, kept a mistress. After the American occupation, the new Catholic hierarchy determined that a thorough reform was necessary. The attempt to reestablish the Church's authority was initiated in 1853, with the appointment of Jean Lamy as bishop of New Mexico. The austere Frenchman was zealous in his efforts to accomplish his charge, as was his successor, Jean-Baptiste Salpointe, who became bishop in 1885. Both reformers, though united in their disdain of local religious observance and ethnic culture, accomplished a good deal, paramount being the foundation of a solid Catholic educational system in the Territory.

Other reforms met with stiff resistance, most notably the attempt to rein in the Penitentes, who represented a mystical brand of religious zeal which has always threatened the Church as an institution. Its annual practice of corporal penance, however, was the reason the Church gave for its opposition. As the Penitentes were persecuted, they increasingly went underground and succeeded in maintaining the allegiance of the villages of northern New Mexico and southern Colorado well into the twentieth century. Its members looked to the brotherhood to provide a modicum of economic security as well as to administer to their spiritual needs, undoubtedly one reason why mutualistas were less popular in the northern Hispano villages than they were in other parts of the Southwest. By the late nineteenth century, the Brotherhood, while continuing its religious and social activities, also began to organize politically. In many rural areas it was impossible to win an election without its blessing. Its foray into the political area, more than anything else, illustrates its transformation into a vehicle for the protection of traditional village culture.

Ultimately, the preservation of a land base proved to be impossible, especially after the turn of the century, when much of the land in the territory was taken over by the federal government and transformed into national parks. Hispanos, though, had better success in protecting their traditional way of life. The historian Marc Simmons puts it best: "Gradually, of course, by a process of accretion, American ways made inroads. Yet the framework of Hispanic culture was kept intact and continued to serve as the principal point of reference by which the people viewed their past and measured the future."[27]

TEXAS

Texas was the area where Anglo-Mexican relations were at their worst during the second half of the nineteenth century. Mutual animosity was evident since at least the time of the Texas Revolt and persisted throughout the era of the Lone Star Republic, but it intensified during the Mexican-American War. Texans made up a good part of the invading American force into Mexico, and when they committed numerous atrocities there, some Tejanos, probably the majority of the eleven thousand residing in the state, found themselves in sympathy with their old homeland, where many of them still maintained family ties. Naturally, the violence before the war continued afterwards. The conflict was most pronounced along the Mexican border, where flagrant attacks on the Spanish-speaking community were waged with impunity.

Diversity characterized the Mexicanos in Texas, just as it did in the rest of the Southwest. As Arnoldo De León ably demonstrates in a number of excellent studies, their experiences were markedly different in the three major zones of Tejano occupation: San Antonio and surrounding areas (Central Texas), the Lower Rio Grande Valley (South Texas), and El Paso and neighboring communities (West Texas).[28] These experiences were largely dictated by economic considerations.[29]

In Central Texas, Anglos came to dominate political and economic life immediately after its acquisition in 1836; certainly, this hegemony was established in San Antonio before the Mexican-American War. In the postwar period, when Tejanos lost their numerical edge, the rate of interethnic marriages declined, and the Tejano elite in San Antonio was able to preserve some semblance of power only with the greatest of difficulties. Oftentimes, in fact, they were forced to sacrifice the interests of the community in order to maintain their own status. "They comprised probably the most reactionary and sycophantic leadership to be found in the Southwest," according to Juan Gómez-Quiñones.[30]

The erosion of the Tejanos' land base continued after the war, and, as in other parts of the Southwest, it was accomplished in a variety of ways, including litigation, taxes, and outright violence. Moreover, as marginal farmers and ranchers, the bulk of the Tejano population was especially vulnerable to economic downswings, necessitating land sales at below market prices.

Tejano merchants fared no better. They had a difficult time competing against more aggressive Anglo rivals from the very outset, and their financial plight became precipitous after the so-called Cart War in 1859.[31] Throughout the early nineteenth century, Tejanos had established a flourishing overland trade between San Antonio and the Gulf Area, the merchandise transported on carts. This lucrative enterprise continued to be their exclusive preserve even after Texas entered the Union in 1845. In an attempt to break the Tejano monopoly, Anglo competitors initiated a series of physical attacks on the *carreteros* (teamsters) in 1859. By the time this violent campaign of harassment was stopped, many wagon owners had been forced to abandon their livelihood. The subsequent decline of the cart trade was a major catastrophe for San Antonio's Tejano merchants, who had invested heavily in the enterprise.

The Mexican population of South Texas, the Lower Rio Grande Valley, managed to retain economic and political power much longer than in the Alamo City, mainly because Anglos were slow to enter the region. Still, by the end of the century they too came to be seen as second-class citizens.

The aftermath of the Mexican-American War saw a trickle of Yankee immigrants into the region, most of them ex-servicemen. These newcomers tended to marry into the local elites. Typical was Richard King, who arrived in the 1850s and acquired enormous holdings. A benevolent patrón, King maintained the loyalty of his Mexican ranch hands, the *Kineños*, until his death in 1885. The first significant penetration by Anglos into South Texas, however, came at the time of the American Civil War. Their arrival signaled the beginning of the dispossession of native rancheros. Land was acquired through the usual methods, including marriage with the native elites. By the turn of the century, Anglo dominance in South Texas was not only economic but also political, as the machines that characterized political life along the border were controlled by the newcomers, Jim Wells of Brownsville being only the most successful of a host of ambitious carpetbaggers.

Anglos entering South Texas were attracted primarily by the prospect of acquiring lucrative cattle ranches. The cattle industry in the United States boomed after the Civil War ended. The heyday of the Texas cowboy occurred between 1865 and 1885, when longhorns raised on the southern Texas grasslands were driven to northern railheads. During these two decades, beef prices soared and South Texas ranches prospered. However, the gradual expansion of the railroad network ultimately made the long drive superfluous. The cattle boom was over. Many ranchers went under, with Tejanos, owners of smaller holdings, being especially vulnerable.

The end of these bonanza days was a catastrophe in more ways than one for the Mexican population of the Lower Rio Grande Valley. With ranching no longer profitable, farming slowly emerged as the economic mainstay of the area. By now many technological innovations had been made in agriculture; and in order to compete, the expanding farms needed to modernize. By the late 1880s, commercial farming had made its appearance in some of the southern counties, initiating an economic revolution which would continue to unfold almost to the outbreak of World War II. Tejano ranchers, land rich but money poor, were at a distinct disadvantage during this transitional period. Only a few of them managed to preserve sizable holdings, among them Hipólito García and Dionisio Guerra.

The fate of the rancheros was mirrored by that of their workers. Increasingly Tejano vaqueros, some of whom were ex-landholders already forced to accept a decline in status, were reduced to working as wage laborers on large farms, a process well illustrated by sociologist David Montejano. By the turn of the century, the proletarianization of the bulk of the Hispanic community, continuously reinforced now by impoverished Mexican immigrants from across the border, was complete.

Racial subjugation in South Texas was accompanied by massive violence. Dispossession of Mexican holdings was often the result of physical attacks on native inhabitants. The Texas Rangers, instead of helping the situation, only made it worse since this constabulary was blatantly anti-Mexican, and selective law enforcement succeeded in inflaming passions on both sides of the border.

Some of this endemic border violence took the form of resistance to Anglo domination by Tejanos. The rise of Juan Nepomuceno Cortina (1824–1892), the most famous of the Texas bandidos, must be seen in this context.[32] Born in the Mexican state of Tamaulipas, Cortina was a member of a prominent ranching family with holdings on both sides of the border. Already embittered by the theft of local ranches by unscrupulous newcomers, Cortina was in Brownsville on 13 July 1859 when he spotted an Anglo city marshal pistol-whipping a Mexican prisoner. Attempting to protect the hapless victim, Cortina killed the lawman and fled across the border. Enraged by the incident, Anglo citizens of Brownsville initiated a reign of terror against "greasers." Cortina, at the head of a small army, responded with a raid on the city in September, an attack that initiated a long period of virtual warfare between Anglos and Mexicans. The so-called Cortina War took many lives on both sides of the border; but its chief victims were Tejanos, most of them innocent men, women, and children caught in the crossfire. Border lynchings and other atrocities became commonplace throughout the 1860s.

While much of the fighting by Mexican raiders was mere banditry, motivated primarily by the quest to gain wealth, or occasions for personal vendettas, Cortina himself had a loftier goal: he believed he was fighting to vindicate the rights of his people. Most Chicano scholars attribute genuine revolutionary potential to Cortina's movement. That the campaign never achieved this potential was due not only to the strength of the opposition—the Rangers were ruthless in their fury—but also to the divisions among the oppressed people, who were separated by both class and, since they lived on both sides of the border, by nationality. His ultimate failure notwithstanding, Juan Cortina, the Red Robber of the Rio Grande, became a hero among the residents of South Texas during his lifetime. Perceived as a champion against Anglo injustice, he was immortalized in a number of *corridos* (folk ballads), some of them still current today.

Another Tejano of the time who also achieved immense renown, and apparently for the same reasons, was Gregorio Cortez (1875–1916), the subject of some of the most popular corridos along the Texas-Mexican border.[33] Born in Mexico, near Matamoros, Cortez moved with his family to Manor, Texas, in 1887. There, on 12 June 1901, he shot Sheriff Harper Morris dead after the lawman tried to arrest him for a crime he had not committed. Cortez fled, initiating the longest manhunt in Texas history. The fantastic ten-day flight, the subject of intense media coverage, ended when Cortez was tracked down by Texas Rangers. He was brought to trial and sentenced to life imprisonment. After years of fighting the unjust verdict, the celebrated prisoner was pardoned by Gov. Oscar B. Colquitt in 1913. The ballads commemorating Gregorio Cortez represent a protest against Anglo injustice on one level, but on another level, they are a tribute to all Mexicans who had the courage to stand up for their convictions.

Catarino Garza (1859–1902) is a third symbol of resistance from South Texas. Like Cortina and Cortez, Garza was born in Mexico, but he was raised in Brownsville, which he considered his home. A journalist, he constantly inveighed against Anglo injustice at home and political tyranny in Mexico, where Porfirio Díaz ruled the country with an iron hand. In 1891, Garza recruited a small army in South Texas and captured the Mexican village of Guerrero, hoping to initiate a popular uprising. The masses failed to respond. Disillusioned, Garza and his men returned to Texas. Harassed by the authorities for the next few years, the hapless crusader eventually fled to Cuba, then to Colombia, where he died.

Anglos did not penetrate into West Texas in massive numbers until the railroad arrived in El Paso in 1881. Nevertheless, even before this date, they exerted a significant influence on the area's economy. In 1848, the Mexican population of the El Paso Valley was clustered along a series of small settlements along the river, of which El Paso del Norte was the largest. El Paso had had a strategic importance from the very beginning since it connected the New Mexican towns of the Upper Rio Grande with central Mexico. The opening up of the Santa Fe Trail had increased the volume of goods flowing back and forth along the Chihuahua Trail, augmenting the commercial importance of the city. Mexicans poured into the valley during the last years of the Mexican period to take advantage of the new opportunities.

The Treaty of Guadalupe Hidalgo established the Rio Grande River as the international border, leaving El Paso del Norte on the Mexican side. Given the great economic potential of the area, it was not long before five small American settlements were established on the opposite bank, the most substantial of which were Magoffinsville and Franklin. These villages grew slowly during the next few years. When El Paso County was established in 1850, San Elizario, a larger Mexican town downriver, was made county seat. Franklin became the nucleus of a city soon to be called El Paso (incorporated as such in 1873), creating a problem of identity with its sister city nearby, a confusion cleared up only when the Mexican town adopted the name Ciudad Juárez, in honor of Mexico's most revered president, on 16 September 1888.

After the Mexican-American War, the Chihuahua trade was hurt by Mexican tariffs on American goods. The Apache were also a major threat during these years. Under these adverse circumstances, the area attracted only a small number of Anglo entrepreneurs. The arrival of John Butterfield's Overland Mail in 1858, however, revived the sagging economy of the El Paso Valley, encouraging immigration from the east.

W. W. Mills, an early pioneer, recalled years later that relations between Anglos and Tejanos were remarkably cordial in the valley in the period between the Civil War and the arrival of the railroad.[34] In fact, the area was spared the racial strife that was endemic in other parts of the state during this era, as Anglos integrated well into local society. Like their predecessors, many Anglo newcomers during the Civil War married into *Paseño* society, thus creating a bicultural environment, which characterizes the valley to this day. Of course, these contacts were established almost exclusively with the native ranching and mercantile elites.

However, the advent of the railroad would drastically alter the relations between the two ethnic communities in the El Paso Valley. A harbinger of things to come was the Salt War of 1877. The source of this conflict was a recent Anglo monopoly of the Guadalupe lakes east of El Paso and the salt they produced, a commodity which the local Mexican community had traditionally collected free of charge. When angry Paseños protested, one of their spokesmen was killed, inciting the marchers to violence. The war took on racial overtones, much to the dismay of El Paso's Anglo population, which constituted only one-tenth of the city's eight hundred residents. After several Anglos were killed, Texas Rangers were called in and promptly took bloody reprisals. For a time, it appeared that Mexico and the United States might go to war over the incident. In the end, Tejanos regained their rights to the salt beds, but the two ethnic communities remained estranged for many years.

The Southern Pacific arrived in El Paso on 19 May 1881, and it was soon united with the Texas and Pacific Railroad, which linked the west Texas town to San Antonio. The coming of the railroad was undoubtedly the most significant event in the history of West Texas. As in other parts of the Southwest, the railroad increased property values and stimulated the local mining interest, which in turn attracted the inevitable parade of Anglo entrepreneurs and speculators. The city's population surged in the next few years.

El Paso was transformed into an Anglo town almost overnight. In 1884, the county seat was transferred from Ysleta, a city located in the midst of a string of Mexican settlements to the south, to the mushrooming railroad center, a change that signified the end of Tejano political power in El Paso County.

Economically, local workers were increasingly proletarianized and their wages depressed by the influx of impoverished immigrants from Mexico—the arrival of the Mexican Central in 1884, linking the Mexican interior to the El Paso Valley, was perhaps as consequential as that of the Southern Pacific—who were recruited to toil both in mines and on railroads. Immigration from the south increased steadily throughout the 1890s, when El Paso became the major American port of entry from Mexico; and by the turn of the century, the city, with a population of almost sixteen thousand, was again predominantly Mexican.

One of the most valuable contributions made by Carey McWilliams in *North from Mexico* was to explode the myth of what he called the Fantasy Heritage.[35] As pointed out in this pioneering work, during the late nineteenth century, especially in California, there developed the popular romantic notion, promoted for economic as well as sentimental reasons, that before Anglo entry into the Southwest, frontier society consisted of two basic classes: the "Spanish Dons," a white ranchero elite, and "Mexican peons," the Indianized masses. Those elements of the culture judged to be positive came to be identified with the former; negative characteristics were seen as typical of the latter. As McWilliams notes, there are many problems with this popular analysis. Historically, he has shown, the Spanish/Mexican dichotomy has been used to justify the selective discrimination of lower-class members of the Spanish-speaking community, while at the same time glorifying the Spanish presence in America. Moreover, the portrayal of the Hispanic elite was highly inaccurate. In point of fact, Indian blood permeated Hispanic society, from top to bottom, though clearly mestizaje was more complete among the lower classes.

Another criticism of the Fantasy Heritage, one which McWilliams does not emphasize enough, is that the class system was much more complex than the popular perception would have us believe. There were pobres and there were ricos, but by the second half of the nineteenth century there was also a significant middle class throughout the Hispanic Southwest.

Although some of the middle-class elements were native to the area, notably in the Upper Rio Grande Valley, many of them were recent immigrants, lured north by the prospect of wealth and security. Despite the common perception, Mexican immigration into the Southwest was not exclusively a twentieth-century phenomenon; Mexicans entered the United States throughout the second half of the nineteenth century. While most of these immigrants were impoverished, they were accompanied by more fortunate compatriots who had education and entrepreneurial skills, especially from the border states of Chihuahua and Sonora.

THE GREAT MIGRATION

1900–1930

5

The dominant theme of Chicano History in the twentieth century is immigration. With the one exception of the 1930s, every decade has witnessed a significant influx of Mexican immigrants into the United States, and there is little reason to believe that this movement will be stemmed in the near future. The first major push of immigrants occurred during the first three decades of the twentieth century. Although statistics pertaining to immigration from the south are highly unreliable, it appears that over one million Mexicans entered the country at this time, joining the half million already in residence. Most settled down in the Southwest, though Mexican settlements began to appear in other sections of the country as well. Given the magnitude and impact, Chicano historians have labeled this transnational influx "The Great Migration."[1]

MOTIVES FOR MEXICAN IMMIGRATION

It is entirely possible, as some students of American immigration suggest, that more Mexicans have immigrated into the United States than any other single national group, including both Germans and Italians. One observer recently went so far as to conclude that Mexican movement north constitutes "the greatest migration of people in the history of humanity."[2] This statement appears rather grandiose, but Mexicans may indeed rank first among peoples who have made the United States their home. It is a claim, however, which is hard to substantiate, given inadequate statistics relating to the Mexican population. As hard as record-keeping is today, it was even more difficult prior to 1930.[3] The primary problem, then as now, was the surreptitious nature of much of the exodus. In fact, probably most Mexican immigrants in 1900–1930 entered illegally, or at least through irregular channels.

During and immediately after the First World War, a series of laws were passed, culminating in the Reed-Johnson Immigration Act of 1924, regulating immigration into this country. While this legislation was aimed primarily at stemming the massive influx of southern and eastern Europeans, immigration from the Western Hemisphere was also affected by literacy requirements and entry fees. However, given the labor needs in the country during the economic boom of the war and postwar periods there was no serious attempt to enforce these laws as they applied to Mexicans, who were only too glad to bypass the bureaucratic red tape. Consequently, many of them entered the country without official authorization, a trend that continues today.

The best way to look at Mexican immigration in 1900–1930 is still, as Carey McWilliams did in his pioneering work on Mexican Americans, as a movement motivated by a push-pull process; that is to say, there were certain factors in Mexico forcing citizens to leave the country and simultaneously there were other factors in the United States, specifically the Southwest, attracting them.[4]

THE MEXICAN REVOLUTION

Let us look at Mexico first. Recent interpretations of the Mexican experience in this country have tended to accentuate the problems encountered in American society. There can be no denying that incoming Mexicans have faced severe problems, more than most immigrant groups, including racial prejudice and discrimination. Yet the fact remains that since the turn of the century, Mexicans have willingly entered the United States in huge numbers, as they continue to do even today when they are under no illusions about what life holds in store as they head north; and many have opted to remain in this alien environment, so far from the psychological security of their native villages and cities. Why have they come? Why do they continue to come? An impartial observer must recognize, at the very least, that with all their problems, the United States still offers the immigrant advantages over the Old Country. It would seem, life in Mexico is even more oppressive than life in the United States.

Certainly, this was the case in the first decades of the twentieth century, a period of Mexican history dominated by the Revolution, a conflict which in itself indicated massive discontent among the populace. In contrast to a purely political uprising, a true revolution impacts every aspect of life: politics, economics, culture, society itself. The upheaval that Mexico experienced in 1910–1920 qualified in every respect; it was one of the few true revolutions of the twentieth century. Its origins were rather modest. It began as a protest movement initiated by Francisco I. Madero, a bespectacled intellectual and member of the landholding elite from the state of Coahuila, on 20 November 1910, after he lost a fraudulent election for the presidency to the incumbent, Porfirio Díaz (1830–1915). While Madero's motives were almost completely political, the revolt quickly escalated into a full-fledged social revolution, so profound was popular dissatisfaction with the Porfiriato.

The roots of the 1910 revolution can be traced far back into Mexican history. Some scholars today find its genesis in the agrarian discontent already in evidence by the late eighteenth century. Popular disaffection increased throughout the following century as the peasant masses were gradually incorporated into world capitalist markets, a trend culminating during the late nineteenth century, a period dominated by General Díaz. A partisan of liberalism and a lieutenant of Benito Juárez, Porfirio Díaz gained immense popularity early in his military career when he helped General Zaragoza repel the French invasion at Puebla in 1862. The death ten years later of Juárez, by now a political rival, paved the way for the ascendancy of Díaz, who gained the presidency in 1876. Determined to end the chaos that marked the political life of the struggling republic—the presidency changed hands seventy-five times from 1821 to 1876—Díaz gradually consolidated his position, ultimately establishing a one-man dictatorship which he maintained until his ouster in 1911.

The Porfiriato had popular support in the beginning. Mexico had paid dearly for the political and economic instability that prevailed after its independence in 1821. The loss of its northern territories to the United States in 1848 was only one, albeit the most catastrophic, of the setbacks encountered by the young nation. Corruption at all levels of government was rampant, years of weak and ineffectual leadership encouraged the breakdown of law and order, the economy was in shambles, and social problems abounded. Díaz was determined to resolve the most pressing of these problems, and Mexicans, tired of years of violence and insecurity, were sympathetic to these efforts. Still, divisions were typical. The Church, in particular, fought frantically to preserve its privileges against the "godless" liberals. Díaz was forced to impose his will over recalcitrants using strong-arm methods. Lacking a democratic tradition, many Mexicans were convinced that there were no viable alternatives to these measures. Moreover, Díaz's policies appeared to work reasonably well in the beginning.

The top priority of the new administration was to restore the power of the central government at the expense of the state legislatures, something which was accomplished by the 1880s. Díaz then turned to strengthening the economy. Mexico was rich in subsoil resources and cheap labor but lacked technological expertise and capital. Díaz sought to remedy the situation by turning to foreign entrepreneurs, especially British and even American investors, the latter not very popular given the recent war. Foreign capital, enticed by generous grants of land and favorable tax laws, poured into the country; and, as Mexico was inexorably incorporated into the global market under the aegis of capitalism, the economy did improve dramatically. The mining industry was revived, with copper now rivaling silver as the most valuable ore. Oil production began in 1901, and nine years later some thirteen million barrels were produced, mostly for export. A vast network of railroads was constructed linking the most strategic state capitals to one another and to American border towns, notably Laredo—a crucial link to San Antonio—and El Paso. By 1892, Mexico had built 6,876 miles of railway; and by 1910, the figure reached 12,000 miles. After the turn of the century, the government also succeeded in establishing an iron and steel industry centered on the northern city of Monterrey. Díaz had promised order and progress, and even his enemies were forced to concede that he had been able to deliver the goods to a surprising extent by the last years of his presidency.

By this time, however, there were many dissidents who had come to question whether the impressive material gains warranted the immense sacrifices asked of the masses. No doubt Díaz had brought his people more security, but at the expense of liberty. Moreover, while a significant minority in Mexico, the Europeanized upper class, was able to share the material benefits of Díaz's reforms with foreign entrepreneurs, the great majority of the citizenry found that its economic status had hardly improved at all or had even deteriorated, in part because Mexico's population soared during the Porfiriato—from 8.7 million to 15 million inhabitants. The railroads themselves, as George J. Sánchez has argued, while helping to integrate formerly isolated villages into the larger community, also disrupted traditional patterns of life, causing widespread discontent in peasant society.[5]

The most unfortunate victims of progress were Indians. At the end of the nineteenth century, the indigenous community in Mexico was still enormous; more than a third of the people were listed as Indians in official records, and some two million of them spoke native dialects exclusively. Díaz, who ironically was part Mixtec himself, was convinced by his advisors, above all his treasury secretary José Ives Limantour, that the native population was hopelessly backward and that their very existence posed a grave obstacle to modernization. *Ejidos* (Indian communal holdings) were rapidly divided under Díaz and the land redistributed, the chief beneficiaries being foreigners and the Mexican upper class, mostly whites. Luis Terrazas of Chihuahua, for instance, amassed lands totaling nearly five million acres by 1910, at a time when only 3 percent of the Mexican population owned any land at all. Generally, Indians were reduced to working as peons on large haciendas, where they lived in squalor as virtual slaves, one of the most disruptive effects of the rapid incursions made by capitalism into Mexican agrarian society. Those who refused to cooperate were dealt with in severe fashion. Among the intransigents were Yaquis from Sonora who were shipped off to toil in the henequen haciendas of Yucatán after the turn of the century. Making matters worse, the alienation of ejido lands was accompanied by growing anti-Indian prejudice, the Mexican variation of the racism that increased everywhere in the Western world as the nineteenth century waned.

Serious resistance to the regime began to develop after the turn of the century. Anti-Díaz sentiment focused on the border states of the north, which became the seedbeds of rebellion. It was here that Ricardo Flores Magón (1873–1922), the most important precursor of the Revolution, got his start, as a co-founder of the Partido Liberal Mexicano (PLM) in 1901. Dedicated to overthrowing the Díaz regime, and ultimately the capitalist system, party leaders, including Ricardo and his brothers, were exiled to Texas within a few years. Headquartered first in Laredo and later in San Antonio, now becoming the center of exile politics, the *magonistas* initiated a series of rebellions in northern Mexico in 1906. Persecuted by the U.S. government for violating neutrality laws, PLM leadership fled first to St. Louis, Missouri, then, in 1910, to Los Angeles. In the meantime, Ricardo Flores Magón had abandoned liberal ideas and had begun to espouse anarchism, a transition that can be traced in his influential newspaper, *Regeneración* (founded in 1900). In 1911, magonistas attempted an invasion of Baja California from their base in the north, where Ricardo Flores Magón remained to direct operations. The uprising proved to be abortive as the insurgents failed to arouse popular support among the masses. Crestfallen, the survivors retreated to the United States, where they suffered ongoing persecution by U.S. authorities. During this period, the uncompromising opposition leader also worked to construct a working-class movement, based on anarchist principles, among the Mexicans of the Southwest.

In February 1915, an attempt to overthrow U.S. rule and reclaim the Southwest was initiated in southern Texas. The insurrection was announced in the mysterious *Plan de San Diego*—a document apparently drawn up in the Duval County town of San Diego—the origins of which remain obscure. Mexican insurgents, some from across the border, others U.S.-born, numbered as many as five thousand individuals. Their leaders included Aniceto Pizaña and Luis de la Rosa. The 1915–1917 revolt, however, dissipated in the face of repression in Texas, during which hundreds of Mexicans were killed, and the disavowal of the irredentist movement by President Carranza of Mexico.

While this bizarre episode seemed to be fueled by the loss of lands to aggressive Anglo entrepreneurs, made possible by the recent arrival of the railroad into South Texas, and leadership was provided by local Mexican elements, the magonistas, despite their denials, were apparently implicated in the plot; the San Diego manifesto was vaguely anarchist in spirit. The U.S. government, determined to eradicate the PLM, stepped up its efforts to prosecute party chiefs; Ricardo Flores Magón spent the last years of his life in a Kansas prison, where he died under suspicious circumstances in 1922. The magonista movement failed, mostly for the same reasons that all anarchist-inspired movements have floundered—lack of organization and an unrealistic program. Its legacy, however, as recent scholarship has demonstrated, was profound.[6] It was Ricardo Flores Magón who first openly challenged the Díaz regime, exposing its vulnerabilities and laying the foundations for the Great Revolution of 1910.

Francisco Madero, scion of a wealthy hacendado family from Coahuila, was no friend of anarchism, but he was able to tap the discontent that the magonistas had accentuated when he launched the Revolution with his *Plan de San Luis Potosí*, issued in San Antonio in November 1910. The bulk of his support came, however, from the middle class rather than the workers. While the bourgeoisie, which constituted a little less than 10 percent of the population, had fared relatively well under the Porfiriato, a financial debacle in 1907 had abruptly altered their prospects for the future, alienating them from the government. According to the historian Ramón Eduardo Ruiz: "One event, as so often happens, ignited the fuse of rebellion. The financial crisis of 1907, which marked the swan song of prosperity, revealed the flaws in Mexico's economic and social fabric and became the watershed of rebellion. Until the depression paralyzed mining, commerce, and industry, the people paid homage to the Mexican success story; with its onset, even disciples of the Old Regime began to listen to the disciples of change."[7]

The ease of his initial success must have surprised Madero. Taking over power, however, was one thing; consolidating that power was an entirely different matter. Madero unleashed forces he could not control. Ascending to the presidency on 6 November 1911, he was assassinated by counter-revolutionists three months later, the beginning of a lengthy period of intermittent civil strife, at times bordering on complete chaos. While political principles may have been paramount at the beginning, the rebellion soon deteriorated into a series of power struggles as one caudillo after another attempted to gain control of Mexico City. Efforts generally resulted in political assassination. Emiliano Zapata, the most dedicated of the revolutionists, an Indian leader who fought for land and liberty, was assassinated in 1919; as was Venustiano Carranza, the Coahuila strongman and architect of the famous 1917 Constitution, one year later; and in 1923, Pancho Villa, from Chihuahua, as much a bandit as he was a revolutionary. These executions were simply the tip of the iceberg. Between 1.5 and 2 million men, women, and children lost their lives during the Revolution.[8] This cataclysmic figure contradicts the common stereotype in the United States of the "cowardly" Mexican.

Despite the obstacles, many Mexicans were able to flee the country even during the periods of most intense violence. Some eight thousand refugees, for example, crossed the border from Piedras Negras, Coahuila, to Eagle Pass, Texas, in a single day in October 1913; and in one week in June 1916, almost five thousand Mexicans poured into El Paso. The numbers increased dramatically, however, once the violence abated.

The Revolution created as many problems as it solved. Massive destruction, the result of pillage, looting, and burning, was everywhere, especially in the areas west and north of the capital, the Bajío. Mexico City was the objective of the various rebel armies and their leaders, most of whom swept down from the north—Madero and Carranza from Coahuila, Villa from Chihuahua, and Alvaro Obregón from Sonora—and it was in the Bajío that the heaviest fighting took place as government troops, the *federales*, moved north to defend the capital. These strife-torn states—which included Guanajuato, Michoacán, and Jalisco—were also among the most heavily populated in Mexico, and the destruction of their crops left the population on the verge of starvation.

Difficulty in acquiring land in an area where the hacienda system was so firmly entrenched also compounded peasant discontent. The end of the Revolution in 1920, with the triumph of Obregón, alleviated the situation somewhat, but it did not solve the basic problems. Agrarian reform, the most popular demand of the landless peasants, was enacted all too slowly by the triumphant Sonoran faction headed by Obregón and Plutarco Elías Calles. In the end, it was clear, there was not nearly enough arable land to meet the needs of the desperate rural population.

Peasant disillusion with agrarian reform was in part responsible for the Cristero Rebellion which broke out in western Mexico in 1926–1929, but there were other factors that added to the crisis. The most immediate cause of Catholic dissatisfaction was the anti-clerical legislation of the postrevolutionary period. The Catholic Church had made itself unpopular with the revolutionaries by its support of conservative elements during the conflict. A champion of the status quo, the Church found itself extremely vulnerable with the fall of the Porfiriato. President Calles, Obregón's successor, was determined to weaken the institution through a series of measures, including the expulsion of foreign clergymen and the closing of parochial schools. The attempt to curtail clerical privileges produced an unanticipated reaction in the countryside. Government leaders had miscalculated the extent to which parish priests influenced the peasantry, generally the most conservative element in any society. Devoted to their priests, mestizos and Tarascan Indians ("purépechas") in Jalisco, Michoacán, and Colima rallied to their defense.

Violence swept through the towns and villages of western Mexico as the government eschewed a policy of reconciliation and insisted on fighting fire with fire. It is estimated that some eighty thousand lives were lost in this holy war. Peasants, many of them innocent bystanders, were driven off their small plots of land, their only means of survival. In Arandas, Jalisco, for example, 1,300 inhabitants fled north for fear of reprisals by government troops.

The decade of the 1920s, the years immediately after the revolutionary upheaval, witnessed the largest exodus from Mexico, particularly from the western states of Guanajuato, Jalisco, and Michoacán. Flight was facilitated by the reconstruction of the railroad lines, which had been largely destroyed during the years of heavy fighting. Altogether, during the Revolution and its aftermath, a million people, some of them political exiles representing every class of society, most of them starving peasants, moved north to seek a better life across the border.

In fact, significant numbers of Mexicans had been entering the United States even before the Revolution. As Chicano historians have discovered recently, beginning in the 1880s, with the arrival of the railroad in the Southwest, many immigrants, mostly from the northern border states, had moved north from Mexico.[9] These early immigrants, like later arrivals, found economic conditions in the Old Country stultifying. Dissatisfied with the Porfiriato, some political malcontents preferred life abroad. After the turn of the century, the numbers of people moving north increased sharply. The historian Lawrence A. Cardoso believes that as many as half a million Mexicans entered the United States during the first decade of the twentieth century.[10]

While political exiles before the Revolution were exclusively liberal in their sentiments, those who came during the upheaval itself—when they made up about 10 percent of the total—and especially in the aftermath, tended to espouse conservative positions. Whatever their politics, however, these émigrés, mostly of urban and professional backgrounds, came to be the backbone of the small middle class that developed in the *colonias* of the Southwest. Their most popular destination was San Antonio, where they settled in the Mexican barrio on the West Side. In these ethnic enclaves, as Arnoldo De León persuasively argues, these elites came to play a significant role in preserving traditional culture:

> They promoted a Mexican past through the distribution of Mexican books, magazines, musical records, and Spanish-language newspapers from Mexico City. They sponsored speaking engagements and theatrical performances and editorialized or extolled the virtues of *la patria* (Mexico, their native country). Meantime, they formed their own clubs and held exclusive cultural activities. They maintained a commitment to preserving Mexican nationalist sentiments within the community of immigrants.[11]

THE ECONOMIC DEVELOPMENT OF THE SOUTHWEST

The immigrants, whether they came in the 1880s or the 1920s, set their sights on the American Southwest. The most attractive destination was Texas, whose Mexican population increased from 71,062 in 1900 to 683,681 in 1930, according to official statistics (the actual numbers would have been significantly greater). California, the second leading magnet, had 368,000 Mexican residents by this time.

There were a variety of factors which drew these immigrants into the borderlands. For one thing, Mexican colonies were already established here and there throughout the region. Once a part of Mexico, the Southwest continued to be familiar territory, especially for the residents of the northern Mexican states, where the climate and terrain were virtually identical to those of the arid lands north of the border. In fact, as John R. Chávez argues, Mexicans saw themselves as indigenous to the region, a perception that made it easier for them to make the move.[12] Distance was another factor. The Southwest was the most accessible part of the United States. Railroad lines linked the teeming population centers of central Mexico with American cities like El Paso and Laredo, both of them directly to the north, and eventually Nogales, where a railway line to Guadalajara was completed in 1927. Also, as Chicano scholars have emphasized recently, based on their studies of participant narratives, many immigrants were lured into the area by encouragement and financial aid extended by family members who had previously made the journey; that is, many newcomers were part of a chain migration.[13] Oftentimes, large numbers of people from the same village in Mexico came to live together in the United States.

Still, the most significant attraction exerted by the Southwest was the abundance of jobs. Mexicans found work as laborers on construction sites, public works systems, service and food establishments, lumbering camps, and ranches. The overwhelming majority, however, came to work in three main industries: mining, railroad construction and maintenance, and agriculture.

At the turn of the century, the best employment opportunities were to be found in the mines. The pacification of the Apache in the mid-1880s had permitted Americans to enter the heart of the Southwest, the territories of New Mexico and Arizona, where they discovered a superabundance of mineral wealth—coal, silver, and copper. Southern Arizona was particularly rich in precious metals. Acquired as part of the Gadsden Purchase in 1853–1854, the area south of the Gila was thought to be worthless by both governments, except as a corridor through which a railroad connecting Texas and southern California could be built. By the mid-1880s, though, Tombstone was the hub of a thriving silver mining industry. Difficult to reach from other parts of the United States, a lack of labor was all that prevented the full exploitation of the territory.

Just across the border, in Sonora, was a reservoir of cheap labor with a long tradition of mining going back to 1640. In Sonora, moreover, a mining resurgence, centered at Cananea after 1899, drew large numbers of workers from the

Mexican interior at the end of the Porfiriato. Eventually, these miners became the backbone of the Arizona silver and copper mining industry. By the mid-1920s, Mexicans composed 43 percent of the state's copper mining work force. New Mexico, too, developed a flourishing mining industry, especially in the southern region. Soon after the turn of the century, nearby El Paso became the site of the largest smelting operation in the world.

As they had during the time of the California gold rush, Sonorans came to dominate many mining areas, notably along the border. In contrast to the earlier period, they now worked for large corporations, among them Kennecutt and Phelps Dodge, under a highly regimented system of contract labor. The hazards they faced in the tunnels and pits, as well as the smelters, only begin to describe their plight. Segregated from white miners who earned more than they did for the same jobs—the infamous dual wage system—and at the mercy of employers who forced them to live in substandard housing in company towns and pay exorbitant prices at company stores, Mexican miners endured the worst conditions of any of their countrymen in the United States. And yet, they continued to perform their duties; Carey McWilliams estimated that 60 percent of the mine workers in the Southwest in 1900–1940 were Mexicans.[14] They were also well represented in the mining fields of Oklahoma, Colorado, Utah, and Nevada during these years.

By the first decade of the twentieth century, Mexicans were beginning to compete in another industry which required heavy physical labor—railroad work. The railways of the Southwest, first and foremost, the Southern Pacific and the Atchison, Topeka and Santa Fe, were constructed in the 1870s and 1880s, mostly by recent European immigrants, particularly the Irish, Greeks, and Italians. In an effort to take advantage of generous subsidies, the lines were built hastily and sometimes very carelessly. Maintenance became a pressing problem almost immediately. Finding better job opportunities in other occupations or moving up the railroad career ladder into skilled positions as conductors, engineers, firemen, and machinists, the old immigrants tended to abandon the track crews as soon as they could; and the more recent arrivals from Europe were reticent to make the long trek across the continent, once again opening up opportunities for Mexican workers. Since repairing railroad lines did not require special skills, there were no real impediments to employing the predominantly inexperienced laborers, who were needed to unload rails, lay switches and ties, and level roads. From 60 to 90 percent of the section and extra gangs employed on eighteen western railroads in 1900–1940 were Mexican. This dominance was most pronounced in the Southwest, where, according to a 1922 survey, they composed some 85 percent of the track workers.

While most of these laborers remained close to the Mexican border, residing either in boxcars or labor camps situated at regular intervals along the railroad lines, some were transferred to other sections of the country by railroad companies in dire need of a cheap and pliable labor force. They ended up in major rail terminals like Omaha and the twin cities of Kansas City, Kansas, and Kansas City, Missouri. Undoubtedly, the most popular destination outside the Southwest was Chicago, where during the late twenties, Mexicans represented more than 40 percent of the track labor force.

In the early decades of the twentieth century, however, it was the Southwest that attracted the overwhelming bulk of immigrants from the south, for it was at this time that the region experienced an amazing transformation from a pastoral to an agricultural economy, a development that became heavily dependent on cheap Mexican labor. By the 1920s, when immigration from Mexico assumed flood proportions, neither the mines nor the railroad lines could compete with agriculture in attracting the Mexican immigrant.

While significant farming enterprises had appeared before the turn of the century, notably in the cotton fields of Texas, the sugar beet fields of Colorado, and the wheat fields of the Great Valley of California, the true beginning of agricultural development in the Southwest dates from the enactment of the Newlands Reclamation Act of 1902.[15] This legislation provided for a series of irrigation projects that were to transform arid lands into rich farming country.

By 1929, the Southwest was producing 40 percent of the total fruit and vegetable output in the United States. The enormous cost of irrigation required massive outlays of capital, which ensured the dominance of large corporate enterprises rather than the small family farms typical of the Midwest. Factory-farms required huge numbers of workers, and by the 1920s, only Mexico was in a position to provide them.

Europeans continued to enter the United States at the turn of the century. Indeed, they came in record numbers. But most of them were not attracted to agriculture; and those who were, preferred to settle in the Midwest, where, taking advantage of the Homestead Act (enacted in 1862), they were still able to acquire their own farms. During the First World War, European immigration waned; and after the war, the Immigration Acts of 1921 and 1924, which imposed quotas on Old World migration, effectively stopped the influx of virtually the only Europeans still willing to make the transatlantic journey.

Asians were the other potential source of competition for farm work, but after the turn of the century they slowly disappeared from the fields. The Chinese Exclusion Act had shut off the most substantial source of Asian field labor in California, as well as other Pacific Coast states; and under the terms of the Gentlemen's Agreement, a series of notes in 1907 and 1908 between the United States and Japan, immigration from the latter nation was also curtailed. In the 1910s, laborers were brought in from India, the so-called Hindus, but their numbers were modest, and they displayed the same propensity for climbing the socio-economic ladder as their predecessors had. As Asians remaining in the United States abandoned the fields, some becoming farm owners, others leaving agriculture altogether, the labor shortage intensified, especially during the Great War, when agricultural production in the West expanded rapidly.

By the 1920s, Mexicans dominated farm labor in the greater Southwest. Their only competition came from Filipinos, who arrived in California after 1923, but who were at a distinct disadvantage given the vast distance separating their island homeland from the American mainland. By 1930, they were outnumbered by Mexicans ten to one in the fields of California.

The expansion of southwestern agriculture produced a wide variety of crops. Over two hundred products would ultimately be cultivated in California itself. Each crop required an enormous amount of labor. Cotton was the best example. Unlike the harvest of other commodities, such as sugar beets or melons, which required only brute strength and therefore discouraged the use of women and children, cotton picking could be done by the entire family, one reason why more Mexicans were employed in this crop than any other.

Before the twentieth century, cotton culture was largely confined to the Deep South, where African Americans performed most of the physical labor. During the last twenty years of the nineteenth century, cotton culture spread into Central Texas, where Mexicans were recruited as sharecroppers. By 1900, however, Texas cotton was being harvested by migratory laborers, most of them Mexicans who found employment over a seven-month period by making the "big swing" from the southern part of the state into central and northern areas, before returning home via western counties.[16]

The expansion of cotton from Texas into the heart of the Southwest coincided with the period of the Great Migration. By 1910, cotton was being cultivated in both West Texas and the Imperial Valley of southern California. Shortly thereafter, the Mesilla Valley of New Mexico and the Gila River Valley in Arizona began to produce the valuable commodity. After the turn of the century, as Devra Weber documents in her fine study *Dark Sweat, White Gold* (1994), cotton was reintroduced into California's San Joaquin Valley, where the first "Mexican harvest" occurred in 1920. In the six years from 1924 to 1930, from September to February, an average of 58,000 Mexicans made the seasonal trek into the Central Valley, where cotton had become the dominant crop, and Mexicans constituted more than three-fourths of the total work force. During the twenties, cotton production throughout the state of California increased by 400 percent. Until the cotton harvest was mechanized in the 1950s, huge farms employed tens of thousands of *campesinos* (farmworkers), who picked the crop by hand three times seasonally.

The harvest was the most labor intensive task, but there were many other jobs that had to be performed before the cotton could be picked: once the land was cleared, the cotton had to be planted, thinned and spaced by hoe, weeded, and irrigated. The entire operation up to the ginning process was done by unskilled labor. The same kinds of tasks were required for each and every crop. The amount of work to be performed was staggering. Given the magnitude of the labor problem, then, one can appreciate why Mexicans were considered indispensable to the economic life of the Southwest by the 1920s.

THE IMMIGRANT

Driven out of Mexico and attracted to the Southwest for political, religious, economic, and a variety of other reasons, thousands of immigrants, most of them destitute peasants, made the hazardous trek north during the halcyon years of the early twentieth century. What was life like for the immigrant during the period of the Great Migration? Each experience was undoubtedly unique, and yet certain thematic motifs emerge over and over again. On the basis of these common threads, it is possible to construct a composite biography of the immigrant during this momentous thirty-year period, and thus understand how this immigrant experience differed so radically from that of other newcomers to America.[17]

José Martínez, our typical modal immigrant, was born at around the turn of the century in a small village in western Mexico, a town like Arandas in Jalisco or Jacona in Michoacán.[18] He was a mestizo, like the great majority of his friends and neighbors. His schooling was rudimentary; impoverished, the Martínez family saw education as a luxury, and young José was soon pulled out of school to help provide income. Too young to take part in the early stages of the Revolution, José made a living as a *peón* (peasant), much like his father had. Illiterate and unskilled, he faced the prospects of living out the rest of his life toiling on a hacienda. As the military campaigns dragged on, and generals grew desperate for men, he and other youths were recruited as foot soldiers by either the federales or their opponents. Politically apathetic, like most villagers, he was ignorant of the larger issues and preferred to be left alone. Neither a coward nor a hero, José did as he was told.

Fighting alongside his boyhood friends and relatives, he gradually convinced himself of the righteousness of the cause. However, as the conflict deteriorated into a bloodbath, and it became impossible to tell friends from foes, his faith began to waver, and eventually survival became his overriding objective. The chaos during the closing stages of the Revolution allowed José to return to his native village, one of the fortunate survivors. He now married his childhood sweetheart María and tried to a resume normal life.

But for many people, especially ex-fighting men, a return to the status quo ante bellum proved impossible. On the one hand, some things had changed dramatically. Old rancors from the Revolution now divided communities and violence, though diminished, continued to permeate society. On the other hand, other things had not changed enough. Poverty was still rampant, and perhaps even worse than before, given the massive destruction and a population increase—notwithstanding the high mortality caused by the bloody civil war—that put a strain on limited resources. The much- anticipated agrarian reform proved a major disappointment. If and when land did become available, the plots were often insufficient in size and of poor quality. The old elites resurfaced, and little changed for the masses.

José, unable to make a good living, but convinced that a better life was possible, one of the most positive legacies of the Revolution, was prepared to try his luck in the United States. Friends and acquaintances, most of whom had never been there themselves, assured him there was plenty of work to be found in *el norte* (the north). In fact, the postwar depression of 1921–1922 was over in the United States and labor needs were soaring in the Southwest. His wife, who was destined to remain behind, living with her in-laws, was less enthusiastic. Eventually, however, María was won over to the idea. She was reassured that José would return soon, with enough money to acquire a small business, possibly even a ranch. Borrowing money from relatives, he purchased a railroad ticket for about twenty dollars (several months' wages) and headed north with high hopes. The year was 1923.

Several days later, the weary traveler arrived in El Paso and entered the United States without any trouble whatsoever. It was Mexican immigrants like José who would increase the population of this west Texas town, the Queen City of the Southwest, from a little over 39,000 to about 58,000 during the decade of the twenties. While he was required to pass a literacy exam and pay a modest head tax of eight dollars, there was minimal effort to enforce these regulations, even after the establishment of the Border Patrol a year later. It was well understood along the border that cheap labor was essential for the success of large-scale capitalistic enterprises, such as the railroad.

On his way to El Paso, José met and befriended countrymen bound for New Mexico, where, they had heard, they could find jobs on *el traque* (literally, "the tracks"), repairing railroad lines. His new friends invited him along, and soon José found himself working on railroad maintenance crews for "el SP," the Southern Pacific. Later, he did a variety of other jobs requiring a strong back and few skills. On one occasion, he was recruited to go to southern Colorado, where he worked in the coal mines near Trinidad. There were plenty of jobs available, and he was a good worker. Nevertheless, it took José two years before he could save enough money to send for his wife. By now, he had abandoned his original plan. It had become clear that his family would have to work several years in the United States before they could raise enough money to live comfortably in Mexico.

By the time José met María at the bridge linking El Paso and Ciudad Juárez, he had purchased a secondhand Model T Ford. He now chose to live the life of an agricultural worker, an occupation more congenial to his peasant upbringing, rather than return to the backbreaking and hazardous job of repairing railroad tracks. For the next few years, José, María, and their children worked as migratory farm laborers following the crops throughout the Lone Star State. During the periods of seasonal unemployment, they made their home in the predominantly Mexican communities of the Lower Rio Grande Valley, in Mercedes, let us say, where they became part of a growing Mexican subculture.[19] It was in "the Valley," too, that most of their children were born. As the family grew, they came to rely increasingly on the cotton harvest, making the "big swing" that took them through the cotton belt to the northeast. While the wages were meager, given the enormous labor pool consisting of African Americans as well as Mexicans, cotton, grown throughout the state, provided work for the entire family.

After the Depression, as Texas agriculture increasingly mechanized, the Martínez family, having by now abandoned the notion of ever returning to Mexico, would often follow the migratory trails out of state. They ventured throughout the Southwest and even beyond, on occasion. In the spring, they would chop cotton at home. In the summer, they journeyed to California's Central Valley, where there was an abundance of jobs, especially on the Westside, where agricultural empires were being developed by such powerful land barons as J. G. Boswell in Corcoran (Kings County) and Russell Giffen in Mendota (Fresno County). The family might move north in time for the berry harvest in Oregon's Willamette Valley. The beet fields of northern Colorado were another option. Some of their friends preferred midwestern destinations. Yet autumn found the family back home in Texas picking cotton, when other migrants were doing the same in California or working in the sugar beet harvest in the Great Lakes region or in the nearby Red River Valley of Minnesota or picking potatoes in southern Idaho. Eventually, after World War II, the Martínezes tended to gravitate more toward the Golden State, where wages were significantly higher than in Texas, before finally settling down in one of California's agricultural valleys in the 1950s.

Life for Mexican migratory laborers like José Martínez and his family in the years before the Depression was not easy. What they contributed to the American economy was much more than they received in return. Year in and year out, they toiled in the fields under the most trying of circumstances. They did monotonous stoop labor, often under adverse climatic conditions. Given the seasonal nature of the jobs, they were forced to travel vast distances and to endure frequent periods of unemployment. When they found jobs, hours were long, especially when work-ing with perishable crops, and wages were pitiful, the lowest of any job category in the United States. There was no overtime pay nor health benefits.

The living conditions of migrant workers were equally wretched. They typi-cally lived in isolated labor camps, some of them populated by thousands of tem-porary residents. In the 1920s, they were generally housed in tents or one-room shacks. Sanitation was usually poor. Living next to the fields where they worked, they endured not only the stench of rotting crops, but also invasions of insects and rodents attracted by the agricultural waste. Disease was rampant, especially tuberculosis, which reached endemic proportions prior to World War II; and health care was sadly deficient. Education for the children was nearly impossible under these woeful conditions, so there was little social mobility from one generation to the next.

There were exceptions to this cycle of poverty. One of them was Anthony Quinn, the eminent actor, who was brought to the United States via El Paso as an infant of four months by his mother on 2 August 1915. Manuela Oaxaca Quinn herself appears to have been an extraordinary person, according to her son's auto-biography, *The Original Sin* (1972), a valuable memoir chronicling a vital aspect of the Mexican experience. Born in the state of Chihuahua in dire poverty, Manuela fell in love with a young man from a moderately well-to-do family, Francisco Quinn, son of an Irish immigrant and a Mexican mother. She joined him as a *soldadera* (a woman soldier) when he went off to fight in the Revolution as an officer under Pancho Villa.[20] After he got her pregnant, Francisco, under pressure from his widowed mother, who looked down on Manuela for her humble Indian origins, refused to see the young girl. Leaving her in the city of Chihuahua, he went off to Texas when the Revolution took a turn for the worse. Confused and left utterly destitute with her infant son, Manuela began her search for the father of her child. After experiencing many hardships, she found him in El Paso. Im-pressed by her devotion and persistence, Francisco agreed to accept Manuela as his wife; in time, he even grew to love her.

During the next few years, the family of five, which now included Anthony's younger sister as well as his grandmother, traveled throughout the Southwest as Francisco eked out a living performing a variety of backbreaking jobs. Manuela's life was not much easier than it had been in Chihuahua, but she rarely com-plained as the family moved from one railroad or mining camp to another. Not only did she perform her duties as wife and mother but, like most lower-class Mexican women in her position, she was forced to work outside of the home to make ends meet. On one occasion, she even toiled alongside her husband repair-ing railroad tracks in southern California! Anthony Quinn recalls his mother tell-ing him: "I suppose nowadays all this sounds unbelievable. It might even sound strange, a young girl working on the railroad, but we Mexican women were used to it. We fought beside our men and found it only normal to work beside them. I loved working hard beside Francisco. When we came home at night we were both tired and hot. We understood each other's pains. That is almost more important than sharing each other's happiness."[21]

When her husband died at the age of twenty-nine in an accident, Manuela was left in East Los Angeles with two young children and a mother-in-law to support. She made it through this difficult period by working the night shift at a Goodyear Rubber plant. In many ways, Manuela cuts a heroic figure, and there can be no doubt, even making allowances for a son's natural partiality, that she was an usually strong figure. But she was hardly unique; during these tumultuous times, thousands and thousands of Mexicanas were forced to make extraordinary and incredible sacrifices.

THE CONTRATISTA

Anti-Mexican sentiment was pronounced wherever Mexicans went, a bitter legacy from the nineteenth century. The most extreme animosity occurred in Texas, where the memory of the Alamo combined with the exaggerated racial attitudes of Southerners to make life especially difficult for the immigrant. However, living in their own isolated communities and segregated from whites in the work force, most Mexicans had few contacts with Anglos during the 1920s. In many parts of the Southwest, they remained an "invisible minority" until well after World War II. The discrimination they suffered was inflicted institutionally by large mining, railroad, and agricultural concerns rather than directly by individual citizens. As was true of practically all immigrants, the capitalist economy took advantage of Mexicans, who—despite well-intentioned efforts by Chicano scholars to stress their "agency," their ability to shape their situation—were almost completely at the mercy of their employers. Despised as Mexicans, the immigrants, as Chicano scholars have shown, increasingly developed a sense of ethnic nationalism; that is, they came to identify with Mexico rather than their native villages.[22]

Not all the injustice came at the hands of the dominant society. Like other newcomers to the United States, Mexicans often discovered that the most shameful exploitation came from within their own ethnic communities. This should not be too surprising since the massive influx of new immigrants predictably created tension with established Mexican communities. Problems were most severe in New Mexico and southern Colorado, where the native Spanish-speaking population, anxious to be accepted as "Americans" and afraid to be confused with recently arrived *cholos* (lower-class immigrants), came to identify themselves as "Spanish" or "Spanish-Americans" in the years preceding the Great War. This mindset, predicated on the false notion that the Indian heritage was negligible in their own development, was pervasive among Hispanos until the 1960s, and continues to have some currency even today. Generally, however, this haughty attitude did not translate into major conflict between old-timers and newcomers given the relative absence of labor-intensive agriculture in New Mexico.

Undoubtedly, the worst abuse from within the ethnic community emanated from *contratistas* (labor contractors). Sometimes immigrants themselves, though more often native-born, contratistas served as intermediaries between Mexican laborers and their employers. They were indispensable to the workers since they had access to the one thing the newcomers needed most—jobs.

Some contratistas had a genuine concern for the welfare of their workers—as was true, too, of some farmers—and it cannot be denied that at times real bonds of affection were forged between the worker and his patrón. But the extreme vulnerability of the immigrants and their own considerable power over the workers invited exploitation, a temptation few contratistas were able to resist. The greatest opportunities for abuse occurred in agriculture, where the transient work force made it especially susceptible to coercion. The contratista, who was generally given a lump sum of money by the grower to have his crop harvested, tried to pay his workers as little as possible to increase his own profits. One way this might be done was by paying workers an hourly wage during the height of a season, when the harvest was plentiful, then switching to piecemeal wages (paid by the unit) when *la pisca* (the picking) thinned out. In this way, the cards were stacked against the unfortunate workers. Yet what was to prevent them from abandoning the fields before the entire crop was in? It was not unusual in this case for the contratista to withhold a percentage of the wage until the last day of the picking season to ensure that employees would stay to the end. This money, popularly called *los bonos*—though it was hardly a "bonus" at all—reverted to the contratista if workers failed to meet their obligations, whether it was their fault or not.

There were many other ways of taking advantage of the powerless. For example, a cotton contractor, when weighing a sack of cotton, might claim a weight much lower than that registered on the scale. Since it was considered bad form to check the scale, which always faced the contractor, the hapless worker might not realize he (or she) had been bilked. An incredulous and unusually bold worker who might question the accuracy of the reading would simply be told that, yes, it had weighed more, but a few pounds had been deducted to compensate for cotton that was too wet or a canvas sack that was too heavy. Protests were useless; the contractor had the final say. At times, less subtle methods were employed. Tampering with scales was not uncommon. There were extreme cases, too, when a contratista would simply abscond to Mexico with the entire payroll.

There were more subtle means by which a contratista could turn a nice profit. Most of the workers were *solos*, married men traveling alone, or *solteros*, bachelors, so room and board (*borde*) was often provided. Since the contractor had a monopoly on the food concession in the fields, he could charge as much as he pleased, often an exorbitant rate. He might also pay his workers in scrip, which could be redeemed only at *his* store. Many contractors were entrepreneurs who owned businesses, especially *cantinas* (bars). In addition, when the contratista did favors for his workers, altruism was rarely the dominant motive. He would bail a worker out of jail, write a letter for him to his relatives in Mexico, drive him from the labor camp to attend mass on Sundays—all for a price.

RURAL LIFE

The exploitation Mexicans suffered in industry and agriculture was galling, but the options for workers were extremely limited. Unable to speak English and ignorant of their legal rights, most were forced to endure indignities in silence. Those who protested found themselves blackballed or, worse still, expelled from the country as illegal aliens, a lesson others took to heart. Moreover, as Mario T. García has pointed out, rather than acknowledging their position at the bottom of the socioeconomic ladder in the Southwest, this first generation of immigrants tended to compare their present status with that which they had occupied in the Old Country, a perspective which softened the sting of injustice. It is important to remember that the overwhelming majority of immigrants came believing that they would soon return to Mexico, with plenty of money, so they felt that the sacrifices they were asked to make would not be more than they could bear. This resignation was most pronounced among laborers in the countryside.

The historian Gilbert G. González has recently noted that Chicano colleagues in the discipline tend to display an urban bias in their research, often neglecting the rural environment that typified the lives of their forebears.[23] Certainly this is true of studies done on the period of the Great Migration. For example, it is sometimes pointed out that the 1930 census indicated that 50.8 percent of immigrant and native-born Mexicans lived in urban areas. Yet this statistic is extremely misleading. Mexicans living in the countryside, many of them migratory, were prone to be undercounted. Moreover, there is an enormous difference in the lifestyle of a Mexican living in Los Angeles in the 1920s and one living in a small town in the Lower Rio Grande of three thousand inhabitants. But both individuals would be considered urban dwellers by the U.S. Census Bureau in 1930 because both communities had populations exceeding 2,500.

Unquestionably, most Mexicans in the United States lived in rural settings as late as the 1920s. To be sure, there were those who resided in true urban communities (which will be discussed in the next chapter), places like Albuquerque, El Paso, San Antonio, Tucson, and Los Angeles. But this was not true of miners, railroad workers, or the majority of agricultural workers, especially migratory farm laborers. In fact, some Mexicans lived in labor camps on a permanent basis. For example, workers in the citrus industry of southern California, as Professor González shows, worked year-round and were expected to maintain permanent residence near the orange and lemon groves. However, not even migrant workers, like José Martínez, could be expected to spend their entire existence living exclusively in labor camps. On the eve of the Depression, the majority of Mexicans resided in small country towns at least part of the year. These rural communities displayed considerable diversity, depending mainly on the kind of economic function they served, but they could hardly be called "urban."

To achieve an accurate picture of what life was like for Mexicans between 1900 and 1930, it should be recognized that the population was highly transient. Farm and railroad laborers had seasonal jobs, and it was not unusual during this time, a point emphasized by Devra Weber, for a person to work in agriculture, mining, and railroad maintenance, all within a span of a few months, which of course necessitated considerable mobility.[24] Even urban dwellers reflected this impermanence; many workers residing in major urban areas, notably the suburbs of Los Angeles, would follow the crops seasonally.

By the 1920s, most Mexicans continued to live in rural environments and consequently out of the American mainstream, but they were not completely isolated from outside influences. To be sure, they rarely interacted with Anglos. Still, despite segregationist policies, they sometimes worked alongside European immigrants in the mines and railroads in the Southwest; and in Chicago and other cities outside of the borderlands, in other industries as well. They were familiar with African Americans, not only in the cotton fields of Texas, but also in California, where blacks worked in the Imperial Valley as early as the 1910s. Mexicans also came into intimate contact with Asians, who worked in the fields as wage earners or small farmers.

A good example of this intimacy occurred in the Imperial Valley. Immigrants from the Punjab—Hindus, Moslems, and especially Sikhs—arrived on the Pacific Coast shortly before the turn of the century. Some 6,800 entered the United States between 1899 and 1914. Most settled in the agricultural valleys of California, where the men—the immigration was almost exclusively male—often married Mexican women. The phenomenon occurred first and remained most pronounced in El Centro and the surrounding area, where 93 percent of "Hindu" marriages before 1949 were with Mexican women. As Karen Isaksen Leonard has discovered, "Family life and the development of a Punjabi-Mexican community began and flourished best in the Imperial Valley, with settlement in other regions of California and the western states fanning out from there."[25] Interestingly, while the children of these mixed marriages were more intimately impacted by their Mexican rather than their Indian heritage, they identified with the latter as they grew older, so entrenched were anti-Mexican feelings in the community at large.

MEXICANS BEYOND THE SOUTHWEST

Several Chicano scholars, notably Juan R. García, Louise Año Nuevo de Kerr, Zaragoza Vargas, and Dennis Nodín Valdés, have indicated that even during the period of the Great Migration, a significant percentage of the Mexican population ventured beyond the confines of the old Spanish borderlands. Their history is yet to be incorporated into the larger American mosaic. Some went directly to urban centers, where they worked in industry, but most were migratory farm laborers.

The initial movement of Mexican-origin agricultural workers out of the Southwest occurred in the South Platte River Valley at the turn of the century. Stimulated by the 1897 Dingley Tariff, which imposed heavy taxes on imported sugar, the culture of sugar beets spread rapidly throughout the United States at this time, and northeastern Colorado became one of the leading producers. Workers from the south flocked to the fields. Some of these newcomers were Hispanos from New Mexico and the San Luis Valley in southern Colorado, others were Mexican immigrants, many of them from western and southern Texas, which served as vital staging areas for the industry. Entire families were contracted to do the labor-intensive job of harvesting sugar beets by large agribusiness concerns, notably the Great Western Sugar Company.[26] By the 1920s, immigrant and U.S.-born Mexicans had effectively displaced the old work force, consisting mostly of Belgians, German-Russians, and Japanese.

By this time, too, many *betabeleros* (Mexican sugar beet workers) had begun to move into other Rocky Mountain states, notably Utah and Idaho, as well as the North Platte Valley of western Nebraska. Most of these migrants returned to homes in the Southwest seasonally, but eventually some of them settled in the intermontane plateaus, which now became bases for other migratory circuits.

The chief thrust, according to the Chicano historian Erasmo Gamboa, was westward into the Pacific Northwest. In the twenties, the first Mexican families entered the Yakima Valley of eastern Washington from the Mountain states. During the following decade, they were joined by a second wave, workers from South Texas, mainly from the area around Edinburg. Mexican rural communities were well established in the Pacific Northwest by World War II, notably in the Yakima and Willamette valleys.

Eventually, Mexicans made their way as far north as Alaska. By the mid-1990s, an estimated twenty thousand Mexicans would settle in Juneau, Fairbanks, and other mainland cities, working mostly in hotels and restaurants; and a sizable colonia was to be found on Kodiak Island, working in salmon canneries. Unfortunately, this immigration into the Far North has attracted little scholarly interest.

The other major migration northward occurred east of the Rockies, via the Great Plains and into the Great Lakes region. The primary crop attracting Mexican labor to the Midwest was sugar beets, once again. Betabeleros first entered the region in significant numbers during World War I, lured by higher wages than they could extract in the borderlands. By 1927, some 58,000 Mexicans worked in the sugar beet farmlands extending from Colorado to Ohio. At this time they composed more than three-quarters of the beet workers in Michigan, Ohio, Indiana, Minnesota, Iowa, and the Dakotas.

The first Mexican migrants were foreign-born, but by the twenties, they were gradually replaced by the native-born. In either case, they came primarily from Texas, where they were heavily recruited by agents of the sugar industry. The main enlistment center was San Antonio, which had the largest Mexican population in the country before the mid-1920s. Other major recruitment sites included El Paso, Fort Worth, and even Dallas, which began to see the appearance of barrios as early as the 1870s and 1880s. As in other parts of the country, migrants quickly established networks to help one another. "Mexican migration to the Midwest," according to Zaragoza Vargas, "was not haphazard; each sequence of the journey was well planned by the migrants and involved consultation with family members or friends and especially with those who had already made the extended trip north."[27] During the Depression, Tejano penetration of the northern beet industry would be helped by the formation of an AFL-sanctioned agricultural workers' union among European beet workers in the upper Midwest. The union threatened to raise wages, prompting growers to recruit more heavily in the Lone Star State.

By the Depression, many midwestern cities, notably Detroit and Chicago, had witnessed the growth of large Mexican barrios, as field workers increasingly chose to settle down closer to the farms employing them or abandoned agricultural work altogether. Northern migration was only just beginning. By 1930, the estimated three hundred colonias of the Midwest contained less than 6 percent of the Mexican population in the United States, more than three-quarters of them from Mexico's central plateau. During this early period, according to the historian Juan R. García, in contrast to the Southwest, men vastly outnumbered women in these northern enclaves.[28]

MEXICAN AND EUROPEAN IMMIGRATION: A COMPARISON

The massive influx of Mexicans into the United States which came to an end during the Depression has often been compared to the European immigration which ended abruptly about a decade earlier, when the Golden Door swung shut. In point of fact, the immigrant experience of Mexicans in 1900–1930, especially in the Midwest, was quite similar, in many ways, to that of Europeans entering the country from about the mid-nineteenth century to the First World War, a view best articulated by John Bodnar.[29] The contratista, for example, had his counterpart in the Italian *padrone* and the Irish politician. All were liaisons with the host society. Immigrants, whatever their origin, shared common motives for emigrating, notably the disruption of village economies caused by encroaching capitalism, and they experienced similar problems in adjusting to American society. Both relied on the same kinds of institutions as coping mechanisms, like mutual benefit societies and, above all else, the family. The differences between Mexicans and the various European ethnic groups, however, were more striking and ultimately much more significant.

One major difference was the mindset of the two groups. The overwhelming majority of Europeans entering the United States came expecting to become permanent residents or quickly adopted that orientation. Separated by vast distances from their homelands, and a difficult ocean voyage, they tended to burn their bridges psychologically once they left their native villages. It is true that many newcomers grew disillusioned and ultimately returned to their homelands. According to the immigration scholar Walter Nugent, some 40 percent of Europeans who migrated to Argentina, Brazil, Canada, and the United States in the half-century before World War I eventually repatriated.[30] Still, these "birds of passage" were a distinct minority within every ethnic group; the decided majority chose to make America their home.

In contrast, most Mexicans did not sever their ties with the Old Country psychologically. Close family bonds and other sentimental reasons, as well as the ill-treatment many of them experienced in an alien environment, kept the attachment strong. Moreover, the proximity of Mexico made it relatively easy to return home. And because legal restrictions aimed at Mexicans were few in number and badly enforced, a unique pattern of immigration developed, as Emilio Zamora has observed, with Mexicans crossing back and forth between the two countries on a regular basis, sometimes seasonally.[31]

Geography is pivotal as well in another way: it dictated, to a large extent, the kind of jobs immigrants would perform. Europeans landed in the East. Early arrivals, like the Germans, were able to penetrate into the Midwest; but most remained in the mushrooming eastern cities, where they were employed in the rapidly expanding industrial job market. While wages were low and the work monotonous, these "urban villagers" were able to establish roots, mainly in ghettos, permitting their children to gain an education. Conditions would soon improve because the first effective labor unions appeared in industrial centers, especially in the Northeast. On the other hand, Mexicans entering the Southwest found employment opportunities largely restricted to mining, railroad maintenance and repair, and agriculture: occupations that required hard physical labor and oftentimes a migratory existence. Working conditions improved very slowly and social mobility was limited within these occupational categories.[32] What little progress was achieved was wiped out by the onset of the Great Depression.

While many European peasants managed to purchase land as they entered the American heartland, Mexicans were unable to acquire a land base, a salient characteristic, according to the labor historian Ernesto Galarza:

> As a small farmer, as a husbandman, as a yeoman, the Mexican failed. Even though he was unquestionably a dedicated and industrious worker of the land, he acquired none of it for his own in the United States. And this was not because of a prejudice in American society working notoriously and exclusively against him. It was because even small-family farming—the only kind accessible to the landworking Mexican—was beyond his means, and because family farming was proving no competitor for agribusiness.[33]

The nature of entry into the United States was very different for the two groups. Europeans were overwhelmingly legal immigrants. They arrived at government reception centers—the most famous being Ellis Island in New York Harbor, established in 1892, which saw 12 million immigrants pass through its waiting rooms—and after a lengthy certification process, only those eligible for entry were admitted. Mexican immigration was largely unregulated. Most immigrants from the south entered the country without their papers—Devra Weber estimates the figure to be as high as 80 percent among migrant workers at this time—a status which was not a problem through the 1920s (except for the 1921–1922 economic slump), a decade when severe labor shortages required the importation of cheap Mexican labor. Beginning in 1929, however, when federal legislation made it a felony to enter the United States illegally, their pattern of irregular entry created many difficulties for *indocumentados* (unauthorized immigrants).

Race is an obvious difference: Europeans are white and Mexicans, in general, are not.[34] This is significant. Although most European immigrants after the 1840s suffered intense and widespread discrimination, especially those who represented religious traditions other than the Protestantism of mainstream Anglo society, their skin color was rarely a factor (notwithstanding sporadic attempts made by nativists to label the Irish and Italians *racial* minorities). The same cannot be said of Mexicans. Those who immigrated to the United States were peasants, for the most part, and therefore predominantly mestizo and Indian, a fact that nativist organizations never tired of broadcasting. The nonwhite status of Mexicans would not have been a problem if U.S. society were color blind; but this was, and remains, far from the truth. From the very birth of this nation, beginning with our Founding Fathers, Americans have been absorbed with race, which has always been "at the very center of America's social and political history."[35] In fact, as critics of the dominant Eurocentric perspective argue, out and out racism, rather than simply a disinterested fascination with race, has been characteristic of this history. More pronounced at certain times than at others, it was particularly virulent during the 1920s, when the belief that whites were superior to nonwhites was so pervasive that even some people of color came to accept it. Racism not only provided a justification for the exploitation of Mexicans—and other racial minorities—but it also accounted for much of the ill-treatment they received. In this respect, the plight of Mexicans was surely worse than that of their European counterparts.

The intensity of anti-Mexican sentiment among Americans had much to do, too, with the unique relationship that had been forged historically between the United States and Mexico. Having enticed Mexico into a major war through a Machiavellian policy and having forcefully divested Mexicans of half their territory, Americans found justification for their aggression by blaming the victims. Moreover, the economic penetration of American capitalism into Mexico during the Porfiriato, based as it was on the exploitation of cheap native labor, fortified the widespread belief that Mexicans were meant to be subservient to whites. Unlike their European counterparts, Mexicans entering the United States found themselves marginalized from the very outset.

The many differences between European and Mexican immigration into this country—as well as the fact that the major waves of Europeans came several decades before the Great Migration—help to explain the notable discrepancy between the two groups today in terms of social, economic, and political power. While the Irish, Italians, and Jews have been absorbed into the middle class, Mexicans, at least three-quarters of them, continue to be predominantly working-class people.

This apparent lack of socioeconomic progress has been especially frustrating to Chicano intellectuals who predicted some years ago, based on favorable demographic trends, that the 1980s would be the Decade of the Chicano. It never materialized. The standard explanation given by most Chicano historians for this failure to fulfill their potential is that Anglos have consciously and callously kept Chicanos in a state of subservience.[36] Although vastly overstated, there is something to be said for this point of view. Certainly, the policies of the Republican administrations of Ronald Reagan and George Bush go a long way in explaining the depressed status of Chicanos and other working-class people today. Nor should the needs of corporate capitalism be minimized as factors contributing to racial and other kinds of oppression. But there is a more basic problem, namely the gigantic influx of Mexican immigrants into the United States at present. As long as this immigration continues on the same massive scale—and given Mexico's burgeoning population and the continuing affluence of the United States, there is every indication it will—the Mexican community in this country will continue to occupy a position at the lower end of the American socioeconomic spectrum.[37]

Still, as is often the case, there is a silver lining. While most Mexican Americans will continue to make modest gains or no gains at all, some Mexican immigrants will raise their standard of living significantly, as will some middle-class elements. Moreover, from a broader perspective, America can only benefit from the large numbers of people entering the country. After all, while other Americans may give lip service to the work ethic, it is the immigrants who are prepared to make the sacrifices, a point of view sustained by immigration experts Alejandro Portes and Rubén G. Rumbaut, "Above all, immigrant laborers provide a source of highly motivated, hardworking men and women whose energies expand the human resources of the nation."[38] As was true during the Great Migration, Mexican immigrants will continue to be of vital significance in many sectors of the American economy.

THE
DEPRESSION
1930–1940

6

The 1930s was a decade of economic hardship for the United States. All segments of the American population suffered from the shrinking job market. Mexicans were no exception. Material deprivation was only part of the story. Prior to this decade, anti-Mexican sentiment had been on the rise, but in many parts of the country "the Mexican Problem" was hardly a major issue. With the onset of the Depression, however, Mexicans became a popular scapegoat. By now many Mexicans had begun to move into towns and cities; no longer were they an invisible minority. Even their traditional defenders, the large mining, railroad, and agribusiness interests of the Southwest, were reticent to speak out on their behalf. Employers had access to a huge reservoir of cheap domestic labor thanks to the influx of Dust Bowl immigrants; Mexican workers were now expendable.

By the thirties, though, many Mexicans were beginning to view "los Yunaites Estaites," as they called it, as their home. Indeed, many were now citizens by right of birth. Their means of resistance were limited. Not surprisingly, then, many Mexicans joined the struggling labor movement, now radicalized by the desperate conditions of the working masses. In the end, the unions were forced to their knees by their powerful enemies. For Mexicans, the defeat was especially vexing. By the mid-1930s, thousands repatriated to Mexico. Some did so voluntarily, others were forced to leave. The legacy of this humiliation is still felt in Mexican communities to this day.

THE DEPRESSION

The Great Depression is generally dated from the collapse of the New York stock exchange in October 1929; but the roots of the economic slump, the most catastrophic in history, can be traced back to the Great War itself. The global conflict had witnessed a vast increase in American economic production, since the United States had to supply its allies (their dwindling resources practically exhausted) as well as meet its own escalating needs. American factories continued to produce at a fantastic rate even after the devastating conflict. However, an agrarian crisis in the twenties severely hampered the buying power of farmers, leading to overproduction. Most Americans hardly realized the difficulties that beset the farming community at the time; they were too busy enjoying life during the Jazz Age. Unfortunately, much of the affluence which seemed to characterize the period was based on credit, a form of gambling. During the 1920s, Americans discovered the luxury of buying on the time plan, and they took advantage of their opportunities with a vengeance. As businesses began to fold and workers lost their jobs, they were unable to meet their financial obligations. Many debtors lost everything, including their homes. By 1932, the nadir of the slump, about a quarter of the American work force was jobless, and many more were only marginally employed. By this time, world production had been cut in half. Investments in industry practically ceased, falling from ten billion dollars in 1929 to one billion dollars in 1932. The most heavily industrialized countries were the most vulnerable. Germany and the United States were hit the hardest.

Less industrialized than other sections of the United States, the Southwest, where the great majority of Mexicans resided, appeared better able to weather economic fluctuations. Both mining and railroads, however, were forced to make major cuts, and southwestern farmers, whose operations were already heavily mechanized and who sold their products nationwide, were not much better off.

The collapse of the economy left Mexicans in dire straits, whether they were found in the Southwest or other sections of the country. Even those retaining jobs found that wages were barely enough to make ends meet. Many Anglo Americans who had previously shunned the difficult and low-paying jobs Mexicans were accustomed to now found themselves with no alternatives but to enter these fields. Wages inevitably plummeted as competition for jobs increased.

URBANIZATION

One of the most momentous consequences of economic dislocation for Mexican *obreros* (workers) was that many were forced from the countryside and into cities. While food was more difficult to access there, urban centers offered compensating advantages. Work remained scarce, but there was a wider array of opportunities, and people could make ends meet by going from one subsistence job to another. The welfare programs that were established as part of President Roosevelt's New Deal were mostly city-based. Of course, large numbers of Mexicans were ineligible for welfare because they were indocumentados or because they failed to meet residency requirements; and, in point of fact, the government was not very sympathetic to their plight. Nonetheless, welfare services helped many Mexican families survive, especially in the winter, when rural jobs tended to vanish.

The Depression was only a catalyst, however; urbanization among Mexicans antedates the 1930s by many decades. Indeed, some Mexicans were to be found in an urban environment from the time of the Treaty of Guadalupe Hidalgo. Reacting to a popular misconception that Mexicans became city dwellers only after World War II, Chicano historians like Richard Griswold del Castillo and Albert Camarillo have pointed out in recent years that the Southwest contained sizable urban populations by 1900. In truth, the number of Mexicans living in urban barrios was rather modest at that time. However, significant demographic changes begin to occur shortly after the turn of the century. The number and size of barrios increased dramatically during World War I, thanks to immigration from Mexico, as well as the influx of rural laborers seeking to improve their lives in the expanding urban-industrial sector occasioned by the war itself. True urbanization among Mexicans began at this time. During the 1920s, the movement accelerated at a rapid pace, particularly in the Midwest, and continued into the following decade.

Perhaps the Mexicans most impacted by the Depression were the Hispanos of northern New Mexico and southern Colorado. During the course of the early twentieth century, as their land base contracted, villagers in this impoverished area found themselves fighting to survive. The men were forced to make ends meet by turning to wage labor, which meant seasonal migrations into the sugar beet and mining industries of Colorado. The decline of these enterprises during the Depression, though, cut off these vital sources of revenue, causing a major crisis. Unable to pay taxes and conservation district assessments, some eight thousand Hispanos lost their farms and ranches. The collapse of the regional economy in the early 1930s, well documented by the historian Sarah Deutsch, inevitably forced many families to abandon village life for the cities.[1] In Denver, for example, the Mexican population tripled during the troubled decade.

While the transformation of traditional Mexican culture was not as dramatic in other parts of the Southwest, urbanization was a regionwide phenomenon. The main destinations of citybound immigrants continued to be the major barrios created in the previous century. By 1940, the largest of these were found in the West Side of San Antonio, El Paso's Chihuahuita in the southern part of the city, and, most of all, in Los Angeles, particularly east of the downtown area.

The City of Angels illustrates the dynamics of the urbanization experience for Mexicans better than anywhere else, and today it contains the largest Spanish-speaking population in the United States. Special attention has been given to the evolution of *Angeleños* by many Chicano historians. Founded in 1781, Los Angeles remained a Mexican pueblo until the giant land boom of the 1880s transformed it into a flourishing Anglo metropolis. By the turn of the century, the Mexican population, a small minority, was mainly confined to the area slightly west of the Los Angeles River, centered on the old plaza. The site of the original pueblo, the plaza was now the city's central business district. After about 1910, "Sonoratown," as it was known to outsiders, was rapidly transformed into a modern commercial center. As real estate prices skyrocketed, Mexicans fanned out in several directions, aided by the expansion of the interurban railway system, creating a host of new barrios, which grew along with the city (the population of Los Angeles mushroomed from about one hundred thousand in 1900 to over a million in 1930). The main thrust from the city center went east, to and beyond the river. By the outbreak of the war, Mexicans had entered the Belvedere-Maravilla area; and in the 1920s, they were in the process of penetrating neighboring Boyle Heights, lured by economic opportunities created by the construction of factories nearby. By 1930, more Mexicans resided in East Los Angeles, the collective name for the eastern barrios, than in the historic central plaza barrio. The population grew not only because of natural increase but also because the barrios there came to serve as a magnet for the migratory farm labor force from throughout southern California. In addition, some residents arrived directly from Mexico, which was also the case in a number of other southwestern cities—notably San Antonio and El Paso—which served as distribution centers for Mexican labor to the north. By 1930, Los Angeles, with 97,116 Mexicans living within its city limits, had the second largest Mexican population in the world, surpassed only by Mexico City itself.

The way of life in the Mexican barrios of East Los Angeles and other parts of the city in the 1930s was not much different than in other barrios scattered across the Southwest. Life was extremely difficult during the Depression—a sense of stultifying poverty was the first and most vivid impression made on the visitor. In fact, social and economic conditions were wretched even before, as the Mexican Fact-Finding Committee commissioned by Gov. C. C. Young, which focused on Los Angeles County, made clear in its oft-quoted 1930 report. The Depression accentuated all the problems. Housing was dilapidated and overcrowded. Few residents owned homes, though Mexicans in Los Angeles were better off in this regard than in most other places. Sanitation was deficient, not much better than in underdeveloped Mexico itself. Other woes included seasonal employment at low wages and a rudimentary education for the children, usually in segregated schools.

Problems abounded in the community, and yet barrio life represented a multitude of positive features, even in the depths of the economic slump, as old-timers looking back on their experiences years later remembered.[2] The barrio offered—and still offers—the kind of security that immigrants and their children could find in no other place. The surroundings were familiar, the reason barrios were often labeled "Little Mexicos" by both friendly and hostile observers. Spanish was the dominant language. It was heard everywhere—at home, in the streets, in businesses, and at church. Much of the social life of the barrio revolved around the Catholic Church, especially for *la gente decente*, the "more respectable elements," though Protestant denominations were also beginning to administer to the needs of the community. While women spent a good deal of time in church, men preferred cantinas and pool halls, where drinking and gambling were the most popular pastimes. Everyone enjoyed fiestas, dances, parades, and picnics in the park. Movie houses, showing the latest films from Mexico as well as the United States, and touring *carpa* theaters, which also helped to preserve ties with the Old Country, were generally packed. Community life was vibrant.

The barrio population was highly transient—even in the more industrialized colonias of the Midwest—as a large number of residents were migratory workers much of the year. This spatial mobility would suggest that the community was certainly not a restrictive environment where inhabitants felt trapped and alienated. Chicano scholars today generally see the barrio in a positive light, challenging the widely held belief that ethnic ghettos are predominantly breeding grounds for crime and poverty. In the words of the Chicano historian Ricardo Romo: "[T]he distorted ghetto image of barrios ignored the fact that the majority of Mexican immigrants, for reasons of language, kinship, and folk customs, chose to live together in barrios. These barrios provided a sense of identity with the homeland and a transition into American society. Thus modern ghettos or barrios are not necessarily homes for losers and sinners."[3]

URBANIZATION IN THE MIDWEST

The most urbanized Mexican population by the Depression was to be found in the Midwest. The history of Mexicans there, only now being studied in a systematic way by Chicano scholars, begins at the turn of the century, when a small number of migrants made their appearance in the sugar beet fields which began to proliferate throughout the region.[4] By World War I, Mexican railroad workers had also arrived in the area following the rails from Texas to Chicago via Dallas, Omaha, and other railroad towns on the plains. The greater metropolitan area of Kansas City, for example, a major railroad center on both sides of the Missouri-

Kansas state line, already had a Mexican population of three thousand by 1914. Since farm labor and railroad work were highly seasonal, both contributed heavily to emerging urbanization.

In the beginning, factory owners found this spontaneous migration satisfactory for their needs. During and immediately after the war, though, labor agents began to actively recruit workers directly from Mexico and Texas and to ship them into the urban-industrial centers by rail, so acute was the labor shortage. Not only had wartime industries expanded, but the global conflict and the 1917 Immigration Act had cut off the flow of European immigrants, previously the mainstay of heavy industry in the North. Some Mexicans were brought in as strikebreakers, most notably during the nationwide steel strike of 1919—which resulted in their recruitment as far east as Bethlehem, Pennsylvania. Mexicans found employment in the industries with the most urgent need: steel, automobile, cement, and meat-packing plants. Omaha, St. Louis, and Kansas City witnessed the steady growth of colonies during or soon after the war. Such was the case in the industrial cities of the Great Lakes as well. In Detroit, the center of automobile manufacturing, the country's biggest industry, Mexicans made their appearance in 1918, when the Ford Motor Company began to recruit them successfully by offering the same wages it paid white workers. Two years later, the Motor City had a Mexican population of three thousand, with the largest barrio located southwest of the downtown area. Other automobile manufacturing centers in Michigan, like Flint, Pontiac, and Saginaw, also enticed Mexican labor.

The greatest concentration occurred, however, in the Chicago metropolitan area, where there were almost twenty thousand Mexicans on the eve of the Depression, mostly young foreign-born males. The hub of the nation's railroad network, it was inevitable that the Windy City would attract a significant Spanish-speaking population. Other Mexicans, however, found work in the packing plants and steel mills of the city and its suburbs. In Chicago proper, already the second largest metropolis in the country, barrios surfaced in three areas. The largest was in the Near West End, where Italians were the predominant ethnic group. South Chicago, where Mexicans lived and worked with Poles, had a smaller though better integrated Mexican population. The smallest community was in the Back of the Yards district, where they got along best with their neighbors.

Mexican communities immediately began to expand eastward from the southern part of the city along the southern shores of Lake Michigan (the Calumet) into East Chicago and Gary, steel centers in northwestern Indiana. By 1930, these two satellite cities and surrounding communities reported the presence of some nine thousand Mexican residents, with the largest colony located in Gary's southside. Many Mexicans in the Calumet region worked at the Inland Steel Company in East Chicago's Indiana Harbor, the largest employer of Mexicans in the Midwest after the Ford Motor Company.

Other Mexicans lived in medium-sized towns like Davenport, Iowa; Omaha, Nebraska; Lansing, Michigan; and Toledo, Ohio. By 1930, according to census figures, there were approximately 58,000 Mexicans in the Midwest, of which the overwhelming majority were urban dwellers. Most of the men (53.6 percent) worked in manufacturing jobs.

Mexicans residing in the Midwest had experiences which differed significantly from those of their compatriots living in the border area. There were many reasons. First, midwestern Mexicans were more heavily urbanized, which means they generally received higher wages and a better education.

Second, midwestern Mexicans were less isolated from outsiders, often living and working with European immigrant populations. Of course, there was also ongoing tension, even violence, as both groups competed for the same jobs during periods of adversity. Moreover, beginning in 1919, as the labor historian Lizabeth Cohen has illustrated in her study of Chicago workers during the interwar period, factory owners encouraged racial tensions by employing both Mexicans and African Americans as strikebreakers.[5] However, conditions improved in time, a situation which promoted interethnic marriages between Mexicans and other Catholic populations. Exogamy was much more pronounced among midwestern Mexicans than among their compatriots who settled in other regions. The presence of African Americans, who also initiated their great migration to the industrial cities of the North during World War I, served to mute somewhat the racism that Mexicans experienced.

Third, their distance from Mexico made it harder for midwestern Mexicans to maintain ties with their native roots, which, together with the other differences mentioned, resulted in a greater degree of assimilation than occurred in the borderland. The use of English, as University of California economist Paul S. Taylor reported in the 1920s, was significantly higher in the northern cities. All in all, it is difficult to disagree with the historian Dennis Nodín Valdés when he asserts: "Early twentieth-century Chicano/a history in the Midwest has more parallels to European immigration history than in the American Southwest."[6]

Yet, the Mexican assimilation rate lagged behind that of the European immigrants they worked and often lived with, as many contemporary observers noted at the time. Of course, the bulk of the Europeans preceded the majority of Mexicans into midwestern cities, but this is only one reason for the disparity. Discrimination against Mexicans ("spicks"), the presence of African Americans notwithstanding, was significant. Other immigrants feared economic competition and felt superior to the dark-skinned newcomers. Furthermore, Mexicans made a concerted effort to maintain their cultural traditions, setting up a variety of patriotic, religious, mutualist, and other associations. Mexican nationalism was zealously defended in barrios—more so with the immigrants than their children— in part as a reaction to the mistreatment they encountered from their neighbors. Ironically, too, nationalism at this time was more pronounced among these and other Mexican communities in the United States than it was in Mexico itself, where village and regional allegiances continued to be more vital than national sentiments for many more years.

THE "MEXICAN PROBLEM"

As might be expected, the collapse of the economy in the 1930s increased racial tensions, which augured ill for Mexicans, both in the Southwest and outside of that region. In fact, anti-Mexican sentiments, as the account above indicates, were evident well before the Depression. In the 1920s, during the aftermath of the Great War, nativism was pervasive. Many people felt the need to keep America "pure." The Ku Klux Klan—with a membership of some five million in the mid-1920s—was only the most outspoken of a large assortment of white supremist organizations, which included the American Legion, the Daughters of the Golden West, and other patriotic groups. Although these animosities mirrored the impoverished conditions among some segments of the American population in the 1920s, nativism may have had more to do with the xenophobia engendered by the war. It was these sentiments which were primarily responsible for the legislation enacted after 1917 restricting European immigration.

Nativist fears fed the growing perception of Mexicans as a problem in the 1920s, a concern intensified by the appearance of Mexicans in cities. The "Mexican Problem" was a popular topic in the national press throughout the interwar period. Spearheading this anti-immigrant campaign was the widely read *Saturday Evening Post*. Although statistical evidence was rarely presented, the "Mexican element" was accused of increasing community crime rates, lowering educational standards, and creating slums. Mexicans were viewed as a foreign and unfriendly people who were lazy and unassimilable. There was just enough truth in the arguments to sway public opinion. The naturalization rate of the Mexican—less than 6 percent in 1930—was the lowest of any immigrant group, and problems abounded within the colonias (though detractors rarely mentioned that Mexicans were more often victims than perpetrators).

Stereotypes of Mexicans invariably had a racial basis. A classic example is provided by Dr. Roy L. Garis, an economics professor at Vanderbilt University, who saw Mexicans as "human swine" and described them in this way in 1930:

Their minds run to nothing higher than animal functions—eat, sleep, and sexual debauchery. In every huddle of Mexican shacks one meets the same idleness, hordes of hungry dogs, and filthy children with faces plastered with flies, disease, lice, human filth, stench, promiscuous fornication, bastardy, lounging, apathetic peons and lazy squaws, beans and dried chili, liquor, general squalor, and envy and hatred of the gringo. These people sleep by day and prowl by night like coyotes, stealing anything they can get their hands on, no matter how useless to them it may be. Nothing left outside is safe unless padlocked or chained down.[7]

The popular aversion to Mexicans in the racially charged atmosphere of the 1920s was not unique. All ethnic Americans were suspect. The lingering stereotype of the Italo-American as a Mafia gangster, for example, has its origin in the interwar period.

The so-called Mexican Problem was both a cause and a consequence of a campaign waged in Washington throughout the 1920s to stem the flow of immigrants from south of the border by the enactment of restrictive legislation. The Quota Acts of 1921 and 1924 had exempted immigration from the Western Hemisphere, thanks to the efforts of southwestern business interests, who insisted that Mexican labor was vital to their survival. Critics demanded that this exemption be terminated. Nativist groups were the leading supporters of this concerted anti-immigrant campaign, but organized labor was a powerful ally. Though racism played a role, unions generally opposed New World immigration on economic grounds: the new immigrants, it was feared, would depress wages and steal jobs. The leading spokesman for labor in the fight to exclude Mexicans was Samuel Gompers, president until 1924 of the American Federation of Labor (AFL).

In Congress, the campaign to restrict Mexican entry was led by Representatives John Box (D-Tex) and Albert Johnson (R-Wash) and Senator William Harris (D-Ga), all of whom sponsored bills to curtail immigration during the twenties. Their opponents in Congress agreed that Mexicans were racially inferior, but they countered with the argument that Mexican labor was indispensable. In the end, as is usually the case, the economic argument prevailed. However, while the representatives of southwestern corporate interests were ultimately able to defeat the exclusionary bills, popular opinion was so adamant that Congress was forced to pass legislation in 1929 making illegal entry a criminal offense.

REPATRIATION

The restrictionist campaign did not end in the 1920s, but the Depression made additional immigration laws unnecessary: the economic slump choked off immigration from the south. Mexicans, after all, had been attracted to the United

States by the prospect of making money, but now jobs were virtually nonexistent. Although it had problems of its own, agrarian Mexico, on the periphery of the world economy, looked far more attractive to its citizens than an industrial United States apparently on the verge of collapse. Moreover, it seemed foolhardy to make the hazardous journey to the north, where anti-Mexican sentiments were pronounced and discrimination was widespread, when Mexicanos could remain in the familiar and secure environment of their native villages, close to friends and relatives. In fact, in the 1930s, many Mexicans living in the United States returned to their homeland.

Altogether, it has been estimated that about one-third of the Mexican population in the United States left the country during the Depression, though some authorities, according to Lawrence A. Cardoso, believe that the true figure may be closer to half.[8] The most intense period of repatriation occurred in 1929–1935, when Abraham Hoffman, the leading authority on the subject, estimates some 400,000 Mexicans were involved.[9] Not all of these repatriations were voluntary. Possibly, as many as half of those who left did so against their will. Some of the methods employed to get Mexicans to return home were subtle, some were heavy-handed, and occasionally some were even illegal. County, state, and federal government agencies were all involved. During the course of this popular campaign, civil liberties were violated on a regular basis, as American-born children of immigrants, now U.S. citizens, were often denied the option to stay in the country when their parents were deported. Harassment and discrimination against remaining Mexicans were also common.[10]

The exodus began in the first months of 1931, when the federal government launched a massive deportation drive centered on southern California. By the end of the year, somewhere between 50,000 and 75,000 Mexicans had left the southland for Mexico, most of them intimidated by government scare tactics. During the next few years, Los Angeles would lose roughly one-third of its Mexican residents.

Mexican communities in the Midwest, however, witnessed the most losses relative to the total population. A 1934 study by Paul S. Taylor found that while only 3.6 percent of Mexican nationals in the United States lived in Indiana, Michigan, and Illinois, this region provided over 10 percent of the *repatriados* (repatriates).[11] By this time, Chicago had lost 30 percent of its Mexican population.

The plight of Mexicans during these tumultuous times was perhaps worst in Texas, where repatriation, heightened racial tensions, and a depressed economy—only intensified by the Agricultural Adjustment Administration policy of eliminating hundreds of thousands of acres from cotton production—forced them out of the state in droves. Although many Tejanos headed south of the border, others scattered throughout the United States, a diaspora that paralleled the better-known migration of so-called Okies from the Dust Bowl.

THE DUST BOWL MIGRATION

Between 1929 and 1933, farm income in the United States dropped by two-thirds. Already weakened by the financial reverses of the Depression and threatened by growing mechanization—the tractor, first and foremost—tenant farmers in the lower Great Plains were struck a death blow by mother nature in the mid-1930s. Drought conditions, which actually appeared as early as 1931, combined with windstorms, made life in what had once been labeled the Great American Desert precarious at best. A single storm—on 11 May 1934—carried away some 300,000 tons of topsoil from the plains states. Thousands of destitute families were forced to abandon their homes. Some parts of the Dust Bowl lost up to 40 percent of their population. Eventually, more than a half million people were involved in this exodus. Some moved into the industrial centers of the North, but work was difficult to find there. The number of jobs had shrunk dramatically, perhaps more than in any other part of the country. Moreover, the mass migration of black laborers from the South, initiated during World War I, was well under way and these northern cities were now witnessing a phenomenal growth of African-American communities. Lacking industrial skills, Dust Bowl immigrants were reluctant to compete for jobs in the unfamiliar northern metropolises. The only other alternative was to move west.

Car caravans began in 1935. Entering the Southwest via Texas and New Mexico, some families found jobs and established roots in those states. Others settled down in Arizona. Most, however, perhaps 350,000, continued on to the promised land, California, a trek graphically described by the novelist John Steinbeck and, more recently, the historian James Gregory. A few ventured beyond, into the Pacific Northwest. The agricultural valleys of the Pacific Coast were soon swamped with poor white farmers looking for work. While, as Professor Gregory has shown, almost half of the Okies entering the Golden State settled in Los Angeles or the San Francisco Bay Area, the most popular rural destination proved to be the Great Valley, especially the southern section.[12] Bakersfield and the rest of Kern County grew a whopping 63.6 percent from 1935 to 1940.

The impoverished status of Mexicans, already extreme, was only worsened by the new arrivals, who often settled down in the very places Mexicans had previously dominated—the agricultural valleys. Whereas Anglos had accounted for only 20 percent of the state's migratory labor force in 1929, they represented about 85 percent of the total by 1936. Problems were bound to surface, since, as regional writer Gerald Haslem has pointed out, "many Okies were Southerners in their racial attitudes, and some had left their native states rather than do 'nigger work'."[13] Tensions remained high between both groups for decades, a situation that was only exacerbated when Okies moved out of the fields to better-paying jobs in packing sheds, canneries, ice plants, and cotton gins, which they then attempted to monopolize, with considerable success.

LABOR STRIFE

The adverse conditions caused by the Depression led to a prolonged period of intense labor unrest in factories and fields throughout the country. "In fact," one astute observer has noted, "for five years, from the middle of 1933 to early 1938, America witnessed a full-scale outbreak of class warfare such as had not been seen for generations."[14] The Southwest was among the bloodiest battlefields. As Emilio Zamora, Juan Gómez-Quiñones, and other Chicano labor historians have documented clearly, Mexicans were active participants in the strikes that characterized the region during this tumultuous period. This activism, though, did not originate during the Depression; as Gómez-Quiñones has shown, obreros had fought to raise wages and improve living conditions from the nineteenth century and even before.[15] The beginning of the twentieth century witnessed accelerated efforts by Mexicans to improve their economic status. A brief account of this movement from 1900 to 1930 will suffice to illustrate an essential Mexican contribution to American history that continues to be neglected by mainstream historians. Literally hundreds of strikes took place. Only the most well-chronicled episodes will be covered here.

It should be made clear at the outset that Mexicans have had to struggle to improve their lives without much help from established labor unions. The U.S. labor movement was in its infancy at the turn of the century. Less political and ideological than their European counterparts, the first American unions concentrated on organizing skilled workers. Only after the First World War were half-hearted attempts made to incorporate unskilled workers. Bastions of white supremacy, unions took little interest in organizing African Americans, and even less effort was put into organizing immigrants of color, including Mexicans. The only exception of any consequence was the Industrial Workers of the World (IWW), a socialist union formed in 1905, but this short-lived association became a casualty of the postwar Red Scare. In the first decades of the twentieth century, unionized labor was dominated by the American Federation of Labor. A craft union, the AFL was exclusively concerned with skilled workers. This strategy and the racism that was evident among many of its members precluded any real interest in mobilizing Mexicans, the great majority of them unskilled. Mexican workers had to look, instead, to their own associations; in other words, to the mutualistas. Although these organizations were not primarily intended to fight for economic gains when they emerged in the nineteenth century, mutualistas, in the absence of other alternatives early on, came to play a key role in the struggle to improve working conditions.

Some of the worst abuses were to be found in the mining industry of the Southwest, which by the first decade of the twentieth century centered on the copper fields of Arizona, where Mexicans—the largest of the immigrant groups in the work force—toiled in mines, mills, and smelters under disgraceful conditions. The Western Federation of Miners (WFM)—which would affiliate with the AFL in 1911—was the only viable mining union in the region, but its membership was reticent to include Mexicans and other immigrants. Dissatisfied with their conditions and unable to break into the WFM, Mexicans began to organize on their own by 1900, when they initiated a strike in Ray, Arizona, near the important mining center at Globe. Three years later, they joined with Italians to plan, lead, and carry out the great strike at the Clifton, Morenci, and Metcalf mines in eastern Arizona. The WFM stood on the sideline, only one of many reasons the strike failed.

After the 1903 strike, the WFM, divided between those who wanted to recruit immigrants and those who opposed, labeled "inclusionists" and "exclusionists," respectively, by the labor historian Phil Mellinger, reluctantly began to organize foreign and Mexican miners.[16] For their part, Mexican miners were not eager to enroll in the WFM, looking instead to the Partido Liberal Mexicano. Dissension in the ranks of the labor movement and the panic of 1907 ensured that little would be accomplished in the years before the First World War.

In 1914 and 1915, Mexicans struck again at Ray. While mutualistas were involved, real leadership now came from the Comité por Trabajadores (Committee for Workers), a Mexican grassroots association, though not a mutualista. The July 1915 strike was a modest success, in part because Anglo miners were willing to play a supporting role—a harbinger of things to come.

In September 1915, an even bigger strike was initiated at Clifton and Morenci. Once again, Mexican miners took the initiative, though the leadership was approximately half Anglo and half Mexican. The agitation lasted four months. In the end, miners won meaningful concessions, but the true significance of these strikes is that Anglos and Mexicans finally began to work together in the WFM, a milestone in the annals of the working-class movement in the mines of the Southwest.

The victory was short-lived. During and after the war, mining operators went on the offensive, resulting in the infamous Bisbee Deportations in 1917—when more than one thousand strikers were unceremoniously dumped in the middle of the New Mexican desert by vigilantes after an unsuccessful work stoppage in Arizona—and a series of crushing defeats inflicted on the miners in the aftermath of the Red Scare of 1919. During this "Time of Troubles," however, Mexicans preserved their greatest gain—they had joined the mainstream of American organized labor.

Labor organization in the railroad industry was also considerably difficult for Mexicans prior to the Depression. The problems they encountered in railroad maintenance were similar to those in mining camps. The work was hard, dangerous, and ill paid. Moreover, there was a wage differential that worked to their detriment: most Mexican rail workers were paid about one dollar for a ten-hour day, while Anglos received seventy-five cents more. Housing was equally dismal; oftentimes, Mexican families were forced to live in box cars.

Organizing was more daunting in railroad work than in mining, mainly because the labor force was constantly on the move. Nonetheless, Mexicans began to organize at the turn of the century—by which time they had come to dominate railroad construction and maintenance in the Southwest—again without the help of the fledgling American union movement. The first noteworthy agitation occurred in Los Angeles in the spring of 1903, when Mexican tracklayers launched a strike against Henry Huntington's Pacific Electric Railroad. Mexicans were making less than eighteen cents an hour. They demanded higher wages. Leadership was provided by the Unión Federal Mexicanos (Mexican Federal Union), "probably the first union of Mexican track workers in the United States."[17] In the end, the strike was a complete disaster because Anglo workers refused to back the Mexicans and because management was able to recruit strikebreakers.

Much more work needs to be done by Chicano scholars on Mexican attempts to organize track workers. Preliminary studies, however, indicate that workers' efforts to form unions and win concessions were no less active here than in other industries. It is equally clear that victory was elusive given the many obstacles facing labor organizers, on the one hand, and the strength of the railroad industry—judged to be vital to the national interest by both the government and the public—on the other hand.

The most vigorous field of labor activity by Mexicans in the first three decades of the twentieth century was in agriculture, mainly because their numbers were so much greater here than in other areas of employment. Moreover, the perishable nature of many crops provided a lever they could use to their advantage, despite the many obstacles facing unionization in the fields. The most persistent efforts occurred in southern Texas and southern California, the two most advanced areas of agricultural production in the Southwest.

Thanks to Emilio Zamora, Chicano historians have recently become aware of the significant amount of labor activity—as well as other forms of working-class organization—in southern Texas shortly after the turn of the century.[18] As in other regions, this initial organization owed a great deal to the much-neglected mutualistas. However, as Zamora indicates, the impetus also came from left-wing political organizations on both sides of the border, more specifically, the Texas Socialist party (established in 1903) in the first decade of the twentieth century, on the American side; and the PLM, during the second decade, on the Mexican side. While these working-class associations did not confine their efforts to agricultural organization, they are noteworthy primarily because they represent the first systematic efforts to unionize Mexican workers in the fields of South and Central Texas.

In the Golden State, efforts to create effective working-class unity with the aim of improving conditions have long been the subject of historical study. The initial attempt to chronicle this activity goes back to 1939, when Carey McWilliams published *Factories in the Fields*. The first strike in California agriculture where Mexicans played a significant role was in Ventura in 1903, when they joined Japanese workers in a futile effort to gain concessions from beet farmers. Strikes continued sporadically for the next three decades—many of them instigated by the IWW—culminating in the Imperial Valley Cantaloupe Strike of 1928. This confrontation was led by La Unión de Trabajadores del Valle Imperial (The Imperial Valley Workers' Union), formed early in that very year, largely through the efforts of mutualistas, although the Mexican consulate also lent a hand. The strike, which began in May, was prompted not only by a desire for better wages but also by the need to curb the worst abuses of the contratista system. Despite adverse public opinion and the threat of deportation, strikers achieved most of their objectives, the first victory ever recorded in the fields of California, according to the historian and State Librarian Kevin Starr.[19]

Given this legacy of labor militancy, it is not surprising that the 1930s saw a resurgence of labor agitation by Mexican workers. While strikes occurred throughout the Southwest, they centered on California agriculture. It was here that the American Communist party focused its efforts, targeting the factory farms that dominated the industry; and it was party members, at least at the outset, who were most active in providing leadership. Agitation lasted throughout the decade, but the most turbulent year was 1933, when there were thirty-seven strikes involving some 47,500 workers from the Sacramento Valley in the north to the Imperial Valley in the south. Two clashes, in particular, are noteworthy: the El Monte Berry Strike and the San Joaquin Valley Cotton Pickers' Strike.

El Monte, a small agricultural community in the San Gabriel Valley, near Los Angeles, was characterized by small farms, many of them leased by Japanese farmers, who grew a variety of berries. The labor force was mixed, but Mexicans were the largest single ethnic group, and it was they who initiated the strike on 1

June 1933. Some five thousand workers were involved before it was all over. Eventually, on 6 July, the strikers won a minor victory, mainly because the targeted farmers were nonwhite and because the Los Angeles Chamber of Commerce, fearful of losing their business, backed the workers. Unfortunately, the picking season was virtually over by the time of the settlement. Moreover, during the strike, a major schism had developed among the workers which would have far-reaching consequences. Initiated by a small Mexican union, the strike had quickly been taken over by the Cannery and Agricultural Workers Industrial Union (CAWIU), a member of the Communist Trade Union Unity League (TUUL). Encouraged by the Mexican consul, Alejandro Martínez, Mexicans soon affiliated with La Confederación de Uniónes de Campesinos y Obreros Mexicanos (CUCOM, The Confederation of Mexican Farmworkers' and Workers' Unions), an ethnic union recently created by leaders of an older mutualist-inspired association. The split in the ranks of the obreros would provide agribusiness in the next few years with the opportunity to employ the tactics of divide and conquer, which they used with enormous success.

The CAWIU instigated most of the labor agitation in 1933, including the Cotton Pickers' Strike in October, "the longest, largest, and most highly publicized of the many strikes" that year.[20] The work stoppage centered on Corcoran, a small community in the heart of the state's expanding cotton kingdom in the southern San Joaquin Valley, and involved some twelve thousand workers, mostly Mexican. Strikers were immediately put on the defensive as growers, using red-baiting tactics, convinced the local citizenry that social revolution was imminent. As Kevin Starr points out, however, "If a revolution was occurring in the cotton fields of California, it was a revolution from the right, a *putsch* driven by American Legionnaires and deputized vigilantes, railroading DAs and judges and their shamelessly cooperative juries."[21] Racism played a role, as well. Vigilante violence, which took the lives of three strikers, and the cooperation of local police authorities ensured the complete subjugation of the workers, an omen of things to come in the next few years. Government repression of the CAWIU in the mid-1930s and the subsequent influx of Okies, newcomers who harbored pronounced anti-unionist sentiments and strong racial prejudices, meant that serious efforts to organize farmworkers were essentially over.

Mexican field workers did attempt to resurrect the movement in 1937–1938, when another round of strikes broke out in California. Much of this activity was directed by a new nationwide union, the United Cannery, Agricultural, Packing, and Allied Workers of America (UCAPAWA), formed in Denver in July 1937. Less radical than the Communist CAWIU, the UCAPAWA was nevertheless subject to red-baiting. Moreover, it faced formidable adversaries. By now, agribusiness, fortified by a statewide organization to champion its interests, the

Associated Farmers of California (created in 1934), was clearly in the ascendancy. While growers decried workers' efforts to organize, then and later, they themselves, as Devra Weber expertly depicts in her scholarly investigations, achieved an organization which their counterparts in industry could only envy.[22] The next twenty-five years would be the Golden Age of Agribusiness in California.

The 1930s strikes are significant for a number of reasons. For one, they illustrate the aggressive role played by the Mexican government in protecting the rights of its citizens in the United States. This tradition goes back to the nineteenth century, but the consulates expanded their advocacy activities enormously after the Mexican Revolution, when patriotism surged among expatriate communities. Their numbers also increased; by 1928, there were fifty-eight consulates scattered throughout the country. During the repatriation movement, as Francisco Balderrama has argued, consuls served as advocates and benefactors for their compatriots who were harassed by American authorities.[23] Although most Chicano scholars tend to be critical of what they perceive to be modest efforts at best, consuls deserve acknowledgment and credit for alleviating the hardships experienced by the beleaguered community. The aid they lent to the organization of Mexican workers is one of the least appreciated of their contributions. Especially during the Depression, Mexican consular offices energetically defended the rights of workers, a reflection of the pro-labor sympathies of the Cárdenas administration (1934–1940). Enrique Bravo, the consul at Monterey, for example, was actively involved in the 1933 San Joaquin Valley strike. Joaquín Terrazas, the consul of Calexico, supported Mexican strikers in the Imperial Valley in 1934. Strikers in the southern California citrus industry in 1935–1936 received valuable assistance from the consul of Los Angeles, Ricardo Hill. Undoubtedly, too, consulate activity in the thirties was prompted by fear that without their intervention, the emerging working-class movement would come under Communist domination.

Conditions became so appalling during the Depression that for the first and only time in American history Communists became significant players in efforts to organize labor. Red unions proved to be much more receptive to the idea of recruiting Mexicans than the traditional unions had ever been. Heirs of the IWW, the CAWIU too chose to recruit from the ranks of the working class regardless of color. Moreover, Communist unions like the CAWIU, despite doctrinal precedence given to mobilizing the industrial proletariat, were willing to enter the agricultural fields of California and the Southwest. Generally speaking, Mexican workers were receptive to CAWIU overtures. Dorothy Ray Healey, who began her long career as a Communist leader by organizing for the CAWIU in the 1930s, later recalled, "Despite charges by the growers that the Communists were conspiring to destroy California's agricultural economy, we were rarely the instigators of these strikes. They usually broke out spontaneously and then the workers would come and find us. Most of the workers we encountered in the early 1930s were Mexican, with some Filipinos, and a scattering of Blacks and Anglos."[24]

Extreme situations call for extreme solutions, and many Mexicans in desperate straits came to see that there was little to lose in supporting radical unions. Some had recently arrived from Mexico, where the fledgling labor movement had strong left-wing roots, so they were not averse to working with Communist associations. Most Mexican workers, however, even those in red unions, had little real understanding of Marxist ideology; they needed relief and they joined Communist unions because mainstream labor unions had failed to cultivate Mexicans.[25] To many of them, it seemed that only radical organizations were willing to extend a helping hand.

In the end, the strikes of the 1930s failed not because of dissension in the ranks of the strikers, though this was certainly a factor, but because the opposition had preponderant strength. The forces of corporate capitalism, though weakened, turned out to be remarkably resilient. Moreover, the American public, especially the middle class, generally supported Big Business, seeing in it a bastion against Communism, widely perceived as a threat to the American Way. Class and race considerations also dictated that public opinion would be opposed to the organization of farmworkers, many of them thought to be unassimilable aliens. What little support the workers had garnered was soon undermined by the revival of the economy stimulated by the Second World War.

Beginning with Carey McWilliams, scholars who have studied the history of Mexicans in the United States have gone to great lengths to illustrate that their subjects have been very active throughout the twentieth century in combating labor exploitation by setting up unions and initiating strikes. Chicano scholars, in particular, especially those influenced by Marxist perspectives, have emphasized these struggles. Like McWilliams, they have stressed labor history in an effort to demolish the myth of Mexican docility, a popular stereotype of the Mexican as a lazy and unprogressive peon. Chicano historians have done well to combat this pernicious view. It seems that in every society there is a need to attribute negative qualities, especially laziness, to some group to promote a more positive self-image among insiders.

The truth of the matter is that Mexicans have had an unusually strong work ethic. Although Mexico has ostensibly been a welfare state since 1917, when the Constitution instituted a social transformation, in actuality its economy is so fragile that citizens who fail to work risk starvation, hardly a situation calculated to encourage sloth. Anyone who is intimately familiar with Mexican immigrants today recognizes them as people who are willing to do an honest day's job for an honest day's pay, one of the reasons many American employers prefer them over local labor pools. The related, though more generalized, picture of Mexicans as innately docile hardly needs refutation.

On the other hand, the recitation of a long litany of Mexican strikes by sympathetic and well-meaning scholars has left a distorted view of Mexican labor militancy, as Mario T. García has aptly pointed out, especially in agriculture. "Some Mexicans did resort to strikes as an expression of discontent," García observes, "but most Mexicans shied away from such activity and saw no reason for these 'radical' manifestations. Accommodation rather than resistance characterized the Mexican immigrant experience."[26] Historically, and in spite of blatant exploitation, labor agitation among Mexicans has been the exception, not the rule. "Despite the need for rigorous self-protection," as Mark Reisler has justly observed, "Mexican unions were more ad hoc than permanent."[27] In fact, Mexicans were used as strikebreakers on many occasions, both in industry and in agriculture.

There are many reasons why the Mexican masses have failed to live up to the revolutionary expectations of activist university professors, none of them having to do with innate deficiencies of character. In the nineteenth century, there was little possibility of protesting working conditions, quite aside from the absence of an effective labor union movement. There was the class division between old "Spanish" residents and the newer "Mexican" immigrants, the strength of anti-Mexican animosity in the host society, and the relatively modest numbers of Hispanics vis-à-vis Anglos. During the period of the Great Migration, efforts at labor organization were initiated but remained weak. The peasantry is reputed to be the most conservative social class in an agrarian society, certainly the most tradition-bound, and most Mexican immigrants came from these social origins. Furthermore, during the first decades of the twentieth century, while laborers recognized that they were being exploited by mining, railroad, and agribusiness enterprises, they compared their life in the United States with what it had been in Mexico. Even after the Revolution, there was no question that the standard of living was higher in this country than back home. After all, Mexicans came—and they continue to come—to the United States, where many took up residence, of their own volition. Only after they admitted to themselves that they were here to stay—a conclusion that many recent immigrants have still not made—did the immigrants and their children come to appreciate their underprivileged status in American society and the need to change it through their own efforts.

Even with this awareness, it was difficult to translate discontent into a viable movement to improve wages and working conditions. The problems were formidable. This was especially true in the fields, where most of the newcomers eked out a living. To begin with, agricultural work traditionally paid the lowest wages of any job, in part because the work was seasonal and, consequently, migratory. Impoverished workers could not afford to pay union dues. Indeed, they tended to be preoccupied with simply meeting their daily needs. Secondly, the workers lacked education, a luxury they could ill afford given their dismal wages and migratory existence. Many could not speak English. These conditions made it difficult, at best, to develop a cadre of leaders, a prerequisite to any organization. Thirdly, most Mexican immigrants working in the fields had entered the country illegally, which was relatively inconsequential at first, but became a major problem during and after the Depression. Fearing deportation, undocumented workers strove to maintain a low profile. Lastly, and perhaps most crucial in explaining Mexican failures in the fields, was the enormous power of agribusiness, both before the Second World War and especially afterwards. Most of these problems were evident in the industrial sector, though not to the same degree as in agriculture. Given these obstacles, it is surprising that Mexican workers mobilized at all and, in time, accomplished as much as they did.

MEXICAN WOMEN AND THE LABOR MOVEMENT

The strikes of the 1930s are important because they illustrate that Mexicans were often active agents in determining their fates, not mere pawns in the hands of powerful economic interests. Ultimately, though, the most momentous significance of these activities, as Chicana scholars like Vicki L. Ruiz have argued, is that they show the dynamic role played by women. Mexicanas, of course, had always been active in contributing to the economic well-being of the family even outside the home. This was particularly the case in lower-class households, where the woman's income was often essential for survival. Financial necessity ultimately overcame the prejudice so pervasive in the culture that a woman's place was in the home. During the Depression, though, a new assertiveness became evident among Mexicanas.

By the thirties, women played a significant role in the emerging union movement in the Southwest. This phenomenon was not totally unprecedented. The first in a long line of Mexicana labor leaders was Lucy Gonzales Parsons (1852–1942), a native of Johnson City, Texas, who helped found the IWW shortly after the turn of the century. She has been described as "a figure of great stature," by Martha Cotera, the foremost chronicler of the history of Mexican women in the United States.[28] Some unions were dominated by Mexicanas, especially in the canning industry where, as the historian Vicki Ruiz and the anthropologist Patricia Zavella have shown, they established a culture of their own.

Mexicanas were often found among the rank and file of the unions, but a measure of the progress they had made within the traditional Mexican family and Anglo society—institutions that often placed barriers to their advancement—was the degree to which they contributed to the leadership of the organizations. Chicano and Chicana historians have only recently brought to light the contributions made by these remarkable women. Since they are not yet household names—only Dolores Huerta seems to have achieved this kind of recognition—something should be said about the most influential of these labor organizers.

Strictly speaking, Luisa Moreno (1906–1992) was not Mexicana, having been born in Guatemala; however, this Latina worked intimately with Mexicanas during her long career as an organizer and came to be accepted by them as one of their own. Moreno immigrated to the United States in 1928 to pursue an education. After graduating from the College of Holy Names in Oakland, California, she developed a passion for labor reform. She worked as a professional organizer on the East Coast for both the AFL and the Congress of Industrial Organizations (CIO), a more progressive coalition of unions which split from the AFL in 1937. Eventually, she found her way to Texas and California, where she made her mark recruiting Mexican farmworkers and cannery workers for the UCAPAWA, the most progressive agricultural union of the day. Many of the leaders of the UCAPAWA were members of the American Communist party. It is not clear whether Moreno shared that affiliation, but she was certainly sympathetic to the party's humanitarian program. Ultimately, she was elected UCAPAWA vice-president, the first woman to achieve this office in any major American labor organization.[29]

Although most of her efforts were focused on labor issues, Luisa Moreno was also active in the fight for civil rights, notably the campaign to end segregation in the Southwest. Perhaps her most meaningful contribution in this regard was the establishment of El Congreso del Pueblo de Habla Española (The Spanish-Speaking Congress) in 1938, a coalition of middle- and working-class associations in Los Angeles created to protect the civil liberties of the Hispanic population. Retired from public life shortly after World War II, Moreno was forced back into the limelight when she was accused of subversion during the McCarthy witch hunts. She was deported in 1950. It is only during the past generation that Luisa Moreno, thanks to the efforts of Chicano and Chicana scholars, has received the credit she so richly deserves.

Another early crusader for the rights of Mexican workers was Emma Tenayuca (1916–), who was born in San Antonio, and whose brief career as a union activist was confined to the state of Texas. She initiated her life as a labor organizer in 1934, her senior year in high school. During the next decade, despite her youth, she became the undisputed leader of the labor movement in her native city. She gained national prominence in 1938, when she led a strike of local pecan-shelling workers, most of them Mexicanas. There were occasional victories, but in Texas, as elsewhere, the prosperity brought on by the war undermined the fledgling labor movement. Like Moreno, Tenayuca retired from union activity in the late 1940s, when she left for California. Emma Tenayuca was a pioneer in more ways than one: a reentry student, she eventually graduated magna cum laude from San Francisco State College, one of the first Mexicanas to earn a college degree.

Another Mexicana who made a lasting impact on the labor movement was Josefina Fierro de Bright (1920–). Born in Mexico, Josefina was raised in Los Angeles by her mother, a single parent, who introduced her to the anarchist teachings of Ricardo Flores Magón. After working in the fields of the San Joaquin Valley, she enrolled as a student at UCLA but abandoned her studies to marry John Bright, whose left-wing views would reinforce her mother's influence. Entering the workers' movement, the young idealist immediately drew the attention of Luisa Moreno, who encouraged her in her efforts at labor and community organization. Fierro soon became the prime mover behind the Congreso. The organization, which aimed at the betterment of Hispanic peoples, drew widespread support from many sectors of southern California society, including the film industry. Among early supporters were Anthony Quinn, Dolores del Río, and John Wayne. Fierro was only one of several women comprising the Congreso's leadership. She herself later estimated that about 30 percent of the organization's activists were women.[30] After the war, she helped organize the Independent Progressive party in California, before voluntarily repatriating to Mexico to escape persecution during the McCarthy era.

The 1930s is generally described in very negative terms by Chicano historians. Clearly, there is good reason to be critical, for on the surface, at least, it was a time of unmitigated disaster for Mexicans. Economic conditions, as bad as they had been before, now deteriorated in both rural and urban areas. Many Mexicans suffered the humiliation of deportation, others were subjected to intense discrimination. Mexican efforts to organize into unions and to combat the escalating exploitation collapsed.

By the thirties, though, a ray of hope could be discerned. By now, Mexicans, many of them born in the United States, were beginning to realize that there would be no returning to the Old Country. This growing awareness was especially evident in the emerging barrios in and out of the Southwest. As Mario T. García demonstrates, the 1930s witnessed the emergence of a significant Mexican middle class, both in numbers and influence, determined to protect the rights of its people as citizens of the United States, perhaps the most portentous accomplishment in an otherwise dismal period in the history of Mexican Americans.

THE SECOND
WORLD WAR AND
ITS AFTERMATH

1940–1965

7

In the annals of American history, the Second World War was probably not as momentous in its consequences as was the Great War a generation before, but such is not the case for Mexicans in this country. World War II altered life in the Mexican community profoundly. Its heaviest impact was on the fledgling middle class, which grew in both size and influence. In the aftermath of the war, this middle sector, largely composed of children of immigrants rather than immigrants themselves, was eager to win acceptance into American society, but only on its own terms. Much maligned by Chicano historians in the past for its lack of concern for the welfare of the ethnic community at large, this middle class, thanks largely to the efforts of the brothers Mario T. and Richard García, Guadalupe San Miguel, Jr., and like-minded historians, is currently being reevaluated in a much more positive light. Given the intellectual and moral climate engendered by the war, it is clear that options available to this generation were rather limited. Moreover, there is mounting evidence that a significant number of the middle class did attempt to ameliorate working and living conditions for the Mexican community at large, with some success.

MEXICANS IN THE MILITARY

The Japanese attack on Pearl Harbor on 7 December 1941 forced the United States into the war. For Mexicans, the colossal conflict represented an opportunity to enter the American mainstream. By the 1940s, there were many more of them in the country than there had been during World War I, so their participation was much higher. Ultimately, between 250,000 and 500,000 Mexicans, both immigrants and native-born, out of a population of 2.7 million, engaged in active military service. Like their compatriots, most Mexicans were drafted into the service. Many of them, however, were volunteers. Indeed, as is true of other conflicts in the twentieth century, notably Korea and Vietnam, the Mexican enlistment rate was probably greater than that of the population at large. There were a number of reasons for this apparent enthusiasm. First of all, the service represented one of the few opportunities for Mexicans to improve their low socioeconomic status. Often isolated in small communities or trapped in the barrios of larger cities, poorly educated and lacking job skills, they saw the military as the easiest and most immediate way of improving their position. Secondly, while some of them still fostered notions of returning to Mexico, many newcomers, as was typical of immigrant communities, felt a sense of gratitude to their new homeland and joined up out of a sense of sincere patriotism. Finally, the high enlistment rate owed something to the macho ethic permeating Mexican society; military service represented a way of proving their manhood.

In contrast to World War I, when they were recruited almost exclusively in the Southwest, many Mexican soldiers now came from outside that region. The Midwest was well represented. The Illinois town of Silvis, near Moline, for example, sent 110 Mexicans off to war, which, according to the U.S. Defense Department, was more than any other comparable town of its size.

As the historian Raúl Morín, a native of Lockhart, Texas, and himself a veteran of the war, has illustrated, Mexicans were one of the most highly decorated ethnic groups in the U.S. Armed Forces. They served with distinction both in the Pacific and the Atlantic theaters, where they won scores of medals, including the Silver Star, the Bronze Star, the Distinguished Service Cross, the Purple Heart, and the most prestigious military citation of all, the Congressional Medal of Honor. The last award, conferred by the U.S. Congress for valor, was first established in 1861. Since that time some 3,400 individuals have been recognized as Medal of Honor winners, more than three-quarters of them posthumously. Among the recipients have been thirty-eight Hispanic soldiers, mostly of Mexican descent. During World War II, twelve Hispanics, apparently all of Mexican ancestry, were bestowed this honor: Luciano Adams, Macario García, Silvestre Herrera, José M. López, and Cleto L. Rodríguez from Texas; Harold Gonsalves, David M. Gonzales, and Ysmael R. Villegas from California; José P. Martínez, Alejandro R. Ruiz, and José F. Valdez from New Mexico; and Manuel Pérez, Jr., from Oklahoma.[1]

The largest number of Mexicans who served overseas were probably sent to the Pacific theater, where they were engaged in battle from the very outset. Hispanos composed a large proportion of the New Mexico National Guard, which was stationed in the Philippines on the eve of the war, and many of them were among the 36,000 troops forced to surrender to the Japanese. Hundreds of these prisoners died on the infamous Bataan Death March, the murderous eighty-five-mile forced march through the island jungles in April 1942. Almost three years later, in January 1945, they returned to the Philippines with Gen. Douglas MacArthur and subsequently saw heavy action in the great island battles, notably Okinawa, that would finally bring the cataclysmic war to an end.

Mexicans were also active on the other side of the globe, in North Africa and Europe, where they participated in all major battles. Perhaps their most telling contribution occurred during the Italian campaign, which was initiated on 10 July 1943, with the invasion of Sicily. Company Z of the 141st Regiment of the 36th Division, consisting entirely of Tejanos, most of them from El Paso, was one of the premier American units in Italy. Many members of the company performed heroically, but two individuals in particular stand out: Lieut. Gabriel Navarette from El Paso and Sgt. Manuel S. Gonzales from Fort Davis, Texas, both of them recipients of Distinguished Service Crosses.

Mexicans also figured prominently in the assault on "Fortress Europe," which was launched on the beaches of Normandy on D-Day, 6 June 1944. Among the many heroes of the final assault on Germany was Medal of Honor winner Sgt. José M. López, from Brownsville, Texas. A machine gunner with K Company of the 23rd Regiment, 2nd Division, López killed more than one hundred Germans in the Krinkelt Wald, in Belgium, on 17 December 1944. He has the distinction of having killed more enemy soldiers than any other American in World War II. In general, Mexicans performed valiantly in battle, making sacrifices well beyond what one would expect. It is reported that the heaviest battlefront casualties during the entire war were suffered by the 3rd, 36th, and 45th Infantry Divisions. All contained generous numbers of Mexicans in their ranks. California Congressman Jerry Voorhis observed at the time: "As I read the casualty lists from my state, I find anywhere from one-fourth to one-third of these names are names such as Gonzales or Sanchez, names indicating that the very lifeblood of our citizens of Latin-American descent in the uniform of the armed forces of the United States is being poured out to win victory in the war. We ought not to forget that."[2]

Mexicans who survived the war gained immeasurably by the experience. Perhaps the most valuable benefit was psychological. Morín explains:

> These *Chicanos* were different from the Mexican-Americans that we had known before we left the States and went overseas. Although still full of fun and deviltry as ever, they now were well-seasoned and experienced American soldiers. No longer were we chided and shunned by other GI's and Army officers. Where we had been held in contempt by others who disliked us because of our constant Spanish chatter or our lax [sic] in military discipline, we were now admired, respected, and approved by all those around us including most of our commanding officers.[3]

Military service did wonders for self-esteem, but it was meaningful for many young Mexicans in other ways. Some were forced to deal with Anglos for the first time, and the experience in interethnic relations was generally positive. Cooperating against the common enemy tended to break down mutual prejudices. Some of the friendships forged in battle undoubtedly continued to be cultivated after the war. Although discrimination was not entirely done away with, there was less of it in the service; and Mexicans and other minorities found career opportunities opening up. Some of them even succeeded in breaking into the officer corps. Manuel Chávez (1910–1996), for example, better known as the poet and historian fray Angélico Chávez, achieved the rank of major while serving in both Europe and the Pacific in 1943–1946. An even larger number picked up job skills that would be useful in civilian life. Finally, veterans' benefits offered Mexicans unprecedented opportunities to better their lives by providing education and job training, as well as facilitating the purchase of homes. The G.I. Bill, in particular, stands out. Signed into law by President Roosevelt on 22 June 1944, this pathbreaking act, one of the most powerful legislative forces for social change in American history, paid for the education of 7.8 million soldiers reentering civilian life, many of them Mexican veterans. Beneficiaries included José Antonio Villarreal (1924–), among the most gifted of contemporary Spanish-speaking writers; Ramón Eduardo Ruiz (1921–), a leading authority on Latin American history; Américo Paredes (1915–), one of the most prolific scholars of the century; Octavio Romano (1932–), founder of El Grito, the most influential Chicano literary magazine; and Ralph Guzmán (1924–1985), noted educator and civil rights activist. Mothers and widows of young soldiers killed in action also received financial aid from the government, a source of family income which often represented the difference between a life of poverty and a relatively comfortable existence.

As neglected as Mexican men are in conventional histories of the Second World War, the role of Mexican women has been even more obscure. Indeed, it is not much of an exaggeration to state that *mujeres* (women) have been totally absent from these accounts. Like their male counterparts, however, they contributed mightily to the war effort. Some of them, especially *Hispanas* (Spanish-speaking women from New Mexico and Colorado), served in the military. Their major contribution, though, was on the home front, where they sold war bonds and set up numerous organizations to assist servicemen and servicewomen. The activities of one such organization, Tucson's El Club de Madres y Esposas (Club of Mothers and Wives), has been thoroughly documented by the historian Christine Marín.[4] Like other American women, Mexicanas helped to fill the labor vacuum created by servicemen. They continued to toil in the fields, as they had from the very beginning, but now they increasingly discovered opportunities in industry. Some of them even gained employment in defense plants, where jobs were opened

Habitants de Californie, a lithograph by Louis Choris of neophytes in Alta California, which appeared in the artist's *Voyage pittoresque autour du monde* (Paris: Imprimerie de Firmin Didot, 1822). California Historical Society, North Baker Research Library, Templeton Crocker Collection, FN-30510

Juan N. Cortina, "the Red Robber of the Rio Grande," 1886. The UT
Institute of Texan Cultures at San Antonio, Texas Southmost College
Library, Brownsville, Texas, 78-842a

Mariano Guadalupe Vallejo and members of his family in the 1880s.
California Historical Society, FN-30504

Antonio Coronel, a leading citizen of Los Angeles in the nineteenth century.
Seaver Center for Western History Research, Los Angeles County
Museum of Natural History

Carlos Velasco, founder of *La Alianza Hispano-Americana*, and his family about 1880. Courtesy of the Arizona Historical Society/Tucson, AHS#61,860

Mariano and Dolores Samaniego, prominent Arizona pioneers. Courtesy of the Arizona Historical Society/Tucson, AHS#28,995

Juana Elías, member of one of Tucson's ranking families,
in 1901. Courtesy of the Arizona Historical Society/Tucson, AHS#2,138

Mexican miners in Arizona in the early 1900s. Courtesy of the Arizona
Historical Society/Tucson, AHS#64,323

Jovita Idar, *tejana* feminist, ca. 1905.
The UT Institute of Texan Cultures at
San Antonio, courtesy of A. Ike Idar,
684-596

Ricardo and Enrique Flores Magón, precursors of the Mexican Revolution,
in 1922. *Los Angeles Times*

Campesina in the spinach fields of Robstown, Texas. Library
of Congress, USF34-24829-D

Mexican cotton pickers ca. 1920. Fresno Historical Society Archives

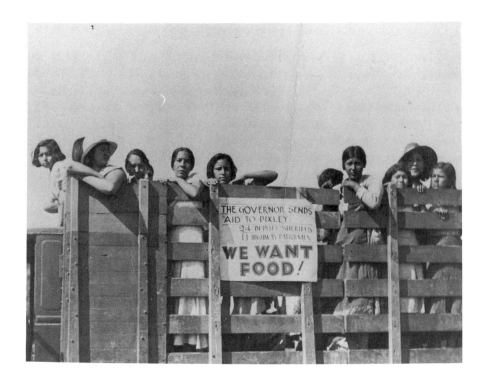

Mexicanas protest during the 1933 cotton strike in California.
Powell Studio Collection, courtesy of the Bancroft Library,
University of California, Berkeley

Santa Fe Railroad track layers, Calwa, California, 1937.
Fresno Historical Society Archives

Women railroad workers in Arizona during the Second World War.
Courtesy of the Arizona Historical Society/Tucson, AHS#63,527

Ben Garza, LULAC leader, in 1929. Benson Latin American Collection, University of Texas, Austin

M. C. Gonzales, LULAC leader, in the 1930s. Benson Latin American Collection, University of Texas, Austin

M. C. GONZALEZ
Regional Governor of Texas
San Antonio, Texas

Mexican funeral, Fresno, California, ca. 1935.
Courtesy of Mrs. Carmen Acuña

Emma Tenayuca, *tejana* labor leader, in 1938. The UT Institute of Texan Cultures at San Antonio, The San Antonio Light Collection, 1575-C

Dr. Hector García, founder of the American G.I. Forum. Dr. Hector P. García Papers, Special Collections & Archives, Texas A&M University—Corpus Christi Bell Library

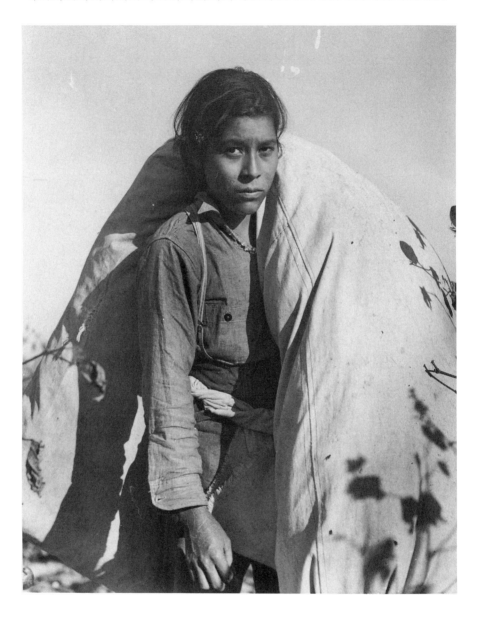

Young cotton picker in the San Joaquin Valley in 1936.
Library of Congress, USF34-9950-C, FSA project,
photograph by Dorothea Lange

up to minorities thanks to Executive Order 8802, which established the Committee for Fair Employment Practices in 1941. Most mujeres in the industrial sector, however, had to settle for less lucrative jobs, such as working in the mushrooming food-processing plants of the Southwest.

URBANIZATION: TRIALS AND TRIBULATIONS

The best jobs were found in cities. Consequently, during the war years, there was a massive influx of the Mexican population into urban centers. This was true not only along the border but in other parts of the country as well. In the Midwest, the greater Chicago area saw the Mexican community surge in numbers, a trend that was evident in Detroit as well. In the Pacific Northwest, the war witnessed the beginning of Mexican urbanization as campesinos began to arrive in Portland and Seattle from the Willamette Valley, the Yakima Valley, and other agricultural areas.

As Mexicans moved into cities in large numbers during the war years, their standard of living began to improve slowly. Some were even able to move beyond the barrio, where, for the first time, they established significant contact with Anglos outside of a work environment. However, this migration was not an unmixed blessing. Discrimination continued to be rampant. Deficient housing, limited economic opportunities, and segregated schools were only the most glaring of the chronic problems plaguing the newcomers. Moreover, in the urban environment, external pressures began to have an adverse impact on the bulwark of Mexican life, the family.

Chicano nationalists today tend to have a highly idealized picture of the Mexican family. In fact, this positive assessment is common both within and outside of the Mexican community. To a large extent, this perception is a myth. Domestic violence, alcoholism, extramarital affairs, abandonment, and divorce have taken their toll on the modern Mexican family. These developments are not recent. If one is to believe Ramón Ruiz, social ills were widespread in Mexico even before the Revolution: "In 1910, more than one out of three births were illegitimate, and the malady, up from 22 percent a decade before, was obviously getting worse."[5] The Revolution was bound to exacerbate the deteriorating situation given the massive population movements it spawned, as well as the high mortality.

Still, in rural Mexico, as in preindustrial economies in general, the family took on special significance. "The extended family," Alan Riding has observed, "is the principal safe haven where emotions can be shown without risk, where unquestioning loyalty is guaranteed, where customs are maintained."[6] Moreover, among the immigrants—most of whom came to toil in rural areas in the Southwest—the family was revitalized; it was the most immediate source of security in an alien and unfriendly environment, as well as the basic economic unit, a point emphasized by the anthropologist Robert R. Alvarez, Jr., in a recent study.[7]

Urban living was bound to weaken traditional family ties. In the countryside, largely isolated from American influences, the man, as father and husband, could continue to demand that unquestioned obedience—more theoretical than real—he was used to in the Old Country. In the city, though, his wife and children encountered a dominant society which called into question many of their traditional beliefs and relationships. No longer was the ultimate authority of the male unquestioned. Moreover, as economic opportunities opened up to women, a trend accentuated by the war, they naturally demanded more rights, and, as Vicki Ruiz has shown, generally received them.[8] Still, changes came amidst staunch resistance, often accompanied by domestic violence. The demand for greater freedom, though inevitable, proved highly disruptive to the family, in part because it occurred so quickly. In his autobiographical novel *Pocho* (1959), José Antonio Villarreal gives a graphic illustration of this corrosive process, which ultimately leads to the complete disintegration of a Mexican family making a transition from rural to urban life in California's Santa Clara Valley in the thirties and forties.

The advent of pachuco gangs in the early 1940s mirrors the breakdown of the traditional family, as well as the discrimination experienced by Mexican youths in an urban environment. Pachucos, or "zoot-suiters," who apparently first appeared in El Paso on the eve of the war, were youths who represent an interesting subculture in the Mexican community. Much maligned at the time, both in and out of the ethnic community, the pachuco is best known today through Luis Valdez's sympathetic portrayal in his popular and justly acclaimed play *Zoot Suit* (1978).

The pachucos, never very numerous, exerted an enormous influence on a whole generation of Mexican youths in the 1940s and 1950s. Children of immigrants, for the most part, pachucos (and pachucas) felt alienated from their parents, who held on to Old World values hoping to return to Mexico. Misunderstood by the older generation, they also found themselves at odds with the dominant society; Anglos, who denied them jobs and educational opportunities, rejected them as outsiders and criminals. Caught between two worlds, pachucos rebelled by creating their own unique society. They wore a distinctive uniform, consisting of a long, loose-fitting coat, high-waisted, baggy pants, and a feathered broad-rimmed hat. Their hair was made up in a ducktail. Dressed in short skirts, pachucas used heavy make-up and wore their hair in a pompadour. Pachuco/a fashions were not unique; these were popular contemporary styles, as any Hollywood movie of the time will attest. What *was* unique was the degree to which the styles were exaggerated, the extremes the youths embraced as a symbol of their defiance. They developed a patois, a strange and fascinating mixture of Spanish, English, and black slang which came to be called *caló*. More extreme was the occasional use of marijuana and a proclivity for tattoos, especially by males. In short, pachucos tried very hard to "shock the bourgeoisie" with their flamboyancy, and did so with a good measure of success.

In his masterpiece on the Mexican national character, *The Labyrinth of Solitude* (1961), Nobel Prize winner Octavio Paz devoted a controversial chapter, "The *Pachuco* and Other Extremes," to the subject. The Mexican intellectual, who betrays a not-too-subtle class bias, drew a very unflattering portrait of zoot-suiters. Scorned for his loss of identity, the pachuco, Paz wrote, "is an impassive and sinister clown whose purpose is to cause terror instead of laughter. His sadistic attitude is allied with a desire for self-abasement which in my opinion constitutes the very foundation of his character."[9] Unfortunately, Paz, like many Anglos in the United States, tended to identify pachucos with the entire Mexican-American community, which was patently unfair. In fact, zoot-suiters experienced enormous contempt in their own neighborhoods, if one is to believe Manuel Servín, himself a severe critic, who writes: "This writer has yet to find an older, pre-world [sic] War II Mexican or Mexican-American defending or offering an apology for the pachucos."[10] However, Paz's view of the pachucos themselves as deeply alienated and insecure is not far off the mark, though he might have been more sensitive to their plight. After all, pachuco youth were more deserving of pity than scorn. While the trend toward victimization has been taken too far recently, pachucos—as educator George I. Sánchez, pointed out at the time—*were* victims.[11] Through no fault of their own, they found themselves assailed and rejected on all sides. Left to their own devices, they took refuge in *carnalismo* (brotherhood).

While pachucos and pachucas elicited some sympathy in the barrio where Mexicans, as Paz notes, felt an ambivalence toward them, beyond their community they found only enmity. The war unleashed acute racial tensions in American society, as the internment of the Japanese-American population in 1942, a product of intense xenophobia, amply demonstrates. Unfortunately, for Mexicans in general and pachucos more particularly, animosity was soon directed at other ethnic minorities as well. Given the intense racial antipathy of the period, it was predictable that there would be a reemergence of "the Mexican Problem." In fact, a climate of repression soon surfaced, to a marked extent the product of a well-orchestrated campaign waged by William Randolph Hearst and the newspaper media of Los Angeles. The main targets were pachucos, ideal scapegoats given their distinctive appearance and small numbers.

Two incidents in southern California particularly illustrate the virulence of anti-pachuco sentiment during the war: the Sleepy Lagoon Case in 1942 and the so-called Zoot Suit Riots a year later. The Sleepy Lagoon was a small reservoir situated on the eastern outskirts of Los Angeles, where, in early August of 1942, the body of José Díaz was discovered. The young man, a member of a local gang, had apparently been slain the previous evening, possibly by a rival Mexican gang, the 38th Street Club. Although the evidence was purely circumstantial, authorities were determined to make an example of them, and charges of murder were soon filed against twenty-two members of the 38th Street gang. Except for one youth, all were Mexican Americans.

Spurred on by the local press, which decried a crime wave by "the Mexican element" and advocated a get-tough policy, public opinion was firmly on the side of the prosecution. The trial was conducted under an atmosphere of mass hysteria. Nor did it help that the judge, Charles W. Fricke, had concluded that the gang was guilty beforehand and prejudiced the case in a number of ways throughout the proceedings. For example, he denied the defendants the right to groom themselves properly; they came into the courtroom looking like "criminals." Predictably, no Mexicans were allowed to sit on the jury. Under these adverse circumstances the verdict was a foregone conclusion. Seventeen youths were found guilty of a variety of crimes. Twelve were charged with first or second degree murder: Jack Melendez, Victor Thompson, Angel Padilla, Gus Zamora, John Matuz, Ysmael Parra, Manuel Reyes, Bobby Telles, Manuel Delgado, Chepe Ruiz, Henry Ynostroza, and Henry Leyvas, the leader of the gang.

The Sleepy Lagoon Case is very consequential in the annals of Mexican-American history for a number of reasons, not the least of which is the fact that it resulted in the first effective mobilization of the Mexican community in southern California. Mexicans quickly perceived that it was the entire community, not just pachucos, who were being judged in the case. Racism, it was clear, had a great deal to do with the outcome of the trial.

Perhaps the best indication of racist sentiments during the court proceedings was the testimony presented before the grand jury by Lieut. Edward Duran Ayres of the Los Angeles Police Department. Ayres felt that Mexican youth were criminally inclined for genetic reasons. Descended from the bloodthirsty Aztecs, themselves of Mongoloid stock and therefore having "an utter disregard for the value of life," these youths, he argued, had inherited a predisposition toward violence. Ayres explained: "The Caucasian, especially the Anglo-Saxon, when engaged in fighting, particularly among youths, resorts to fisticuffs and may at times kick one another, which is considered unsporting, but this Mexican element considers all that to be a sign of weakness, and all he knows and feels is a desire to use a knife or some lethal weapon. In other words, his desire is to kill, or at least let blood."[12] Convinced that the problem was genetic, Ayres concluded that there was little the authorities could do to combat the malaise ("basically it is biological—one cannot change the spots of a leopard"), save to sentence offenders to lengthy prison terms.

The oft-quoted testimony presented by Ayres—who, ironically, appears to have had been Hispanic himself—reflected racial attitudes widely held by the Los Angeles Police Department. In fact, there is some suspicion that Ayres did not author the report at all. However, these views were also shared by a large segment of the American population at the time. And if the root of the problem was indeed biological, it was not only pachucos who stood indicted, but the entire Mexican community.

The trial was so outrageously unjust, given the dubious procedures that were followed, as well as the racist premises which informed the verdicts, that efforts to overturn the decision were initiated almost immediately. Spearheading the campaign, which focused on the Mexican barrios of the southland, was a small but determined band of white radicals, notable among them Carey McWilliams, and leaders of the Mexican community, like Josefina Fierro. They were assisted by the Spanish-language press, including *La Opinión,* the city's most respected ethnic newspaper, an organ of the more affluent members of the Mexican community. Ultimately, the indefatigable efforts of the Sleepy Lagoon Defense Committee paid off: in 1944, the convictions were finally reversed and the defendants released.

In the meantime, Los Angeles was at the center of another series of events that sharply divided the Mexican and Anglo communities. The Sleepy Lagoon Case brought to the surface underlying racial tensions. The string of defeats that the United States encountered in the first months after Pearl Harbor, especially at the hands of the Japanese in the Pacific, undoubtedly exacerbated the situation back home. Indeed, during the war, race riots between blacks and whites broke out in Detroit, New York, and other cities around the country. Violence erupted between Mexicans and Anglos as well. However, the "Zoot Suit Riots," as these clashes have been labeled, hardly qualify as riots in the usual sense of the word.

There was no love lost between pachucos and U.S. servicemen in southern California, site of a number of military training camps, during the early months of the war. It is hard to imagine two lifestyles so completely at odds. Furthermore, as Mauricio Mazón has argued in his pathbreaking psychohistorical study *Zoot-Suit Riots: The Psychology of Symbolic Annihilation* (1984), pent-up frustrations and the humiliation experienced in boot camps predisposed the servicemen to acts of violence which would restore their manhood and a sense of community with the civilian population. Given these underlying conditions, confrontation was inevitable. The result was a series of sporadic clashes between the two groups. These culminated on 3 June 1943, when, after a relatively minor skirmish, servicemen stationed in San Diego determined to teach the "greasers" a good lesson.

Immediately, a small army, mostly sailors and marines on leave, descended on the barrios of Los Angeles. Victims included Mexican youths, both boys and girls, having little or nothing to do with pachucos but having the misfortune of being in the wrong place at the wrong time. During the next few days, violence escalated, spurred on by the press, which pinned the blame for the so-called riots on the Mexicans, and tolerated by the police, who simply looked the other way. Local authorities were unable or unwilling to effectively rein in rampaging servicemen. Before too long, similar acts of aggression were launched against Mexicans in other parts of California, eventually spreading as far as the barrios of the Midwest. The outrages went on for a week, and might have continued longer, except for the intervention of the federal government. The violence stopped only when President Roosevelt had the military revoke passes and order its men back to their bases. But real credit for the termination of this bloody episode belongs to the Mexican government, which lodged a strenuous protest condemning the mistreatment of its people, some of them Mexican citizens, north of the border. Reluctant to antagonize a valuable ally in the crusade against the Axis Powers— Mexico had declared war on 22 May 1942—FDR was compelled to intervene.

For many Mexicans living in this country, the Zoot Suit Riots, like the repatriations of the 1930s, left a scar which never completely healed. They wondered how it was possible that they should be subjected to verbal and physical abuse at home at the very time that so many members of their community were fighting overseas to preserve the American Way. The events of the 1930s and 1940s go a long way in explaining the disaffection of the Mexican population with both the dominant society and the government. For years and years, even those among them who were citizens of the United States would continue to see and identify themselves as "Mexicans," not "Americans."

THE BRACERO PROGRAM

The Bracero Program was another major consequence of World War II. Braceros were Mexican nationals recruited to work in the western United States on a temporary basis as part of a U.S. government–sponsored project during and after the war. The managed migration, an unprecedented and radical solution to America's labor needs, was occasioned by the enormous manpower shortage created by the war. This problem was especially severe in the agricultural fields of the Southwest due to the rapid expansion of the farming industry there and the tendency of farmworkers to move to the cities nearby.

The war effectively eliminated Europe as a source of competition on the world market, opening up fabulous opportunities for American farmers. It was the Southwest which benefited most. Growing by leaps and bounds, this region, with its seemingly endless supply of land and its greater propensity to mechanize, forged ahead of the Midwest to become America's breadbasket; by 1945, California had replaced Iowa as the leading agricultural state in the Union. The agricultural boom in the Southwest continued after the war, for the massive destruction wrought by the long conflict left Europe, outside of the Russian sphere of influence, heavily dependent on American imports.

The need for campesinos in the Southwest increased not only because of the growth of the agrarian sector, but also because traditional sources of farm labor were abandoning the countryside for the cities during and after the war. The creation of defense industries served as a catalyst for the transformation of the Southwest into an urban society. Industrial work, more secure and better-paying, was an irresistible magnet for many people living in rural poverty. The expansion of the industrial sector in California, in particular, was so vast that even racial and ethnic minorities found the opening of economic opportunities.

Already by the time of Pearl Harbor, it had become apparent that a new source of labor was imperative if American agriculture was to meet the emerging challenges successfully. Mexico was the obvious answer. Indeed, it was practically the only solution after Pearl Harbor, when the Pacific was transformed into a Japanese lake, cutting off any possibility of Asian workers. Still, not everyone was enthused about this prospect. Nativists were alarmed over the racial and socio-economic implications of migration from the south, albeit on a temporary basis. Even the large-scale growers of the Southwest who were slated to be the chief beneficiaries had reservations. The last bastion of rugged individualism in America, agribusiness feared the prospects of government regulation that the program entailed. These concerns were most evident in Texas, where farmers were more receptive to the idea of an open border, the absence of any bureaucratic controls at all, for the duration of the war.

So severe was the labor shortage, that in the end, and despite the objections of the Texans, an accord was signed on 23 July 1942, by FDR and Mexican President Manuel Avila Camacho and ratified in Mexico City shortly thereafter. The first braceros arrived in California on 29 September. Thanks to this binational agreement, some quarter of a million Mexicans, all of them male, were employed as braceros throughout the West before its expiration in April 1947. During the war itself, some of these men were permitted to work in the railroad industry; however, with this single exception, the agreement specified that workers were restricted to harvesting agricultural products.

Intended as a wartime expedient, the Bracero Program proved to be so efficacious that it was maintained after the defeat of the Axis, albeit in modified forms. Although the original legislation expired, the program itself continued as a series of informal agreements—and was even expanded into Texas, which had refused to participate initially—with slight alterations until the Korean War (1950–1953).

The guest worker program was revitalized in the early fifties, thanks, once again, to a shrinking labor market in the fields. This time, however, Mexican officials were anxious to provide more safeguards for their citizens, especially in the Lone Star State, where abuses were most flagrant. Public Law 78 (PL78), passed by Congress in July 1951, reenacted the program. The new agreement took into account Mexican concerns; though as the years went by, the Mexican government increasingly lost its ability to influence the pact. Administration continued in the hands of the Department of Labor, where it had been placed three years before, instead of with the Department of Agriculture, notoriously pro-farmer. While agribusiness was not totally satisfied with the revised legislation, the results were so successful that PL78 was extended every two years, thanks to the efforts of its representatives in Congress. Altogether, the Bracero Program lasted twenty-two years, from July 1942 to December 1964.

Although there were adjustments every time legislation was renewed, the basic outline of the program remained unchanged. Recruitment of workers was the responsibility of the Mexican government. Quotas were set up for the various Mexican states. Because there were so many more volunteers than were needed, a problem that increased over time, the authorities generally resorted to a lottery system. Men fortunate enough to be selected were taken to one of a select number of screening centers in northern Mexico, where criminal records were checked and medical examinations administered. At the height of the program, in the late 1950s, Mexican centers were located in Hermosillo, Chihuahua, and Monterrey. These hurdles cleared, successful applicants were taken across the border to U.S. recruitment centers located in places like El Centro and El Paso, where, after further medical examinations, employer representatives made the final selection. Typically, workers who failed to secure employment at the end of one week were sent back across the border, to make their way back to native villages at their own expense. Workers who were chosen signed a standard contract and were then transported north to work sites.[13]

The contract spelled out the obligations of the two parties involved, the employer and the employee. The farmer was to provide housing, transportation, and work. The bracero was responsible for health insurance, Mexican social security, and food, all costs that would be deducted from his paycheck. The pact also guaranteed certain conditions of employment, basic living and health needs, and the protection of the worker's civil rights. These stipulations were part of every agreement. Contracts, however, differed in terms of the crop, or crops, to be picked, the county, and the length of tenure (usually three to six months), according to the individual. The U.S. and Mexican governments were responsible for making sure that the contract was honored on both sides.

According to official estimates, the Bracero Program employed approximately 4.8 million Mexican nationals during its twenty-two years in existence (the actual figures were more modest, since many men participated year after year). The highwater mark occurred in 1957, when more than 450,000 workers were recruited. Three-quarters of all braceros found employment in Texas and California, but the program was not confined to the Southwest. Significant numbers of workers were transported to the Pacific Northwest (before 1947) and the Midwest.

Given the scope of the program and the weakness of government bureaucracy, it was inevitable that abuses would occur. The greatest single complaint by workers was the quality of the food; in an effort to save money, farm owners, generally through their contratistas, provided food and drink that was cheap but often unfamiliar to the Mexican—spaghetti, sandwiches, kool-aid, and so forth. Wages were low, housing often inadequate, and race discrimination severe, especially in the states bordering the South. "Although the Bracero agreement contained stipulations with regard to health, housing, food, wages, and working hours," critics charge, "most were disregarded by both the U.S. government and the growers."[14] These chronic abuses have been chronicled in minute detail by Erasmo Gamboa, who has written the most thorough study yet on the workings of the program in a specific area, *Mexican Labor and World War II: Braceros in the Pacific Northwest, 1942–1947* (1990). Interestingly, in the Pacific Northwest, in contrast to other areas, braceros often went out on strike, which may reflect the difficulty growers experienced in finding alternate sources of farm labor in that particular region.

In spite of the program's shortcomings, it was not difficult to recruit braceros, who clearly derived advantages from the arrangement. The Mexican government, too, found the program profitable. Its social security system received a much-needed boost, and, even more propitious, bracero earnings were sent home, where they pumped up local economies. However, the most obvious beneficiaries, as Ernesto Galarza, one of the most respected Chicano scholars and an early critic of the program, has shown in a variety of studies, were the farmers, particularly the large growers of Texas and California.

Although there was some resistance to the bilateral accord at the outset—and in some quarters there was never complete acceptance—the program was a bonanza for the big farmers, who quickly came to that realization. One of their major concerns historically was the recruitment of labor. How to find workers to harvest crops when needed and to leave the area thereafter, thus avoiding a burden on local schools and public relief funds—this question had never been resolved before. But now that nagging problem was solved at the expense of the government, i.e., the taxpayer. Moreover, braceros were ideal laborers when compared to alternative sources of labor: migrant families, undocumented workers, and "winos" (alcoholic derelicts), the last category notoriously unreliable, though the cheapest of all options. Braceros came to the United States for one reason—to make money. Consequently, they were highly efficient and unusually reliable. Unlike local laborers, braceros were unlikely to go on strike (the Pacific Northwest was clearly an exception), nor miss work after a weekend of celebration, nor leave the area as the harvest season wound down and became less lucrative. These men, most of them in their twenties and thirties, were picked—usually by a contratista, who found a comfortable niche in the program—solely on the basis of their ability to do the best job possible. The length of the Bracero Program is a testimony to the considerable power wielded by agribusiness in the United States.

On the other hand, the binational program had stalwart opponents, who called for its dismantling by resorting to racist and economic arguments. Nativist organizations were uniformly opposed, of course. Labor unions also found braceros offensive for racist reasons, but economic considerations were predominant. There was widespread fear among union leaders that guest workers remaining in the United States illegally (less than 10 percent of the total) would find their way into the industrial sector—which organized labor saw as its domain—depressing wages and displacing American citizens. Finally, there were small farmers who did not employ braceros but had to compete nationally and internationally against factory farms having the unfair advantage of cheap Mexican labor. Not surprisingly, the campaign to terminate the agreement in Congress was led by George McGovern (D-SD) and Eugene McCarthy (D-Minn), spokesmen for the family farmers of the Midwest. In the end, PL78 was allowed to expire, not only because of pressure exerted by a powerful coalition of opponents but also because of increasing mechanization in the fields. As the labor historian Dennis Nodín Valdés argues: "By the late 1950s, as the effect of mechanization offset the demand for workers in cotton, growers could less easily justify their demand for braceros. Consequently, when the political attack on the bracero program intensified in the late 1950s, traditional bracero users were not as united as before."[15]

The attitude of the Mexican community in the United States toward the Bracero Program, a managed migration, was as ambivalent as their attitude toward recent Mexican immigration in general. In theory, the program had safeguards protecting the rights of native-born farmworkers. For example, the U.S. government was required to certify that there was a genuine labor shortage before local farmers would be eligible to request braceros; and these braceros, once employed, had to be paid "the prevailing wage," that is, the wage that was generally paid for harvesting the particular crop in the particular area—not less than local workers received. In practice, however, given the funding and size of the government bureaucracy and the politics of agricultural communities, where large land-holders wield extraordinary power and influence, braceros often displaced native-born workers and tended to depress agricultural wages. This suggests that the attitude toward braceros would likely be more negative among the Mexican-American working class, which was adversely affected by the program, and more positive among the ethnic middle class, people whose jobs were secure. In general, this may have been the case. However, it should be pointed out that, without exception, Mexican-American civil rights organizations, predominantly middle class, took a stand against braceros.

More critical than class considerations was ethnic identification. Those Mexicans living in the United States, regardless of class, who felt a strong sense of Mexican nationalism (*mexicanidad*) were more likely to identify with the newcomers and accept them, especially if they themselves were immigrants. On the other hand, native-born Mexicans with weak sentimental ties to the Old Country were likely to reject the guest worker program. In the Mexican communities of the Southwest, the most consistent and disparaging criticism of the program came from New Mexico's Hispanos, not so much because of competition—agribusiness, concentrated in the Mesilla Valley, was not as strong here as in other states—but because the population, given its long-term residency, was more estranged from its Mexican roots than in other areas. Among southwestern congressmen, New Mexico Senator Dennis Chávez (1888–1962) was the most vociferous critic of the Bracero Program.

OPERATION WETBACK

Factory farmers were also willing to dispense with braceros, albeit reluctantly, because by the 1960s they had easy access to other sources of labor that were almost as attractive, notably indocumentados, sometimes referred to as *mojados* (wetbacks) or, less often, *alambristas* (fence-jumpers). Illegal immigration from the south had always been a fact of life along the border, but following the Second World War, it became much more significant, reaching flood proportions by the time PL78 was allowed to lapse in the mid-1960s. Some five million illegals were apprehended and returned to Mexico by the U.S. Border Patrol during the twenty-two years of the Bracero Agreement. In fact, it was the contract-labor program itself, as Manuel García y Griego argues, more than any other single factor, which seems to have stimulated the huge wave of indocumentados.[16]

The increase in illegal entry into the United States, especially in the immediate postwar period, was also a result of the rapid economic development of Mexico. Beginning with the war, a vast economic transformation was initiated. As the economy expanded, Mexicans rushed into the cities to take advantage of new job opportunities. By 1960, the urban population had surpassed the rural population. Unfortunately, while the Mexican bourgeoisie made sizable gains in the 1940s and 1950s, the same could not be said of the lower class. Wages were unable to keep up with inflation. Moreover, a spiraling population ensured that the standard of living would remain low. In 1934, Mexico's population was about 16 million; by 1958, it had skyrocketed to more than 32 million. This phenomenal growth and the problems it fostered were most apparent in the cities, where slums proliferated. The historians Michael Meyer and William Sherman explain: "Drawn by the lure of industry, hundreds of thousands of rural Mexicans flocked to the cities in hope of a better life, but few found it. The industrial revolution required skilled, not unskilled, labor. The need for more jobs, schools, health services, sewage disposal plants, streets, and houses in the cities was now taxing even the extraordinary postwar prosperity."[17] Mexico City, in particular, experienced the problems associated with urban poverty as the population of the Federal District jumped from 3 million in 1952 to 4.5 million in 1958. The devastating impact of overpopulation and industrialization on the capital's sprawling *vecindades* (slum tenements) during the fifties has been thoroughly investigated in the classic studies of the American anthropologist Oscar Lewis.

The northern periphery of Mexico became another source of illegal immigration. After the war, this tier of states experienced a rapid economic transformation thanks to irrigation projects initiated during the administration of Miguel Alemán (1946–1952), notably the Morelos Dam on the Colorado River, near Mexicali, and, in the northeast, the Falcón Dam in the Lower Rio Grande Valley. The prospects of employment stimulated a steady northward movement of people from the densely populated central states. The norteño agrarian economy, however, was unable to absorb all the newcomers, resulting in the spectacular growth of border cities. From 1940 to 1967, Ciudad Juárez grew from 55,024 to 501,416; Mexicali from 44,399 to 540,300; and Tijuana from 21,977 to 347,501.

Once on the border, Mexicans found it relatively easy to make the crossing to the United States, where jobs were abundant and wages high compared to Mexican standards. Unable to meet the stipulations legal entry required, the overwhelming majority crossed illegally. Since it was virtually impossible to police the international divide, given its length of almost two thousand miles and the modest size of the Border Patrol—deliberately kept understaffed by congressional representatives of southwestern business interests—Mexicans found it easy to avoid detection. The volume of traffic increased steadily. In 1950, the number of illegal entrants apprehended and returned to Mexico reached an unprecedented high of 469,000.

In the competition for jobs, undocumented workers held their own against braceros. The sociologist Julián Samora, a specialist on the subject, explains, "Wetback labor is even cheaper [than bracero labor]—no need for contracts, minimum wage, health benefits, housing, transportation, etc. Since the workers are illegal aliens, they have few rights before the law and can be dismissed at a moment's notice."[18]

While corporate farmers may have welcomed the rising tide of undocumented workers, other Americans grew apprehensive. By the early 1950s, anti-immigration fears were exacerbated by the xenophobia accompanying the Cold War. The result was a massive campaign waged by the Immigration and Naturalization Service (INS) to deport undocumented Mexicans. Labeled "Operation Wetback," the program was initiated on 17 June 1954, and lasted for several months.[19] Conducted as a military operation by the Border Patrol, and often employing the intimidation tactics of the thirties, it focused on the Southwest, but eventually it was extended nationally. Over one million people (1,075,168) were apprehended and returned to Mexico in 1954. Operation Wetback was hailed as a huge success, and it is true that in the late 1950s, apprehensions declined noticeably. However, by the following decade the number of apprehensions made it clear that illegal entries were on the rise again. Once the Bracero Program was terminated, this immigration exploded.

With the growth of illegal immigration came the advent of a thriving smuggling operation, a major service industry today from Brownsville to San Diego. At one time, Mexicans could cross the border routinely, no questions asked. As entry became more difficult, as was the case at the time of Operation Wetback, many undocumented immigrants sought help in crossing the border and finding work while escaping detection. Men and women involved in this dangerous and nefarious enterprise came to be known as *coyotes* and *coyotas,* respectively. Some did little more than guide their clients, or *pollos* (chickens), as they came to be called, a few hundred yards under cover of darkness. Others, more fearless, transported hidden clients across checkpoints in motorized vehicles. For a higher fee—about two hundred dollars in the fifties—they were willing not only to smuggle aliens into the country but to transport them to work sites at a safe distance from the border. On rare occasions it was possible to secure transportation beyond the Southwest, something which became more common after 1965. Oftentimes, the client would be provided employment, invariably a low-paying job, since some smugglers either worked for or were themselves contratistas. During this period of illegal immigration, the overwhelming numbers of indocumentados were men, but women occasionally entered the migratory stream, some of them smuggled in to work as *cantineras* (barmaids) and prostitutes. Because the traffic was illicit and because the clients were virtually powerless, the business of smuggling tended to attract an unusually large number of unsavory and unscrupulous individuals. As has been observed on more than one occasion, border populations tend to have more than their share of such predatory types.

THE MEXICAN AMERICAN GENERATION

Until recently, Chicano historians have found little to compliment in the emerging middle class in Mexican communities of the United States, if they bothered to deal with them at all. By and large, the bourgeoisie has been written off by some critics as a pack of opportunists motivated exclusively by self-interest, often at the expense of poorer Mexicans in the barrios. Calling themselves "Latin Americans," "Mexican Americans," or "Spanish Americans," they seemed to be willing to win acceptance into the dominant society at any cost. This exceedingly bleak portrait of the middle class is familiar to anyone who has read the works of Rodolfo Acuña, the leading exponent of this view. Most Chicano scholars, products of the 1960s, an age when the downtrodden were glorified and anti-establishment views reigned supreme, share this perspective, to a greater or lesser extent.

During the last decade, however, this simplistic interpretation has come under increasing criticism by a growing minority of Chicano scholars, led by Mario T. García, one of the most respected historians in the academic community. Calling for a radical reevaluation, García sees the middle class in a positive light. As he points out, more affluent members of the Mexican community have periodically been in the forefront of the fight for civil liberties. This was particularly true of the middle class during the years from 1930 to 1960, a cohort that he and other like-minded colleagues refer to as the Mexican-American Generation. Consisting primarily of the native-born, the middle class by the thirties began to identify primarily with the United States rather than Mexico; in contrast to the previous generation, which consisted of immigrants whose identity was overwhelmingly conditioned by their love of the Old Country, *México lindo* (beautiful Mexico). Consistent with this new orientation—what the historian Richard García calls the "Mexican-American mind"—the second generation, rather than resigning themselves to their degraded condition, as their immigrant parents had been wont to do, began to seek political solutions to the many problems that beset the ethnic community.

Mario García sees the Great Depression as something of a watershed in this process; however, there was more continuity than he suggests. The League of United Latin-American Citizens (LULAC), for example, which was formed in 1929 and was the most significant of all the organizations constructed by the Mexican-American Generation, is lauded by Professor García as "the oldest Mexican-American civil rights association in the United States." Yet, LULAC itself was an outgrowth of a number of older organizations, including the Orden Hijos de América (Order Sons of America) founded in San Antonio in 1921, which Professor García, in an apparent contradiction, describes in this way: "Comprised of mostly lower middle-class professionals, the Sons stressed socializing Mexican Americans to their rights as U.S. citizens and obtaining equal rights for them."[20] LULAC, it could be argued, was the product of developments that can be traced back to World War I, and even further back. The Primer Congreso Mexicanista (First Mexican Congress), which was convened by the influential newspaper editor Clemente N. Idar in Laredo in 1911, was an early champion of the rights of Mexicans. Indeed, it is clear that even in the nineteenth century, Mexicans were concerned with protecting their civil liberties and were willing to use political weapons.

Yet it is during the Second World War, as most Chicano scholars conclude, that most Mexicans in the United States begin to see the advantages of remaining in this country rather than returning to Mexico. Moreover, with the war came the rise of a middle class with sufficient interest and ability to provide effective political leadership beyond Texas. It is partly for these reasons that Juan Gómez-Quiñones, in his thorough study of contemporary political life *Chicano Politics: Reality and Promise* (1990), sees the period between 1941 and the 1960s as a distinct stage of cultural development.

In order to appreciate the political advances that were made from the forties to the sixties, however, it is necessary to briefly recap key factors in Mexican-American life prior to the Second World War. By the turn of the century, many mutualistas, though primarily immigrant organizations interested in ameliorating the social and economic conditions of their members, were realizing that civil rights could be guaranteed only by entering the political arena. Certainly, this perspective was in evidence, as we saw previously, in the Alianza Hispano-Americana. The First World War spawned a number of mutualistas that aped the Alianza in their concern for social and political action, notably the Liga Protectora Latina in Phoenix and the Liga Protectora Mexicana in Kansas City. The Alianza, however, remained the most active and influential mutualista as it expanded its lodges throughout the Southwest, reaching the pinnacle of its popularity in the twenties. During the thirties and forties, under conservative leadership, it shied away from controversy, but it resumed its fight for civil rights after World War II. Kaye Briegel reports that "even as late as 1968 the Alianza remained the best-known Mexican-American organization in Los Angeles."[21] Nevertheless, by this time, it had long since been superseded by more dynamic associations.

The most energetic and respected of these other organizations was undoubtedly LULAC, which, as mentioned above, grew out of an association that was more obscure but historically meaningful nonetheless, the Orden Hijos de América.

The latter was founded in 1921 by prominent leaders of the San Antonio Mexican community. The association excluded immigrants. "This limitation of membership to American citizens," writes Miguel David Tirado, in a pioneering article, "indicated a growing realization by Mexican-American leaders that political power is essential for the achievement of the minority's aim in this country, and that the political power only arises with the organization of a solid voting bloc of citizens."[22] Although it managed to set up lodges in South Texas, the Orden was soon beset by a multitude of difficulties, not the least of which was ethnic infighting and ultimate schism.

It was some of the more militant members of the Orden who took the initiative resulting in the founding of LULAC in Corpus Christi on 17 February 1929.[23] Its program was very similar to that of its predecessor. The most effective and charismatic of its first leaders was Alonso S. Perales (1899–1960), who was ably assisted by Manuel C. Gonzales (1900–1986) and Ben Garza (1892–1937). Mirroring the assimilationist attitudes of the time, LULAC too confined its membership to U.S. citizens, and therefore to the middle-class elite. Its stated objective was to inculcate American values among its members. Consistent with this philosophy, it adopted English as its official language. However, it vowed to protect the Mexican community—not just its own membership—from the discrimination that was rampant at the time. To a surprising extent, it was successful in keeping its promise. Although in public it claimed to be apolitical—its membership included both liberals and conservatives—politics was one avenue it was willing to pursue.

In the past, Chicano historians have been hard on LULAC because of its middle-class orientation and assimilationist tendencies. However, while conceding that a strong class bias permeated the organization, Mario García rightly points out that the aim of *Lulacers* was not to deny their Mexican heritage. What they hoped to accomplish, he avers, was "some functional balance between mainstream Anglo-American culture and the culture derived from their Mexican roots."[24]

The success of LULAC was due to its dynamic leadership, its incorporation of youth and women's auxiliaries, and its willingness to change with the times. After the war, LULAC became increasingly active in combating racial prejudice and discrimination in Texas, always its stronghold despite forays into other sections of the country. During the postwar period its effectiveness was aided by its ability to work with a number of powerful Anglo politicians in the state, notably Lyndon B. Johnson.

Perhaps LULAC's most lasting contribution, as Guadalupe San Miguel has shown in *"Let All of Them Take Heed": Mexican Americans and the Campaign for Educational Equality in Texas* (1987), was in the area of school desegregation, a major problem in Texas and throughout the Southwest. Mexican children began to be segregated into "Mexican" schools at the turn of the century. The nation's first successful legal challenge to this discriminatory practice occurred in California in 1931, when angry Mexican parents sued the San Diego County community of Lemon Grove, after their children were barred from Anglo schools, and won a favorable verdict. Some years later, in 1945, Mexican parents in Orange County, California, led by Gonzalo and Felicitas Méndez, filed a class action suit against several school districts in an effort to integrate local schools. *Méndez et al. v. Westminster School District of Orange County* (1947), "one of the most significant legal cases in the history of the Southwest," according to Gilbert G. González, effectively ended de jure segregation in California.[25]

Lulacers, while only peripherally involved in the *Méndez* case, were in the forefront of the effort to desegregate Texas schools which culminated in *Delgado v. Bastrop Independent School District* (1948), which did for the Lone Star State what the former had done for California. While de facto segregation survived until the 1960s in some areas of the Southwest, both of these cases served as notable precedents for the landmark *Brown v. Board of Education of Topeka* (1954), the Supreme Court decision that mandated school desegregation in the United States and launched the civil rights movements of the sixties.

Finally, the last Mexican association with a substantial political agenda to emerge before World War II was the Congreso del Pueblo de Habla Española, a federation of Mexican associations founded, as previously mentioned, in Los Angeles on 4 December 1938. Like all other organizations which aimed at achieving first-class citizenship for Mexicans, the Congreso mirrored the concerns of the time. Spawned by the Depression, it was a progressive-radical body with a marked Communist influence, as witnessed in the labor unions active in its creation. The association sought to ensure both economic benefits and civil liberties for Mexicans.

The Congreso differed from most Mexican organizations of the interwar period not only because of its radical social program but also because of the degree to which mujeres were involved. Mexican women have been a significant minority in almost all associations mentioned previously, sometimes segregated into auxiliaries of their own, sometimes integrated into the general membership, as the Chicana historian Cynthia Orozco has chronicled so well recently.[26] Rarely, though, had they played a leading role. The Congreso was an exception. From the very outset, women were among the most active members; the Congreso itself was the brainchild of Luisa Moreno and its executive secretary for most of its short history was Josefina Fierro de Bright.

The California-based organization had only one national convention, in 1939, before disappearing three years later. Its brief existence can be attributed to two main causes: its political radicalism, which though within the reformist tradition, was considered too extreme by most Americans, including many Mexican obreros themselves; and the onset of the war, which required that all Americans work together for the common cause and generated a multitude of jobs, effectively countering worker dissatisfaction. While the Congreso eschewed electoral politics, it was memorable nonetheless because it provided valuable leadership training for many Mexican men and women, among them Eduardo Quevedo and Bert Corona.

Despite its efforts to expand its membership nationally or at least regionally, the Congreso remained a California organization with Los Angeles as its power base. Its demise in 1942, on the eve of the Zoot Suit Riots, left a void at precisely the time when a coordinated effort on behalf of civil liberties was most essential. Distressed by the vehemence of anti-Mexican sentiment, Mexicans in southern California began to set up grassroots organizations for the protection of their communities. Immediately after the war these efforts led to the formation of Unity Leagues, the first of which arose in the Pomona Valley, east of Los Angeles, in 1946. The effort was guided by a respected champion of the ethnic community, Ignacio L. López (1908–1973), editor of a local Spanish-language newspaper, *El Espectador,* in the nearby San Gabriel Valley. Unlike most of the organizations mentioned previously, the Spanish-Speaking Congress being the outstanding exception, the Unity Leagues, which soon proliferated throughout the Los Angeles area, were as interested in mobilizing the working class as they were the middle class. Although their primary mission was to combat discrimination, especially the segregation of schools and other public facilities, Unity League members also sought political office. In 1946, they managed to elect the first Mexican to a California city council since the nineteenth century, Andrés Morales in Chino. While encountering only moderate success in achieving their goals, they did lay the foundation for the Community Service Organization (CSO), the most effective Mexican-American association to appear in California during the postwar period.

The chief link between the two organizations was Fred W. Ross, a professional organizer and arguably the most important non-Hispanic ever to advance the cause of the Mexican community. After the war, Ross, a USC graduate, came under the sway of Saul Alinsky (1909–1972). Using Alinsky's techniques of community mobilization and leadership development, Ross exerted an enormous influence on the Mexican middle class of the City of Angels.

CSO, which was founded in East Los Angeles in September 1947, grew out of efforts to elect Edward Roybal (1916–) to the Los Angeles City Council in that year (1881 was the last time a Mexican served on the council). Although he lost the election, Roybal, using Ross's organizational techniques, transformed his small but enthusiastic coterie into an association with more ambitious goals. As its title suggests, the Community Service Organization was intended to meet the many needs of the Mexican community, but given its genesis as an electoral vehicle, it is not surprising that the nonpartisan group emphasized political action from the very beginning. During its first years, CSO managed to expand throughout the state, successfully electing a number of candidates to school and government positions, notably Roybal himself, who was elected to the Los Angeles City Council in 1949. By this time, though, America was in the throes of the Cold War, and CSO leaders, many of them veterans, grew reluctant to advance political candidacies. While continuing to sponsor voter registration drives, during the 1950s, CSO focused on educational and police issues. Eventually, even these questions came to be seen as too controversial, and the organization was virtually transformed into a mutual-aid society by the sixties.

In addition to CSO, the other major community-based organization that developed among Mexicans in the postwar period, and one that was considerably more effective in achieving its stated goals, was the American G.I. Forum.[27] Founded in Corpus Christi in 1948, the G.I. Forum was confined exclusively to veterans, which meant that the membership would be highly patriotic and heavily committed to assimilation. On the other hand, given its conservative origins and composition, the association's devotion to the American Way was beyond reproach. Consequently, reasonably immune to red-baiting during the McCarthy years, it was less prone to compromise on questions of racial discrimination than its California counterpart. Although its lodges were largely confined to Texas, the G.I. Forum would be the most celebrated champion of Mexican civil rights in the country before the advent of the Chicano movement.

Perhaps the key reason for the G.I. Forum's early prominence was the leadership provided by Dr. Héctor Pérez García (1910–), one of the most charismatic personalities to emerge from the Mexican community. Born in Tamaulipas, García was raised a Tejano. He received his B.A. from the University of Texas in 1936 and eventually became a physician. He served with distinction in the war, winning a Bronze Star, before returning to South Texas, where he immersed himself in Democratic politics and gained a solid reputation as an indomitable defender of the civil rights of Tejanos. The founder of the Forum, he served as president for many years. He was also active in LULAC and a variety of other ethnic organizations. In 1984, culminating a long and distinguished career of community service, Dr. García was awarded America's highest civilian honor, the Presidential Medal of Freedom.

The most valuable accomplishments of the G.I. Forum came in the area of discrimination, a special concern since there was so much of it in the Lone Star State. Indeed, the organization was founded in the first place as a result of a clamorous example of racial injustice in 1948, when a Mexican soldier, Félix Longoria, killed in the Philippines was refused burial in the Live Oak County town of Three Rivers, Texas. After a heated campaign, and with the help of Sen. Lyndon Johnson—the beginning of a long and fruitful association—Dr. García and the G.I. Forum were able to secure Longoria a burial at Arlington National Cemetery.

Segregation, the most blatant form of discrimination, was widespread in Texas during the forties, not just against blacks but also "Meskins," who were generally perceived as a nonwhite population, as they were in other parts of the country. During the forties and fifties, the G.I. Forum initiated a series of class action suits aimed at desegregating schools, recreational facilities, and transportation. It encountered many victories in this area, especially after the 1954 *Brown* decision.

Like CSO, the G.I. Forum was, and remains, officially nonpartisan, but it has always encouraged members to run for elected office and has endorsed candidates. Undoubtedly, the influence of the G.I. Forum goes a long way in explaining why Tejanos have been so much more assertive in politics than have Mexicans in California and other states during the past half century.

CSO and the G.I. Forum, though falling short of their lofty goals, were nevertheless able to survive, in contrast to another Mexican civil rights association that was founded in the forties: the Asociación Nacional México-Americana (ANMA, the National Mexican American Association). Founded in Phoenix in February 1949, ANMA functioned only through 1953. Organized by a militant mining union with heavy Mexican representation, the International Union of Mine, Mill and Smelter Workers (Mine-Mill), ANMA, like the Spanish-Speaking Congress before it, was almost exclusively working class in its membership. Like the old organization, too, its politics were markedly left of center. Dedicated to protecting the rights of Mexicans, both native- and foreign-born, ANMA was willing to work through alliances with other progressive working-class groups, including the American Communist party, as well as other persecuted ethnic minorities. Another striking similarity with the Congreso was the concern with feminist issues, which was reflected in its leadership, where many key positions were held by Mexicanas. Among the members of the first national executive board were Isabel Gonzales, vice-president; Xochitl Ruiz, secretary-general; Virginia Ruiz, executive secretary; and Florencia Luna, secretary-treasurer. Women, too, were conspicuous in leadership roles at the local level.[28] At least two of them, Carmen Contreras and Dolores Heredia, were presidents of important local chapters, in San Francisco and Chicago, respectively.

One of ANMA's most notable campaigns was in support of the famous 1950–1952 miners' strike in Bayard, New Mexico. The fifteen-month work stoppage—immortalized by the film classic *Salt of the Earth* (1954)—was initiated by Mine-Mill. The striking miners, most of them Mexicans, succeeded only when their wives insisted on participating, in spite of their husbands' objections, snatching victory from apparent defeat.

Never very numerous—at its height, membership was a few thousand—ANMA was plagued throughout its brief history by unfounded charges of Communist affiliation, which eventually led to its demise during the McCarthy era. "ANMA eventually declined," recalls Bert Corona, one of its most active members, "because the FBI intimidated its members and destroyed its organization."[29] The radical tradition of Mexican political activity, represented by the Congreso and ANMA, would resurface during the Chicano movement in the sixties. Given the temper of the times, however, the only realistic hope for reform during the postwar years rested with more traditional middle-class organizations.

By the late 1950s, winds of change were beginning to sweep through the United States. The Cold War began to thaw out, and African Americans, led by Dr. Martin Luther King, Jr., initiated a powerful civil rights movement. These momentous changes were reflected in the Mexican community with the creation of the Mexican American Political Association (MAPA), a middle-class association that unabashedly called for political action by its members. More specifically, this initiative was a direct result of Hispanic dissatisfaction with the Democratic party. To the extent that they had participated in the electoral process, Mexicans tended to support the Democrats beginning in the days of FDR (their vote was pretty evenly split between both parties before the Depression). Since Republicans displayed scant interest in courting them, Mexican votes automatically went to the Democrats, still considered the party of immigrants. Unfortunately, Mexican support was taken for granted and patronage for barrio politicos was weak or nonexistent. The final disillusion came with the defeat of Henry ("Hank") López for California secretary of state in 1958, after lukewarm support from the Democratic party leadership.

Meeting in Fresno, California, disgruntled Mexican leaders organized MAPA on a statewide basis in April 1960. Founders included Roybal and Quevedo, but the most dedicated and respected single individual was Bert Corona (1918–), who came to dominate the organization. Born in El Paso, Corona received his education in California. He attended USC briefly, but dropped out during the height of the Depression to work as a labor organizer for CIO. As mentioned previously, he was one of the leaders of the Congreso, where he worked with Quevedo. Both men continued to collaborate in CSO.

Set up as a bipartisan political association, MAPA pledged to support Mexican candidates to public office and non-Mexican candidates who promised to work for the Mexican cause. While *Mapistas* met with some success at the polls during the next decade—the election of Roybal to the U.S. House of Representatives in 1962 was especially gratifying—efforts were hampered by internal dissension, a failure to adequately cultivate the working class, and, despite the rhetoric, an unwillingness to abandon the Democrats.

The tendency to support the Democratic party became apparent almost immediately, in the Viva Kennedy movement that helped elect JFK to the presidency in 1960. Led by Tejanos Dr. Hector García, elected National Coordinator, and Congressman Henry B. González (1916–), this campaign mobilized the Mexican community solidly behind the youthful Catholic candidate. Mapistas in the Golden State, with few exceptions, were enthusiastic supporters.

The Viva Kennedy clubs were so effective in bringing Mexicans together that in 1961 it was decided to use the successful campaign as a springboard for the creation of an umbrella organization that would unite the various Mexican civil rights associations. A precedent had been set ten years before by the American Council of Spanish-Speaking People (ACSSP), but the attempt was abortive and the organization failed to survive into the sixties. The new initiative was taken by the ubiquitous Dr. Hector García, who became the founder and first president of the Political Association of Spanish-Speaking Organizations (PASO or PASSO). The organization got off to a good start in Texas; however, attempts to promote PASSO in the rest of the Southwest floundered, and ultimately the organization petered out. It experienced the obstacles that Mexican political and cultural associations have always had to overcome at the local level—power struggles, lack of money, class differences, and so on—but apparently the overriding problem was regionalism, the tendency toward parochialism, which translated into an unwillingness of Mexicans in one section of the country to work with those in another. Although PASSO went through difficult times, it scored occasional victories, among them the stunning election of five Mexican candidates to the city council of Crystal City, Texas, in 1963.

Political gains made by Mexicans before the mid-1960s appear rather modest to many critics of the Mexican middle class. Certainly, it is true that from a purely political perspective little had been gained in terms of representation at any level of government—municipal, county, state, or federal—outside of New Mexico. By 1965, despite a population of between four and five million, Mexicans had only four representatives in the U.S. Congress: Joseph Montoya (D-NM) in the Senate and Henry B. González (D-Tex), Eligio ("Kika") de la Garza (D-Tex), and Edward R. Roybal (D-Calif) in the House. It is important, however, to appreciate the difficulties leaders faced as they tried to mobilize the ethnic community.

First of all, the immigrant community held a thoroughly negative attitude toward politics. Democracy has never worked well in Mexico. Corruption has been rife, a recurring problem in Mexican political life, as Ramón Eduardo Ruiz's studies show so conclusively. One can hardly blame Mexicans for being cynical, especially peasants who were traditionally excluded from the political process. Second, Mexican immigrants came to the United States typically believing that they would return home someday. Third, a large number, possibly the majority, of immigrants entered the country without their papers, which meant they were ineligible for citizenship. Fourth, nationalism came to be so deeply embedded that even immigrants who came in legally and had no intention of returning home had a difficult time giving up Mexican citizenship. Fifth, the socioeconomic level of the community made it difficult to form political associations. Mexicans were generally impoverished and often illiterate. Sixth, though there were occasional respites, anti-Mexican feeling was generally pervasive, which meant that the dominant society, consistently maintaining an attitude of ethnic and cultural superiority, discouraged political participation through a variety of tactics including the poll tax, gerrymandering, and at-large elections.

And yet, from a broader perspective, and in spite of these nagging problems, middle-class leadership achieved significant progress by 1965, notably in the field of civil rights. The supreme accomplishment of Mexican leaders between World War II and the mid-1960s was the effective end of *legal* forms of oppression, a significant achievement which paved the way for future gains.[30] Few scholars today would agree with Manuel Servín who, speaking before the Western History Association in 1965, concluded that "the post–World War II Mexican Americans have been a nonachieving minority."[31]

THE MEXICAN-AMERICAN INTELLIGENTSIA

Another positive trend in the period 1940–1965 was the rise of an intelligenstia, a measure of how far the Mexican middle class in the United States had progressed by the mid-twentieth century. During the nineteenth century, there were a number of individuals who would qualify as intellectuals. Generally, they were clergymen, like Father Antonio José Martínez, or newspaper editors, like Francisco P. Ramírez. These were isolated cases, however. After the turn of the century, during the Great Migration, immigrants, especially political refugees, included some well-educated men and women, people of high culture; but many of them were in the country temporarily, and the others were influential only at the local level.

The Depression witnessed a fateful departure. Among the most powerful intellects emerging from the barrios were Ernesto Galarza (1905–1984), awarded a Ph.D. at Columbia University, an educator, union organizer, and specialist in labor history; the aforementioned Américo Paredes, a folklorist, poet, and novelist who received his Ph.D. from the University of Texas, where he taught for many years; and a person whose contributions are only now being appreciated, Jovita Mireles Gonzales, a folklorist and historian, the first Hispanic to be elected president of the Texas Folklore Society.

Three other names, however, deserve special attention because, as Mario García points out, they "helped shape a Mexican-American intellectual culture and scholarship that played a role in the academic world while providing some direction in the realm of ideas to the struggles of the Mexican-American Generation," thus anticipating Chicano scholars who came after: Carlos Castañeda, Arthur Campa, and George Sánchez.[32]

Carlos Eduardo Castañeda (1896–1958) was born in Ciudad Camargo, Chihuahua, but was raised in Brownsville, where his family moved when he was ten. He enrolled at the University of Texas as an Engineering major, but influenced by the renowned historian Eugene C. Barker, switched to History, earning three degrees in that field, including a Ph.D. in 1932. His academic career was spent at his alma mater, where he taught from 1933 to 1958. The best-known of his dozen historical works was a massive six-volume study entitled *Our Catholic Heritage in Texas* (1936–1950). The first major historian to write about the history of Mexicans in the Southwest, Dr. Castañeda is also credited with encouraging American scholars to take an interest in Latin American studies.

Arthur León Campa (1905–1978), too, was an immigrant to Texas. Born in Guaymas, Sonora, where his parents were Methodist missionaries, he grew up near El Paso. Later, his mother moved the family to Albuquerque, where the youth received his early schooling. Campa pursued his college education at the University of New Mexico, earning two degrees, before continuing his graduate studies at Columbia University, where he was awarded a Ph.D. in languages in 1940. He served in the Second World War, winning a Bronze Star. Subsequently, he turned to an academic career and taught at the University of Denver from 1946 until his retirement in 1972. Although not the first student of Mexican folklore in the Southwest to achieve fame—the New Mexican Aurelio M. Espinoza, Sr., merits that honor—Campa soon acquired a reputation as the outstanding authority in this field. Published posthumously, *Hispanic Culture in the Southwest* (1979) is a summary of Dr. Campa's scholarship during the course of a long and celebrated career.

George I. Sánchez (1906–1972), the dean of Mexican-American scholars, was born in Albuquerque. After receiving his B.A. at the University of New Mexico, he continued his studies at the University of Texas and the University of California at Berkeley, where he was awarded his Ed.D. in Educational Administration in 1934. A scholar, writer, and educator, Dr. Sánchez first achieved prominence with his impressionistic history of Hispanos, *Forgotten People,* published in 1940, the very year he joined the University of Texas faculty. He is best remembered, though, as a pioneer in the field of bilingual education. An indefatigable worker, Dr. Sánchez also left a mark as a civil rights leader. He was a stalwart member of LULAC, serving as president in 1941. Ten years later, he founded the short-lived ACSSP, the umbrella organization of Mexican organizations in Texas.

Probably the outstanding trend in Mexican-American history in the period between 1940 and 1965 was the rise of a middle class from virtual anonymity. A generation ago, this assessment would have encountered fierce resistance in emerging Chicano Studies departments. The pioneering Chicano historians of the 1960s generally provided a very unflattering portrait of the fledgling middle sector. Its very weakness, given its low educational level and lack of capital, invited scorn. Moreover, the assimilationist tendency the middle class displayed historically was completely at odds with the Chicano movement's demand for cultural regeneration at a time when Chicano scholarship was beginning. Not surprisingly, the popular view of the Mexican-American middle class as vendidos was mirrored by young scholars of the time.

During the past few years, however, the Chicano perception of these professionals, merchants, and artisans has undergone a major shift, though not one universally endorsed. Now, there is growing appreciation of the fact that during the years between 1940 and 1965, and in spite of the adverse political climate created by two major wars and the fear of Communism, the middle class waged an unremitting struggle to win citizenship rights for all Mexicans living in the United States. The gains made in the field of civil rights—impressive accomplishments considering the temper of the times—were made primarily because of pressure exerted by middle-class associations, notably LULAC, CSO, and the G.I. Forum. These organizations, even a long-time critic of the middle-class elitism like activist-scholar Juan Gómez-Quiñones is forced to admit, had a "creditable record of activity between the forties and the midsixties."[33]

The revisionism apparent today in Chicano historiography reflects a greater maturity on the part of Chicano scholars. Most of them were intellectual heirs of the 1960s and 1970s, with Ph.D.s generally earned in the middle of the latter decade (Chicanas somewhat later). Some were militants at the time. Virtually all of them, however, were influenced by Chicanismo whether they were active participants in the movement or not—which is why they are recognized as Chicano and Chicana scholars—and accepted its natural repugnance of elites. The bias against the bourgeoisie was also reinforced, in many cases, by exposure to Marxist ideas, a tendency more evident at the University of California than elsewhere—and one of the reasons why minority historians trained in California tend to be more militant than their colleagues from Texas. Finally, it should be noted that the overwhelming majority of these scholars have working-class origins.

What accounts for the more sympathetic view of the Mexican middle class by the scholarly community? The new revisionism reflects a natural swing of the pendulum—when historians move so far in one direction there is no place to go but in the other direction—but also demographic and socioeconomic changes in the Mexican community. The middle class today is becoming larger. Moreover, Chicano professors in the nation's major universities—or even in community colleges, for that matter—are realizing that their students are or will soon become middle class, albeit with increasing difficulty. Last, and not least, the aging professors themselves have entered into the ranks of the once despised bourgeoisie, which of necessity has softened their attitude toward it.[34]

THE CHICANO MOVEMENT

1965–1975

8

The decade comprising the mid-sixties to the mid-seventies was a period of extraordinary ferment in the Mexican communities of the United States. Significant social changes were in the air. Immigration from Mexico, for example, increased markedly, a trend that tended to push many of the older residents of the Southwest into other parts of the country. The most momentous changes, though, were political and psychological.

Following the lead of the African-American community, which initiated a far-reaching movement for civil liberties in the fifties, many Mexicans, now calling themselves Chicanos and Chicanas, embarked on their own campaign to improve socioeconomic conditions and win full recognition of their rights as U.S. citizens.[1] While these concerns had been articulated before, notably by the Mexican-American Generation of the post–World War II period, after the mid-sixties a new aggressiveness developed in the barrios. Socioeconomic gains made in past years seemed woefully inadequate. Many Mexicans began to demand immediate reform. Some called for revolution. Convinced that changes of whatever kind could be instituted only through the acquisition of power, political action was emphasized as never before. Moreover, in contrast to their postwar predecessors, the leaders of the so-called Chicano Generation stressed pride in their ethnic roots while deemphasizing assimilation into the American mainstream. "A Chicano," Rubén Salazar, a journalist on the periphery of the movement, once said, "is a Mexican-American with a non-Anglo image of himself."[2] Tired of apologizing for their ethnic origins, Chicanos looked to Mexico, especially Indian Mexico, for inspiration. While there was much disagreement on specific methods—indeed a significant minority stood on the sidelines—most of the community was in general agreement with the goals formulated by barrio leaders: cultural regeneration and political power. Since these twin objectives are the crux of the emerging Chicano movement (also called Chicano Power or Brown Power), the struggle for Mexican-American civil rights, it seems reasonable to see this decade in terms of Chicanismo.

THE MEXICAN COMMUNITY IN THE MID-SIXTIES

A portrait of the Mexican population on the eve of the Chicano movement is helpful in explaining why Chicanismo became so appealing to large segments of the population. The best source of information on Mexicans in the early sixties, indeed the most comprehensive work on the subject up to this time, was *The Mexican-American People: The Nation's Second Largest Minority* (1970) by Leo Grebler, Joan W. Moore, and Ralph C. Guzmán, a product of research conducted by the Mexican-American Study Project at the University of California at Los Angeles in 1964–1968. The study was based on data taken from the 1960 U.S. census, so the information is very appropriate for our purposes.

The use of government statistics was not without its pitfalls. Since the census had no separate category for Mexicans but identified them on the basis of "Spanish-surname," a rubric that would include Cubans, Puerto Ricans, and others, it was difficult to interpret the findings. Furthermore, this census, like most government statistical records, was criticized for heavily undercounting Mexicans, mainly because of the difficulty in keeping track of migrant workers and illegal aliens. Still, the 1960 census and the Grebler study based on it are invaluable demographic sources useful in tracing emerging trends. Making allowances for the deficiencies alluded to, they present a fairly clear overall portrait of the community.

The total Mexican population in 1960, according to Grebler and his colleagues—who interpreted and adjusted the official census figures—was 3,842,000, of which 87 percent (3,344,292) resided in the Southwest and the remaining 13 percent (497,800) in other parts of the country. Texas and California, with about equal numbers, accounted for over 80 percent of the southwestern total. Urbanization was advancing at a brisk pace. By 1960, about two-thirds of the population was urban. Somewhat surprisingly, urbanization was more pronounced in the Southwest, where the proportion approached 80 percent. Roughly one-third of all Mexicans lived in four cities in this region: Los Angeles, San Antonio, San Francisco, and El Paso. Whether living in cities or the countryside, however, Mexicans displayed a striking tendency to reside in segregated ethnic communities. Some of these barrios were in the middle of large cities, as was the case in Los Angeles and Albuquerque; some were on the periphery, as in Fresno; some encompassed the entire community (oftentimes a labor camp), as was true of many agricultural towns of the Lower Rio Grande Valley and, to a lesser extent, the San Joaquin Valley.

During the previous decade, the most trenchant demographic trend was the immigration from throughout the Southwest, especially Texas, to California. There was also heavy immigration into the United States from Mexico. During the fifties, over 290,000 Mexicans entered the country legally. Illegal immigration may have been four times greater. Nevertheless, over 85 percent of the Mexicans were born in the United States. Indeed, over half of the Spanish-speaking people in the Southwest were native-born of native-born parents; that is, they were at least second-generation U.S. citizens. The fertility rate was very high. Consequently, the population was relatively youthful. The median age was a little over nineteen years, compared to twenty-eight years for the total white population (excluding Spanish-speaking people) in the Southwest. The high fertility rate and immigration combined to bring about rapid growth: during the fifties, the Mexican population of the Southwest increased by a swooping 51 percent. By 1960, Spanish-speakers, almost all of them of Mexican origin, made up 12 percent of the total population in the region.

Impressive social and economic gains had been registered by this time. During the decade of the fifties, the percentage of Latinos in the Southwest classified as laborers declined from 42 to 30 percent. Another positive trend was the entry of Mexican women into the labor force. Their rates of employment outside the home were higher than among Anglos. During the fifties, median income for Mexican households rose at a substantially higher rate than that of Anglos. Home ownership went up, as well.

Educational levels were improving. During the fifties, the proportions of Spanish-speaking people in the Southwest who completed high school increased almost 75 percent, with California making more progress than other states. The educational gap between Mexicans and Anglos actually narrowed slightly at this time. Greater numbers of Mexicans were enrolling in institutions of higher learning. Though brown faces were difficult to find in major universities across the United States, or even in the Southwest, for that matter, the emerging community colleges provided minorities, including Hispanics, an opportunity to improve their socioeconomic status. Prominent Mexicans benefiting from a junior college education—many of them in this period—include scholars Renato I. Rosaldo, Ralph Guzmán, Américo Paredes, Julián Nava, Carlos Muñoz, Jr., Oscar J. Martínez, and Patricia Zavella; writers Ron Arias, Gary Soto, Denise Chávez, and Floyd Salas; civil rights activists Ignacio López, Dolores Huerta, Cruz Reynoso, José Angel Gutiérrez, and Edward James Olmos; political leaders Eligio de la Garza, Philip Sánchez, Henry B. González, and Gloria Molina; educators Tomás Rivera and Cecilia Preciado de Burciaga; artists Manuel Neri, José Montoya, Rupert García, and Michael J. López; newspaper publisher Mónica Cecilia Lozano; and Tom Flores, the popular athlete and coach.

In general, the decade of the fifties, based on census records, indicated a gradual improvement in the community's socioeconomic condition, this in spite of ongoing immigration from Mexico which skewed the statistics against this trend.

Nevertheless, there were many problems. The best indicators of socioeconomic status are education, occupation, and income. According to the Grebler study, Mexicans ranked close to the bottom in all three categories. In all southwestern states, Mexicans averaged three to four years less education than Anglos. Roughly 50 percent had less than eight grades of schooling, a lower rate than African Americans. Moreover, the statistics do not indicate the severity of the problem, for they tell us nothing about the quality of education. "These years of education," according to the sociologist Joan Moore, "probably were obtained disproportionately in rural, small town, and other schools of inferior quality."[3] In institutions of higher learning, the record was dismal. Less than 6 percent of Mexicans had some college education, half the percentage of the black population and a quarter of the Anglo population. Naturally, the problem was most serious at the university level. In the Golden State, for example, where Mexicans made up about 10 percent of the population, no branch of the University of California had as many as one hundred Mexican students as late as 1967.

In part because of their educational deficiencies, most Mexicans were employed as unskilled or semiskilled workers in low-wage or marginal jobs, what social scientists call a secondary labor market. Within a particular job category, they tended to be at the bottom, earning the lowest wages. Unemployment rates for Mexicans were twice as high as for Anglos of comparable ages in 1960. The census of that year indicated that incomes were considerably lower among Spanish-speaking people than other segments of the population. Grebler, Moore, and Guzmán state: "Mexican Americans had only 47 cents for every dollar of Anglo income, and they were worse off than nonwhites."[4] The rural population was significantly more disadvantaged in this respect than the urban population, a disparity that widened during the previous decade, which helps explain the continuing migration to the cities. According to government criteria, over one-third of the Spanish-speaking population fell under the poverty level (an annual income of three thousand dollars per family). In Texas, over half the Mexican population was officially poor. Juan Gómez-Quiñones, the dean of Chicano historians, puts the picture in clear perspective: "Despite the organizational challenge by Mexican Americans to discrimination in the forties, fifties, and sixties and economic gains resulting from postwar economic booms, the unequal position between Mexican Americans and Anglo Americans probably expanded rather than contracted. Mexican advances in education, income, employment, occupational status, and political representation were dwarfed by the much larger gains of Anglo Americans."[5]

The gloomy picture described here had a variety of causes, among them recent immigration, lack of job skills, a scarcity of capital, and language problems. Equally important, though, was discrimination—based on class, religion, and especially race. Moreover, demographic changes in the Mexican community worked to increase the climate of intolerance.

ORIGINS OF THE CHICANO MOVEMENT

Still, the socioeconomic condition of the Mexican community was not notably worse in the early sixties than it had been in the past. Indeed, demographers indicate that steady progress had been made in this regard. Furthermore, despite widespread hostility, *overt* forms of racism were fading. Discrimination was less blatant than before, thanks in part to the efforts of the Mexican-American Generation, as well as the waning of the Cold War and the demand for conformity that it fostered. Even Mexican participation in Vietnam, with its widespread disaffection, is insufficient to explain the rise of Chicanismo; Mexicans had fought and died in other U.S. wars without turning to militant anti-establishment activity. What made the difference was the changing intellectual climate in America, especially the rise of the black civil rights movement.

Brown v. the Board of Education of Topeka encouraged a new assertiveness by blacks, whose civil rights movement began in 1955, when Rosa Parks, a black woman, refused to give up her bus seat in Montgomery, Alabama. This campaign launched the career of Dr. Martin Luther King, Jr. (1929–1968), a young Baptist minister, arguably the most powerful voice for racial justice in the annals of American history. Influenced by Mohandas Gandhi and Henry Thoreau, Dr. King preached the philosophy of militant nonviolence, which had a profound and lasting impact on his contemporaries. Dr. King and the Southern Christian Leadership Conference (SCLC) spearheaded the drive for desegregation and together with the National Association for the Advancement of Colored People (NAACP) dominated the swelling movement during its first years.

By 1966, however, dissatisfied with the seemingly glacial pace of reform, more militant leaders emerged from the African-American community, particularly in northern urban ghettos, where Dr. King was less influential. They included Stokely Carmichael, head of the Student Nonviolent Coordinating Committee (SNCC); Bobby Seale, Huey P. Newton, and Eldridge Cleaver of the Black Panthers; and the most charismatic of the new leaders, Malcolm X (1925–

1965), who emerged from the ranks of the Black Muslims. Labeling their movement "Black Power," they called for permanent racial separation and the use of violence.

Both moderate and radical wings of the black civil rights movement, and the riots that broke out in African-American ghettos across the country in 1964–1967, had a significant impact on American society. One of the most immediate responses was the War on Poverty, which was launched by President Lyndon B. Johnson in a quixotic attempt to create the Great Society. A myriad of federally funded programs—Job Corps, Volunteers in Service to America (VISTA), Neighborhood Youth Corps, Head Start, and Upward Bound, among them—were set up to affect the change. While not completely successful, LBJ's domestic programs did ameliorate the plight of many poor people in the country, and they also took the wind out of the sails of black militancy, which had faded by the seventies.

The black civil rights movement, though, left a powerful legacy. One of its most momentous consequences was the stimulus it provided for other people of color to stand up for their rights. These included Mexicans, who now initiated their own movement of self-awareness.

CHÁVEZ, HUERTA, AND THE UNITED FARMWORKERS

The Chicano movement consisted of hundreds of organizations focusing on a variety of issues. Broadly speaking, these groups were found in barrios, schools, and prisons. In terms of their approaches, they could be divided into those associations that sought to work through the system and those that called for a major restructuring of the system, the moderate and radical wings of the movement respectively. As the Chicano movement began, in the mid-sixties, the moderates predominated. The key organization representing their perspective was undoubtedly the United Farm Workers (UFW).

The history of labor organization among field workers goes back to the early part of the twentieth century, as we have seen. Both the IWW, before and during the Great War, and the American Communist party, in the thirties, made abortive attempts to win concessions for farmworkers in the agricultural valleys of the West. Before the rise of the UFW, the last serious initiative in the fields was taken by the National Farm Labor Union (NFLU), formed in 1945 and led in California by Ernesto Galarza. In the late forties, the NFLU launched a series of strikes in California, where it centered its activities. These initiatives failed not only because of the many difficulties inherent in organizing workers in the fields but also because the Bracero Program made it impossible to win concessions from growers. The termination of the Bracero Agreement in 1964, however, set the stage for the most ambitious unionization attempt to date, the UFW campaign begun in California's San Joaquin Valley during the following year. It was led by two extraordinary people: César Chávez and Dolores Huerta.

Despite his rejection of the term *Chicano,* César Chávez (1927–1993) is the single most important representative of the movimiento; indeed, he is the most well-known figure in the Mexican community, in general.[6] A legend in his own lifetime, it is difficult to separate fact from fiction in relating the outlines of his long and productive career. César Estrada Chávez was born on 31 March 1927, on a small family farm near Yuma, Arizona. During the Depression, his grandfather lost the farm, and the Chávez family was reduced to working as migratory farm laborers. For the next few years, they traveled up and down California eking out a living. Education for the Chávez children was sporadic, given their nomadic existence, and young César was forced to abandon school altogether after the eighth grade. During World War II, he joined the Navy and served in the Pacific. Upon his release in 1946, he returned to the fields, joining the ill-fated NFLU.

Eventually, Chávez settled down with his wife Helen and their growing family in San Jose, California, where he continued to do farm work. It was here that he met and was influenced by Fred Ross, who recruited him into the Community Service Organization in 1952. Hardworking and dedicated, Chávez made his way up the organizational ladder very swiftly, becoming CSO regional director in 1958. In this capacity, he tried to steer the association toward advocacy of the rights of farmworkers. He met fierce resistance among CSO members who preferred to focus attention on urban and middle-class concerns. Exasperated, Chávez quit CSO in 1961 and took his family to Delano, his wife's hometown. Using his life savings, he initiated a new union, the Farm Workers Association—known later as the National Farm Workers Association and, later still, the United Farm Workers—which was founded in Fresno on 30 September 1962.

Because the UFW always focused on the family unit, women came to play prominent roles in union activities. Among them, Helen Chávez and Jessie López de la Cruz stand out. From the very outset, though, César Chávez's most trusted lieutenant—often considered cofounder of the union—was Dolores Huerta (1930–). Although eclipsed by Chávez throughout most of her life, Huerta remains in many ways, as her biographer Richard A. García has argued, a better symbol of Chicanismo than her friend and mentor.[7]

Dolores Fernández Huerta was born in Dawson, New Mexico, in 1930. Her parents divorced when she was five; and her mother, the seminal influence on her life, took the family to California. Unlike Chávez, Dolores emerged from a middle-class background. Her mother, who started off as a waitress and cannery worker, eventually came to own a hotel in Stockton, California, where Dolores was raised in an integrated neighborhood, received her early education, and met her first husband, an Anglo. After her marriage, she earned a provisional credential by attending community college and taking night classes at College of the Pacific, and became a grammar school teacher.

In the mid-fifties, however, she determined to devote herself to fighting for the rights of the underprivileged. She joined CSO, where she received her initial training as an organizer under Fred Ross, who taught her the mobilization techniques associated with Saul Alinsky. "The emphasis of Alinsky's message," writes Richard García, "coincided with hers—a pragmatic non-ideological approach to life and change."[8]

It was in CSO in 1955 that she met Chávez, initiating a lifelong though sometimes turbulent friendship. A conservative Catholic, somewhat puritanical in his value system, Chávez would always have difficulty accepting her two divorces and the apparent neglect of her children. These personal difficulties, however, rarely impeded effective collaboration by two individuals equally dedicated to the cause of ameliorating the lives of the downtrodden. When Chávez bolted CSO in 1961, Dolores Huerta followed. Together, they forged the new union. She was in Delano when the strike began. During the next few years, it would completely consume her life.

THE DELANO STRIKE

The strike against local grape growers in the Kern County city of Delano, just north of Bakersfield, was initiated by the Agricultural Workers Organizing Committee (AWOC), a Filipino union affiliated with the AFL-CIO, on 8 September 1965. Led by Larry Itliong, Filipinos struck to gain higher pay and recognition as a union, a right given to industrial workers by the National Labor Relations Act of 1935 but denied to agricultural laborers. Since most of the field hands in the area were Mexican—by the sixties, they constituted at least two-thirds of the agricultural work force in the state—Chávez was asked to join and help conduct the strike. Fearing that his own fledgling union was unprepared, he agreed with some reluctance. However, given his union's superior numbers and his characteristic determination, Chávez soon became the acknowledged leader of the entire operation.

UFW tactics and strategy at Delano mirrored Chávez's personal philosophy. Profoundly impacted by both Gandhi and Dr. King, he had come to embrace the philosophy of militant nonviolence. Like his two renowned mentors, Chávez, a devout Catholic, was against violence on principle; but he also realized, as they did, that violence was self-defeating when directed at a power with a monopoly on armed force. On the other hand, the idea of turning the other cheek, while praiseworthy as a Christian ideal, was calculated to preserve the status quo. It was essential, he felt, that the oppressed unite and assert themselves, using a variety of strategies to gain their ends. In the case of farmworkers, those objectives were better working conditions, including higher wages, and recognition of their union. Unlike many other militants of the time, Chávez believed that the American middle class was basically responsive to the needs of poor people and would support them if given the opportunity.

During the long struggle, Chávez recruited help from various disparate sources. These included the trade union movement, especially the AFL-CIO, with which he affiliated in 1966; Christian organizations, both Protestant and Catholic; radical student associations, including the Students for a Democratic Society (SDS); and other civil rights groups. Aside from alliances, he relied, too, on demonstrations, prayer sessions, marches, and fasts. His basic tactic was the strike, the *huelga,* the time-honored weapon of organized labor. Eventually, though, he discovered that a work stoppage had limited potential in small agricultural towns like Delano, where powerful growers could generally count on the support of the local citizenry, including the Mexican petite bourgeoisie, and even many of the farmworkers themselves. Beginning in 1968, Chávez came to rely on the boycott, a consumer strike, which meant that his success would depend to a large extent on winning support in urban areas throughout the country. His boycott of non-union grapes in 1968–1975, the first nationwide boycott of any kind, was highly successful. Some 12 percent of the adult American population (17 million people) honored the appeal, effectively wiping out grower profits. Still, the strike was long and hard. It finally ended in 1970, when growers reluctantly agreed to recognize the union and sign contracts with it.

Flushed with victory, the UFW had visions of organizing farmworkers throughout the country. Inspired by Chávez's example, a campesino strike had already occurred in the cantaloupe fields of Starr County in Texas in 1966, the beginning of the Chicano movement in that state. Chávez immediately dispatched Antonio Orendain, an able lieutenant, to mobilize the farmworkers of South Texas. Similar developments would soon take place in Arizona, Colorado, Washington, and other states. Even the Midwest felt repercussions. In 1967, the Toledo-based Farm Labor Organizing Committee (FLOC) was founded by Baldemar Velásquez, a native of Pharr, Texas, to fight for the rights of migrant workers.[9] Concentrating its efforts on Ohio and Michigan, the FLOC achieved its most notable victory in 1986, after an eight-year strike and boycott of the Campbell Soup Company. In neighboring Indiana, the Farm Labor Aid Committee (FLAC) was established by a number of activists, including Gilbert Cárdenas, later an eminent Chicano scholar. California, however, was the key, as Chávez knew, and he next tackled the lettuce growers of the Salinas Valley, where labor conditions were as abominable as they had been in the Great Central Valley. Relying on the same tactics as before, the union achieved moderate success.

The UFW was suddenly forced to return to Delano in 1973. Upon the expiration of the old contracts, growers, ignoring Chávez, chose instead to sign new agreements with the Teamsters Union. The International Brotherhood of Teamsters had been expelled by the AFL-CIO in 1957. A maverick union, under the leadership of Jimmy Hoffa, it would be the only major working-class organization to support the Republican party in the post–World War II period. Moreover, it was the only labor union to support the Bracero Program. Efforts to organize field hands were blatantly cynical since the Teamsters had little interest in these workers themselves; their overriding concern was the welfare of the truckers, who would be out of work without fruits and vegetables to transport. The Teamsters were intent on mobilizing campesinos to keep them *from* striking. Since their interests coincided with those of growers, the latter were anxious to end their association with the UFW and sign sweetheart contracts with the Hoffa union.

During the next few years, an acrimonious jurisdictional dispute erupted throughout the agricultural valleys of the West between the two competing unions. It was not resolved until California Governor Jerry Brown, whose sympathies lay with Chávez, entered the fray and forced a compromise: the Teamsters would have jurisdiction over cannery and packing shed workers, the UFW would have free rein over field workers. Surprisingly, the truce held. The 1975 Agricultural Labor Relations Act (ALRA), which Governor Brown guided through the state legislature, helped the UFW initially—it won almost half the 406 elections decided in the first few months—but Republican administrations in California, particularly under Governor Deukmejian, subsequently undermined its effectiveness, causing Chávez to regret his initial support of the legislation.

Unfortunately, successes were few and far between for Chávez during the next few years, as the public mood grew increasingly conservative, boding ill for both trade union and civil rights movements. The upsurge of undocumented workers brought unwelcome competition for agricultural jobs. Internal dissension compounded union problems. When Chávez died in 1993, the union was moribund. The UFW rebounded under his son-in-law, Arturo Rodríguez, but by 1995, when there were an estimated 1.6 million farmworkers in the country, membership was only 26,000, a stark contrast to the 70,000 members during the union's peak years in the mid-1970s. The difficulties in organizing farm labor had proved insurmountable. Growers were as strong as workers were weak; it truly was a David and Goliath battle. Mechanization, especially, had hurt unionization efforts.

Still, the failure to unionize farm labor should be seen in a wider perspective. Chávez brought about much-needed reforms in the fields, including medical, pension, and unemployment benefits. The determined UFW leader served as an important catalyst in this regard. He was also responsible for focusing national attention on the abuses of agribusiness interests, particularly monopolistic tendencies vis-à-vis land and water.

Moreover, it is a mistake to see and measure Chávez solely in terms of union activity. His movement was much more than an attempt to organize farmworkers; it was a vital wing of the civil rights movement, which partly accounts for the widespread support he found among churches. Chávez was concerned about the plight of Mexicans generally, not just those among them who happened to be campesinos. He succeeded in politicizing a large part of the ethnic community, his paramount contribution to the Chicano movement. Indeed, he even found this expanded focus to be too constricting. Like Gandhi and King, he eventually came to espouse the entire gamut of human rights, irrespective of race, perhaps his most enduring legacy.

In recent years, it has become fashionable to criticize Chávez's deficiencies both as man and leader. Even sympathetic observers have pointed out that he sometimes made poor decisions and fostered authoritarian tendencies within the union.

Among his own people, Chávez has been criticized from both ends of the political spectrum. Most Mexicans who dislike him allege that his movement is un-American. Often products of the Cold War era and middle class in background, these conservative critics are embarrassed by his emphasis on Mexican ethnicity, use of the tactics of confrontation, and alliances with radical groups. Even some farmworkers, usually with economic ties to agribusiness, have withheld their support. Though less evident, there is some criticism of Chávez from the other end of the political spectrum, Chicanos who assail him for his conservatism. These have generally been student radicals, often schooled in Marxist ideas, who felt that his nonviolent approach was misguided, who objected to his emphasis on Catholic symbols, or who were embittered by his rejection of La Raza ("The Race," a term used by Chicano cultural nationalists as a self-referent) as a new form of racism. Notwithstanding these criticisms from both political extremes, though, Chávez has been and remains the most respected Mexican American among his own people, three-quarters of whom, at a minimum, see him as a hero. Not surprisingly, at his death, his name was given to a variety of streets, schools, parks, and community centers, often in the face of outraged Anglo opposition. The most publicized instance occurred when Chicano students at UCLA, after a lengthy hunger strike, succeeded in getting university officials to set up a César Chávez Center for Interdisciplinary Study and Chicano and Chicana Studies.

OTHER EARLY CHICANO LEADERS

During the sixties, another extraordinary individual emerged from the ranks of the Mexican community who received national attention and, for a short while at least, had a profound impact on young Chicano activists, Reies López Tijerina (1926–).[10] Tijerina is assuredly the most fascinating and controversial of movement personalities. Born near Fall City, Texas, the son of migrant farm laborers, he was raised by his father and grandmother after his mother's premature death. At eighteen, he embraced a fundamentalist form of Protestantism and enrolled in the Assembly of God Bible Institute at Isleta (now part of El Paso), where he studied for the ministry. Expelled from the school, he became an itinerant Pentecostal evangelist. His travels took him throughout the country. In 1950, Tijerina and his coreligionists set up a utopian community near Casa Grande, Arizona, but this experiment in communalism did not last long. In 1957, he left Arizona, a fugitive from the law, and headed south, broadening his interests during his brief stay in the country of his forefathers. "Entering Mexico as an itinerant religious leader, he left it deeply motivated by the philosophy of the Mexican revolution."[11] In 1960, Tijerina made his way to New Mexico, where he championed a new cause—the crusade to recover lost Hispano lands. Toward that end, he founded the Alianza Federal de Mercedes (Federal Alliance of Land Grants) in 1963.

This improbable crusade led by an unlikely champion gained surprising support among Hispanos, people notoriously Catholic and conservative. The reasons are largely historical. During World War II, continuing the trend initiated during the Depression, Hispanos were forced to leave their traditional villages in northern New Mexico and southern Colorado in increasing numbers. Many displaced villagers headed to California, but the majority made their way to the cities nearby, notably Albuquerque. This disintegration of village life caused profound alienation. Moreover, poverty continued to be a major problem for both rural and urban residents. The war also saw the continued immigration of Anglos into the state. Now a minority within the population—by 1960, only 28.3 percent of the state population was Spanish-speaking—Hispanos saw their political clout dissipate rapidly. The rise of Tijerina, an outsider, has to be seen in the context of these desperate and deteriorating conditions.

Disillusionment was most severe in northern New Mexico, where angry villagers blamed their problems on the loss of land. Moreover, it was here that seemingly irresponsible policies established by the National Forest Service threatened the grazing and water rights of the rural Hispano populace. It was in this northern peripheral area, centering on Río Arriba County—where half the residents were on public relief—that Tijerina built a power base. Ultimately, Alianza membership reached twenty thousand.

Tijerina believed that all the problems of "Indo-Hispanos" in the Southwest stemmed from the loss of their patrimony. He charged that this land was taken illegally. The Treaty of Guadalupe Hidalgo, he argued, guaranteed Mexicans in the United States citizenship rights, including those relating to property. Even land alienated through sale had been taken illegally. Mexicans, he concluded, needed to organize to win redress through the American court system. The repossession of lost grants was to be a prelude to an even more ambitious and utopian scheme: the creation of a free city-state, the independent Republic of Chama, that would be established in northern New Mexico. Vague and backward looking, the Alianza, as Nancie L. González insightfully notes, represented a "nativistic cult movement."[12]

During the first years, from his headquarters in Albuquerque, Tijerina pursued a moderate path in his efforts to achieve victory. For the most part, he placed his faith on legal avenues; he hoped to regain lost lands through litigation. His research into land grants took him to the archives of Spain and Mexico, where he gathered materials to sustain his claims. He got nowhere; U.S. courts refused to hear the case.

In desperation, Tijerina sought to bring national attention to the plight of Hispanos and to force the government to hear him out through extralegal means. Increasingly, the Alianza resorted to fence-cutting and arson. In 1966, Tijerina occupied Echo Amphitheater, formerly an old land grant, now part of Kit Carson National Forest, arresting forest rangers for trespassing. On 5 June 1967, he and his supporters invaded the courthouse at Tierra Amarilla, county seat of Río Arriba, in an attempt to free jailed Alianza members and make a citizen's arrest of the local district attorney. A shoot-out ensued, with *aliancistas* making a getaway by taking two hostages. The largest manhunt in New Mexico history resulted in the arrest of Tijerina and his closest associates. The chief prosecution witness, a deputy sheriff, was found mysteriously beaten to death in early 1968. Later that year, Tijerina was put on trial for kidnapping and assault during the 1967 shoot-out. While admitting to being present at the courthouse, he denied having anything to do with the shooting. A forceful and charismatic speaker, Tijerina handled his own defense and, in a stunning turn of events, succeeded in winning acquittal.

Rey Tigre (King Tiger), as his admirers now called him, was soon in trouble with the law again, and this time his luck ran out. Tried on charges stemming from the Amphitheater episode and for destruction of federal property at a second incident at Kit Carson National Forest, he was found guilty in June 1969 and sentenced to prison. Jailed for two years, he was released on parole from federal prison in Springfield, Missouri, in July 1971, and placed on probation for five years. One of the conditions of his parole was that he sever all ties to the Alianza. He returned to public life, but the old fire was gone. Counseling moderation, he was no longer in the forefront of the Brown Power movement. Soon, even his supporters in New Mexico fell away. Accused of being an Elmer Gantry, a religious charlatan, Tijerina remains an enigmatic figure today. His most meaningful contribution was to dramatize the plight of the impoverished Hispano communities in New Mexico.

Unlike Chávez and Tijerina, Rodolfo ("Corky") Gonzales (1929–) realized that the future of the Mexican community would be in urban areas and that the focus should be on young people.[13] Raised in the barrios of Denver, Gonzales first achieved national prominence as a prize fighter in the early fifties. When he left the ring, he turned to Democratic politics in his hometown. In 1960, he acted as Colorado coordinator of the Viva Kennedy clubs. He then served in a variety of War on Poverty programs. "In no time," according to Stan Steiner, "he was a one-man directory of poverty agencies."[14] Like many other barrio leaders, Gonzales gradually became disillusioned with conventional party politics, and in April 1966, he founded an organization that would permit him to better serve Mexicans in Denver, La Crusada Para la Justicia (the Crusade for Justice).

An organization to mobilize the ethnic community, the Crusade focused on young people and their problems. It established a whole host of services—school, nursery, gym, art gallery, and community center—as well as its own newspaper, *El Gallo.* During the course of the late sixties, as the political climate became more radical, the Crusade embraced a more militant posture. Gonzales, an ex–G.I. Forum member, began to emphasize cultural nationalism. Before too long, he came to espouse a form of separatism. Adopting a widely held view of the time among nationalists, Corky Gonzales became the foremost champion of the idea that Aztlán, the mythical homeland of the México, was to be found in the Southwest, which he and others called "occupied America." The Crusade, going beyond Tijerina, called for the restoration of their ancestral land to Chicanos. In the meantime, Gonzales focused on direct action in the schools, launching a series of student walkouts in Denver. The Crusade also participated in Dr. King's 1968 Poor People's March on Washington, D.C., where Gonzales and Tijerina led the Chicano contingent.

By now, the idea that militant student groups throughout the country needed a unified organization had gained currency; and Gonzales, the self-appointed leader of the movement, took the initiative in sponsoring a Chicano Youth Liberation Front, a national convention of barrio youth, in Denver on 27–31 March 1969. The convention attracted more than 1,500 Chicanos. It was there that the *Spiri-*

tual Plan of Aztlán, a call for an autonomous Chicano homeland, was unveiled, and the formation of an independent Chicano party was projected.[15] A second youth conference met in Denver in May of the following year. Gonzales was now firmly committed to the idea of a separatist political party, and immediately after the 1970 conference, he and his allies launched the Colorado Raza Unida party.

The genesis of La Raza Unida occurred four years earlier. On 28 March 1966, a number of prominent Mexican delegates walked out of a conference in Albuquerque sponsored by the Equal Employment Opportunity Commission (EEOC) in protest of that organization's failure to address the pressing problems of the barrios. "The walkout in Albuquerque," it has been observed, "marked the first time that the middle-class leadership had engaged in an act of collective protest against the government."[16] President Johnson, looking to placate the dissidents, promised a White House conference of Hispanic leaders to deal with Mexican-American issues.

But it soon became obvious that LBJ was having second thoughts about the promised meeting. He had other worries at the time, first and foremost, the conflict in Vietnam. Moreover, he realized that at the proposed meeting, delegates would pressure the administration on a number of potentially embarrassing issues, including the war itself and recognition of the UFW. As the historian Julie Leininger Pycior has ably demonstrated, while LBJ was sympathetic to many Mexican causes—a sympathy stemming from early teaching experience at a "Mexican" school in Cotulla, Texas—he also had to assuage conservative Democrats and political supporters back home who represented agribusiness and ranching interests.[17] Moreover, he realized that many Hispanics, especially outside of Texas, were leaning toward his rivals for the Democratic nomination for the presidency, Senators Eugene McCarthy and Robert Kennedy. Mexican leaders pressed for the conference, but the administration was evasive. Frustration set in. Even his most staunch Mexican allies in Texas, Dr. Félix García, Vicente Ximenes, and other G.I. Forum leaders, counseled that he extend some kind of olive branch.

Eventually, the beleaguered Johnson offered a compromise. He would establish an Interagency Committee on Mexican American Affairs, to be chaired by Ximenes. The Committee, in turn, would sponsor a conference in El Paso in late October 1967, when LBJ was scheduled to meet Mexican president Gustavo Díaz Ordaz to sign a treaty returning a small piece of disputed land to Mexico. The compromise package was accepted, and one thousand representatives of Mexican community organizations throughout the country were invited to El Paso.

These delegates, however, were disappointed that the meeting would not be held at the nation's capitol. Moreover, Johnson alienated them by excluding many of their most prominent, and radical leaders, including Corky Gonzales and Reies López Tijerina. César Chávez, a zealous Kennedy supporter, was asked to attend, but he turned down the invitation because the El Paso conference refused to deal with farmworker issues.

The meeting was held as scheduled on 27–28 October 1967. Gonzales, Tijerina, and other uninvited radicals, intent on embarrassing the administration, chose to have their own meeting in El Paso, in the Mexican barrio on the southside. The radicals were joined by a number of representatives who had attended the official meeting but walked out in protest, among them Ernesto Galarza. At the alternate meeting, labeled *La Raza Unida,* the Johnson administration was roundly condemned, and delegates resolved to set up a nationwide organization that would represent Chicano interests in the coming elections. Finally, the delegates endorsed the *Plan de La Raza Unida,* a manifesto affirming Chicano solidarity. A follow-up meeting of La Raza Unida was held in San Antonio in January 1968. It drew 1,200 delegates representing fifty organizations, both middle-class and student-oriented groups.

The emerging party was mainly the brainchild of José Angel Gutiérrez (1944–), still another of the influential leaders of the Chicano movement. While Chávez and Gonzales might be considered transitional figures from the Mexican-American Generation to the Chicano Generation, Gutiérrez, because of his younger age, was firmly rooted in the latter (the idiosyncratic Tijerina belonged in a category all his own).

Gutiérrez was born in the Texas town of Crystal City, in Zavala County, the heart of the Winter Garden area. A dedicated student, he earned his B.A. at Texas A&I University in Kingsville, before moving on to graduate studies at St. Mary's University, a Catholic college in San Antonio. In 1967, while still in graduate school, he became one of the founders of a Chicano student organization, the Mexican American Youth Organization (MAYO).[18] Two years later, Gutiérrez and other MAYO leaders, including Mario Campeán and Willie Velásquez, initiated the Winter Garden Project, a Ford Foundation–funded campaign to maximize Mexican political power in a ten-county area along the Rio Grande, centered in Crystal City. Concurrently, Gutiérrez and his MAYO confederates were among the most active promoters and participants at the El Paso and San Antonio La Raza Unida conferences, where they eagerly embraced the concept of a Chicano political party.

In January 1970, translating the widespread aspiration into concrete reality, MAYO created El Partido de la Raza Unida, popularly called La Raza Unida party (LRUP).[19] Established in the Winter Garden area, it was intended to serve as an electoral vehicle in local school board and city council contests. In the spring elections, Gutiérrez and other LRUP leaders ran for office. The party had a spectacularly auspicious beginning: Crystal City Mexicans won two council seats and three school board seats, one of them belonging to Gutiérrez. These successes were repeated in two other predominantly Mexican communities nearby, Cotulla and Carrizo Springs. His good fortune prompted the hardworking Gutiérrez to expand his political horizons. He was determined to make LRUP a national association, a third party for Chicanos in competition with the two traditional choices.

In Colorado, meanwhile, Corky Gonzales had similar plans. As we have seen, in the spring of 1970 a Colorado LRUP was established in Denver just a few months after Gutiérrez had initiated his regional organization of the same name in South Texas. Beginning in late 1970, under the Tejano's influence, LRUP chapters began appearing in California. It was Gonzales, however, who took the initiative for a nationwide party first. At his urging, three thousand delegates from throughout the Southwest and parts of the Midwest met in El Paso on 1–4 September 1972. The result was the establishment of a national Raza Unida party.

Unfortunately, this first national convention would also be the last. Problems surfaced immediately, as the meeting was marred by massive internal dissension. Two factions emerged, a moderate group looking to Gutiérrez, who saw the party as a vehicle to achieve political power, and a radical contingent headed by Gonzales, who wanted the party to take a more ideological path by dealing with issues of class and gender. Additionally, moderates were willing to consider electoral alliances with the established parties in the coming elections. Radicals were vehemently opposed to this kind of interparty cooperation. Tensions were exacerbated by personal animosity between the two ambitious leaders. The moderates ultimately won out; Gutiérrez was elected chairman of the new party.

Work began immediately on extending LRUP into other parts of the Southwest in preparation for the 1972 primary and general elections. While LRUP was able to gain a small following in New Mexico, Arizona, and California, results at the polls were almost uniformly disappointing. In fact, electoral victories were confined to South Texas.

The party never came close to meeting the lofty expectations of its founders. LRUP declined for the same reasons that the entire Chicano movement, which it claimed to head, fell apart. There were also causes that were particular to its situation. The reticence of Mexicans, both the leadership and the rank and file, to abandon the Democratic party was one. Democrats continued to get about three-quarters of the Mexican vote. Chávez, in particular, was wedded to the Democrats; and in California, his power base, he was constantly at odds with LRUP. Older middle-class organizations, like the G.I. Forum, LULAC, and even MAPA, kept their allegiance to the Democrats, despite their professed nonpartisan stances. Moreover, using confrontational tactics, LRUP leaders managed to alienate many potential allies. Regionalism also played a role: the Tejanos, who controlled the party, found that other Chicanos in the Southwest were anxious to maintain their freedom of action. Finally, there was the inability of leaders to work together. As would be true in virtually all Chicano and Mexican-American organizations, personality clashes were grave impediments to effective teamwork. Increasingly alienated by Gutiérrez, Gonzales left LRUP in 1974, taking his followers with him. Shortly thereafter, the Tejano was challenged for control of the party even in the Winter Garden, his old stronghold. By the mid-1970s, the party was in shambles.

THE CHICANO STUDENT MOVEMENT

To a large extent, the Raza Unida party, notably through the agency of MAYO, reflected the influence of Chicano students. By 1970, the Chicano movement, it appeared, was increasingly dominated by young people, students in high schools and universities concerned especially with the multitude of problems they experienced in these institutions. Among the issues were de facto segregation, racist instructors, the tracking system, and, in institutions of higher learning, inadequate recruitment and funding.

Student activism among Mexicans was not altogether a recent phenomenon. As with other aspects of the Chicano movement, there were notable historical roots. According to Carlos Muñoz, Jr., who has written the most complete study of the Chicano movement to date, the origins of Mexican student activism "can be traced to 1929 when Ernesto Galarza, then a twenty-four-year-old graduate student in history at Stanford University, spoke out in defense of Mexican immigrant workers."[20] More significantly, in 1942 the Mexican-American Movement, Inc. (MAM), a student association which grew out of YMCA-sponsored Mexican Youth Conferences in Southern California, was formed. Led by Paul Coronel and Félix Gutiérrez, it was dedicated to the promotion of educational opportunities for the Mexican community. The main precursor of the Chicano student movement was undoubtedly MAM.

By the mid-sixties, the ferment of the youth movement had impacted Chicanos, who eagerly embraced militant forms of protest. The intellectual sources of student militancy among Chicanos were varied. Almost any form of resistance to oppression was appealing. Students looked to their more militant elders for inspiration, preeminent among them being Chávez and Tijerina. The Black Power movement was a second major contributor. The Mexican Revolution, personified by Pancho Villa and Emiliano Zapata, was still another source of intellectual inspiration. Many students came under the sway of socialism. They looked to Marx, Mao, and especially the heroes of the Cuban Revolution, Che Guevara and Fidel Castro. The Vietnam antiwar protest had an impact, as well.

By 1970, after its formative stage, perhaps the cardinal influence on the growing youth movement was that of indigenismo. By now, students were heavily committed to the idea of cultural regeneration, which, as in the case of blacks, meant a glorification of the motherland. It was the Indian legacy, however, that they found attractive, rather than that of the Spanish, who were doubly condemned for being white and imperialist.

The Chicano *student* movement—as contrasted to other aspects of *La Causa* (the Cause)—began in the mid-sixties; that is, it emerged simultaneously with the other Chicano efforts previously described. The first of the student organizations espousing some form of Chicanismo was the Student Initiative founded at San Jose State College by Armando Valdez in 1964. Three years later, in 1967, several other militant campus organizations appeared. Texas and California took the lead. In the Lone Star State, besides the aforementioned MAYO in San Antonio, there was the Mexican American Student Organization (MASO) at the University of Texas at Austin. In southern California, the Mexican American Student Association (MASA) appeared at East Los Angeles Community College. It was overshadowed at the outset, however, by the United Mexican American Students (UMAS), which established chapters at UCLA, USC, Loyola, and a number of state colleges. In northern California, where the student movement was more radical than in the southland, the dominant organization was the Mexican American Student Confederation (MASC), which grew out of the Student Initiative at San Jose. MASC established chapters at Fresno State, Sacramento State, and Hayward State in 1967, and UC Berkeley the following year.

These student groups all tried to extend their authority beyond their immediate area. The most fortunate in this regard was UMAS, which was able to spread beyond California, opening up chapters at the University of Colorado at Boulder in 1968 and penetrating other parts of the Southwest the following year. Soon it also entered the Midwest. Its first chapter there was set up by Gilbert Cárdenas at the University of Notre Dame in South Bend, Indiana.

Beginning at the college level, student militancy quickly spread to younger students. On 3 March 1968, Latino dissatisfaction with the school system became evident at the high school level. On that fateful day, Chicano students in East Los Angeles, in an effort to get school administrations to address their many problems, walked out of several local high schools. They were led by Sal Castro, a Lincoln High School teacher. These "blowouts," as they were called, soon spread to other schools in what was then the largest school district in the country. Altogether, over fifteen thousand students were involved. Eventually, thirteen strike leaders, including UMAS members Moctezuma Esparza, from UCLA, and Carlos Muñoz, Jr., an ex-serviceman, now chapter president at Los Angeles State College, were indicted on conspiracy charges (dropped two years later).

The Los Angeles strike received national attention. It also stimulated student activism in other cities. During the next few months, walkouts occurred in high schools throughout the Southwest and beyond. Those in Denver and South

Texas were the largest and received the most media attention. Student demands included the hiring of Mexican instructors, counselors, and administrators; bilingual and bicultural education; and closer cooperation between schools and the barrio.

However, the repercussions of the East Los Angeles blowouts went beyond the high school. A few months later, Mexican students at San Jose State walked out of their graduation, the first protest activity by Chicanos on a college campus. Other Chicanos participated at the massive strike instigated by the Third World Liberation Front (TWLF) at San Francisco State in November 1968. A TWLF strike ensued at UC Berkeley during the first half of 1969. Chicano students, who had played only a supporting role at San Francisco, were among the most active supporters of the Berkeley demonstration. By now, it was clear, the Chicano student movement was rapidly moving to the left and increasingly involved with issues that concerned other radical students.

In early 1969, Chicano students, dispersed in a number of student clubs, sought to achieve a measure of cohesion through the establishment of a nationwide organization. The opportunity arose at a conference held in April at UC Santa Barbara, one of the strongholds of the mushrooming movement. The conference was called by the Chicano Coordinating Committee on Higher Education (CCHE), formed in 1968 by a group of concerned college students and professors. About one hundred delegates—students, instructors, and administrators—were present. They came from throughout the state of California and other parts of the Southwest. Among the most dynamic participants were Jesús Chavarría, a young professor at UCSB and the dominant personality at the meeting; Juan Gómez-Quiñones, who had been one of the prime movers of the meeting; and the ubiquitous Carlos Muñoz, Jr., the future chronicler of the Chicano student movement. The three-day Santa Barbara convention had two meaningful results: (1) the drafting of the *Plan de Santa Bárbara,* a program of educational reform calling for the institution of Chicano Studies programs, and (2) the establishment of El Movimiento Estudiantil de Aztlán (MECHA or MEChA, The Student Movement of Aztlán), an organization intended to supersede all other student groups by uniting them under the banner of cultural nationalism.[21] The convention, and the organization it spawned, mirrored the increasingly radical notions espoused by Corky Gonzales, whose appeal was at its height at this time. Several weeks before, a number of the delegates at Santa Barbara had attended the Denver Youth Conference, where the Spiritual Plan of Aztlán had been formulated. Gómez-Quiñones had been one of its principal authors.

Naturally, educational issues were of paramount importance to MECHA, as they were to other student associations. Like them, too, it put major emphasis on community involvement, working with a variety of local Chicano community service and political action groups. *Mechistas* were especially active in support of the UFW and LRUP, in spite of the bad blood between the two organizations.

MECHA went into a serious tailspin between 1971 and 1973, from which it never completely recovered. There are many reasons for this diminished status. The enthusiasm that inspired the organization initially could not be sustained after the original leaders left college. Internal divisions took their toll, as well. The dominant nationalist emphasis was challenged in the early seventies by a social-ist-inspired wing insisting that class issues receive priority over ethnic consider-ations. This point of view was ultimately rejected, and distraught socialists abandoned the organization in droves. The same went for frustrated Chicanas who found MECHA reluctant to deal with feminist issues.

Given its numerous problems, it is easy to see why MECHA failed to achieve its ambitious program. It remains today a loose federation of chapters scattered throughout California. The failure of MECHA parallels the ultimate decline of the Chicano student movement in general. Its strengths and weaknesses are best sum-marized by Juan Gómez-Quiñones, whose participation gives his insights par-ticular cogency: "At its best, the work of student activists has been seminal in its influence on much later activity as well as generously courageous in its militancy; at its worst, it has been anarchic and self-indulgent, given to rhetoric and organi-zational inconsistency."[22]

THE CHICANO MOVEMENT IN THE COMMUNITY

The Chicano Power movement was not confined to students; Chicanismo was also pervasive in barrios, where it was particularly evident among the work-ing class. The most important of the militant barrio organizations was the Brown Berets. A paramilitary group, it was founded in East Los Angeles in 1967 by David Sánchez, Carlos Móntez, and Ralph Ramírez, all of them college students at the time. The Brown Berets, however, were relatively unconcerned with the univer-sity; their focus was on the barrio, where they targeted police brutality and drug use in the community. They also took a special interest in the youth and played a conspicuous role in the 1968 school walkouts. Sánchez, Móntez, and Ramírez were among the strike leaders put on trial afterwards. In 1969, they claimed to have chapters in twenty-seven cities other than Los Angeles, including Denver and San Antonio. By this time, the Vietnam War had become a major priority.

During the previous year, antiwar sentiment in the country had been trans-formed into a massive movement uniting students and communities throughout the country, and Chicanos were in the forefront of the protest. Not all Mexicans opposed the war—the G.I. Forum was a firm supporter of U.S. involvement, especially under LBJ—but Chicano students found that their opposition was generally shared by their families in the barrios. This contestation was understand-able: the war had escalated steadily since August 1964, when the infamous Tonkin Resolution gave LBJ carte blanche to stop Communist aggression in Southeast Asia; and, as in World War II and Korea, Mexicans played a leading role.

Inspired by patriotism, machismo, and the chance to escape dead-end jobs in rural towns and urban barrios—the primary motives cited by the soldiers them-selves in Charley Trujillo's absorbing series of interviews, *Soldados: Chicanos in Viet Nam* (1990)—many Mexican youths volunteered for service. A high percent-age entered high-risk branches of the service, such as the U.S. Marine Corps. The majority were drafted. Undereducated, and often ignorant of their rights, Mexi-cans were prime targets for draft boards. Hispanos, for example, made up 27 percent of the New Mexican population in 1970, but they supplied 69 percent of all draftees from that state. Even more than most wars, Vietnam was fought by poor people. Studies conducted by Prof. Ralph Guzmán in 1969 indicated that Mexicans and other Hispanics were overrepresented in Southeast Asia—on the battle front and on the casualty lists. Constituting about 11 percent of the popu-lation in the Southwest in 1960, Mexicans apparently represented close to 20 percent of the region's soldiers killed in battle during the following decade.

By the war's end, according to Rubén Treviso, an ex-intelligence case officer in Southeast Asia, "One of every five Hispanics who went to Vietnam was killed in action."[23] This is clearly an exaggeration. However, while it is impossible to deter-mine precisely, impressionistic evidence suggests, as Treviso and minority schol-ars claim, that Hispanics did indeed make a disproportionate contribution to the war effort. The Vietnam War Memorial in Washington, D.C., for example, indi-cates that 103 Garcías, 86 Gonzálezes, and 75 Martínezes (the three most com-mon Hispanic names on the monument) died in battle, compared to 660 Smiths, 523 Johnsons, and 346 Joneses (the three most common "Anglo" names).[24] But Hispanics, according to the 1960 census, constituted only about 5 percent of the U.S. population, so one would expect the ratio of deaths to be closer to 20:1 rather than the less than 7:1 disparity. Fresno State University professor Lea Ybarra—who had eighteen cousins serving in Vietnam, as well as her only brother—claims that more than ten thousand Hispanics died in the war.[25]

Many Mexicans distinguished themselves on the field of battle. Thirteen Hispanics were awarded the Medal of Honor, among them Marine Sgt. Alfredo González from Edinburg, Texas, who died in battle in 1968. Twenty-eight years later, he became the first Mexican American to have a destroyer named after him by the U.S. Navy. In general, the war was fought by minorities and working-class whites. It was not long before the white middle class, who had hailed the war as a moral crusade against Communism at the beginning, came to the conclusion that the escalating conflict was morally indefensible—after most deferments were abolished in early 1970 and the burden of financing the war fell increasingly on to their shoulders. The irony was that those youths being asked to lay down their lives to protect the American Way, the poor of the nation, were largely the very individuals who had gained least from it.

Spearheading Mexican opposition to the war was the Chicano Moratorium Committee, consisting of both students and members of the community in southern California. The Brown Berets was the most conspicuous of the barrio groups. David Sánchez, Brown Beret prime minister, was cochair of the Chicano Moratorium Committee, together with Rosalio Muñoz, former UCLA student body president. The Moratorium Committee was responsible for a series of protest marches in East Los Angeles in 1970–1971.

The most memorable demonstration occurred on 29 August 1970, when thirty thousand people gathered at Laguna Park to protest U.S. involvement in Vietnam and the disproportionate loss of Latino lives in the conflict. Chicano representatives came from all over the Southwest. Corky Gonzales was one of the featured speakers. Intended as a peaceful demonstration, the crowd got out of hand when provoked by the police. In the aftermath, three Mexicans were killed. These included Rubén Salazar, who died under mysterious circumstances.[26] Salazar, a reporter for the *Los Angeles Times* and news director of KMEX-TV, was sitting at a bar with some friends when he was struck in the head by a tear-gas projectile fired by a deputy sheriff. Since he was in the process of preparing an exposé on law enforcement in Los Angeles, the circumstances of his death aroused instant suspicion. Even staunch defenders of law and order condemned the injustice: "Whatever the rights and wrongs of what Chicano activists called an Anglo police riot, there was no excuse for what, according to the coroner's inquest, was the unprovoked killing of Salazar."[27] The incident incensed the Latino community in Los Angeles—the officer who shot Salazar was never charged with a crime, though negligence was obvious to many—and angry demonstrations continued for months.

Like the Black Panthers, after whom they patterned themselves, the Brown Berets were subject to intense police repression during this time, and like the black militant group, they gradually changed their emphasis from confrontation to more productive and concrete forms of community service, including educational projects and soup kitchens. Beset by internal dissension, the Brown Berets announced their disbandment in 1972.

Most barrio-based organizations were considerably less conspicuous than the Brown Berets. Yet one of the most effective of these was the Centro de Acción Social Autónoma–Hermandad General de Trabajadores (CASA-HGT, Center of Autonomous Social Action–General Brotherhood of Workers), called by one Chicano scholar, "the most salient progressive organization functioning in the

Mexican community" during the seventies.[28] Set up in Los Angeles in 1968 and headed by Soledad ("Chole") Alatorre and Bert Corona, CASA stressed working-class interests. Moreover, it advocated the transnational organization of ethnic Mexican workers without reference to formal citizenship status, a logical orientation given the development of a regional capitalism that seemingly made the Mexican-U.S. border superfluous. However, during the early 1970s, increasingly dominated by "Young Turks" like Magdalena Mora, CASA moved steadily to the left, becoming a bulwark of Marxism before its demise in 1978. In spite of its brief existence, it influenced many other organizations, even after the heyday of the movimiento. Alatorre and Corona, meanwhile, eschewed the more ideological orientation of CASA, choosing instead to focus their efforts on assisting indocumentados in combating deportation and gaining permanent residency through La Hermandad Mexicana Nacional (The Mexican National Brotherhood), an organization established in the early fifties.

Not all community organizations were run by working-class residents. Some of the most influential and enduring were Chicano organizations set up by professionals. Perhaps the two most productive associations of this type were the Mexican American Legal Defense and Education Fund (MALDEF) and the Southwest Council of La Raza (SWCLR). MALDEF was conceived in 1967 by Chicanos in Texas who hoped to provide much-needed legal services to the community. Founders included Peter Tijerina, Gregory Luna, and Mario Obledo. Eventually, MALDEF was able to prosper not only because of its effectiveness in securing funding from private foundations and by winning cases but also because of its excellent leadership, notably executive directors Vilma Martínez, Joaquín Avila, and Antonia Hernández. Its impact has been profound. "MALDEF," according to the political scientist Maurilio E. Vigil, "has done more to address the problems, needs and concerns of Chicanos than any other contemporary Chicano organization."[29]

The SWCLR was established in 1968 in Phoenix to provide technical assistance and help fund community-based organizations in border states. Four years later, it went national, changing its name to the National Council of La Raza (NCLR) and establishing its headquarters in Washington, D.C. Aided by Hermán Gallegos, Henry Santiestevan, and Maclovio Barraza, Raúl Yzaguirre, from San Juan, Texas, took the initiative in forming the influential advocacy organization, which he continues to lead. Other prominent Chicanos identified with NCLR were Bert Corona and Ernesto Galarza, both of whom seemed to have been involved with virtually every major civil rights initiative during these halcyon years.

From the old SWCLR came the idea, in 1975, for the Southwest Voter Registration Education Project (SWVRP), a Texas-based organization that was extremely effective, under the leadership of ex-LRUP leader Willie Velásquez

(1944–1988), in mobilizing Mexicans to participate in the political process. The SWVRP eventually turned its attention to litigation, working closely with MALDEF.

Educators were some of the most active professionals in the Chicano movement. The oldest of their organizations was the Association of Mexican American Educators (AMAE), established in California in 1965 among teachers and administrators to promote quality education for Mexican youth. Sal Castro was one of the founders. During its first years, AMAE campaigned vigorously for bilingual and bicultural educational programs.

A more militant educators' organization was the National Association for Chicano Studies (NACS). The idea of a national Chicano association of activist scholars emerged in 1972–1973. Among the founding fathers were Carlos Muñoz, Jr., José Cuéllar, and Jaime Sena-Rivera. A series of informal meetings culminated in the first annual convention in May 1974 of the National Association of Chicano Social Scientists, as the group was first called, at UC Irvine. During the first years, the most dedicated members, in addition to those cited above, included Tomás Almaguer, Lea Ybarra, Adaljiza Sosa Riddell, José Limón, and Mario Barrera, who are today all prominent scholars.

Although NACS has survived to the present, it has always experienced internal disputes due to both personality clashes and differences in philosophical approaches. The most recent threats to unity, according to the historian Ignacio M. García, have come from members advocating lesbian-feminism, neo-Marxism, or a militant form of Latinoism.[30] These same difficulties have beset Chicano Studies programs, which NASC has unsuccessfully attempted to coordinate into a cohesive network. Since the early 1980s, these programs have suffered a steady decline in enrollment.

THE CHICANA MOVEMENT

After about 1970, a new force began to surface within the movement: feminism. While feminism has a history in the Mexican community that can be traced at least as far back as the Liga Femenil Mexicanista (Mexican Feminist League), established in 1911 by Jovita Idar (1885–1946) in Laredo, the movimiento at its inception in the sixties had little concern for women's liberation, a neglect it shared with other civil rights movements. Although advanced in their political ideas, many Chicanos were very traditional in their views of women and the family.[31] Consequently, in the various Chicano organizations, active participation by Chicanas was discouraged; it seemed that they were inevitably relegated to subordinate positions, such as secretaries, cooks, and janitors. Outright sexual harassment of female members was not uncommon. Many Chicanas gradually came to realize that they were worse off than their *compañeros* (male comrades) since they were subject to triple oppression: exploitation based on race, class, *and* gender. As they sought a greater voice in the movement, they encountered considerable resistance. At the 1969 National Chicano Youth Conference in Denver, delegates, mostly male, resolved that Chicanas were opposed to their own liberation! Middle-class Chicanas also had a difficult time gaining a forum for their views. In 1970, efforts to establish a Chicana caucus at the annual convention of MAPA proved premature.

Some of the feminist criticism came from the ranks of their own sisters. As Anna Nieto-Gómez, herself an early feminist champion, has pointed out, women within the Chicano movement soon came to be divided into two general categories, which she calls the "loyalists" and the "feminists."[32] The first recognized that mujeres were oppressed within their own ethnic communities but felt that ultimately Anglo institutions were to blame. Moreover, they believed that criticism of Mexican men would serve only to sow the seeds of dissension. Feminists argued that the oppression they experienced within their own communities was as bad as that encountered from the dominant society. They felt that in returning to their cultural roots, many Chicanos had unfortunately come to glorify all aspects of the culture indiscriminately, including misogynistic elements. They insisted on speaking out against the machismo and sexual abuse rampant in the movement.

This widening schism among women activists came out in the open at the First National Chicana Conference, *Mujeres Por La Raza* (Women for La Raza), in May 1971, when six hundred delegates from the Southwest and Midwest met in Houston. The debates were extremely animated and the two sides polarized. Eventually, loyalists, almost half the delegates in attendance, walked out of the meeting in protest, ostensibly because of alleged neglect of mujeres in the barrio.

At first, feminists were put on the defensive by charges of being sellouts. Labeled traitors, they came to identify with La Malinche, who though much maligned historically for helping Cortés conquer her own people, was now adopted as a symbol of womanhood and revered as the mother of the Mexican mestizo. Moreover, their critics tried to discredit them by identifying emerging feminism with the small lesbian minority within their ranks, thus cashing in on the homophobia that pervades Mexican culture.

Undaunted, Chicana feminists began to form their own caucuses within Chicano conferences. They also initiated their own publications. While not exclusively feminist in its orientation, one of the earliest and most influential was *Regeneración,* which appeared in Los Angeles beginning in 1971. *Encuentro Femenil,* published by Nieto-Gómez and Adelaida del Castillo in 1973–1974, was the first major student publication. Chicana feminists worked with community-based women's service organizations, and before long they created their own associations distinct from those of other members of La Causa. In fact, some of them antedated the Houston Conference. Among these early women's groups were Las Chicanas at San Diego State University and Hijas de Cuauhtémoc at Long Beach State University. The Chicana movement—i.e., the movement championing the rights of Mexican women—was emerging from the shadow of the Chicano movement.

As they encountered increasing hostility by some segments of the Mexican community, some Chicana groups attempted to make common cause with their counterparts in the white feminist movement which had resurfaced in the early sixties. In 1973, for example, they formed the Chicana Women's Political Caucus within the National Women's Political Caucus. For the most part, though, these early attempts at cooperation turned out to be disillusioning. Alfredo Mirandé and Evangelina Enríquez explain:

> The Anglo women's movement showed itself to be indifferent to the unique needs of Chicanas, assuming that it could unite all women in the struggle against sexism but minimizing or neglecting the issues of race and poverty. . . . What Anglo feminists failed to see was that it was not possible for Chicanas to conceive of a separate women's movement independent of their racial-cultural struggle, just as it had not been possible for them to separate their problems as women from their racial oppression.[33]

Several dynamic leaders emerged from the early Chicana movement. Some of them tended to focus their efforts on the community, others on the schools. Community involvement was particularly strong among Tejanas, but perhaps the most talented and respected barrio activist of this period was Francisca Flores, from Los Angeles. Together with Ramona Morín, Flores founded the California League of Mexican American Women, a political action association, in the mid-sixties. Beginning in 1963, she and Delfino Varela published *Carta Editorial* to keep the community informed on issues relating to Mexicans. When the paper changed its name to *Regeneración* in the seventies, Flores became its chief editor. In October 1970, she was one of the cofounders of the L.A.-based Comisión Femenil Mexicana Nacional (CFMN, National Commission of Mexican Women), the first major national feminista organization, and one which played a leading role in organizing the Houston Conference. A representative of the women's auxiliary of the Pomona G.I. Forum, Flores was among the most outspoken defenders of the feminist perspective at Houston, a defense she continued in the pages of *Regeneración*. Another Flores initiative was the Chicana Service Action Center (CSAC), an employment counseling and manpower training program. For years, she and Alicia Escalante, who founded the East Los Angeles Welfare Rights Organization in 1967, remained the most authoritative voices of Chicana feminism in southern California.

Among the many academicians who were pioneers in the movement, several stand out. Perhaps the most productive and persevering was Martha P. Cotera (1938–). Born in the state of Chihuahua, Cotera was brought to the United States at the age of eight. After receiving her education at Texas Western University (now the University of Texas at El Paso) and Antioch College, she worked as a librarian in Austin until 1968. Two years later, together with her husband, she was one of the founders of Jacinto Treviño College—now defunct—which specialized in preparing teachers for bilingual education programs. By now, Cotera was heavily involved in the Chicano movement and had enough support to run for public office as a member of LRUP, where she joined Rosie Castro and Virginia Músquiz as one of a small group of women in the party leadership. María L. Hernández (1896–1986), a community activist since the twenties, now an LRUP stalwart, served as her mentor. A staunch feminista, Cotera helped found the Texas Women's Political Caucus in 1973, and a year later, she set up a nonprofit Chicana Research and Learning Center in Austin, an umbrella organization which encouraged and helped fund projects aimed at empowering minority women. Her publications on feminism have gained widespread acclaim, making Marta Cotera one of the leading educators involved in the Chicana movement.

Chicanas were active in championing all the causes Chicanos espoused, but their focus was consistently on women's issues. These included welfare rights, child care, sexual discrimination in employment, abortion, and birth control. Throughout the seventies, they were also adamant in their opposition to involuntary sterilization programs that victimized poor minority women. In colleges, their main contribution was the establishment of Chicana Studies classes beginning in 1968 and Chicana Studies programs a little later. These feminist programs were rapidly adopted by institutions of higher learning throughout the Southwest. Their greatest success was in California, the stronghold of Chicana feminism, where Nieto-Gómez, Gracia Molina de Pick, and Corinna Sánchez led the way in their foundation. But in the early seventies, the Chicana movement was only in its infancy. Ultimately, it was to survive the hard years ahead much better than the Chicano movement.

THE DECLINE OF CHICANISMO

The heterogeneous nature of the movement, given the community it represented, was inevitable; but problems were bound to surface. It was very difficult to get organizations and individuals to lay aside their specific agendas for the common welfare. The growing rift between Chicanos and Chicanas was only the most glaring example. Even *within* organizations, personal squabbles worked against unity. The same factionalism that characterized LRUP was evident in the

Brown Berets and MAPA. The authorities were only too happy to encourage this state of affairs. One well-informed scholar states, "Police provocation to commit not only violent acts but more frequently counterproductive actions was a fact; and of course led to the promotion of dissension within or between groups as well as individuals."[34] Moreover, no one leader emerged from the pack to give direction to the movement—not even Chávez, whose modest education and social conservatism ill suited him for the role that Dr. King played among blacks.

It should also be noted that not all Mexicans bought into the movement. As might be expected, many older and more affluent Mexican Americans, especially Hispanos in New Mexico and Colorado, had difficulty identifying with the goals of the movement, let alone endorsing the tactics. Called *tapados* (literally "stuffed up people," i.e., those who refuse to hear the truth) or, worse still, *vendidos* by Chicano sympathizers, they were quickly alienated by what they perceived to be the excesses of the militants. In truth, even elements within the movement— among them, some of the most active defenders of Mexican rights, including César Chávez, Bert Corona, and Anthony Quinn—decried extremist tendencies. The point of view of more moderate Chicanos was best expressed by Rodolfo de la Garza, then on the Political Science faculty of Colorado College, as the movement lost its impetus:

> I am convinced that American society has never dealt justly with Mexican Americans and that Anglo politicians have systematically deprived us of our political rights. Nonetheless, it is also my belief that we must accept some of the responsibility for the situation in which we find ourselves. . . . Too many of us, however, have ignored the example Chávez and the farm workers have given us and instead have resorted to rhetoric and have blamed others for all our problems. We must never allow Anglo society to deny the oppression imposed upon us, but we must also recognize that unless we admit our own weaknesses we can never correct them.[35]

Some working-class people expressed reservations also. Most immigrants, for example, especially recent immigrants, shied away from the movement. To some extent, this reservation reflects the subtle tension that has always existed between the Mexican immigrant and the native-born Mexican American—as is true historically of almost any immigrant community in American society. Recent immigrants are generally preoccupied with making a living. Moreover, despite their problems, they are grateful for the opportunity to improve their lives.

But ultimately, the failure of the movimiento needs to be seen in a broader context. Despite its deficiencies and weaknesses, the fact of the matter is that all the civil rights movements faded, not just the Brown Power movement. The political and intellectual climate of the country changed drastically with the end of the Vietnam War in 1975. Problems, perceived and real, with the economy altered priorities, as well. As Americans approached the eighties, the concern for human rights was eclipsed by the desire for financial security. Mexicans were forced to fight hard just to retain their recent gains in a period of conservative ascendancy.

THE CHICANO LEGACY

Writing about the Chicano movement in the early 1990s, one observer tersely commented, "Nothing remains of it now but a handshake practiced by middle-aged men."[36] Granted, there does not appear to be much militancy among Mexicans today, either in the barrios or in the schools. Even the term *Chicano* has fallen upon bad times. Nevertheless, it could be argued that the legacy of the movement is very much alive.

Chicano activists were correct when they acted on the premise that American institutions respond to the needs of a minority community only when they are forced to. A good example was the War on Poverty. The programs emanating from that government-sponsored campaign were initially concessions to the black community, thanks in part to the riots of the mid-sixties, but also to the efforts of the black civil rights movement. It was largely Chicano militancy that forced LBJ to include Mexicans, who received many benefits, not the least of which was the opportunity for leadership training in government-supported programs.[37] There are literally hundreds of community service organizations today serving the Mexican community that trace their roots to the turbulent decade between 1965 and 1975.

The Brown Power movement had other benefits as well. Reform legislation was one. Bilingual and bicultural education, for example, owes its existence to Chicano pressure. In terms of higher education, the single most important contribution may well be Chicano and Chicana Studies programs, strongholds of Chicanismo, instituted in more than one hundred universities throughout the nation. A monument to the efforts of student militants, these programs continue to exist—those at UCLA, UC Berkeley, and the University of Texas at Austin seem to be the most active—serving the student community and producing innovative scholarly research on a host of topics. Virtually all Latino college professors, in or out of Ethnic Studies departments, were impacted by the movement. Through them, its values continue to be transmitted to a powerful audience, the future leaders of a multicultural society.

The movement has had a profound influence on artists. Beginning with El Teatro Campesino, established by Luis Valdez as an adjunct to the UFW in the mid-sixties, Chicanismo became a vital force in the arts. Ultimately, it spurred a cultural renaissance which continues to enrich not only the Mexican community but American society as a whole. Finally, there is the sense of pride that it fostered among Mexicans, both men and women, especially the youth. Undoubtedly, this is its single most beneficial contribution.

Themselves products of La Causa, most Chicano historians who have studied the Chicano movement tend to see it as the culmination of Mexican-American history. In point of fact, the movimiento was an episode in that history, albeit a very important one. The movement has come and gone, as scholars David Hayes-Bautista and Gregory Rodríguez rightly conclude, but the people are still there.[38]

It is a mistake to identify Chicanismo solely with students. Armando Navarro, who has done the most comprehensive study on MAYO to date, is representative of this tendency.[39] But this proclivity is most obvious in the work of another political scientist, Carlos Muñoz, Jr., himself an ardent activist in his student days, as has been made abundantly clear.[40] Professor Muñoz makes a good point when he insists that students were on the cutting edge of the Causa; however, his propensity to define Brown Power entirely in terms of a youth movement is much too restrictive. He neglects the middle-class associations created by the Mexican-American Generation, organizations like LULAC and CSO.

Moreover, the exclusion of other activists of the sixties is highly suspect. For example, in assessing César Chávez, Muñoz avers, "In fact, Chávez has been and remains the leader of a labor movement and later a union struggle that was never an integral part of the Chicano movement."[41] An LRUP member at one point, apparently Muñoz is unwilling to look for unifying factors. To exclude Chávez, Tijerina, and leaders of that ilk is to do grave injustice to them and their contributions.

In sum, the movement was extremely varied. Indeed, it would be more accurate to describe several Chicano movements. Although the students were more vocal and radical, consequently grabbing the headlines, most militant organizations were not student-centered. In fact, as the historian Ignacio García argues, despite appearances, "a closer look at the Movement reveals that it remained dominated not by students or youth but by adults who had experienced Anglo-American prejudice for an extended period."[42] These activists were to be found in a variety of community groups, some operating in urban barrios, others in rural settings. Most catered to the working class.

Contrary to Muñoz's interpretation, however, middle-class organizations were also well represented in the movement. In the decade between 1965 and 1975, older middle-class associations like LULAC, CSO, MAPA, and even the G.I.

Forum embraced the concept of La Raza, albeit reluctantly at times. The spectrum within the movement extended from the moderate position endorsed by the G.I. Forum to the radical philosophy of the Brown Berets, with student groups—who were more moderate than their rhetoric would suggest—somewhere in the middle. What these various organizations had in common was that they all sought, through the tactics of confrontation, to gain political representation in order to protect their civil rights, and they all rejected breakneck assimilation into the American mainstream, opting instead for some form of cultural pluralism.

PAIN AND PROMISE

1975–1998

9

Unlike other social scientists, historians approach the study of contemporary events with some trepidation. While the factual record may be relatively clear, it is extremely difficult to interpret significant trends. Nevertheless, in this chapter an attempt will be made to discover these currents as they relate to Mexicans in the United States. The political generation that emerged in barrios after the mid-1970s, labeled the Post-Chicano Generation—or the Hispanic Generation, given its more conservative nature—by Chicano historians, has lived in a time of rapid and confusing change. Most Chicano scholars, influenced by the high expectations of the preceding decade, have tended to accentuate the negative. The political gains from the mid-1970s to the mid-1990s, for the most part a period of Republican ascendancy, appear minimal. Socioeconomically, too, the vast promise held out by the Chicano movement never seemed to materialize. And yet, upon closer examination, it is possible to detect more hopeful signs for the future. This chapter will try to present a balanced portrait of the contemporary Mexican community in the United States by focusing on its frustrations and achievements, on its pain and promise.[1]

DEMOGRAPHICS

Mexicans maintained a high profile in American society after the 1970s. There were many reasons for this emerging trend—bilingualism, affirmative action, and so on—but perhaps the most salient was the enormous increase in numbers. Hispanics—a government category used by the U.S. Census Bureau that included Mexicans, Puerto Ricans, Cubans, and other Latin Americans—increased by 61 percent between 1970 and 1980, and 53 percent between 1980 and 1990. By the latter date, according to census data, these communities numbered 22.4

million, about 9 percent of the total American population (exclusive of indocumentados).[2] About 60 percent of Hispanics, some 13.5 million people, were Mexican.[3] In California alone, according to the census, 109 towns and cities had achieved a Hispanic majority by 1990. This dramatic increase reflected an extraordinarily high birth rate. There were 3.8 persons per family, compared to the 3.2 for a typical American family. A youthful population, Hispanics had a median age of 26.2 years, compared to the 33.0 years for the total population.

By the 1990s, Mexicans could be found picking citrus fruit in Florida, harvesting tobacco in North Carolina, collecting mushrooms in Pennsylvania, tending poultry in Maine, packing orchard crops in Washington, cleaning fish in Alaska, and working in slaughterhouses in Iowa. As the decade opened, some 200,000 Mexicans lived in New York City. Clearly, they had become a national rather than a regional minority. Still, 83 percent of them continued to reside in the Southwest. The greatest number, 6,118,996, lived in California, where the 7.7 million Latinos represented 25.8 percent of the total population, about the same percentage as in Texas (25.5) though lower than New Mexico (38.2). In New Mexico, interestingly, the trend was different than in other parts of the Southwest. Here the Anglo population was growing at the expense of the Hispano population. For example, in Santa Fe County, the Hispano share of the population fell from 65 percent to 45 percent between 1970 and 1990. Outside of the Southwest, the largest number of Mexicans was found in the Midwest. Over 1.5 million of them resided in Chicago and Detroit and their surrounding areas.

By 1990, 90.5 percent of the Mexican population in the United States was urban, a higher percentage than the population at large. The highest concentration of Latinos as of 1992, 4,779,000, was found in the Los Angeles metropolitan area (32.9 percent of the total population)—where they constituted the majority of students in the public school system— especially in greater East Los Angeles and the San Fernando Valley. At this time, the Mexican community of Los Angeles was the fourth largest in the world, after Mexico City, Monterrey, and Guadalajara. In Texas, there were several major cities with heavy Hispanic (overwhelmingly Mexican) representation, including San Antonio (47.6 percent), Corpus Christi (52 percent), El Paso (69.6 percent), and Laredo (93.9 percent). In Houston, Latino students made up roughly half of the school population. By 1990, Mexicans, and other minorities, were part of a major movement leaving city centers for outlying suburbs, a shift motivated by a number of factors, notably the desire to escape violence in the barrios.

IMMIGRATION

In addition to the high birth rate, the second major cause of changing demographics, and another obvious reason why Mexicans maintained a high profile,

was massive immigration from Mexico to the United States. Beginning in the
1960s and accelerating greatly in the 1980s, the movement of people across the
border was a source of continual and often acrimonious controversy throughout
the nation. This influx, according to Jeffrey Passel, a demographer for the Urban
Institute in Washington, D.C., constitutes the greatest historical mass migration
to the United States from a single country.[4] While no one can calculate the volume of traffic with any certainty, the number of Mexicans apprehended by the
Immigration and Naturalization Service for illegal entry exceeded one million in
the sixties and seven million in the seventies. Between 1980 and the early 1990s,
when apprehensions of all illegals grew by two-thirds nationwide, according to
official records, over one-third of them took place in the San Diego area. By the
mid-1990s, the INS estimated that 54 percent of the more than five million illegal
immigrants in the country were Mexican nationals. As was true of previous waves
of immigration from the south, this influx, though generally excluding the absolutely destitute (people with no resources at all), was propelled, as Jorge Durand
of the University of Guadalajara, Laura González of the University of Guanajuato,
and other Mexican demographers have shown, mainly by the inability of Mexico
to provide a decent living for many of its citizens.

The outstanding fact of the history of Mexico since World War II was an
incredible demographic explosion. By the mid-nineties, the population exceeded
93 million people, an increase of over 30 million in twenty years. Up until the late
1970s, the economy had been growing at a steady pace, and the problem of a
burgeoning population was reasonably contained. But after this time, severe
financial and economic problems surfaced; and in 1981–1982, the economy, beset by a fall in oil prices, high inflation, and an unmanageable foreign debt, suddenly plummeted. According to official figures, the number of Mexicans living in
poverty mushroomed from 32.1 million to 41.3 million in 1980–1987. The government of President Carlos Salinas de Gotari (1988–1994) responded by instituting severe cost-cutting measures and by integrating the Mexican economy with
that of the United States. Both policies met with vehement opposition, especially
from nationalists and the beleaguered working classes.

At first, the neo-liberal reforms of Salinas and his successor Ernesto Zedillo
Ponce de León seemed to be working in spite of massive popular discontent;
however, government optimism proved completely unfounded in December 1994,
when the peso suddenly crashed. Only U.S. aid in the form of a $13.5 million
rescue package put together by the Clinton administration saved the Mexican
economy from total collapse. To pay for the bailout, Mexico was forced to reduce
the standard of living for most of its citizens by 20 percent. By 1996, according to
a study by the Colegio de México, 80 percent of the Mexican population lived in
poverty. Popular dissatisfaction was inevitable, given the country's huge uneven
distribution of wealth. Political scientist Howard Handelman notes that by the

mid-nineties, income was more highly concentrated in Mexico than in many considerably poorer countries, such as Pakistan, India, Indonesia, and Peru.[5] The Partido Revolucionario Institucional (PRI) was further discredited by its failure to carry out democratic political reforms. Government corruption was dramatically exposed during the 1994 presidential elections, when intraparty strife led to widespread violence and the assassination of the party's official candidate, Luis Donaldo Colosio. It was only the safety valve provided by American immigration, many knowledgeable observers have noted, that kept Mexico from plunging into the throes of revolution.

Some Mexicans entered the United States through legal channels. The 1965 Immigration Act amended the Immigration and Nationality Act of 1952 by putting a cap, for the first time, of 120,000 a year on immigration from the Western Hemisphere. Eleven years later, immigration from Mexico was restricted to 20,000 a year, a quota which was always filled. In fact, Mexican immigrants generally exceeded this number substantially since the law allowed additional people to enter under a complicated preference system that gave priority to family reunification. Legal immigration from Mexico in the seventies averaged 60,000 persons per year. Moreover, after the demise of the Bracero Program in 1965, pressure by agribusiness and other economic interests in the border states resulted in legislation allowing Mexicans to enter the country as guest workers under a variety of programs. Some, called commuters, entered on a daily basis; others, "green carders" (their permit was originally green), were given permanent residency, allowing them to travel back and forth across the border.

The majority of immigrants, however, were undocumented workers. Motivation was generally the same as before—economic gain. But, beyond the sheer volume, there were significant differences between recent undocumented workers and those of yesteryear. Now immigrants were much more likely than before to come from urban settings; only about a quarter of the Mexican population worked in agriculture by the nineties. "Contrary to the stereotype of Mexican immigrants as overwhelmingly impoverished peasants," researchers Alejandro Portes and Rubén G. Rumbaut have pointed out, "up to 48 percent of the unauthorized have been found to originate in cities of twenty thousand or more, in comparison with 35 percent of all Mexicans."[6] As the postwar economic boom petered out in the seventies and eighties, masses of displaced peasants were forced to abandon overcrowded villages for the cities. Having made a move once, some newcomers were prepared to relocate again due to failed expectations. Mexico City, possibly the biggest city in the world, was particularly prone to the kinds of pressures that encourage migration, especially after the destructive 1985 earthquake. Many immigrants who left the cities to head north were disillusioned professionals, a class of people largely unrepresented in previous times.

Indians, too, first appeared as a significant component of the immigrant population at this time. California—where some observers feel the foreign-born outnumber the native-born Mexican population—was a favorite destination. They tended to reside close together, which was only natural since immigration was often the result of kinship networks. Tlacolulenses from Oaxaca, for example, could be found in Santa Monica. A Mixteca colony appeared in the hills near Oceanside. This pattern appeared outside of California, as well. Houston developed a significant Mayan colonia. Since the Indian population was the most traditional in Mexico, their escalating immigrant numbers were a barometer of how desperate the economic plight of the lower classes had become.

Anti-Indian sentiment in Mexico was another factor affecting emigration. As Earl Shorris has aptly noted, "In a nation devoted to celebrating its Indian heritage the terrible irony is that Indians are despised."[7] It was mistreatment of indigenous peoples, who constitute between 10 and 15 percent of the Mexican population, that set the stage for the uprising of the Zapatista National Liberation Army in Chiapas on 1 January 1994. Unrest soon spread to other states with large Indian populations, notably Oaxaca and Guerrero.

Women and entire families were much more evident than they had been in prior waves of immigration. One survey suggests, for example, that mujeres constituted between 60 and 75 percent of those arrested with false documents along the Mexico-U.S. border in 1995. This trend may reflect changes in family structure in the Old Country, including the decline of extended family networks and compadrazgo, as well as the increasing number of women forced into wage labor in Mexican villages and cities, the latter a factor emphasized by the sociologist Pierrette Hondagneu-Sotelo.[8] Apparently, many people were more determined at this time to maintain permanent residence in the United States—although a 1997 study of illegal immigration to the Golden State from six states in western Mexico, by the San Francisco–based Public Policy Institute of California, concluded that the majority of indocumentados returned home within two years.[9]

Finally, in contrast to earlier times, many of the recién llegados (recent immigrants) from Mexico were not Mexicans at all, but members of other impoverished and persecuted nationalities. Among them were huge numbers of refugees from Central America, where political violence after 1979 uprooted thousands, especially in Nicaragua, El Salvador, and Guatemala. By the mid-nineties—when the U.S. Census Bureau estimated the Hispanic population was increasing at the rate of 900,000 a year—there were between 500,000 and 1,000,000 Central Americans in Los Angeles, concentrated mainly in the central and south-central parts of the city.

The push-pull paradigm that was so useful in explaining immigration at the beginning of the century had less applicability now, as both Anglo and Chicano students of immigration have noted recently.[10] The current situation was more complicated than the old model suggests. For example, in many regions of Mexico, notably the states immediately north and west of the capital, a tradition of immigration, sometimes having its roots as early as the nineteenth century, had emerged. For many individuals, the movement north was almost a rite of passage. Moreover, many families were now maintaining dual residence, living in Mexico part of the year and in the United States the rest of the time, often establishing "transnational migrant circuits," as the anthropologist Roger Rouse terms them, a complex immigration pattern inconsistent with the traditional push-pull model.[11]

Many illegal Mexican immigrants, like those from other countries, had entered the country legally—on student, work, or tourist visas—then simply refused to return home. By the 1990s, according to some experts, as much as half of illegal immigration from all countries into the United States—estimated at between 300,000 and 400,000 individuals annually—may have been initiated in this fashion.

The destination of indocumentados continued to be the Southwest, though California, where the Hispanic population increased dramatically in the 1980s from 4.5 million to 7.6 million, was now a much more attractive magnet than Texas. By 1990, over half of the Hispanics in Los Angeles were immigrants. However, the borderlands they entered were much different than those encountered by their predecessors in the 1920s, or even the 1950s. No longer were jobs primarily in mining, railroad maintenance, and agriculture. Farm employment, in particular, was difficult to find in the now heavily urbanized Southwest. Moreover, the advent of a so-called postindustrial economy after the sixties meant that available jobs were primarily in the low-wage service sector—typically in restaurants, nurseries, and yard work for men, and child care and paid domestic work for women—rather than in the middle-wage manufacturing area.

In many respects, new immigrants, especially indocumentados (who often worked at two jobs) had it tougher than in the past. One reason was that although there were more artisans, clerical workers, and even professionals represented than before, immigrants for the most part continued to enter the country as unskilled or semiskilled laborers, while available jobs in the service industry increasingly demanded skills, including the ability to speak English. Opportunities were more limited than they had been fifty years earlier, which may be the reason why a sizable percentage of indocumentados maintained dual residence in Mexico and the United States, coming and going seasonally.

Massive illegal immigration predictably sparked a restrictionist campaign in the United States similar to those of the 1920s and 1950s, with the Mexican immigrant as the focus of attention. Much of the controversy centered on the question, basically economic, of whether immigrants, both legal and illegal, augmented or drained national resources.

Defenders claimed that immigrants performed the work U.S. citizens refused to do. More than 92 percent of California's farm-labor force of nearly one million people in the early nineties was foreign-born. Moreover, although conceding they might put a strain on welfare, health, and educational services, sympathetic observers argued that on balance immigrants made a positive contribution. The Urban Institute, a nonpartisan research organization, agreed, concluding in 1994 that foreigners actually contributed far more tax dollars than they used in services. Mexicans, in particular, it was pointed out, were unlikely to use welfare services, since they tended to be illegal immigrants. These services disproportionately benefitted refugees, a category that excluded Mexicans. Chicano and other civil rights groups argued that the immigrant, particularly the indocumentado, was being used as a scapegoat for the multitude of problems plaguing society.

Critics felt that the labor performed by immigrants did not compensate for the services they received. They argued, moreover, that immigrants, many of them illegals, failed to pay a fair share of their taxes. And, of course, there were racist motives at work, though these rarely surfaced in the media and other public forums in overt ways. Racial theories, for example, were widely espoused by members of the Federation for American Immigration Reform (FAIR), the ranking national advocate of immigration restriction.

The attitude of the long-standing Mexican communities in the United States on this heated issue was interesting. Polls indicated that these communities were even more opposed to illegal immigration than was the American population in general. In 1992, for example, the Latino National Political Survey, headed by respected University of Texas political scientist Rodolfo de la Garza, found that 75 percent of Mexicans with U.S. citizenship and 84 percent of Mexicans without U.S. citizenship felt that there were too many immigrants in the country (compared to 74 percent of non-Hispanic whites). Although anti-Asian sentiment in barrios might partly account for these findings, there was little reason to doubt the survey's basic conclusion, highlighting the fact that the controversy was predominantly economic in nature. Mexicans residing in the United States legally, whether they had good reason to believe so or not, suspected that their livelihood was being threatened. Significantly, it was the most recently arrived Mexicans, those who competed for the same kinds of jobs, who were most opposed to a liberal immigration policy. Many Mexican Americans also feared that the backlash against Mexican immigrants would have a detrimental impact on their own communities. For instance, a national identity card, one of the various solutions proposed by restrictionists, would very clearly lead to discrimination against all people of Latino background.

So animated was the popular indignation aroused by both legal and illegal immigration—in some places in California, like Orange County and the San Fernando Valley, it verged on hysteria—that Congress was forced to act, though not without considerable hesitation, given the complexity of the problem and the powerful lobbies participating in the national debate. Probably the major stumbling block to effective legislation was Republican opposition to imposing sanctions on employers, which many critics felt was the only effective means of curtailing illegal entry. Eventually, a compromise solution was reached. The result was the 1986 Immigration Reform and Control Act (IRCA). Essentially, this legislation was an attempt to deal with all the problems of immigration at once. Under the 1986 law, Mexico continued to supply a large number of legal immigrants (126,561 in 1993). IRCA sought to control *illegal* immigration in two ways: (1) it enacted sanctions against employers of illegal immigrants, and (2) it granted amnesty—and eligibility for citizenship—to undocumented workers who had lived in the United States continuously since 1 January 1982; and, through a Special Agricultural Worker (SAW) program, it legalized indocumentados who had worked a minimum of ninety days in U.S. agriculture between May 1985 and May 1986. Approximately 2.4 million indocumentados applied for and were granted legal status under the law.

IRCA *did* diminish illegal entry for several years, but by 1990—when another immigration act was passed, increasing immigration levels by 40 percent and doubling the number of visas for skilled workers—the tide had resumed. After that date, the INS apprehended at least 1.5 million people annually. It was estimated that some 100,000 to 200,000 indocumentados entered the country successfully every year. The total number of Latino illegals in the early nineties was probably around 2 million, though unofficial estimates ranged as high as 12 million—possibly because the first estimate was confined to the settler population while the latter took into account sojourners. A flourishing trade in counterfeit documents made it difficult to enforce the law, but IRCA failed primarily because the U.S. Government was unwilling and/or unable to enforce employer sanctions. Employers were rarely caught in violation of the law, hardly surprising since fewer than 350 agents were responsible for supervising 7 million employers. And when offenders *were* caught, penalties were often avoided. Fewer than half of the 12,714 employer cases reported to the INS from 1989 to 1994 resulted in fines.

The failure of immigration laws to stem the tide once again resurrected xenophobic sentiments, particularly vis-á-vis Mexicans. The fears were most pronounced in California, where denunciations of illegals reached a fever pitch. Violence was common. The backlash created by border problems was so intense that a whole series of measures was introduced in the state assembly to combat Mexican immigration. The drive, spearheaded by Republican assemblymen in southern California, enjoyed popular success. In 1994, Californians, with a resounding 59 percent of the vote, passed Proposition 187, which denied illegal immigrants and their families health care, welfare, and public education. The bill was endorsed by Republican Governor Pete Wilson, a staunch restrictionist, and heavily subsidized by nativist and racist organizations. In Texas, authorities were much more cautious in handling the problem, possibly because the state's economy was relatively healthier in recent years compared to that of California, which had suffered terribly from the drying up of defense industries with the end of the Cold War, as well as from a slump in the real estate business. The Lone Star State also had proportionately fewer illegals—it estimated that 3 percent of its population was illegal compared with 7 percent in California—and a long-established Mexican political presence in many border towns.

THE NORTH AMERICAN FREE TRADE AGREEMENT

The failure of legislation to stymie illegal immigration by 1990 encouraged the supporters of an alternative solution to the problem: those who felt that immigration was inevitable unless the Mexican economy became strong enough to keep Mexicans at home. Efforts in this direction go back to 1965, when American companies, for purely economic motives, began to set up assembly plants, called *maquiladoras,* on the Mexican side of the border to take advantage of cheap labor. Hundreds of thousands of workers were employed assembling parts imported tax-free for appliances, automobiles and other consumer goods, and sending the finished products north, to be sold in U.S. markets. During the 1980s, maquiladoras became increasingly sophisticated in their operations. Some critics, like the sociologist Devon G. Peña, saw them as high-volume sweatshops exploiting the predominantly female labor force, increasingly married women forced to work by the collapsing Mexican economy.

Eventually, the American government, under both Republican and Democratic administrations, became convinced that the encouragement of U.S. business interests in northern Mexico through the creation of a free-trade zone would yield dual benefits: ameliorate the problem of indocumentados by providing Mexicans jobs at home and encourage the economic exploitation of lucrative Mexican markets. By the mid-1980s, the Mexican government, for its part, faced with a glut of unskilled workers and a lack of savings to finance investment, was prepared to wholeheartedly embrace a project which would help modernize the Mexican economy, placate its working class, and stabilize political life. Thus, there gradually emerged on both sides of the border the concept of a North American Free Trade Agreement (NAFTA) linking Canada, Mexico, and the United States, the largest trade bloc in the world.

There were many critics. On the Mexican side, nationalists feared the increasing penetration of U.S. influence, seen as another form of cultural imperialism. On the American side, resistance to the project was centered in labor unions and conservationist groups, an alliance led by populist presidential candidate Ross Perot.

Despite formidable opposition, NAFTA was legislated into law in November 1993 and went into effect on 1 January 1994. Among congressional leaders most responsible for its enactment was Representative Bill Richardson, a Mexican-descent Democrat from New Mexico. Then chief deputy majority whip in the House, Richardson would be appointed American Ambassador to the United Nations by President Clinton in 1997. The variegated Mexican-American communities were divided on NAFTA, but Richardson appeared to reflect a majority opinion. The growing Latino business community was an avid supporter, and found its leading spokesman in the Santa Barbara–based *Hispanic Business* (edited by ex-militant Jesús Chavarría). Among middle-class organizations, the most enthusiastic endorsement came from the Southwest Voter Registration and Education Project, an astute political move, permitting it to gain considerable influence in the Clinton administration.

THE DECADE OF THE HISPANIC: THE UNFULFILLED PROMISE

Despite misgivings by a minority calling for continuing militancy, there was widespread optimism among Mexicans throughout the country during the late 1970s. It was apparent that important gains had been made in the previous decade, and there was a general expectation that progress would continue on all fronts. The 1980s were heralded as the "Decade of the Hispanic" by Raúl Yzaguirre, director of the National Council of La Raza, and others. This potential, though, was never realized. The Post-Chicano Generation, while compiling a creditable record of achievement, found that it had underestimated the resistance to change in society at large and overestimated its own capacity to resolve long-standing problems.

Disappointment was most obvious in the political arena, where, in spite of alliances with fellow Latinos and other underprivileged segments of society, Mexicans failed to register anticipated gains. In terms of elective offices, there were a few significant triumphs at the local and state levels, especially in areas with large Mexican constituencies. Moreover, there was some evidence that political clout was expanding beyond the Southwest; already by the mid-1980s, for example, there were several hundred Hispanic elected and appointed officials in the Midwest. Toney Anaya was elected governor of New Mexico in 1982, continuing a tradition begun in the seventies, when two other Mexican Democrats had won governorships: Raúl Castro in Arizona and Jerry Apodaca in New Mexico. But electoral victories were few and far between. The Hispanic Caucus in Congress, led by Henry B. González, never became a significant force in Washington, despite favorable demographic trends.

One major stumbling block was political apathy in barrios. Yeoman efforts by MALDEF, the National Association of Latino Elected Officials (NALEO), and other Chicano civil rights associations notwithstanding, the voting turnout remained embarrassingly low into the nineties. Year in and year out, depending on the election, less than a quarter of Mexicans eligible to vote actually exercised that privilege.

Internecine squabbles within and between organizations took their toll. Mexican political organizations were notorious for their inability to work together, an unfortunate characteristic best described by journalist Rubén Navarrette, Jr.: "Ethnic solidarity, a successful economic and political tool for American Jews and other ethnic groups, eludes Latinos. . . . For Latinos, there has been little cooperation or camaraderie. And so little progress. Petty competition, personal intolerance and a refusal to let any of our own progress ahead of us make it unlikely that the children of the sun, however numerous, will ever inherit the earth."[12]

Nor, despite repeated attempts, was there significant progress in forming an overall umbrella organization of civil rights associations. Alliances with other ethnic groups, especially African Americans, proved difficult. Although Mexicans aided Jesse Jackson's Rainbow Coalition, support was lukewarm, hardly surprising given racial and economic tensions between the two minorities. Even Pan-Hispanic unity proved elusive. Mexicans, three-quarters of whom continued to vote Democrat, found little common ground with Cubans, who, though attractive as potential allies given their affluence and political clout, remained solidly united under the GOP banner. The Hispanic Congressional Caucus itself was often divided on whether or not to recognize Cuba. In point of fact, there had always been undisguised admiration for Fidel Castro among Chicano intellectuals, a sentiment completely at odds with that of the overwhelming majority of Cuban expatriates, who saw the dictator as the Antichrist himself. Generally speaking, as Peruvian-American scholar Suzanne Oboler has observed, Spanish-speaking peoples in the United States have tended to reject the "Hispanic" label, choosing instead to identify with their particular national group.[13]

The most intractable barrier to Mexican electoral success in the eighties, however, was the radical change in the climate of opinion, as reflected in Republican ascendancy over political life. This conservatism began to make inroads even into the growing Mexican-American middle class. Some of the most damaging criticism of social programs for underprivileged minorities came from members of their ranks, notably the controversial San Francisco–based journalist Richard

Rodríguez (1948–) and a Colorado-born Hispana, Linda Chávez (1947–), an influential Republican affiliated with the Manhattan Institute, a conservative think tank in Washington, D.C.

Educational problems also proved intractable. There was a modicum of progress made in this area, particularly in institutions of higher education, where affirmative action and the Educational Opportunity Program (EOP) helped boost minority enrollment. In the fall semester of 1993, for example, some 14 percent of the 21,593 undergraduates enrolled at UC Berkeley and 17 percent of the 22,892 undergraduates at UCLA were Hispanic (an aggregate category, but overwhelmingly Mexican). Gains were more impressive at the junior college level. By 1996, Hispanics represented 36.3 percent of the 10 million students enrolled in the nation's more than 1,100 community colleges. These numbers, however, were sadly deficient given the burgeoning, and youthful, communities they represented. Moreover, these small but significant gains in higher education were suddenly threatened in the mid-1990s, when the Regents of the University of California, led by Governor Wilson and political ally Ward Connerly, voted to terminate admission policies based on affirmative action. This fateful decision was supported by California voters in 1996, when they overwhelmingly endorsed Proposition 209.

The small numbers of Mexicans in colleges reflected a relatively modest pool of applicants. The high school drop-out rate in the early nineties was over 40 percent—a higher rate than that of African Americans and Puerto Ricans, though slightly better than among native Americans—not much of an improvement over what it had been before the advent of the Chicano movement. Furthermore, brown students receiving high school degrees were not being prepared to go into higher education: Mexicans who took the SAT in 1992 averaged 797, while Anglos averaged 933. This distressing record was compiled in spite of bilingual and a variety of other academic programs meant to remedy the situation. Conservative critics suggested that these programs themselves were part of the problem.

A product of a 1974 Supreme Court ruling, bilingual education (which mandates that immigrant and other children who speak a language other than English as their primary language be taught in their native tongue as well as English), in particular, was anathema to conservative groups, both in and out of educational circles. Leading the campaign against bilingualism was U.S. English, a California-based organization which promoted the learning of English and attempted to convince Congress to adopt a constitutional amendment to make English the official language of government.[14] Founded in 1983 by John Tanton, a Michigan ophthalmologist who was also instrumental in creating FAIR, and led by ex-Senator S. I. Hayakawa, the movement grew by leaps and bounds, reflecting wide-ranging fears of "unassimilable immigrants." One of the national presidents of the organization was Linda Chávez, a champion of the idea that immigrants should assimilate at breakneck speed. Chávez was very vocal in her opposition to all forms of entitlements for minorities because in order to maintain eligibility, she claimed, beneficiaries were encouraged to fail rather than succeed. She and other conservative critics were fond of pointing out the contradiction between segregating students into bilingual programs and the fight for integrated schools that Chicanos and other minorities had persistently waged for most of the twentieth century. The English Only movement, fueled by growing xenophobia and a taxpayers' revolt, flourished in the mid-eighties. A decade later, twenty-three states, including California, had passed English-only amendments, raising serious questions about the future of bilingual education. Nevertheless, in spite of philosophical, financial, and practical difficulties, bilingualism managed to survive, chiefly because of heavy immigration and aggressive advocacy by ethnic rights groups.

Most Mexican educators, like the vast majority of the Latino community, supported bilingualism and other progressive measures. In their view, educational reforms after the sixties had been more theoretical than real. Economic problems and reluctant taxpayers meant, unfortunately, that schools were forced to sacrifice services, and minority-based programs were generally judged to be the most expendable by local school boards. Many Mexicans suspected that American society at bottom had no real sympathy with these reforms, which were conceded reluctantly in the first place.

There was ample evidence to support this point of view. Certainly, many schools were slow to meet Chicano demands. According to a study by the Tomás Rivera Center, a Hispanic policy research institute in Claremont, California, in 1994, a year after Latinos supposedly reached 10 percent of the total U.S. population, only 3.7 percent of all teachers in American public schools represented that ethnic background. Little wonder, Mexican parents complained, that many of their children continued to see school as a kind of prison. The failure of American education to meet the needs of the Mexican-American community was underlined by an exhaustive interdisciplinary project conducted by Carola and Marcelo Suárez-Orozco of the Harvard Graduate School of Education. They discovered that the attitude toward school was more positive among children of Mexican immigrants than among children of Mexican-American parents. The increasing cynicism toward education and poor academic performance of Mexican-American adolescents, the researchers concluded, was attributed to a variety of factors, but especially the disparagement and discrimination to which the youths were subjected, both in and out of the classroom.[15]

Still, though governmental and educational policies had much to do with Mexicans' educational deficiencies, these factors were secondary to impoverished socioeconomic conditions. This depressed status was itself a product of a whole complicated set of circumstances, not the least of which, in recent years, were the public policies of Republican administrations willing to sacrifice the interests of the poor in order to benefit the more affluent segments of American society, thus hastening the trend toward a two-tier society bifurcated largely along ethnic lines. This period, christened "The Rambo Years" by Rodolfo Acuña, is best described by a fellow historian:

> The Reagan era was a period of selfish emphasis, jingoism and chauvinism, and a lack of access. The number of persons in a poverty status increased. The Reagan administration was not only inaccessible; it was generally negative toward the basic social and economic needs of the community, and it undertook specific negative actions concerning immigration and labor. Both antiworker and antiunion policies impacted on the Chicano community.[16]

The reality of poverty was all too apparent. In 1991, according to the U.S. Census Bureau, the median family income for Hispanics was $23,431, as compared to $35,353 for all families in the United States; and the average family income was $29,311, well below the U.S. mean of $42,652. Statistics relating specifically to Mexicans were daunting. More than a quarter of them (28.1 percent) lived below the poverty line. Their unemployment rate exceeded 10 percent during that year. While 85 percent of the general population had medical insurance, only about 20 percent of the Mexican-origin community could afford health coverage. Moreover, many Mexicans were immigrants, which meant that they had language difficulties to contend with, in addition to financial burdens.

In addition, the record of educational failure can partly be attributed to certain aspects of ethnic culture. Most Chicano historians in the past have tended to dwell on the debilitating influences of outside agencies on the Mexican community while deemphasizing internal problems—inadvertently and regrettably encouraging the trend among some segments of the community toward victimization that has been so pronounced since the sixties. As the Súarez-Orozcos suggest, this emphasis is understandable since the harm done by schools, police agencies, government organizations, and other Anglo-controlled institutions—as well as the more pervasive erosive influences that impact all families, Mexican and non-Mexican—has been primarily responsible for the majority of ills plaguing the ethnic community. Nevertheless, it is essential to understand that some of these problems are accentuated by cultural factors, which are, of course, products of a historical rather than a genetic inheritance. Among these historical factors, as the anthropologist Oscar Lewis has shown, is poverty itself.

Perhaps the most serious impediment in Mexican culture to educational success has been the treatment of children. While exemplary in most respects, child-rearing practices, as in many working-class environments, have often fostered an anti-intellectual streak. Mexican historian and social critic Carlos Monsiváis makes this very point when he observes: "It is not uncommon in Mexican homes to hear parents scolding their kids for reading when they 'could be doing something useful, like fixing the door.'"[17] Children's questions, especially abstract ones, are all-too-often discouraged with a "Sólo Dios sabe" (Only God knows) or a "¿Quién sabe?" (Who knows?), leading children to stop asking questions as they grow older, a trait which is hardly conducive to effective scholarship. Mexican parents want children to be *bien educados,* but, significantly, in Latino culture this phrase means "well-behaved" rather than "well-educated." In spite of prejudice and poverty, other ethnic groups, notably Jews and some Asians, have been much more successful in inculcating their children with a healthy respect for education.

All of this suggests that another major area of concern—one touched upon previously—was, and remains, *la familia,* the Mexican family, a subject of heated debate among sociologists and laypersons alike. Contrary to the popular stereotype of the strong Mexican family, the first in-depth studies by Anglo social scientists—Ruth Tuck, Pauline R. Kibbe, Celia Heller, and others—portrayed a dysfunctional unit dominated by the macho though distant male who lorded over his submissive wife and children. During the past generation, Chicano and Chicana scholars have sought to combat this familial deficiency model, condemning it as a pernicious myth perpetrating negative stereotypes.[18] Quite aside from the obvious criticism that there were all kinds of family units in the heterogeneous Mexican community, the studies of these ethnic scholars indicate that while patriarchy represented the theory, the reality was quite different. It was the woman, as wife and mother, who was the glue holding the family together, not the authoritarian male. Moreover, decision-making was much more egalitarian than previously thought. There are many exceptions, but, in general, Anglo academics saw the familia as beset by monumental problems while Ethnic Studies scholars found it a source of immense security.

Unfortunately, however, some minority students of the Mexican family have been overzealous in accentuating the positive, in the process obscuring real problems and creating a mythology of their own. For example, David Hayes-Bautista, director of the Center for the Study of Latino Health at UCLA, concluded in the early nineties that the familia, based on his demographic studies of Los Angeles, was actually quite well adjusted.[19] In many ways, he argued, it was healthier than Anglo families. Presenting statistical data to back up his contention, he claimed, among other things, that 43 percent of Hispanics maintained traditional households (two parents with children) compared to 16 percent for Anglos. These findings, however, contrasted markedly with data presented by other researchers, as well as impressionistic evidence.

Not all Chicano scholars accepted the rosy picture portrayed by Hayes-Bautista, who apparently set about his work in an effort to prove that Mexicans were not part of a permanent underclass, an ongoing controversy among urban sociologists. Rodolfo de la Garza, for one, offered a dissenting opinion. "In the modern world," he argued, "the Hispanic family has experienced all the mainstream disruption that America has and perhaps more."[20]

While Hayes-Bautista's findings might be politically correct, they obscured the reality of the situation. Both statistics and interpretations were highly questionable. His conclusion that more Mexicans than Anglos in Los Angeles lived in traditional households seemed suspect. Certainly, it was not a typical situation nationally. According to the U.S. Census Bureau, in 1991, 69 percent of the 4.9 million Hispanic families in the country were married couples compared to 78 percent for the entire American population (although the first figure was skewed by Puerto Ricans, whose domestic problems were more severe than those of Mexicanos, the second figure was also inflated, by African Americans). This disparity casts doubt on the UCLA study.

Also, statistics don't tell the whole story. The rate of abandonment (difficult to extract from the data) has probably been more pronounced in the Mexican community than among Anglos, because of the high incidence of immigration, if for no other reason. Moreover, there has been a greater aversion to divorce among Mexicans than in society at large. There are two main reasons for this difference: economic considerations and a Catholic value system which stresses the welfare of children, encourages believers to endure adversity and pay for their mistakes, and generally inculcates the notion that divorced people are "losers." Poverty and the widespread persistence of these Catholic beliefs in the Spanish-speaking community would suggest that divorce statistics could be a poor indicator of the true condition of the family unit. As Joan W. Moore has suggested, "A cultural image of the 'strong Mexican family' leads to complete disregard for the bleak statistics on desertion and divorce."[21] By the early 1990s, about 20 percent of families of Mexican origin were headed by a female.

To a large extent, the problems of Mexican families in the United States as the twentieth century drew to a close were those of other American families, and many of the causes were the same as for other groups—urbanization, materialism, drugs, the decline of religion, the influence of television, etc. But there were other factors as well. One of them was discrimination—although admittedly less severe than in the African-American community, where broken homes are endemic and the family is even more fragmented. Discrimination took many forms, from outright police brutality to the destruction of traditional communities through urban renewal or freeway construction.

Poverty, however, was the most salient single problem, one which became increasingly serious among Mexican workers after the 1960s, when middle-income industrial jobs faded, international immigration increased, and the welfare state contracted, as community-based service organizations were dismantled by the federal government. The rise of homelessness in barrios by the mid-1990s reflected these deteriorating conditions. By this time, more than a quarter of the Mexican community in the United States fell under the official poverty line.

But cultural considerations, once again, should not be neglected in exploring factors impacting family instability. Preeminent was the macho ethic. Often resulting in obviously dysfunctional behavior like alcoholism, domestic violence, and marital infidelity, machismo has been the cause of a multitude of family problems, some of them less obvious than others. In his fine autobiography, Anthony Quinn shares many valuable examples of the insidious impact of machismo on traditional working-class households, a persistent reality even today.

One episode in particular is poignant. Quinn recalls that when he was about four, he sat at the table with his family eating a steak—a rarity in that impoverished household—that his father Francisco had brought home. Before finishing his portion, Anthony, too young to know better, demanded more food. His father pointed out that there was still a large piece of meat on the boy's plate, but the child persisted. Francisco, obviously irritated, proceeded to empty his own plate and that of his surprised wife onto little Anthony's. "All right, you eat it all," he said. Then he watched as the child slowly swallowed the food that he and his wife, both still hungry, had provided. Unable to finish, the boy tried to excuse himself, explaining that he had had enough. But Francisco insisted: "You said you wanted it all and you are going to eat it all." Completely full, the child was forced to eat while his father watched impassively. Weeping, Anthony ended up gagging on a piece of meat. The father did not move a muscle to help; he sat sipping his coffee, while his son turned blue. His wife Manuela, horrified, was told to leave the child alone. Finally, Francisco got up slowly and disgorged the meat, saving his son's life. Unperturbed, Francisco asked the terrified child if he wanted more to eat! "Don't cry," he admonished his son. "Take your lesson like a man. Be grateful you've learned something." Anthony survived, but his father had made a point—never ask for more food until you finish what is on your plate.[22]

This lengthy anecdote provides a number of illuminating insights on Mexican working-class culture—Quinn himself used it to illustrate that while a Mexican mother's love is unconditional, the father's love must be earned—but perhaps the most telling has to do with the psychological repercussions of machismo on children. The result of this tyranny was a child's low sense of self-esteem (significantly, his family nickname was "the elephant"), as well as a love-hate attitude toward the father—exactly the impact it had on Anthony Quinn.

The psychological damage described here has often been accompanied by physical violence, another major problem that continues to plague Mexican communities, especially in urban environments. Another reason the UCLA study mentioned above seems unconvincing is that its rosy view of the Chicano family in Los Angeles is inconsistent with the city's reputation as the center of gangs and

the violence associated with *cholos* (gang members). By 1989, authorities estimated that there were some 770 gangs in metropolitan Los Angeles, most of them
Mexican. Southern California is not unique. In Chicago, Hispanic gangs, notably
the Latin Kings and the Latin Disciples, now rival African-American gangs in size
and influence. In fact, gangs proliferated in both rural and urban barrios after the
1960s, a phenomenon mirroring the disintegration of the family. As the anthropologist James Diego Vigil has noted, "The gang has become a 'spontaneous' street
social unit that fills a void left by families under stress."[23] The majority of cholos,
typically second-generation Mexicans, came from single-parent families and many
were raised by grandparents.

Beyond broken homes and weakened families, the escalation of gang life
had other and more profound roots, as the studies of Vigil, Ruth Horowitz, Joan
Moore, and Martín Sánchez Jankowski, among others, have shown. These included poverty, discrimination, and alienation, leading young people into
difficulties with schools and police. Moreover, during the 1980s, most of the
community-based organizations spawned by the War on Poverty disappeared,
destroying a valuable resource that had served to diminish gang activity. Gangs
provided much-needed emotional and social support networks left by this void.
As membership increased, so did gang-related violence, reflecting racial friction,
continuing immigration, the proliferation of firearms, and the popularity of the
drug trade. By the 1990s, some barrios had become war zones. This was particularly true in California, where cholo gangs, divided into *sureños* (southerners) and
norteños (northerners), were engaged in a virtual civil war.

As a result, the Mexican prison population steadily increased. In 1996, when
they represented about 10 percent of the national population, Hispanics constituted 14.3 percent of the prison population. In California, Hispanics were about
28 percent of the population but about 34 percent of the inmate population. It
was clear that Latinos were overrepresented in penal institutions, though admittedly these statistics were somewhat misleading, given legal disadvantages stemming from poverty and inadequate education and a macho proclivity to plead
guilty.

Some cholos eventually graduated to one of two major crime syndicates
operating in and out of the California state prison system: the Mexican Mafia, or
"La Eme" (Spanish for the letter M) and Nuestra Familia (Our Family). The former
was founded in 1957 at Deuel Vocational Institute in Tracy by Mexican prisoners
from southern California as a mutual protection group. Its numbers expanded to
over one thousand members in the seventies, when it came to dominate much of
the underworld economy in barrios—drug smuggling, gambling, prostitution,
and extortion. Eventually, it was even able to infiltrate federally funded social
projects in barrios, notably the Los Angeles–based League of United Citizens to
Help Addicts (LUCHA). Nuestra Familia, a rival organization, was formed at

Soledad Prison in the late 1960s to protect northern California prisoners, mostly of rural background, from La Eme, whose members came mainly from urban southern California. Nuestra Familia, too, had its heyday in the seventies. Both crime syndicates were weakened by intergang warfare and police repression in the eighties, when they lost most of their membership, but both survived into the nineties. Reputedly, La Eme, feeling that its honor had been impugned, put out a contract on Edward James Olmos, the Chicano actor and community activist, who starred in and produced *American Me* in 1992. The film graphically illustrated the ugly side of prison gangs in an effort to discourage Hispanic youth from entering a life of crime.

MEXICAN CATHOLICISM

Finally, like the rest of American society, Mexican communities were beset by a growing spiritual poverty, a void that the Catholic Church was not well equipped to fill. The reasons were partly historical. After their incorporation into the United States in 1848, Mexican Catholics in the Southwest experienced myriad difficulties with the Church. Race was a factor, but equally deleterious, as the church historian Albert López Pulido emphasizes, was the inability of the American clergy to appreciate the folk beliefs and practices, often of Indian and African origin, of their Mexican flocks.[24] The austere religion of the Irish, who came to dominate the American Church, was far removed from that of the mestizo people they encountered. Hispanic Catholicism was much more concerned with sacramentals like rosaries, scapulars, relics, and candles; the festive aspects of religion; and devotions. The saints tended to command more respect, as well, especially the Virgin Mary. Also, church attendance was not considered essential by Mexicans. So vast was the cultural gap that Spanish-speaking parishioners, rather than being treated as practicing Catholics, were often seen by their priests, many of them foreign-born, as pagans requiring missionary activity.

By the first decades of the twentieth century, the unstated policy of the Church was generally to ignore Spanish-speakers. This was a difficult tendency to combat since, unlike their European counterparts, Mexican immigrants did not bring their own priests with them. Moreover, in the United States, the hierarchy failed to attract Hispanics into the priesthood. Although barrio needs were not totally neglected—welfare services and catechetical work were usually available—the institutional Church, now solidly middle class, had apparently forgotten how to be an immigrant church.

It was not until the 1960s, at about the time of the Second Vatican Council (1962–1965), that the institution, in spite of the intransigence of much of the Irish clergy, began to focus attention on Mexicans. Militant activity on the part of Chicano laymen was probably less influential than the escalating numbers of Hispanics and the specter of Protestant conversions in barrios, trends that increased dramatically in the next generation. The latter may have been the most pressing consideration. While Protestant efforts to win over Mexican converts go back to the 1920s, these had met with scant success: in 1960, less than 3 percent of the ethnic community was Protestant. However, during the decade of the sixties striking inroads into Mexican communities were made by Protestant denominations, the most dynamic being Baptists, Mormons, Jehovah's Witnesses, and especially Pentecostals, a source of considerable embarrassment and trepidation to the Catholic hierarchy. The more personal approach to religion and the conservative stance on issues like abortion, crime, homosexuality, and traditional family values within Protestant denominations found a sympathetic audience in barrios. It is estimated that nearly one million Hispanics left the Catholic Church between 1975 and 1990. Though the greatest missionary successes were among Puerto Ricans, some experts feel that between 10 and 20 percent of the Mexican community may have converted to Protestantism, the vast majority of these attracted to Pentecostal or evangelical churches.

Faced by the prospects of losing the allegiance of the barrios, the Catholic Church stepped up efforts to strengthen its ties with its Spanish-speaking congregations in the 1970s.[25] It initiated a series of *encuentros* (encounters) between Hispanic and Anglo Catholics to bridge the cultural gap in 1972, 1977, and 1985. Latinos were also promoted within the clerical hierarchy. By 1983, there were fifteen Hispanic bishops. The first of them to be appointed archbishop was Roberto Sánchez (1934–), who assumed his office in Santa Fe; but the most effective and popular Hispanic spokesman within the Catholic hierarchy soon became San Antonio Archbishop Patrick Flores (1929–).

A native of Ganado, Texas, Archbishop Flores was convinced at the outset that in order to maintain their hold on the barrios, Catholics needed to deemphasize theology and deal with the practical problems plaguing the community. Accordingly, despite opposition from conservative critics within the institution, he encouraged the Church to set up social action programs throughout Texas. Ultimately, Catholics in Texas became major supporters of a variety of minority service programs. The most notable was Community Organized for Public Service (COPS), a grassroots organization founded in the early seventies by Ernie Cortés, Jr. Aided by the Church, COPS, which employed the mobilization techniques of the late Saul Alinsky, quickly expanded its influence throughout the state. In other parts of the Southwest, however, the Church was more hesitant to respond to Mexican needs.

In California, reform efforts centered on Padres Asociados para Derechos Religiosos, Educativos y Sociales (PADRES, Priests Organized for Religious, Educational, and Social Rights). Founded in 1970, this Los Angeles–based association of clergymen was dedicated to aiding the Mexican faithful. These efforts became more effective once Latino leaders within the Church won over powerful Irish prelates to their point of view. Some of them, notably Archbishop Roger Mahoney of Los Angeles, became staunch allies. In 1975, the United Neighborhood Organization (UNO), the California counterpart of COPS in Texas, was established with Church backing. By the mid-1990s, then, when Latinos composed one-third of the U.S. Catholic population, the Church had made visible progress in its campaign to address their needs.

"Traditionally, the greatest single cultural force in Mexican American society has been the Roman Catholic Church," according to the scholar Roberto R. Bacalski-Martínez.[26] This legacy, however, remains ambivalent. On the positive side, Catholicism has provided solace to millions. There are many Mexicans whose entire lives revolve around the Church and who find the experience rewarding and uplifting. The Church has always provided a wide variety of welfare services. More recently, as indicated above, it has immersed itself in social welfare programs—drug rehabilitation programs for *tecatos* (drug addicts), half-way houses for *pintos* (ex-convicts), and the like—even at the expense of alienating more conservative segments of the Catholic community.

In many ways, though, Catholicism has exacted a heavy price. The AIDS epidemic is a case in point. Though Hispanics made up about 9 percent of the national population in 1990, they accounted for over 15 percent of AIDS cases, a percentage which appears to be escalating. Medical officials have targeted the Hispanic population in an effort to deal with the problem; however, the greatest obstacle to this campaign, it has been alleged, is the Catholic Church, which opposes the use of condoms and discourages youths from discussing sex openly.

On a broader plane, some critics attribute much of the responsibility for Mexican poverty to the Church and its traditional teachings, a point made most cogently by Bettina R. Flores in *Chiquita's Cocoon* (1990), a feminist self-help book. Though well-intentioned Chicano scholars have usually painted a portrait of Mexicans as assertive and aggressive, a people who have been ingenious in discovering strategies of resistance, in reality, many members of the ethnic community have not displayed these characteristics at all. Chicano historians have misrepresented the Mexican character, which many commentators, including Octavio Paz and Samuel Ramos, see as flawed by a deep sense of inferiority. Earl Shorris, a perceptive and sympathetic observer of this society, is not misinformed when he notes that Mexicans, both in Mexico and the United States, have traditionally placed a heavy emphasis on the idea of *aguantar*, the virtue of forbearance.[27] A pronounced value in traditional Mexican society, this tendency was largely a product of the culture of poverty that forms the matrix of Mexican-American working-class culture today. It is difficult for the impoverished, those without

resources, without allies, to be assertive. Like other people placed in adverse circumstances, Mexicans and Mexican Americans have often been forced to swallow
their pride in order to survive.

Subservience, too, resulted from the teachings of Catholicism, which has
historically advocated the virtue of humility. Moreover, as Bettina Flores suggests,
traditional Catholic values, anti-materialistic and communal, are, at bottom, profoundly hostile to the spirit of capitalism. The macho ethic, it should be added,
though antithetical in many ways, tends to reinforce the Catholic view in this
instance. Machismo is also opposed to materialism; the values it stresses include
respect, duty, honesty, and bravery—virtues inconsistent with the acquisition of
wealth, the overriding sign of success in American society.

More ambiguous has been the Church's political legacy. Although Chicano
militants have sought to create a different impression, Mexicans are deeply conservative in many respects. Chicano leaders in the sixties—as well as some Chicano
scholars today—have tended to underestimate this conservatism. Mexican-American values today have their roots in a traditional agrarian culture, which still
persists in large parts of Mexico and even the United States. Moreover, the legacy
of Spanish colonial administration, intensely authoritarian, reinforced anti-progressive tendencies. The greatest influence, however, has been exerted by the
Catholic Church, whose very structure, hierarchical and authoritarian, reflects its
conservative bent. This predilection permeates Hispanic society. At the popular
level, we see it today in the fascination exerted by oldies-but-goodies on a generation of youth who were not even born when the music was first popular. There
are more weighty manifestations. Abortion, birth control, busing—the ethnic community tends to endorse conservative solutions to these social problems. In a
1989–1990 political survey of the California population, the Field Institute of
San Francisco found that more Hispanics identified themselves as conservatives
(27 percent) than liberals (25 percent), even though most continue to vote the
Democratic ticket. Whether this traditionalism is a strength or a deficiency is
open to discussion; but to dismiss it is to sadly distort the character of today's
Mexican-descent population.

FEMINISTAS: THE SECOND GENERATION

In spite of the disillusionment voiced by many Chicanos about the glacial
advances experienced by Hispanic peoples generally and Chicanos in particular,
the Mexican-origin community has made meaningful gains during the past generation. The middle class has expanded. Mexicans have become major consum-
ers, together with other Latinos, giving rise to a "Hispanic market," a major target
of business corporations. Social advances, however, are probably more funda-

mental than economic ones. The most significant social trend in Western Civilization during the last few decades has been the progress made by women. Happily, this improvement has been shared by women of color in the United States, including Mexicanas.

During the 1970s, mujeres found that they had more options available to them as traditional attitudes slowly broke down. Urbanization and the mass media were crucial catalysts in effecting this momentous change, though perhaps more telling was the increasing entry of women into the work force. While remaining seriously undereducated and underemployed, mujeres nonetheless experienced greater opportunities for personal growth, a positive gain shared by recently arrived immigrant women, as the studies of Pierrette Hondagneu-Sotelo, Julia E. Curry Rodríguez, and others suggest.

By the early nineties, more Latina women than Latino men were going to college and graduating. In 1991, according to the American Council on Education, Latinas earned 20,455 baccalaureates compared to 16,157 for Latinos, the result of long-term trends of which Mexicanas were a part. By the mid-nineties, there were more Hispanic women in the professions than there were Hispanic men. As educational and career opportunities expanded, some gifted mujeres were able to achieve national prominence in high-profile areas, among them singer Vikki Carr (1940–) in entertainment, golfer Nancy López (1957–) in sports, and astronaut Ellen Ochoa (1958–) in space exploration.

The progress made by Mexicanas in terms of education and careers was mirrored at the political level. The best example was one of the most influential figures in California politics, Gloria Molina (1948–), *Ms.* magazine's "Woman of the Year" in 1985. A Democrat from East Los Angeles, Molina was the first Chicana elected to the State Assembly (1982) and the Los Angeles City Council (1987). In 1991, she won a seat on the Los Angeles Board of Supervisors, the first woman, of any ethnic background, ever elected to that powerful office.

Other mujeres who have enjoyed political success in the post-Chicano era include State Senator Polly Baca Barragán (1941–), from Colorado, elected vice-chair of the Democratic National Committee in 1984; Mari Luci Jaramillo (1928–), an educator from New Mexico, who served as Ambassador to Honduras; and Romana Bañuelos (1925–), Katherine Ortega (1934–), and Catalina Vásquez Villalpando (1940–), Republicans who have been appointed to the office of Treasurer of the United States.

Despite attempts since 1922—when Adelina Otero-Warren unsuccessfully ran for a congressional seat representing New Mexico—no Mexicanas were sent to Congress until 1992, when Edward Roybal's daughter, Lucille Roybal-Allard (1941–), a California Democrat, was elected to the U.S. House of Representatives. An equally significant victory occurred in another House seat election in southern California four years later, when, after a hotly contested race which drew national attention, Loretta Sánchez narrowly defeated nine-term incumbent Bob Dornan, a fiery archconservative, in Orange County, a Republican stronghold. The Democratic newcomer became the 46th Congressional District's first woman and first Hispanic Representative.

The steady, though uneven, progress made by mujeres since the seventies has been mirrored and to some extent shaped by the Chicana movement, though possibly only a minority of Mexicanas identify with feminism at present. A lingering fear in the community at large of the feminist agenda as destructive of traditional family values and a threat to ethnicity has resulted in the domination of the Chicana movement during the past generation by women in academia. Since a lesbian component has become increasingly evident in university-based feminist circles, the movement has grown increasingly distant from the barrio, a trend encouraged by the ascendancy of a conservative political climate in the period under consideration. Chicana lesbians have had a difficult time winning acceptance. "Our culture," one of them lamented, "seeks to diminish us by placing us in a context of an Anglo construction, a supposed *vendida* to the race."[28] Antilesbian tendencies permeated even Chicana feminist groups, according to the sociologist Irene Blea.[29]

In terms of concrete reforms, the most effective women's organizations arose in the barrio, where, in spite of the hostile political climate, they were able to win significant victories. A good example of these kinds of associations, and there were hundreds of them, was Mothers of East Los Angeles (MELA or MOELA), a lay Catholic group led by Juana Beatríz Gutiérrez.[30] MELA waged a long and ultimately successful campaign in the mid-eighties to keep the state from building a prison in East Los Angeles, where residents were tired of being exploited by outside political interests. Mujeres also made progress by working in traditional middle-class ethnic organizations. In 1994, for example, LULAC elected its first woman national president, Belén Robles of El Paso, a forceful personality who enjoyed extraordinary power within the U.S. Hispanic community.

On college campuses, strongholds of Chicana feminism, Chicana Studies programs have steadily proliferated, an indication of the importance accorded women in academic circles. Spearheading this trend has been the University of California, especially the Davis campus, where in the early eighties, inspired by Adaljiza Sosa Riddell (1937–), a Chicana/Latina Research Institute was established. Given its university orientation, it is little surprise that the contemporary Chicana feminist movement, as María Linda Apodaca notes, has been a predominantly middle-class phenomenon.[31]

Without a large popular base, Chicana feminists have generally had to work through other advocacy groups in order to make an impact. Some have chosen to affiliate with white feminist groups like the National Organization for Women (NOW) or with professional organizations of various kinds, like the American Psychological Association or the Modern Language Association, forming Chicana caucuses within the general membership. A more popular option has been to work within Chicano organizations. Typical was NACS, where Chicanas initiated a campaign in 1982 to make their compañeros more responsive to women's issues. A measure of the success of the Chicana caucus, led by the historian Cynthia Orozco, in articulating the feminist agenda was that in 1994 the organization changed its name to the National Association for Chicana and Chicano Studies (NACCS).

Finally, many Chicana academics have felt a need for exclusive associations of their own. These organizations include Mujeres Activas en Letras y Cambio Social (MALCS, Women Active in Letters and Social Change), a national association organized in 1982 by a small group of committed female scholars, foremost among them being Sosa Riddell, as a support and research network for Chicana professors. Another academic association of a similar ilk, though broader in scope, is the Latina Leadership Network, a Hispanic organization of women employed in California community colleges organized in 1988, mainly through the efforts of Olga Arenivár and Betty Cotton, to recognize and foster leadership among its members.

Chicanas have also attempted to create national umbrella organizations, but these have had little lasting success. The first such initiative, on a major scale, was the Comisión Femenil Mexicana Nacional, formed in southern California in 1970. The Comisión was instrumental in setting up the Chicana Service Action Center in Los Angeles two years later, with Francisca Flores as founding director. In the mid-1970s, during the presidency of Gloria Molina, the Comisión tried to extend its sway nationally, but it soon clashed with the Mexican American Women's National Association (MANA), apparently in a jurisdictional dispute. Thereafter, despite its best efforts, it remained confined to California.

Like the Comisión, MANA was one of the few nationwide initiatives that arose outside of academia. Founded in Washington, D.C., in October 1974, as a sophisticated advocate for the rights of Hispanic women (not just Mexicanas), it flourished under the presidency of Elisa Sánchez (1977–1979). By the mid-1980s, according to Sylvia Alicia Gonzales, MANA was "the most prominent Mexican American women's organization nationally."[32] It has become less political in recent years.

By the mid-eighties, the National Association of Hispanic Women (NAHW), another middle-class women's group with national aspirations, was also at its peak. The brainchild of Sylvia L. Castillo (1951–), a clinical social worker, the Los Angeles–based organization was established in order to prepare Latinas for leadership positions in both public and private sectors. Although its membership was modest, about five hundred, the NAHW succeeded in reaching a wider audience through its prestigious journal *Intercambios Femeniles,* founded in 1980.

THE CHICANO RENAISSANCE

Another positive achievement by the Post-Chicano Generation has been a cultural and artistic flowering so vast in scope that the term *Chicano Renaissance* is entirely appropriate. A growing population, better education, and emergent affluence in Mexican communities have led, beginning in the 1960s when the movimiento provided the spark, to a veritable explosion of creativity unparalleled in the annals of Chicano history.

Undoubtedly, the most innovative advances have come in the field of literature, so it is appropriate to begin here before other art forms are surveyed. As in other fields, recent literary achievements have historical roots antedating the 1960s by many decades. These antecedents in the nineteenth century, especially narratives, have attracted the attention of a host of Chicano and Chicana scholars, among them Erlinda Gonzales-Berry, María Herrera Sobek, Rosaura Sánchez, Tey Diana Rebolledo, Genaro Padilla, Ramón Saldívar, José David Salívar, and Juan Bruce-Novoa.[33] However, despite diligent efforts to demolish what Padilla terms "the ethnocentric assumption that Mexican American culture has a meager literary tradition," it must be admitted that this literary output was relatively slight, hardly surprising given the modest socioeconomic conditions of an immigrant population.[34] Imaginative literature, mostly poetry, much of it produced by upper-class political refugees fleeing the Mexican Revolution, generally appeared in the columns of Spanish-language newspapers, which proliferated throughout the Southwest beginning in the late nineteenth century. Among the most popular of these publications were *La Prensa* in San Antonio (1913–1926) and *La Opinión* in Los Angeles (after 1926), both owned by Ignacio Lozano, Sr., a wealthy Mexican immigrant.

The Mexican-American Generation produced little of lasting value in literature, but there was one outstanding exception: *Pocho,* published in 1959 by Doubleday, the first significant novel about the Mexican experience in the United States written by a Mexican American, José Antonio Villarreal (1924–). Largely autobiographical, the work relates the difficulties of growing up the son of a Mexican immigrant in California's Santa Clara Valley during the 1920s and 1930s. Although a vast multitude of themes are covered—some of them universal in scope, others relating specifically to the immigrant experience—the author is most concerned with the search for identity, a major motif in subsequent Chicano literature. Villarreal moved to Mexico in 1973, a surprising turn of events given the assimilationist philosophy that seems to animate the protagonist of his book, and wrote two other novels, *The Fifth Horseman* (1974) and *Clemente Chacón* (1984), neither of which encountered the (belated) success of his initial effort. Given its pioneering features, many literary critics see *Pocho* as the first Chicano novel. Some go so far as to suggest that despite the rapid development of the genre in recent years, it remains the most outstanding novel ever written by a Mexican-American author.

The Chicano movement, with its emphasis on cultural regeneration, encouraged the rise of a whole community of authors—novelists, poets, short-story writers, and dramatists—and determined their choice of themes for years to come. Perhaps the most influential literary effort of these turbulent times was the epic poem *I am Joaquín/Yo Soy Joaquín* (1967) by Corky Gonzales. Written in anger, the work denounced racial oppression, hailed the rise of an awakening minority, and called for the restoration of Aztlán, the lost Chicano homeland. Capturing the mood of the times perfectly, the poem was exalted almost immediately as the leading expression of Chicanismo. Other Chicano poets taking their cue from Gonzales included Abelardo Delgado (1931–), Ricardo Sánchez (1941–), and Alberto Baltazar Urista Heredia (1947–), who writes under the pseudonym Alurista. "This period," according to the literary critic Nicolás Kanellos, "was one of euphoria, power, and influence for the Chicano poet, who was sought after almost as a priest, to give his blessings in the form of readings at all cultural and Chicano movement events."[35]

Another powerful influence on budding Chicano writers was the work of Oscar Zeta Acosta (1936–1974?), a militant Chicano lawyer who wrote two semiautographical novels espousing the philosophy of Chicanismo: *The Autobiography of a Brown Buffalo* (1972) and *The Revolt of the Cockroach People* (1973). The mood of the radical sixties is nowhere better evoked than in this erratic figure, who combined in his personality elements of the *vato loco* (literally, "crazy guy") and the Chicano intellectual. Always living on the edge, addicted to drugs, alcohol, and women, Acosta dropped out of sight in 1974, presumably a drowning victim off the coast of Mazatlán. At the time of his disappearance, Chicano literature was beginning to flower.

The most innovative early Chicano novelists were Tomás Rivera (1935–1984), Rudolfo A. Anaya (1937–), and Rolando Hinojosa (1929–), all of them professors at major southwestern universities. The first of these is generally considered, in spite of his premature death, the preeminent Chicano man of letters. "By any accounts," writes Kanellos, "Tomás Rivera remains the most outstanding and influential figure in the literature of Mexican peoples in the United States, and he deserves a place in the canon of Spanish-language literature in the world."[36] This lofty reputation is largely based on his seminal novel " . . . *y no se lo tragó la tierra"* (1971), which deals with Texas migrant workers, a subject the Crystal City native knew intimately. Anaya, a nuevomexicano, wrote copiously—his output includes a number of plays as well as novels—but like his colleague Rivera, his fame rests largely on a single novel, *Bless Me Ultima* (1972), "the best-selling and arguably the most popular Chicano literary work ever."[37] Hinojosa, on the other hand, has produced a vast body of literature, in both English and Spanish, in the form of a cycle of novels (à la Emile Zola)—what he calls the Klail City Death Trip Series—all of it judged to be uniformly outstanding. The setting throughout is the fictional Texas city named Klail where Hinojosa, himself a native of Mercedes, recreates the life of his people, the Tejanos of the Lower Rio Grande Valley. Other renowned Mexican-American novelists are Lionel G. García (1935–), born in San Diego, Texas, the author of *Leaving Home* (1985); and Alejandro Morales (1944–), a native of Montebello, California, whose most acclaimed work is *The Brick People* (1988), a historical novel.

By the 1980s, Chicanas were becoming highly visible as professional writers, a barometer of the strides mujeres were beginning to make in education. In their work, feminist themes combined with motifs they shared with their male counterparts: cultural conflict, racial oppression, alienation, and the search for identity. Since the late 1980s, Chicana literary achievements have begun to rival those of Chicano authors, especially as regards the novel.[38]

Among the reasons for their popularity was the advent of Women's Studies programs throughout the country which, together with the emphasis on multiculturalism in academic institutions at this time, created a heavy demand for their works. Although almost all were committed feminists, the best of them were able to communicate with a variety of audiences. Lucha Corpi (1945–), born in Mexico, but now based in the Bay Area, evokes the halcyon days of the Chicano movement on college campuses in the 1960s in her novel *Delia's Song* (1989). Among the most prolific Chicana novelists were midwesterners Ana Castillo (1953–) and Sandra Cisneros (1954–), both from Chicago. Castillo began as a poet, but her first novel, *The Mixquiahuala Letters* (1986), an avant-garde epistolary work, firmly established her credentials as a master of that genre among both critics and the public. This reputation was confirmed shortly afterwards with the publication of *So Far from God* (1993), winner of a Carl Sandburg Award. Like Ana Castillo, Cisneros has succeeded in winning contracts with major American publishing firms, a measure not only of her own considerable skill but also of the increasing respect accorded to Hispanic-American literature. Her best efforts include *The House on Mango Street* (1984), a terse semiautobiographical novel; *Woman Hollering Creek, and Other Stories* (1991), a collection of short stories; and *My Wicked, Wicked Ways* (1992), a book of poetry. The San Antonio–based writer was presented the prestigious MacArthur Foundation "genius award" in 1995.[39] Denise

Chávez (1948–), a native of Las Cruces, New Mexico, is probably the most versatile Chicana writer; a playwright and poet, she is also proficient as a short-story writer. Her forte, though, seems to be longer works of fiction, a judgment based on the lavish praise accorded her two novels, *The Last of the Menu Girls* (1986), actually a short-story cycle, and *Face of an Angel* (1993), written in a more conventional format. Chávez has won a multitude of literary prizes for her vivid portraits of ethnic family life and has acquired a solid and well-deserved reputation even beyond Chicano circles.

The short story, "perhaps the strongest genre in Chicano literature today," according to the critic Ray González, is a literary form that has been extremely popular among Mexican authors in the United States.[40] A master of the art is Estela Portillo Trambley (1936–), a Tejana whose short stories—and plays—of the 1970s had a profound influence on feminist writers of the following decade. Though less influential, Helena María Viramontes (1954–), born in East Los Angeles and author of *The Moths and Other Stories* (1985), has also left her mark in this burgeoning art form.

Poetry continued to flourish as the Chicano movement faded. The foremost Chicano poet is undoubtedly Gary Soto (1952–), whose vision transcends Chicanismo. Soto grew up in the central San Joaquin Valley and attended California State University at Fresno, where he became part of a school of poets representing different ethnic traditions. There he studied under Phillip Levine, making him the first Mexican-American literary figure to be trained by a major American poet. His writing output includes short stories, as well as his better-known poetic works. Like Denise Chávez, Soto has won many awards and is highly regarded by academic peers.[41] Albuquerque-born Jimmy Santiago Baca (1952–), an ex-convict, has become one of the Southwest's most respected poets. Pat Mora (1942–), from El Paso, and Lorna Dee Cervantes (1954–), from northern California, are also renowned for their poetry, the first for a whole series of published works, including *Communion* (1991), the second for her *Emplumada* (1981), a collection of narrative poems. Gloria Anzaldúa, a Tejana, has received acclaim not only because of her verses in *Borderlands/La Frontera: The New Mestiza* (1987) but also because of her work as editor of an important anthology, *This Bridge Called My Back: Writings by Radical Women of Color* (1981). Another prominent poet is the multifaceted Cherríe Moraga (1952–), coeditor of *This Bridge Called My Back*. A lesbian and strong feminist, like her compañera Anzaldúa, Moraga is best known for her explorations of sexuality—especially in her early essays and poems published in 1983 under the title, *Loving in the War Years*—a topic finding increasing interest among university-based Chicano and Chicana intellectuals.

Moraga has also made a name for herself in the field of drama, where she has continued to explore gender issues. *Giving Up the Ghost* (1984) remains her most celebrated play. Carlos Mortón (1947–), still another Mexican from Chicago, likewise emphasizes sexuality in most of his dramatic works. The foremost playwright, however, remains Luis Valdez (1940–), perhaps the best dramatist, regardless of ethnic background, currently working in the Southwest. Born in Delano, Valdez attended San Jose State College and studied drama in San Francisco before returning to his hometown to aid the cause of the farmworkers in the mid-sixties. A steadfast supporter of Chávez and the UFW, Valdez used the stage as a vehicle to publicize the plight of farmworkers and strengthen their commitment to working-class unity. El Teatro Campesino, his bilingual theater of farmworkers, was very effective in reaching a wide audience, because it built on a long tradition of popular theater, both professional and amateur, in Mexico and the Southwest, and because it espoused Indianist elements that appealed to Chicano youth.

Ultimately, El Teatro Campesino spawned over one hundred teatro troupes in barrios and universities throughout the Southwest and beyond, some rural and some urban, but all of them exploring raza themes, thus earning Luis Valdez recognition as the father of Chicano theater. Among the most professional of these theatrical groups were the Teatro Desengaño del Pueblo in Gary, Indiana; the Teatro Urbano in Los Angeles; the Teatro de la Gente in San Jose; and the Teatro de la Esperanza in Santa Barbara, later relocated to San Francisco's Mission District.

Desiring to expand his artistic horizons, Valdez left Delano in the late sixties and embarked on a series of productions that would win him popular acclaim far and wide. Many of these projects centered around El Teatro Campesino, which in 1971 made its permanent headquarters in San Juan Bautista, just south of the Bay Area. Through the years, Valdez has gradually moved away from political satire to embrace more mystical and universal themes. His most celebrated theatrical productions have been the musical play *Zoot Suit* (1978) and *I Don't Have to Show You No Stinking Badges* (1986), another mainstream work. He is also an accomplished filmmaker and poet. In fact, "Valdez has no peer in the history of Chicano arts," according to literary critic Ed Morales.[42]

Chicano achievements in film in recent years have been only slightly less meaningful than those in literature. From the very inception of the film industry, movies elicited an enthusiastic response in Mexican-origin communities in the United States. At the outset, the most popular films were those made in Mexico starring Mexican actors. A particularly intimate relationship between audience and actors developed in the Mexican film tradition. It was not unusual, especially in the forties and fifties, to see Mexican matinee idols like Pedro Infante, Jorge Negrete, Pedro Armendáriz, Arturo de Córdova, Tin Tan (Germán Valdez), Cantinflas (Mario Moreno Reyes), Dolores del Río, and María Félix tour the United

States, visiting small communities as well as larger cities like San Antonio and Los Angeles.

Mexicans have always been represented in Hollywood. Up to the seventies, however, it was almost exclusively as actors and actresses, usually in supporting roles—although there were notable exceptions, from Ramón Novarro (José Ramón Gil Samaniego) to Anthony Quinn. Moreover, they were invariably stereotyped into certain "Mexican" roles, mostly negative, as criminal bandits, unfaithful lovers, and immoral mistresses. After the 1960s, however, Mexicans found enhanced opportunities in the acting profession, often in nontraditional roles, and they began to enter into the production side of the industry.

Boulevard Nights (1979), depicting gang life in the barrios, was a landmark film because it featured an all-Latino cast. Since that time, Mexican performers have made steady progress. The most accomplished raza actor, winner of two Supporting Actor Oscars, continues to be the ever popular Anthony Quinn (1915–), one of the most prolific and celebrated names in international cinema. Together with Ricardo Montalbán, another Mexican immigrant who made good in Hollywood, Quinn has also been persistent in promoting Latinos in the mainstream movie industry.

Among the numerous Mexican-American actors and actresses who have become familiar faces to Hollywood audiences in the past few years, Edward James Olmos (1947–) stands out from the rest. His many credits include *Zoot Suit* (1981), based on the Valdez play; *The Ballad of Gregorio Cortez* (1982), a recreation of the popular border corrido; *Stand and Deliver* (1988), where his portrayal of East Los Angeles calculus teacher Jaime Escalante earned him an Academy Award nomination; *American Me* (1992), the controversial depiction of prison life, which he also produced and directed; and *Selena* (1997), a biography of the singing idol.

The most exciting development in the film industry has been the sudden appearance of Chicanos behind the camera, as writers, producers, and directors. Most of this work has been done outside major studios, as independent productions. The first Chicano film, *I Am Joaquín* (1970), based on Corky Gonzales's poem, was made by Luis Valdez, appropriately enough. Other Chicano filmmakers, many of them products of the UCLA film school in the early 1970s, followed in his footsteps. The vanguard included Moctezuma Esparza, Ricardo Soto, Jesús Salvador Treviño, Paul Espinosa, and Sylvia Morales. Together these producer-directors and their Chicano colleagues have developed an impressive array of documentaries and docudramas. These include *Yo Soy Chicano* (1972) by Treviño, *A La Brava* (1973) by Soto, *Chicana* (1979) by Morales, *The Trail North* (1983) by Espinosa, and *Ballad of an Unsung Hero* (1984) by Espinosa and Isaac Artenstein.[43] Artenstein's *Border Brujo* (1990), featuring Mexican performance artist Guillermo Gómez-Peña, is an innovative merger of cinematography and theater.

Outstanding feature films made by independent Chicano artists include Treviño's *Seguín* (1982); Gregory Nava's *El Norte* (1983); *And the Earth Did Not Part* (1992), an adaptation of Rivera's novel, directed by Severo Pérez and produced by Espinosa; as well as the aforementioned *Ballad of Gregorio Cortez,* directed by Robert Young and produced by Esparza.

Some Chicano directors have succeeded in breaking into Hollywood, foremost among them Luis Valdez, who made his play *Zoot Suit* into a feature film in 1981. He followed up this box-office success with a film biography of Ritchie Valens, *La Bamba* (1987), which grossed more than $50 million, sending the signal to the movie industry that Latino movies could be moneymakers. Almost as successful as a commercial and artistic venture was *Born in East L.A.* (1987), a satire by Richard ("Cheech") Marín, who directed and starred in the film. *The Milagro Beanfield War* (1988), coproduced by Esparza; *Stand and Deliver,* directed by Ramón Menéndez; and *My Family* (1995), cowritten and directed by Nava with a strong performance by Jimmy Smits, all contributed to the phenomenon known as Hispanic Hollywood.

Another area of creativity where Latinos have excelled in recent years is in the plastic arts. Here, too, Chicanismo has served to stimulate enormous artistic achievement. The basic themes are similar to those pursued by the literary community. Pre-Columbian Indian influences are pronounced, a reflection of the indigenismo resurrected by the movimiento. Spanish themes are decidedly less evident; however, Catholicism, an Iberian legacy, continues to exert a potent influence on artists, as it does on the community at large.[44] The Virgen de Guadalupe is probably the single most prevalent motif. More recent Mexican influences are evident in the continuing Chicano fascination with the Mexican Revolution, the quintessential symbol of resistance to oppression.

The most popular form of artistic expression has been mural painting, which peaked in the seventies, but continues to prosper in Latino communities throughout the country today. Undoubtedly, the cardinal influence on barrio artists was that of the three great Mexican muralists produced by the Revolution: José Clemente Orozco, David Alfaro Siqueiros, and Diego Rivera. Rivera's wife, Frida Kahlo, a first-rate artist in her own right, has had a profound impact as well, especially on Chicana artists. Although a little-known fact, contemporary Chicano painters have also looked to a home-bred muralist tradition that developed after the 1920s, one best represented by Antonio García and José Aceves, both Mexican immigrants to Texas, and the New Mexican Edward Chávez.

The Chicano mural movement that surfaced in the late sixties was centered in southern California, notably Los Angeles, where the leading representative has been Judith Baca (1946–). A graduate of California State University at Northridge, Baca studied mural painting techniques in Mexico before initiating her career as one of the most prominent women artists in the United States. In 1976, she was a cofounder of the Social and Public Art Resource Center (SPARC), headquartered in Venice, California. Subsequently, as the organization's artistic director, she sponsored many aspiring minority artists.

Another flourishing southern California art hub has been San Diego, where some of the most impressive efforts can be seen in Chicano Park—under the Coronado Bridge—and at the Centro Cultural de la Raza (La Raza Cultural Center), located near the city center in Balboa Park. Many of these San Diego murals were painted by the Congreso de Artistas Chicanos en Aztlán (Congress of Chicano Artists of Aztlán), an art collective previously known as the Toltecas de Aztlán, the brainchild of Salvador Roberto Torres.

The San Francisco Bay Area, a citadel for all the visual arts, also witnessed the proliferation of Chicano murals. Among the most active local groups was Mujeres Muralistas (Women Muralists), founded in 1972 by Texas-born Patricia Rodríguez (1944–), a graduate of the San Francisco Art Institute. Five years later, Susan Cervantes founded the Precita Eyes Mural Arts Center, in the Mission District, the cradle of the mural movement in the city. Stanford University, in nearby Palo Alto, boasts the impressive series of murals done by the multitalented José Antonio Burciaga (1940–1996) at Casa Zapata.

The Chicano Royal Air Force (CRAF), a Sacramento-based artist cooperative, was founded by José Montoya and Estéban Villa. Consistent supporters of Chávez and the farmworkers, they combine mural painting with a variety of other art forms, notably posters.

Outside of California the most innovative murals are to be found in New Mexico and Illinois. In Santa Fe, the Leyba brothers, Samuel, Carlos, and Albert, were instrumental in organizing a group of muralists whose work would win them national recognition. Chicago, with its rich artistic tradition and a relatively prosperous Hispanic population, was soon competing with the barrios of the Southwest as a center of Chicano artistic expression. The chief exponents of the Windy City's muralist movement were two Mexican immigrants, Marcos Raya and José González, the latter the founder of the Movimiento Artistico Chicano (MArCh, Chicano Artistic Movement).

Many muralists eventually expanded into easel painting, a form of artistic expression that developed simultaneously with the mural tradition. These Chicano painters, too, had worthy predecessors whose work largely antedated the turbulent sixties. Pioneers included Melesio Casas of San Antonio, Eugenio Quesada of Phoenix, and Peter Rodríguez of Stockton. Rodríguez also founded the Mexican Museum in San Francisco in 1972. Under the direction of Marie Acosta-Colón, this institution has become the biggest and most prestigious Mexican and Chicano art museum in the nation and a major influence on Latino artists everywhere.

Among artists of the sixties who dedicated themselves to both mural and easel painting were the members of the Los Angeles–based Los Four: Frank Romero, Gilbert ("Magú") Luján, Beto de la Rocha, and Carlos Almaráz. Unwavering advocates of Chicanismo, Los Four concentrated on political themes. Almaráz, born in Mexico City in 1941 and raised in East Los Angeles, eventually went on to become one of the most acclaimed Chicano artists in the country before his untimely death in 1989. Also excelling in both major forms of painting was another Angeleno, Glugio Gronk Nicandro, or simply Gronk (1954–). Beginning his career as a member of the collective ASCO ("nausea")—with Patssi Valdez, Willie Herron III, and Harry Gamboa, Jr.—his superb talents soon placed Gronk in a category all by himself.

While California was indisputably in the forefront of Chicano artistic developments, Texas was not far behind. For Tejanos, the most promising cultural environment was San Antonio, which produced a number of highly regarded painters, including César Martínez (1944–) and Jesse Treviño (1946–). The Gallería Sin Fronteras (Gallery without Borders), an Austin-based art gallery established by the sociologist Gilberto Cárdenas in 1986, offers local artists an excellent marketplace to display and sell their works, while serving as a valuable source of art education for the Spanish-speaking community.

Printmaking is another medium that has attracted Chicano and Chicana artists. The Bay Area continues to be a mecca for graphic artists. Among its principal Latino practitioners have been silk-screen artists Malaquías Montoya (1938–) and Rupert García (1941–), both of whom continue to emphasize movimiento themes, true to their Chicano roots. Carmen Lomas Garza (1948–) and Ester Hernández (1944–), the latter an uncompromising feminist, are other celebrated printmakers based in San Francisco.

Chicanos have also excelled in sculpture, where there is a rich tradition going back to the New Mexican *santeros* (makers of saints' images) of the early nineteenth century. An important bridge linking the traditional santeros with contemporary wood carving was the work of Patrociño Barela (1900–1964), the first Mexican-American artist to receive national acclaim, his sculptures having been displayed in New York's Museum of Modern Art in the mid-1930s. Long neglected by art critics and historians, this solitary genius is now gaining appreciation as one of America's most creative artists of his time. Perhaps the most widely recognized sculptor emerging from the Mexican community since the Second World War is Manuel Neri, born in the San Joaquin Valley town of Sanger in 1930, a professor emeritus at UC Davis. Also significant has been the work of two younger sculptors, the Texas-born Luis Jiménez, whose fiberglass creations are thoroughly modern, and Amalia Mesa-Bains (1943–), whose altars represent a traditional folk artform.

Mexican achievement in music is less obvious than in other art forms, but even here there has been notable progress since the mid-seventies. As in most artistic fields, a rich musical tradition can be traced back to the nineteenth century, notably in the corridos that first became popular at that time. The early twentieth century saw the rise of two other long-term traditions, both of them Texas-based, as the respected ethnomusicologist Manuel Peña has pointed out recently: the *conjunto,* catering mainly to the lower classes, and the *orquesta,* middle-class music, considered *jaitón* ("high tone" or snobbish) by the masses.

Polkas, brought into Texas and Mexico from central Europe during the mid-nineteenth century, are the mainstays of conjunto music, the accordion its trademark instrument. The first great conjunto musician was the accordionist Narciso Martínez, who immigrated to Texas from Tamaulipas, where he was born in 1911. Exclusively instrumental at the outset, eventually conjunto music also became vocal, with one of its most popular interpreters being the legendary Texas songbird, Lydia Mendoza (1916–), among the finest singers ever produced by the borderlands.

Orquesta music, while retaining key Mexican elements, was markedly influenced by American music, notably the Big Band sound, the swing music of World War II. Beto Villa, the "father" of Orquesta Tejana, is representative, though his name is not as familiar today as that of Eduardo ("Lalo") Guerrero (1916–), another musical legend. Born in Tucson, Guerrero is identified with southern California, where he pursued a long and distinguished career as musician and composer after the late 1930s. Asked to perform at the White House on numerous occasions, he was awarded the National Medal of the Arts in 1996 by President Clinton. Prominent in Guerrero's varied repertoire was *música tropical,* a generic term for a variety of Afro-Latin strains—boleros, rumbas, cumbias, cha cha chá, etc.—emanating from the Caribbean. This musical genre has been popular among Mexicans in all regions of the country, especially where they reside in proximity to other Latino communities, as in Chicago and throughout California.

The steady resurgence of Mexican immigration in recent years has meant that musical tastes have undergone a slow metamorphosis in the Mexican communities of the United States. The triumph of conjunto over orquesta music is one consequence; the former has expanded its appeal from its Texas homeland, and today the popularity of the Tex-Mex sound extends well beyond the borderlands. Indeed, some artists, like Flaco Jiménez, have achieved international renown. The rise of *banda* music—a popular musical form related to conjunto, rooted in the brass band tradition, and imported from the northern Mexican states—is another significant tendency, particularly in California, the destination of so many recent norteño emigrants. In general, as the ethnomusicologist Steven

Loza has illustrated in *Barrio Rhythm* (1993), which focuses on southern California, musical styles were much more eclectic in the Golden State than in Texas.

Another musical trend has been the increased popularity of salsa, the latest manifestation of música tropical, especially among the Mexican-American middle class. With roots in the Caribbean, where it merged African and Spanish traditions, it was eventually imported into the United States, where jazz, an African-American musical form, altered it in interesting ways. Salsa has always had its most loyal following in this country in the Cuban and Puerto Rican communities of the East. After World War II, however, its infectious rhythm broadened its appeal to other regions. These included the Southwest, where it began to penetrate into Mexican communities, especially among the nascent middle class which was gradually abandoning conjunto music. As Mexicans and their Latino cousins came into closer proximity, a result of Latin American immigration into the Southwest and Mexican expansion from the borderlands into other regions, the lure of salsa during its boom years of the 1970s proved irresistible, with the Cuban singer Celia Cruz being a particular favorite. Ultimately, it captivated all segments of the Mexican community, save recently arrived immigrants who remained faithful to their more traditional musical forms, like the mariachis of El Mariachi Vargas de Tecalitlán, the ballads of Lola Beltrán, and the rancheras of José Alfredo Jiménez.

Some Mexican artists have crossed over into Anglo musical forms, a tendency which will accelerate as acculturation takes place. From its very inception in the fifties, rock and roll attracted a number of Latino musicians, of whom the most memorable is Ritchie Valens (Ricardo Valenzuela). Born into a migrant farm family in Pacoima, California, the promising pop idol died in an airplane accident in 1959, at the age of seventeen. The crossover tradition has been carried on more recently by Grammy Award winners Tijuana-born Carlos Santana, who combines salsa with rock, and Los Lobos, an East Los Angeles band combining many styles, including norteño music. The tradition is best exemplified, however, by Selena (Quintanilla), the Queen of Tejano, an updated version of Tex-Mex conjunto music. Her rocketing career, then in the process of making a transition to pop, ended tragically in 1995 when the twenty-three-year-old singer was slain by a disgruntled fan. Mexicans have even made inroads into country western music. Tejanos Johnny Rodríguez, Freddy Fender (Andrés Baldemar Huerta), and Tish Hinojosa have all made valuable contributions to this popular sound, while maintaining a distinctively Latino style.

The enormous fascination with Selena which swept across the country after her untimely death highlights what is perhaps the dominant musical trend since the seventies: the increasing popularity of Latino music in general, undoubtedly a reflection of spiraling demographic patterns. An expanding market has encouraged the rise of small Hispanic record companies and a renewed interest by established labels in recording Latino music, giving rise to unprecedented opportunities for Mexican and other Latino artists, and incidentally strengthening this indispensable component of ethnic culture.

In 1987, the eminent black scholar William Julius Wilson published a controversial study of African-American ghettos in Chicago, *The Truly Disadvantaged,* which popularized the notion, current among social scientists for some time, of an urban "underclass." The Harvard sociologist describes a lifestyle typically characterized by chronic unemployment, appalling poverty, dysfunctional families, substance abuse, and violence, much of it gang-related. This growing subculture owes its existence to a variety of factors, including deindustrialization and African-American middle-class flight to the suburbs. The book initiated a heated controversy in the academic community. One of the numerous questions sparked by the debate is whether the underclass model has validity outside the black community. Before too long, Latino barrios, which shared many of the characteristics of black ghettos—among them, crime, alcohol and drug addiction, and elevated school drop-out rates—came under scrutiny. Almost universally, Chicano anthropologists and sociologists have rejected the underclass model as applicable to the Mexican experience.[45]

Among the many trenchant differences between black and Mexican urban neighborhoods is that the latter are continually fed by new waves of immigrants eager to make their way in society, an optimism in marked contrast to the frustration and stagnation which seem to characterize the former. Moreover, while there is a flight by the Mexican middle class to suburbia, ties with the barrios are often maintained through extended families and in a variety of other ways. Cholo gangs, as destructive as they may be, by no means dominate barrio life; the anthropologist Carlos G. Vélez-Ibáñez estimates that only between 3 and 10 percent of barrio youths are gang members, even in Los Angeles.[46] A microcosm of the difference is to be found in southern California, where the despair of Watts—which erupted in the aftermath of the Rodney King decision in 1992—contrasts sharply with the vitality of adjoining Lynwood, a predominantly Mexican community with even more poverty.

Although there are exceptions, Mexican Americans have generally fared better than African Americans; however, there is little reason for complacency. The fact is that there are segments of Mexican society, both in and out of barrios, whose status approaches that of an underclass. Scholars Refugio I. Rochín and Mónica D. Castillo, for example, argue that such is the case in the mushrooming Mexican towns of California's agricultural valleys.[47] Cholo gangs in the cities are also representative of this unfortunate tendency.

There are grave problems in Mexican society, especially in impoverished areas. The family, as we have seen, while it continues to be hailed as a pillar of society by some Chicano scholars, shows serious signs of strain. In fact, by the mid-nineties, Mexican Americans had higher out-of-wedlock birthrates than even blacks. Immigrants are both a blessing and a bane. On the one hand, they replenish the ethnic community with people of unbounded vitality, ensuring the survival of a pluralistic identity; on the other hand, an endless influx of immigrants means Mexican communities as a whole will continue to occupy the lower socioeconomic ranks of U.S. society. Moreover, mobility will be hampered by those anti-progressive aspects of Mexican culture—continually revitalized by immigration, particularly in transnational communities—that have been alluded to before. Given the persistence of these attitudes, the future is not likely to bring radical improvements in the Mexican-American standard of living.

On a more positive note, fears that Mexicans will segregate themselves from the mainstream in the future (part of an ongoing debate on multiculturalism), a common complaint as the twentieth century draws to a close, are completely unwarranted. Certainly, Mexican Americans will continue to maintain a robust ethnic identity. Dr. Celestino Fernández, vice-president for undergraduate academic affairs at the University of Arizona, voices a majority perspective when he states, "I feel Mexican and I behave American."[48]

Still, while insisting on retaining their heritage, Mexicans, both the native-born and the immigrant, look upon life in the United States in a positive light, something that Professors David Hayes-Bautista and Rodolfo de la Garza both agree on. The angst experienced by Guillermo Gómez-Peña in adjusting to life in what he calls "Gringolandia" is hardly typical. Most Mexicans, as researchers Susan E. Keefe and Amado M. Padilla illustrate in their seminal work *Chicano Ethnicity* (1987), have opted for pluralistic solutions, attempting to preserve elements of both Mexican and American culture, though the inevitable pull will be toward the latter. Indeed, even Mexicans in Mexico are becoming more *agringados* (Gringo-ized).

For the middle class, particularly, the future will see growing integration into mainstream society, which, some observers feel, has already occurred to a greater extent among Mexicans than among most other Latinos. This evolution—documented recently by Pepperdine University's Institute for Public Policy—is most evident in southern California.

It seems unlikely that the acquisition of middle-class Anglo values by large segments of the Mexican community will slow down. The most compelling agent of this inclination will undoubtedly be interethnic marriages. It is estimated that during the late eighties and early nineties the rate of exogamy among Mexican Americans was between 15 and 20 percent, higher in certain metropolitan areas like Chicago, Los Angeles, and San Francisco. This tendency may not be as pronounced as it is among other minorities—the Japanese-American out-marriage rate is about 65 percent—but it is more prevalent than at any time in the past, and most observers agree that it will continue to increase in the future.[49] Furthermore, intermarriage, particularly with Anglos, is most evident among the Chicano intelligentsia (artists, writers, college professors, etc.), a powerful group of people who have an exceptional influence on how Mexican Americans define themselves and their interactions with other communities. More than any other trend, intermarriage promises to impact Anglo-Mexican relations in a positive way in the twenty-first century.

NOTES

INTRODUCTION

1. For a review of recent Chicano work in the field, see these historiographical articles: Tomás Almaguer, "Ideological Distortions in Recent Chicano Historiography: The Internal Model and Chicano Historical Interpretation," *Aztlán* 18 (Spring 1987): 7–28; Alex M. Saragoza, "Recent Chicano Historiography: An Interpretive Essay," *Aztlán* 19 (1988–1990): 1–78; Antonia I. Castañeda, "Women of Color and the Rewriting of Western History: The Discourse, Politics, and Decolonization of History," *Pacific Historical Review* 61 (Nov. 1992): 501–33; Richard Griswold del Castillo, "Chicano Historical Discourse: An Overview and Evaluation of the 1980s," *Perspectives in Mexican American Studies* 4 (1993): 1–25; David G. Gutiérrez, "Significant to Whom?: Mexican Americans and the History of the American West," *Western Historical Quarterly* 24 (Nov. 1993): 519–39; Gilbert G. González and Raúl Fernández, "Chicano History: Transcending Cultural Models," *Pacific Historical Review* 63 (Nov. 1994): 469–97; and Arnoldo De León and Carlos E. Cuéllar, "Chicanos in the City: A Review of the Monographic Literature," *The History Teacher* 29 (May 1996): 363–78.

2. Alex Saragoza concludes his excellent essay, "Recent Chicano Historiography," p. 21, by noting, "To press history to yield essentially an epic of heroes, victories, gallant resistance, and labor militancy blurs the everyday struggles of working Mexican men and women to sustain their dignity in a world that has taken a great deal, including, at times, their sense of self."

3. See Carlos Muñoz, *Youth, Identity, Power: The Chicano Movement* (New York: Verso, 1989), pp. 148, 152. The internal colonial model was based on the notion that non-European peoples have been systematically subordinated within Western nations in much the same way that Third World people have been victimized by Western imperialism. Associated with Robert Blauner, a sociologist at the University of California at Berkeley, the internal colonial model enjoyed widespread success among emerging minority scholars in the 1960s and 1970s. During this period Chicano academics, particularly Carlos Muñoz and Mario Barrera, sought to adapt the model as the foremost paradigm explaining the plight of Mexicans in the United States. For criticisms of internal colonialism theories, see Joe R. Feagin and Clairece Booher Feagin, *Racial and Ethnic Relations,* 4th ed. (Englewood Cliffs, N.J.: Prentice-Hall, 1993), pp. 39–40.

4. Carey McWilliams, *North from Mexico* (New York: J. B. Lippincott, 1949).

5. See, for example, Joseph Navarro, "The Condition of Mexican-American History," *The Journal of Mexican-American History* 1 (1970): 25–45. Ralph H. Vigil, on the other hand, calls the book "an impressionistic study that has aspects of New Deal Liberalism mingled with benign condescension." "The Borderlands History: A Critique," *New Mexico Historical Review* 48 (July 1973): 197.

6. *North from Mexico* (New York, Praeger) was revised and updated in 1990 by Matt S. Meier, who added three chapters.

7. Matt S. Meier and Feliciano Rivera, *The Chicanos: A History of Mexican Americans* (New York: Hill and Wang, 1972).

8. Rodolfo Acuña, *Occupied America: The Chicano's Struggle toward Liberation* (San Francisco: Canfield Press, 1972).

9. Richard A. García, "The Origins of Chicano Cultural Thought: Visions and Paradigms—Romero's Culturalism, Alurista's Aesthetics, and Acuña's Communalism," *California History* 74 (Fall 1995): 293.

10. See, for example, Emilio Zamora, "Critical Comments on *Occupied America*," in *Occupied America: A Chicano History Symposium,* ed. Tatcho Mindiola, Jr. (Houston: Mexican American Studies Program, University of Houston, 1982), pp. 41–47. An especially vitriolic criticism of Acuña's perspective is found in Manuel A. Machado, *Listen Chicano!: An Informal History of the Mexican American* (Chicago: Nelson Hall, 1978).

11. Quoted in George Ramos, "In This Fight, Rudy Acuña Has All Angles Covered," *Los Angeles Times,* 22 Mar. 1993. Acuña sued the university after he was denied the post and won an age discrimination suit before a federal court on 30 October 1995.

12. Rodolfo Acuña, *Occupied America,* 2d ed. (New York: Harper and Row, 1981), pp. viii–ix.

13. García, "Origins of Chicano Cultural Thought," pp. 302–3.

14. Saragoza, "Recent Chicano Historiography," p. 10.

15. For a survey of these revisionist trends, see Griswold del Castillo, "Chicano Historical Discourse."

16. In a recent work, *North to Aztlán: A History of Mexican Americans in the United States* (New York: Twayne Publishers, 1996), Richard Griswold del Castillo and Arnoldo De León incorporate some of these revisionist views. In general, they deemphasize the concept of racial oppression, as I do; however, as the title of their important survey indicates—Aztlán has symbolic significance for cultural nationalists—the authors do not entirely abandon the nationalistic school of thought which continues to dominate Chicano historiography.

17. David J. Weber, *Foreigners in Their Native Land: Historical Roots of the Mexican-Americans* (Albuquerque: University of New Mexico Press, 1973).

18. Juan Gómez-Quiñones and Luis Leobardo Arroyo, "On the State of Chicano History: Observations on Its Development, Interpretations, and Theory, 1970–1974," *Western Historical Quarterly* 7 (Apr. 1976): 178.

19. Gutiérrez, "Significant to Whom?" p. 525.

20. The long-awaited study by Vicki Ruiz, *From Out of the Shadows: Mexican Women in Twentieth-Century America,* to be published by Oxford University Press, will go a long way in correcting this deficiency.

21. Angelina F. Veyna, "Chicanas/Latinas: Where Do We Fit in the Curriculum?" *Esperanza: Latina Leadership Network Newsletter* (Fall 1994): 7.

22. These include Sarah Deutsch, *No Separate Refuge: Culture, Class, and Gender on the Anglo-Hispanic Frontier in the American Southwest, 1880–1940* (New York: Oxford University Press, 1987); Vicki L. Ruiz, *Cannery Women, Cannery Lives: Mexican Women, Unionization, and the California Food Processing Industry, 1930–1950* (Albuquerque: University of New Mexico Press, 1987); Camille Guerin-Gonzales, *Mexican Workers and American Dreams: Immigration, Repatriation, and California Farm Labor, 1900–1939* (New Brunswick, N.J.: Rutgers University Press, 1994); Devra Weber, *Dark Sweat, White Gold: California Farm Workers, Cotton, and the New Deal* (Berkeley: University of California Press, 1994); and Lisbeth Haas, *Conquests and Historical Identities in California, 1769–1936* (Berkeley: University of California Press, 1995).

23. Mark McDonald, "Term Limits: Hispanic? Latino? A National Debate Proves No One Name Pleases Everyone," *Dallas Morning News,* 13 Jan. 1993.

1. SPANIARDS AND NATIVE AMERICANS

1. Richard Herr, *Spain* (Englewood Cliffs, N.J.: Prentice-Hall, 1971), p. 36.

2. Eugene K. Keefe et al., *Area Handbook for Spain* (Washington, D.C.: U.S. Government Printing Office, 1976), p. 127.

3. Alistair Cooke, *Alistair Cooke's America* (New York: Alfred A. Knopf, 1980), p. 35.

4. The various interpretations of Columbus are surveyed in Alfred W. Crosby, *The Columbian Voyages, the Columbian Exchange, and Their Historians* (Washington, D.C.: American Historical Association, 1987).

5. Timothy Foote, "Where Columbus Was Coming From," *Smithsonian* 22 (Dec. 1991): 29.

6. John Noble Wilford, "Columbus and the Labyrinth of History," *Wilson Quarterly* 15 (Autumn 1991): 81.

7. Felipe Fernández-Armesto, "Columbus—Hero or Villain?" *History Today* 42 (May 1992): 9.

8. Wilcomb Washburn, *The Indian in America* (New York: Harper and Row, 1975), p. xvi.

9. Arrell Morgan Gibson, *The American Indian: Prehistory to the Present* (Lexington, Mass.: D.C. Heath, 1980), p. 4.

10. An understanding of Mesoamerican people immediately before and after the Spanish Conquest should begin with Eric R. Wolf's provocative *Sons of the Shaking Earth* (Chicago: University of Chicago Press, 1959).

11. Inga Clendinnen, *Aztecs: An Interpretation* (Cambridge: Cambridge University Press, 1991), p. 98.

12. William H. Prescott, *History of the Conquest of Mexico* (New York, Bantam Books, 1967).

13. William H. McNeill, *Plagues and Peoples* (Garden City, N.Y.: Anchor Press/Doubleday, 1976), p. 183.

14. See Hugh Thomas, *Conquest: Montezuma, Cortés, and the Fall of Old Mexico* (New York: Simon and Schuster, 1994).

15. Octavio Paz, "Reflections (Mexico and the United States)," *The New Yorker,* 17 Sept. 1979, p. 140.

16. Jack D. Forbes, *The Indian in America's Past* (Englewood Cliffs, N.J.: Prentice-Hall, 1964), p. 3.

17. In point of fact, many sixteenth-century Spanish jurists and theologians spoke up in defense of native Americans, leading one Spanish scholar to remark: "Never to this day has a colonial empire been built with such a sense of responsibility and self-criticism." Alfredo Jiménez, "The Spanish Colonial Model," in *Handbook of Hispanic Cultures in the United States: History,* ed. Alfredo Jiménez (Houston, Tex.: Arte Público Press and Instituto de Cooperación Iberoamericana, 1994), p. 77.

18. Carlos Fuentes, *The Buried Mirror: Reflections on Spain and the New World* (New York: Houghton Mifflin, 1992), p. 134. It has even been argued by Guillermo Céspedes, *Latin America: The Early Years* (New York: Alfred A. Knopf, 1974), p. 55, that "[c]oming from the racial melting pot of Iberia, Spaniards and Portuguese were not racially ethnocentric," though this seems an exaggeration.

19. Pablo Neruda, *Memoirs,* trans. Hardie St. Martin (New York: Farrar, Straus and Giroux, 1977), p. 54.

20. Richard Rodríguez, *Days of Obligation* (New York: Viking Penguin, 1992), p. 24.

2. THE SPANISH FRONTIER

1. Turner's essay can be found in *Frederick Jackson Turner: Wisconsin's Historian of the*

Frontier, ed. Martin Ridge (Madison: The State Historical Society of Wisconsin, 1986), pp. 26–47; and *Where Cultures Meet: Frontiers in Latin American History,* ed. David J. Weber and Jane M. Rausch (Wilmington, Del.: Scholarly Resources, 1994), pp. 1–18.

2. John Francis Bannon, *The Spanish Borderlands Frontier, 1513–1821* (New York: Holt, Rinehart and Winston, 1970), p. 3. The starting point for a student of the Spanish frontier is David J. Weber's highly acclaimed *The Spanish Frontier in North America* (New Haven: Yale University Press, 1992).

3. David J. Weber, "Reflections on Coronado and the Myth of Quivira," in *Myth and the History of the Hispanic Southwest: Essays by David J. Weber* (Albuquerque: University of New Mexico Press, 1988), p. 4.

4. The Spaniards would continue to explore and settle Florida and other parts of the Southeast during the next few centuries, but this area is not crucial in explaining the roots of the Mexican-American people. Consequently, these eastern borderlands will be dealt with only when they have an impact on the northern frontier of New Spain. Those interested in the Southeast should consult the appropriate sections of Weber's *Spanish Frontier in North America.*

5. The standard biography, a minor classic, remains Herbert E. Bolton, *Coronado: Knight of Pueblos and Plains* (Albuquerque: University of New Mexico Press, 1964).

6. For a fine biography by a historian with sterling credentials, see Marc Simmons, *The Last Conquistador: Juan de Oñate and the Settling of the Far Southwest* (Norman: University of Oklahoma Press, 1991).

7. The importance of the mission on the Spanish frontier was first established by the great borderlands historian Herbert Eugene Bolton. See his 1917 essay "The Mission as a Frontier Institution in the Spanish-American Colonies," reprinted in a slightly abridged version in *New Spain's Far Northern Frontier: Essays on Spain in the American West, 1540–1821,* ed. David J. Weber (Albuquerque: University of New Mexico Press, 1979), pp. 51–65.

8. For a concise description of this revolutionary episode, see Joe S. Sando, "The Pueblo Revolt," in *Handbook of North American Indians,* vol. 9, *Southwest,* ed. Alfonso Ortiz (Washington, D.C.: Smithsonian Institution, 1979), pp. 194–97. See, too, Roberto Mario Salmón, *Indian Revolts in Northern New Spain: A Synthesis of Resistance (1680–1786)* (Lanham, Md.: University Press of America, 1991).

9. Jesús F. de la Teja, "Forgotten Founders: The Military Settlers of Eighteenth-Century San Antonio de Béxar," in *Tejano Origins in Eighteenth-Century San Antonio,* ed. Gerald E. Poyo and Gilberto M. Hinojosa (Austin: University of Texas Press, 1991), p. 37.

10. Robert C. West, *Sonora: Its Geographical Personality* (Austin: University of Texas Press, 1993), p. 43.

11. Jesuit efforts on the peninsula are traced in minute detail by Harry W. Crosby, *Antigua California: Mission and Colony on the Peninsular Frontier, 1697–1768* (Albuquerque: University of New Mexico Press, 1994).

12. Marc Simmons, "Settlement Patterns and Village Plans in Colonial New Mexico," *Journal of the West* 8 (Jan. 1969): 19.

13. Thomas D. Hall, *Social Change in the Southwest, 1350–1880* (Lawrence: University Press of Kansas, 1989), p. 147.

14. Robert H. Jackson and Edward Castillo, *Indians, Franciscans, and Spanish Colonization: The Impact of the Mission System on California Indians* (Albuquerque: University of New Mexico Press, 1995), p. 44.

15. Alicia Vidaurreta Tjarks, "Comparative Demographic Analysis of Texas, 1777–1793," *Southwestern Historical Quarterly* 77 (Jan. 1974): 301.

16. Albert Hurtado, *Indian Survival on the California Frontier* (New Haven: Yale University Press, 1988), p. 22.

17. Adrian Bustamante, "'The Matter Was Never Resolved': The *Casta* System in Colonial New Mexico, 1693–1823," *New Mexico Historical Review* 66 (Apr. 1991): 145.

18. See, for example, Ramón A. Gutiérrez, *When Jesus Came, the Corn Mothers Went Away: Marriage, Sexuality, and Power in New Mexico, 1500–1846* (Stanford: Stanford University Press, 1991).

19. Antonio José Ríos-Bustamante, "New Mexico in the Eighteenth Century: Life, Labor and Trade in la Villa de San Felipe de Albuquerque, 1706–1790," *Aztlán* 7 (Fall 1976): 372–73.

20. Richard L. Nostrand, "Hispano Cultural Distinctiveness: A Reply," *Annals of the Association of American Geographers* 74 (1984): 168 n3.

21. Marc Simmons, "History of Pueblo-Spanish Relations to 1821," in *Handbook of North American Indians,* vol. 9, p. 192.

22. Frances León Swadesh, *Los Primeros Pobladores: Hispanic Americans on the Ute Frontier* (Notre Dame: University of Notre Dame Press, 1974), p. 40.

23. Based on the 1790 census, and taking into account that many mixed bloods were designated *españoles,* Antonio Ríos-Bustamante estimates that "anywhere from 70 to 80 percent of the population of Albuquerque were mestizo in fact, if not in convention by 1790." "New Mexico in the Eighteenth Century," p. 380.

24. Andrés Tijerina, *Tejanos and Texas under the Mexican Flag, 1821–1836* (College Station: Texas A&M University Press, 1994), pp. 7–8.

25. Ignaz Pfefferkorn, *Sonora: A Description of the Province,* trans. Theodore E. Treutlein (Tucson: University of Arizona Press, 1989), p. 284.

26. Manuel Servín, "California's Spanish Heritage: A View into the Spanish Myth," *Journal of San Diego History* 19 (1973): 3.

27. Jack D. Forbes, "Hispano-Mexican Pioneers of the San Francisco Bay Region: An Analysis of Racial Origins," *Aztlán* 14 (Spring 1983): 178; Antonio Ríos-Bustamante and Pedro Castillo, *An Illustrated History of Mexican Los Angeles, 1781–1985* (Los Angeles: Chicano Studies Research Center Publications, University of California, 1986), p. 33.

28. Antonia I. Castañeda, "Sexual Violence in the Politics and Policies of Conquest: Amerindian Women and the Spanish Conquest of Alta California," in *Building with Our Hands: New Directions in Chicana Studies,* ed. Adela de la Torre and Beatríz M. Pesquera (Berkeley: University of California Press, 1993), pp. 23, 29.

29. Frances Hernández, "The Secret Jews of the Southwest," *Outlook* 63 (Fall 1992): 12.

30. David J. Weber, *The Mexican Frontier, 1821–1846: The American Southwest under Mexico* (Albuquerque: University of New Mexico Press, 1982), pp. 278–79. See, too, Oakah L. Jones, Jr., *Los Paisanos: Spanish Settlers on the Northern Frontier* (Norman: University of Oklahoma Press, 1979), p. 253.

3. THE MEXICAN FAR NORTH

1. David J. Weber, "American Westward Expansion and the Breakdown of Relations between *Pobladores* and '*Indios Bárbaros*' on Mexico's Far Northern Frontier, 1821–1846," in *Myth and the History of the Hispanic Southwest: Essays by David J. Weber* (Albuquerque: University of New Mexico Press, 1988), p. 121.

2. Tomás Almaguer, "Interpreting Chicano History: The World-System Approach to Nineteenth-Century California," *Review* 4 (Winter 1981): 482.

3. The status of New Mexican women was even more exalted than that of their counterparts in California, according to Janet Lecompte, "The Independent Women of Hispanic New Mexico, 1821–1846," *Western Historical Quarterly* 12 (Jan. 1981): 17–35. For Anglo views of Hispanas during this period, see Deena J. González, "La Tules of Image and Reality: Euro-American Attitudes and Legend Formation on the Spanish-Mexican Fron-

tier," in *Building with Our Hands: New Directions in Chicana Studies,* ed. Adela de la Torre and Beatríz M. Pesquera (Berkeley: University of California Press, 1993), pp. 75–90.

4. Sherburne Cook, the leading authority on native Americans in California in the early nineteenth century, disagrees. He feels that life improved for Indians after secularization because they had greater freedom, an argument he develops in his 1943 essay "The Indian Versus the Spanish Mission," in Sherburne F. Cook, *The Conflict between the California Indian and Western Civilization* (Berkeley: University of California Press, 1976), pp. 1–194.

5. For the treatment of native Americans by Hispano-Mexican and Anglo masters in the nineteenth century, see Albert L. Hurtado, *Indian Survival on the California Frontier* (New Haven: Yale University Press, 1988), and Douglas Monroy, *Thrown among Strangers: The Making of Mexican Culture in Frontier California* (Berkeley: University of California Press, 1990). The diverse perceptions of the indigenous people by their conquerors at this time are the subject of James J. Rawls, *Indians of California: The Changing Image* (Norman: University of Oklahoma Press, 1984).

6. David J. Weber, *The Mexican Frontier, 1821–1846: The American Southwest under Mexico* (Albuquerque: University of New Mexico Press, 1982), p. 105.

7. David A. Sandoval, "Montezuma's Merchants: Mexican Traders on the Santa Fe Trail," in *Adventure on the Santa Fe Trail,* ed. Leo E. Oliva (Topeka: Kansas State Historical Society, 1988), p. 43. For a comprehensive treatment of Hispanic contributions to the trail trade, see Susan Calafate Boyle, *Los Capitalistas: Hispano Merchants on the Santa Fe Trail* (Albuquerque: University of New Mexico Press, 1997).

8. Patricia Nelson Limerick, *The Legacy of Conquest: The Unbroken Past of the American West* (New York: W. W. Norton, 1988), p. 229.

9. Arnoldo De León, *They Called Them Greasers: Anglo Attitudes toward Mexicans in Texas, 1821–1900* (Austin: University of Texas Press, 1983), pp. 1–13. Raymund A. Paredes, on the other hand, feels that anti-Mexican sentiment among Texans before the War of Independence was largely based on Hispanophobia and anti-Catholicism. "The Origins of Anti-Mexican Sentiment in the United States," *New Scholar* 6 (1977): 158.

10. Juan Gómez-Quiñones, *Roots of Chicano Politics, 1600–1940* (Albuquerque: University of New Mexico Press, 1994), p. 134.

11. Rebecca McDowell Craver, *The Impact of Intimacy: Mexican-Anglo Intermarriage in New Mexico, 1821–1846* (El Paso: Texas Western Press, 1982), p. 75.

12. For a good survey of foreign migration into California during the Mexican period, see Doyce B. Nunis, Jr., "Alta California's Trojan Horse: Foreign Immigration," *California History* 76 (Summer and Fall 1997): 299–330.

13. For a concise review of the pietistic interpretations of the Alamo American historians have generally embraced, see David J. Weber, "Refighting the Alamo: Mythmaking and the Texas Revolution," in *Myth and the History of the Hispanic Southwest,* pp. 133–51. The ambivalent role played by Tejanos in the war, a subject usually neglected in mainstream histories, is the subject of Arnoldo De León, "Tejanos and the Texas War for Independence: Historiography's Judgment," *New Mexico Historical Review* 61 (Apr. 1986): 137–46.

14. This view is shared by most Chicano historians. See, for example, Carlos E. Cortés, "Mexicans," in *Harvard Encyclopedia of American Ethnic Groups,* ed. Stephen Thernstrom (Cambridge, Mass.: Harvard University Press, 1980), p. 701.

15. Michael C. Meyer and William L. Sherman, *The Course of Mexican History* (New York: Oxford University Press, 1979), p. 345.

16. Gómez-Quiñones, *Roots of Chicano Politics,* p. 188.

17. Happily, this historical judgment has been reversed by recent scholarship; today even high school textbooks "recognize American responsibility for the war." Richard Griswold del Castillo, *The Treaty of Guadalupe Hidalgo: A Legacy of Conflict* (Norman: University of Oklahoma Press, 1990), p. 113.

18. Justin H. Smith, *The War with Mexico,* vol. 2 (Gloucester, Mass.: Peter Smith, 1919), p. 311.

19. Walt Whitman, *The Brooklyn Daily Eagle,* July 7, 1846, quoted in Reginald Horsman, *Race and Manifest Destiny: The Origins of American Racial Anglo-Saxonism* (Cambridge: Harvard University Press, 1981), p. 235.

4. THE AMERICAN SOUTHWEST

1. Judith Sweeney, "Chicana History: A Review of the Literature," in *Essays on La Mujer,* ed. Rosaura Sánchez and Rosa Martínez Cruz (Los Angeles: Chicano Studies Center Publications, University of California, Los Angeles, 1977), p. 103.

2. Arthur L. Campa, *Hispanic Culture in the Southwest* (Norman: University of Oklahoma Press, 1979), p. 184.

3. Tomás Almaguer, "Ideological Distortions in Recent Chicano Historiography: The Internal Model and Chicano Historical Interpretation," *Aztlán* 18 (Spring 1987): 15.

4. See Arnoldo De León, "Texas Mexicans: Twentieth-Century Interpretations," in *Texas through Time: Evolving Interpretations,* ed. Walter L. Buenger and Robert A. Calvert (College Station: Texas A&M University Press, 1991), pp. 48–49.

5. Antonio Ríos-Bustamante, "The Barrioization of Nineteenth-Century Mexican Californians: From Landowners to Laborers," *Masterkey* 60 (Summer/Fall 1986): 32.

6. Albert Camarillo, *Chicanos in a Changing Society: From Mexican Pueblos to American Barrios in Santa Barbara and Southern California, 1848–1930* (Cambridge: Harvard University Press, 1979).

7. Manuel Rojas, *Joaquín Murrieta: "El Patrio"* (Mexicali, B.C.: Estado de Baja California, 1986).

8. The complex motives leading to accommodation among the elite are examined in Manuel G. Gonzales, *The Hispanic Elite of the Southwest* (El Paso: Texas Western Press, 1989).

9. Charles Howard Shinn, "Pioneer Spanish Families in California," *The Century Magazine* 41 (Jan. 1891): 385.

10. Rodolfo Acuña, "The Making of *Occupied America,*" in *Occupied America: A Chicano History Symposium,* ed. Tatcho Mindiola, Jr. (Houston: Mexican American Studies Program, University of Houston, 1982), p. 23.

11. Mario Barrera, *Beyond Aztlan: Ethnic Autonomy in Comparative Perspective* (Notre Dame: University of Notre Dame Press, 1988), p. 13.

12. Emilio Zamora, *The World of the Mexican Worker in Texas* (College Station: Texas A&M University Press, 1993), p. 93.

13. Nancie L. González, *The Spanish-Americans of New Mexico: A Heritage of Pride* (Albuquerque: University of New Mexico Press, 1967), p. 76.

14. Ibid., p. 28.

15. Guillermo Lux and Maurilio E. Vigil, "Return to Aztlan: The Chicano Rediscovers His Indian Past," in *The Chicanos: As We See Ourselves,* ed. Arnulfo D. Trejo (Tucson: University of Arizona Press, 1979), p. 3.

16. Frances León Swadesh, *Los Primeros Pobladores: Hispanic Americans of the Ute Frontier* (Notre Dame: University of Notre Dame Press, 1974), p. 133.

17. Marc Simmons, *The Little Lion of the Southwest: A Life of Manuel Antonio Chaves* (Chicago: Swallow Press, 1973), p. 23.

18. Robert A. Roessel, Jr., "Navajo History," in *Handbook of North American Indians,* vol. 10, *Southwest,* ed. Alfonso Ortiz (Washington, D.C.: Smithsonian Institution, 1983), p. 506.

19. Darlis A. Miller, "Cross-Cultural Marriages in the Southwest: The New Mexican

Experience, 1846–1900," in *New Mexico Women: Intercultural Perspectives,* ed. Joan M. Jensen and Darlis A. Miller (Albuquerque: University of New Mexico Press, 1986), p. 100.

20. For a sympathetic biography, see Deena J. González, "La Tules of Image and Reality: Euro-American Attitudes and Legend Formation on a Spanish-Mexican Frontier," in *Building with Our Hands: New Directions in Chicana Studies,* ed. Adela de la Torre and Beatríz M. Pesquera (Berkeley: University of California Press, 1993), pp. 75–90.

21. For biographical information, see Sandra L. Stephens, "The Women of the Amador Family, 1860–1940," in *New Mexico Women,* p. 258.

22. See Simmons, *The Little Lion of the Southwest.*

23. See Richard L. Nostrand, "The Hispano Homeland in 1900," *Annals of the Association of American Geographers* 70 (Sept. 1980): 382–96.

24. David J. Weber, *Foreigners in Their Native Land: Historical Roots of the Mexican Americans* (Albuquerque: University of New Mexico Press, 1973), p. 157.

25. For an engaging study on the brotherhood, see Marta Weigle, *Brothers of Light, Brothers of Blood: The Penitentes of the Southwest* (Albuquerque: University of New Mexico Press, 1976).

26. Fray Angélico Chávez, "The Penitentes of New Mexico," *New Mexico Historical Review* 29 (Apr. 1954): 94–123.

27. Marc Simmons, *New Mexico: An Interpretive History* (Albuquerque: University of New Mexico Press, 1988), p. 164.

28. See, for example, Arnoldo De León, *Mexican Americans in Texas: A Brief History* (Arlington Heights, Ill.: Harlan Davidson, 1993).

29. David Montejano, *Anglos and Mexicans in the Making of Texas, 1836–1986* (Austin: University of Texas Press, 1987).

30. Juan Gómez-Quiñones, *Roots of Chicano Politics, 1600–1940* (Albuquerque: University of New Mexico Press, 1994), p. 270.

31. For a Chicano perspective on this episode, see Mary Romero, "El Paso Salt War: Mob Action or Political Struggle?" *Aztlán* 16 (1985): 119–44.

32. For the first scholarly study of Cortina since the 1950s, see *Juan Cortina and the Texas-Mexico Frontier, 1859–1877,* ed. Jerry D. Thompson (El Paso: Texas Western Press, 1994).

33. See Américo Paredes, *With His Pistol in His Hand* (Austin: University of Texas Press, 1958).

34. W. W. Mills, *Forty Years at El Paso, 1858–1898,* ed. Rex Strickland (El Paso: Carl Hertzog, 1962), pp. 22–23.

35. Carey McWilliams, *North from Mexico: The Spanish-Speaking People of the United States* (New York: Greenwood Press, 1968), chap. 2.

5. THE GREAT MIGRATION

1. The best work on the Great Migration is Mark Reisler's deeply researched and comprehensive *By the Sweat of Their Brow: Mexican Immigrant Labor in the United States, 1900–1940* (Westport, Conn.: Greenwood Press, 1976).

2. Marilyn P. Davis, *Mexican Voices/Mexican Dreams: An Oral History of Mexican Immigration to the United States* (New York: Henry Holt, 1990), p. 4.

3. The difficulties in establishing an accurate demographic record of Mexicans in the United States are examined in Reisler, *Sweat of Their Brow,* pp. 265–73.

4. Carey McWilliams, *The Mexicans in America* (New York: Teachers College Press, 1968), pp. 8–15.

5. See George J. Sánchez, *Becoming Mexican American: Ethnicity, Culture, and Identity in Chicano Los Angeles, 1900–1945* (New York: Oxford University Press, 1993), chap. 1.

6. See James A. Sandos, *Rebellion in the Borderlands: Anarchism and the Plan of San Diego, 1904–1923* (Norman: University of Oklahoma Press, 1992).

7. Ramón Eduardo Ruiz, *Triumphs and Tragedy: A History of the Mexican People* (New York: W. W. Norton, 1992), p. 311.

8. A modest estimate, according to Michael C. Meyer and William L. Sherman, *The Course of Mexican History* (New York: Oxford University Press, 1979), p. 552.

9. Richard Griswold del Castillo and Arnoldo De León, *North to Aztlán: A History of Mexican Americans in the United States* (New York: Twayne Publishers, 1996), p. 23, see a significant rise of Mexican immigration after 1880; consequently, they believe there is a good deal of continuity in Mexican-American history between the nineteenth and the twentieth centuries. This point of view is challenged by Gilbert G. González and Raúl Fernández, "Chicano History: Transcending Cultural Models," *Pacific Historical Review* 63 (Nov. 1994), pp. 488–89, who believe that an entirely new phase of that history is initiated at about 1900 with the beginning of mass immigration.

10. Lawrence A. Cardoso, *Mexican Emigration to the United States, 1897–1931* (Tucson: University of Arizona Press, 1980), p. 34.

11. Arnoldo De León, *Mexican Americans in Texas: A Brief History* (Arlington Heights, Ill.: Harlan Davidson, 1993), p. 71.

12. John R. Chávez, *The Lost Land: The Chicano Image of the Southwest* (Albuquerque: University of New Mexico Press, 1984), p. 1.

13. See, for example, Roberto R. Alvarez, Jr., *Familia: Migration and Adaptation in Baja and Alta California, 1800–1975* (Berkeley: University of California Press, 1987).

14. Carey McWilliams, *North from Mexico: The Spanish-Speaking People of the United States* (New York: Greenwood Press, 1968), p. 186.

15. For the significance of this landmark legislation, see Marc Reisner, *Cadillac Desert: The American West and Its Disappearing Water,* rev. ed. (New York: Penguin Books, 1993), p. 111.

16. See Neil F. Foley, "Chicanos and the Culture of Cotton in Central Texas, 1880–1900: Reshaping Class Relations in the South," in *Community Empowerment and Chicano Scholarship,* ed. Mary Romero and Cordelia Candelaria (Los Angeles: National Association for Chicano Studies, 1992), p. 112.

17. In constructing this composite biography, I have relied heavily on oral interviews found in *The Life Story of the Mexican Immigrant: Autobiographic Documents Collected by Manuel Gamio,* comp. Manuel Gamio (1931; reprint, New York: Dover Publications, 1971).

18. Manuel Gamio attempted to ascertain the home state of Mexican immigrants in the United States in the summer of 1926 by tabulating where they sent their money orders. The top three states, in rank order, were Michoacán (20 percent), Guanajuato (19.6 percent), and Jalisco (14.7 percent). "Sources of Mexican Immigrants and the Distribution of Immigrants in the United States," in *Mexican Immigration to the United States* (Chicago: University of Chicago Press, 1930), p. 13.

19. For this unique society, see William Madsen, *Mexican-Americans of South Texas* (New York: Holt, Rinehart and Winston, 1964).

20. For the role of Mexicanas in the Revolution, and other wars in Mexican history, see Elizabeth Salas, *Soldaderas in the Mexican Military: Myth and History* (Austin: University of Texas Press, 1990).

21. Anthony Quinn, *The Original Sin: A Self-Portrait* (Boston: Little, Brown and Company, 1972), p. 55.

22. See, for example, Sánchez, *Becoming Mexican American;* F. Arturo Rosales, "Mexican Immigrant Nationalism as an Origin of Identity for Mexican Americans: Exploring the Sources," in *Mexican American Identity,* ed. Marta E. Bernal and Phylis C. Martinelli (Encino, Calif.: Floricanto Press, 1993), pp. 43–45.

23. Gilbert G. González, "Labor and Community: The Camps of Mexican Citrus Pickers in Southern California," *Western Historical Quarterly* 22 (Aug. 1991): 298. Professor González explores this topic more systematically in *Labor and Community: Mexican Citrus Worker Villages in a Southern California County, 1900–1950* (Urbana and Chicago: University of Illinois Press, 1994).

24. Devra Weber, *Dark Sweat, White Gold: California Farm Workers, Cotton, and the New Deal* (Berkeley: University of California Press, 1994), pp. 9, 53.

25. Karen Isaksen Leonard, *Making Ethnic Choices: California's Punjabi Mexican Americans* (Philadelphia: Temple University Press, 1992), p. 71.

26. The Colorado sugar beet industry, and the hand-to-mouth existence it generated among Mexican families, with a focus on women, is described by Mary Romero and Eric Margolis, "Tending the Beets: Campesinas and the Great Western Sugar Company," *Revista Mujeres* 2 (June 1985): 17–27.

27. Zaragoza Vargas, *Proletarians of the North: A History of Mexican Industrial Workers in Detroit and the Midwest, 1917–1933* (Berkeley: University of California Press, 1993), pp. 23–24.

28. Juan R. García, *Mexicans in the Midwest, 1900–1932* (Tucson: University of Arizona Press, 1996), p. 89.

29. See John Bodnar, *The Transplanted: A History of Immigrants in Urban America* (Bloomington: Indiana University Press, 1985).

30. Walter Nugent, *Crossings: The Great Transatlantic Migrations, 1870–1914* (Bloomington: Indiana University Press, 1992), p. 35.

31. Emilio Zamora, *The World of the Mexican Worker in Texas* (College Station: Texas A&M University Press, 1993), pp. 15–17.

32. Apparently, a low degree of social mobility was characteristic of urbanized Mexicans, as well. "Among first-, second-, and third-generation semiskilled and unskilled male Mexican laborers in Los Angeles, not a single individual moved upward to a white-collar position during the ten years between 1918 and 1928," according to Ricardo Romo, *East Los Angeles: History of a Barrio* (Austin: University of Texas Press, 1983), p. 122.

33. Ernesto Galarza, "Mexicans in the Southwest: A Culture in Process," *Plural Society in the Southwest,* ed. Edward H. Spicer and Raymond H. Thompson (New York: Weatherhead Foundation, 1972), p. 283.

34. As Peter Skerry has observed in *Mexican Americans: The Ambivalent Minority* (New York: The Free Press, 1993), Mexicans in the United States seem unsure about their racial identity. However, this confusion is more apparent than real; though they recognize and for the most part take pride in their Indian heritage, Mexicans at times identify themselves as white in an attempt to avoid discrimination. And, of course, there is a small minority within the community who *are* white.

35. Michael Omi and Howard Winant, *Racial Formation in the United States: From the 1960s to the 1980s* (New York: Routledge and Kegan Paul, 1986), p. 57.

36. See, for example, Juan Gómez-Quiñones, *Mexican American Labor, 1790–1990* (Albuquerque: University of New Mexico Press, 1994), p. 334.

37. This negative assessment is shared by the respected political scientist Jorge G. Castañeda in "Mexico and California: The Paradox of Tolerance and Dedemocratization," in *The California-Mexico Connection,* ed. Abraham F. Lowenthal and Katrina Burgess (Stanford: Stanford University Press, 1993), p. 42. See, too, Alejandro Portes, "The Longest Migration," *The New Republic,* 26 Apr. 1993, p. 40, who recognizes "the significant progress made by many U.S.-born Mexican-Americans" in the recent past but concludes with this sobering thought: "Their collective achievements get buried in figures skewed by the continuously arriving mass of poor immigrants."

38. Alejandro Portes and Rubén G. Rumbaut, *Immigrant America: A Portrait* (Berkeley: University of California Press, 1990), p. 238.

6. THE DEPRESSION

1. Sarah Deutsch, *No Separate Refuge: Culture, Class, and Gender on an Anglo-Hispanic Frontier in the American Southwest, 1880–1940* (New York: Oxford University Press, 1987), chap. 7.

2. See, for example, Patricia Preciado Martin, *Songs My Mother Sang to Me: An Oral History of Mexican American Women* (Tucson: University of Arizona Press, 1992).

3. Ricardo Romo, *East Los Angeles: History of a Barrio* (Austin: University of Texas Press, 1983), p. 10. "The barrio is not a ghetto," concurs the historian Julián Nava. "It is a haven." Quoted in "Chicanos on the Move," *Newsweek,* 1 Jan. 1979, p. 24.

4. The Midwest, like all geographic regions in the United States, is difficult to define precisely, but for our purposes the area shall consist of the following states: the Dakotas, Illinois, Indiana, Iowa, Kansas, Michigan, Minnesota, Missouri, Nebraska, Ohio, and Wisconsin.

5. Lizabeth Cohen, *Making a New Deal: Industrial Workers in Chicago, 1919–1939* (New York: Cambridge University Press, 1990), pp. 165–66.

6. Dennis Nodín Valdés, "The New Northern Borderlands: An Overview of Midwestern Chicano History," in *Perspectives in Mexican American Studies* 2 (1989): 2.

7. Quoted in Rodolfo Acuña, *Occupied America: The Chicano's Struggle for Liberation* (San Francisco: Canfield Press, 1972), p. 140.

8. See Lawrence A. Cardoso, *Mexican Emigration to the United States, 1897–1931* (Tucson: University of Arizona Press, 1980), p. 144.

9. Abraham Hoffman, *Unwanted Mexican-Americans in the Great Depression: Repatriation Pressures, 1929–1939* (Tucson: University of Arizona Press, 1974), pp. 174–75.

10. For the impact of repatriation on deported Mexicans, see Camille Guerin-Gonzales, *Mexican Workers and American Dreams: Immigration, Repatriation, and California Farm Labor, 1900–1939* (New Brunswick, N.J.: Rutgers University Press, 1994); and Francisco E. Balderrama and Raymond Rodríguez, *Decade of Betrayal: Mexican Repatriation in the 1930s* (Albuquerque: University of New Mexico Press, 1995).

11. Neil Betten and Raymond A. Mohl, "From Discrimination to Repatriation: Mexican Life in Gary, Indiana, during the Great Depression," *Pacific Historical Review* 42 (Aug. 1973): 379.

12. James Gregory, *American Exodus: The Dust Bowl Migration and Okie Culture in California* (New York: Oxford University Press, 1989), p. 17.

13. Gerald W. Haslam, *The Other California: The Great Central Valley in Life and Letters* (Reno: University of Nevada Press, 1994), p. 113.

14. Robert Kelley, *The Shaping of the American Past,* 4th ed. (Englewood Cliffs, N.J.: Prentice-Hall, 1986), p. 608.

15. For a history of labor activism by the Mexican-origin population in the United States, consult Juan Gómez-Quiñones, *Mexican American Labor, 1790–1990* (Albuquerque: University of New Mexico Press, 1994).

16. Phil Mellinger, "'The Men Have Become Organizers': Labor Conflict and Unionization in the Mexican Mining Communities of Arizona, 1900–1915," *Western Historical Quarterly* 23 (Aug. 1992): 323–47.

17. Charles Wollenberg, "Working on *El Traque*: The Pacific Electric Strike of 1903," *Pacific Historical Review* 42 (Aug. 1973): 361.

18. See Emilio Zamora, *The World of the Mexican Worker in Texas* (College Station: Texas A&M University Press, 1993).

19. Kevin Starr, *Endangered Dreams: The Great Depression in California* (New York: Oxford University Press, 1996), p. 66.

20. Ronald W. López, "The El Monte Berry Strike of 1933," *Aztlán* 1 (Spring 1970): 101–2.

21. Starr, *Endangered Dreams*, p. 80.

22. Devra Weber, *Dark Sweat, White Gold: California Farm Workers, Cotton, and the New Deal* (Berkeley: University of California Press, 1994), pp. 118–21.

23. See Francisco E. Balderrama, *In Defense of La Raza: The Los Angeles Mexican Consulate and the Mexican Community, 1929–1936* (Tucson: University of Arizona Press, 1982).

24. Dorothy Ray Healey and Maurice Isserman, *California Red: A Life in the American Communist Party* (Urbana and Chicago: University of Illinois Press, 1993), p. 44.

25. Juan Gómez-Quiñones, *Roots of Chicano Politics, 1600–1940* (Albuquerque: University of New Mexico Press, 1994), p. 394, estimates that Communist party membership "may have numbered approximately five hundred Mexicans."

26. Mario T. García, *Desert Immigrants: The Mexicans of El Paso, 1880–1920* (New Haven: Yale University Press, 1981), p. 235.

27. Mark Reisler, *By the Sweat of Their Brow: Mexican Immigrant Labor in the United States, 1900–1940* (Westport, Conn.: Greenwood Press, 1976), p. 249.

28. Martha Cotera, *Profile on the Mexican American Woman* (Austin, Tex.: National Educational Laboratory Publishers, 1976), pp. 62–63.

29. When Linda Chávez-Thompson was elected executive vice-president of the AFL-CIO in October 1995, she became the first Hispanic, man or woman, to sit on the executive board of that powerful union.

30. Mario T. García, *Mexican Americans: Leadership, Ideology, and Identity, 1930–1960* (New Haven: Yale University Press, 1989), p. 165.

7. THE SECOND WORLD WAR AND ITS AFTERMATH

1. For a complete list of the thirty-eight Hispanic Medal of Honor recipients, see "On the Front Lines," *Hispanic* 6 (Aug. 1993): 39.

2. Quoted in Ronald Takaki, *A Different Mirror: A History of Multicultural America* (New York: Little, Brown and Company, 1993), p. 393.

3. Raúl Morín, *Among the Valiant: Mexican-Americans in WWII and Korea* (Alhambra, Calif.: Borden Publishing Company, 1966), p. 256.

4. Christine Marín, "La Asociación Hispano-Americana de Madres y Esposas: Tucson's Mexican American Women in World War II," *Renato Rosaldo Lecture Series Monograph* 1 (Summer 1985): 5–18.

5. Ramón Ruiz, *Triumphs and Tragedy: A History of the Mexican People* (New York: W. W. Norton, 1992), p. 285. The debilitation of the Mexican family at mid-century is well chronicled by the anthropologist Oscar Lewis in his classic study *Five Families* (New York: Basic Books, 1959).

6. Alan Riding, *Distant Neighbors: A Portrait of the Mexicans* (New York: Vintage Books, 1989), pp. 7–8.

7. Robert R. Alvarez, Jr., *Familia: Migration and Adaptation in Baja and Alta California, 1800–1975* (Berkeley: University of California Press, 1987).

8. Vicki L. Ruiz, "'Star Struck': Acculturation, Adolescence, and the Mexican American Woman, 1920–1950," in *Building with Our Hands: New Directions in Chicana Studies*, ed. Adela de la Torre and Beatríz M. Pesquera (Berkeley: University of California Press, 1993), p. 122.

9. Octavio Paz, *The Labyrinth of Solitude* (New York: Grove Press, 1961), p. 16.

10. Manuel P. Servín, "The Post–World War II Mexican-Americans, 1925–65: A Nonachieving Minority," in *An Awakened Minority: The Mexican-Americans*, ed. Manuel P. Servín, 2d ed. (Beverly Hills, Calif.: Glencoe Press, 1974), p. 173.

11. George I. Sánchez, "Pachucos in the Making," in *Readings on La Raza: The Twentieth Century*, ed. Matt S. Meier and Feliciano Rivera (New York: Hill and Wang, 1974), pp. 122–26.

12. Quoted in "Edward Duran Ayres Report," in *Readings on La Raza,* p. 131.

13. For a firsthand account of bracero life in the late fifties, see the testimony of Manuel Sánchez in Oscar Lewis, *The Children of Sánchez: Autobiography of a Mexican Family* (New York: Vintage Books, 1961), pp. 323–70. For the Bracero Program, see Ernesto Galarza, *Merchants of Labor: The Mexican Bracero Story* (Charlotte, N.C.: McNally and Loftin, 1964); Richard Craig, *The Bracero Program: Interest Groups and Foreign Policy* (Austin: University of Texas Press, 1971); and Kitty Calavita, *Inside the State: The Bracero Program, Illegal Immigrants and the INS* (London: Routledge, 1992).

14. Julián Samora and Patricia Vandel Simon, *A History of the Mexican-American People,* rev. ed. (Notre Dame: University of Notre Dame Press, 1993), p. 140.

15. Dennis Nodín Valdés, "Machine Politics in California Agriculture, 1945–1990s," *Pacific Historical Review* 63 (May 1994): 223.

16. Manuel García y Griego, "The Importation of Mexican Contract Laborers to the United States, 1942–1964," in *Between Two Worlds: Mexican Immigrants in the United States,* ed. David G. Gutiérrez (Wilmington, Del.: Scholarly Resources, 1996), p. 71.

17. Michael C. Meyer and William L. Sherman, *The Course of Mexican History* (New York: Oxford University Press, 1979), p. 647.

18. Julián Samora, *Los Mojados: The Wetback Story* (Notre Dame: University of Notre Dame Press, 1971), p. 9.

19. For the most comprehensive study, see Juan Ramón García, *Operation Wetback: The Mass Deportation of Mexican Undocumented Workers in 1954* (Westport, Conn.: Greenwood Press, 1980).

20. Mario T. García, *Mexican Americans: Leadership, Ideology, and Identity, 1930–1960* (New Haven: Yale University Press, 1989), pp. 25, 29.

21. Kaye Briegel, "Alianza Hispano-Americana and Some Mexican-American Civil Rights Cases in the 1950s," in *An Awakened Minority,* p. 178.

22. Miguel David Tirado, "Mexican American Community Political Organization, 'The Key to Chicano Political Power,'" *Aztlán* 1 (Spring 1970): 56.

23. For a scholarly study of the association, see Benjamin Márquez, *LULAC: The Evolution of a Mexican American Political Organization* (Austin: University of Texas Press, 1993).

24. García, *Mexican Americans,* p.43.

25. Gilbert G. González, *Chicano Education in the Era of Segregation* (Philadelphia: The Balch Institute Press, 1990), p. 149.

26. For the active role played by mujeres in Mexican-American associations, see Cynthia E. Orozco, "Beyond Machismo, La Familia, and Ladies Auxiliaries: A Historiography of Mexican-Origin Women's Participation in Voluntary Associations and Politics in the United States, 1870–1990," *Perspectives in Mexican American Studies* 5 (1995): 1–34.

27. For a well-researched study, see Carl Allsup, *The American GI Forum: Origins and Evolution* (Austin: Center for Mexican American Studies, University of Texas, 1982).

28. See Liliana Urrutia, "An Offspring of Discontent: The Asociación Nacional México-Americana, 1949–1954," *Aztlán* 15 (Spring 1984): 177–84.

29. Bert Corona, *Memories of Chicano History: The Life and Narrative of Bert Corona,* ed. Mario T. García (Berkeley: University of California Press, 1994), p. 189.

30. Juan Gómez-Quiñones, *Chicano Politics: Reality and Promise, 1940–1990* (Albuquerque: University of New Mexico Press, 1990), p. 88.

31. Servín, "The Post–World War II Mexican-Americans," p. 168.

32. García, *Mexican Americans,* p. 232.

33. Gómez-Quiñones, *Chicano Politics,* p. 85.

34. The growing conservatism of aging Chicano Studies faculty is described by Ignacio M. García, who tends to be critical, in "Juncture in the Road: Chicano Studies Since 'El Plan de Santa Bárbara.'" in *Chicanas/Chicanos at the Crossroads,* ed. David R. Maciel and Isidro D. Ortiz (Tucson: University of Arizona Press, 1996), pp. 181–203.

8. THE CHICANO MOVEMENT

1. For the etymology of the term *Chicano,* see Edward Simmen, "Chicano: Origin and Meaning," in *Pain and Promise: The Chicano Today,* ed. Edward Simmen (New York: Mentor, 1972), pp. 53–56.

2. Rubén Salazar, *Los Angeles Times,* 6 Feb. 1970.

3. Joan W. Moore, *Mexican Americans* (Englewood Cliffs, N.J.: Prentice-Hall, 1970), p. 67.

4. Leo Grebler, Joan W. Moore, and Ralph C. Guzmán, *The Mexican-American People* (New York: The Free Press, 1970), p. 19.

5. Juan Gómez-Quiñones, *Chicano Politics: Reality and Promise, 1940–1990* (Albuquerque: University of New Mexico Press, 1990), p. 99.

6. There are a score of Chávez biographies, virtually all of them sympathetic. Though somewhat dated, the most objective biography is John Gregory Dunne, *Delano,* rev. ed. (New York: Farrar, Straus and Giroux, 1971); the most recent, Richard Griswold del Castillo and Richard A. García, *César Chávez: A Triumph of Spirit* (Norman: University of Oklahoma Press, 1995).

7. Richard A. García, "Dolores Huerta: Woman, Organizer, and Symbol," *California History* 72 (Spring 1993): 70.

8. Ibid., p. 65.

9. For a fine study of FLOC, see W. K. Barger and Ernesto M. Reza, *The Farm Labor Movement in the Midwest: Social Change and Adaptation among Migrant Farmworkers* (Austin: University of Texas Press, 1994).

10. For a brief biographical sketch, see Matt S. Meier, "'King Tiger': Reies López Tijerina," *Journal of the West* 27 (Apr. 1988): 60–68.

11. Clark S. Knowlton, "Tijerina, Hero of the Militants," in *An Awakened Minority: The Mexican-Americans,* ed. Manuel P. Servín, 2d ed. (Beverly Hills, Calif.: Glencoe Press, 1974), p. 198.

12. Nancie L. González, "Alianza Federal de Mercedes," in *The Mexican-Americans: An Awakening Minority,* ed. Manuel P. Servín (Beverly Hills, Calif.: Glencoe Press, 1970), p. 202.

13. For a useful biography, see Christine Marín, "Rodolfo 'Corky' Gonzales: The Mexican-American Movement Spokesman, 1962–1972," *Journal of the West* 14 (Oct. 1975): 107–20.

14. Stan Steiner, *La Raza: The Mexican Americans* (New York: Harper and Row, 1969), p. 382.

15. See the *Plan Espiritual* in *Aztlán: Essays on the Chicano Homeland,* ed. Rudolfo A. Anaya and Francisco Lomelí (Albuquerque: University of New Mexico Press, 1989), pp. 1–5.

16. Carlos Muñoz, Jr., *Youth, Identity, Power: The Chicano Movement* (London: Verso, 1989), p. 56.

17. See Julie Leininger Pycior, "From Hope to Frustration: Mexican Americans and Lyndon Johnson in 1967," *Western Historical Quarterly* 24 (Nov. 1993): 468–94.

18. For this key association, see Armando Navarro, *Mexican American Youth Organization: Avant-Garde of the Chicano Movement in Texas* (Austin: University of Texas Press, 1995).

19. For a participant-history of LRUP, see Ignacio M. García, *United We Win: The Rise and Fall of the Raza Unida Party* (Tucson: Mexican American Studies and Resource Center, University of Arizona, 1989).

20. Muñoz, *Youth, Identity, Power,* p. 21.

21. For the *Plan de Santa Bárbara,* see *Introduction to Chicano Studies,* ed. Livie Isauro Durán and H. Russell Bernard (New York: Macmillan, 1973), pp. 535–45.

22. Gómez-Quiñones, *Chicano Politics,* pp. 119–20.

23. Rubén Treviso, "Hispanics and the Vietnam War," in *Vietnam Reconsidered: Lessons from a War,* ed. Harrison E. Salisbury (New York: Harper and Row, 1984), p. 184.

24. Tom Downs, an ex-serviceman, has created a Web site (www.cpeq.com/~wall/) that lists the names on the Washington memorial in alphabetical order.

25. *Fresno Bee,* 24 Dec. 1989.

26. For Salazar's work, see *Border Correspondent: Selected Writings, 1955–1970,* ed. Mario T. García (Berkeley: University of California Press, 1996).

27. L. H. Gann and Peter J. Duignan, *The Hispanics in the United States: A History* (Boulder, Colo.: Westview Press, 1986), p. 301.

28. Gómez-Quiñones, *Chicano Politics,* p. 150.

29. Maurilio E. Vigil, "MALDEF: Chicano Advocate for Educational, Economic and Political Reform," in *Community Empowerment and Chicano Scholarship,* ed. Mary Romero and Cordelia Candelaria (Los Angeles: National Association for Chicano Studies, 1992), p. 231.

30. Ignacio M. García, "Chicano Studies Since 'El Plan de Santa Bárbara,'" in *Chicanas/ Chicanos at the Crossroads,* ed. David R. Maciel and Isidro D. Ortiz (Tucson: University of Arizona Press, 1996), p. 189.

31. "Mexican society," observes Carlos Fuentes, "is founded on very chauvinistic principles inherited from the Aztecs, the Spaniards, and the Arabs. We have a triple misogynistic inheritance that is very hard to overcome." Quoted by Anne-Marie O'Connor, "The Sum of Unequal Parts," *Los Angeles Times,* 24 Oct. 1997.

32. Anna Nieto-Gómez, "La Femenista," *Encuentro Femenil* 1 (1974): 34–47.

33. Alfredo Mirandé and Evangelina Enríquez, *La Chicana: The Mexican-American Woman* (Chicago: University of Chicago Press, 1979), p. 239.

34. Gómez-Quiñones, *Chicano Politics,* p. 140.

35. Rudolph O. de la Garza, "The Politics of Mexican Americans," in *The Chicanos: As We See Ourselves,* ed. Arnulfo D. Trejo (Tucson: University of Arizona Press, 1979), p. 119.

36. Earl Shorris, *Latinos: A Biography of the People* (New York: W. W. Norton, 1992), p. 100.

37. The political impact of Chicanismo is explored in John A. García, "The Chicano Movement: Its Legacy for Politics and Policy," in *Chicanas/Chicanos at the Crossroads,* pp. 83–107.

38. David E. Hayes-Bautista and Gregory Rodríguez, "The Chicano Movement: More Nostalgia Than Reality," *Los Angeles Times,* 17 Sept. 1995.

39. See Navarro, *Mexican American Youth Organization.*

40. See Muñoz, *Youth, Identity, Power.*

41. Ibid., p. 7.

42. Ignacio M. García, *Chicanismo: The Forging of a Militant Ethos among Mexican Americans* (Tucson: University of Arizona Press, 1997), p. 134. See, too, Marguerite V. Marín, *Social Protest in an Urban Barrio: A Study of the Chicano Movement, 1966–1974* (Lanham, Md.: University Press of America, 1991); and Guadalupe San Miguel, "Actors Not Victims: Chicanas/os and the Struggle for Educational Equality," in *Chicanas/Chicanos at the Crossroads,* p. 159.

9. PAIN AND PROMISE

1. A chapter title suggested by Edward Simmen's *Pain and Promise: The Chicano Today* (New York: Mentor, 1972), an anthology of writings on Mexican Americans.

2. The figures relating to the 1990 census in this chapter are taken from *Statistical Record of Hispanic Americans,* ed. Marlita A. Reddy (Detroit: Gale Research Inc., 1993).

3. Most Spanish-speakers prefer *Latinos* to *Hispanics,* although both terms are equally

imprecise, according to Mexican-born writer Ilan Stavans, *The Hispanic Condition: Reflections on Culture and Identity in America* (New York: Harper Perennial, 1996), p. 26.

4. Quoted by Patrick J. McDonnell, "Immigrants Not Lured by Aid, Study Says," *Los Angeles Times,* 29 Jan. 1997.

5. Howard Handelman, *Mexican Politics: The Dynamics of Change* (New York: St. Martin's Press, 1997), p. 176.

6. Alejandro Portes and Rubén G. Rumbaut, *Immigrant America: A Portrait* (Berkeley: University of California Press, 1990), p. 11.

7. Earl Shorris, *Latinos: A Biography of the People* (New York: W. W. Norton, 1992), p. 164.

8. Pierrette Hondagneu-Sotelo, *Gendered Transitions: Mexican Experiences of Immigration* (Berkeley: University of California Press, 1994), pp. 31, 187.

9. *Wall Street Journal,* 29 Apr. 1997.

10. See, for example, Portes and Rumbaut, *Immigrant America,* p. 231.

11. See Roger Rouse, "Mexican Migration and the Social Space of Postmodernism," *Diaspora* 1 (1991): 8–23.

12. Rubén Navarrette, Jr., "Ethnic Envidia: When Achievement Means Selling Out," *Los Angeles Times,* 30 Aug. 1992.

13. See Suzanne Oboler, *Ethnic Labels, Ethnic Lives: Identity and the Politics of (Re)Presentation in the United States* (Minneapolis: University of Minnesota Press, 1995), chap.6.

14. For U.S. English and its relation to the English Only movement, see Luis A. Torres, "The National English Only Movement, Past and Future," in *Community Empowerment and Chicano Scholarship,* ed. Mary Romero and Cordelia Candelaria (Los Angeles: National Association for Chicano Studies, 1992), pp. 217–30.

15. Carola Suárez-Orozco and Marcelo Suárez-Orozco, *Transformations: Migration, Family Life, and Achievement Motivation among Latino Adolescents* (Stanford: Stanford University Press, 1995), p. 188.

16. Juan Gómez-Quiñones, *Chicano Politics: Reality and Promise, 1940–1990* (Albuquerque: University of New Mexico Press, 1990), p. 185.

17. Carlos Monsiváis, "The Immigrants' View of Education," *Los Angeles Times,* 25 Aug. 1996.

18. See, for example, Alfredo Mirandé and Evangelina Enríquez, *La Chicana: The Mexican American Woman* (Chicago: University of Chicago Press, 1979), p. 116, who insist that the familial deficiency model is a myth, arguing instead that "[t]he Chicano family has proved remarkably resilient and impervious to external forces."

19. See Michael Meyer, "Los Angeles 2010: A Latino Subcontinent," *Newsweek,* 9 Nov. 1992, pp. 32–33.

20. Quoted in Adam R. Jacobson, "Changing with the Times," *Hispanic* 7 (Mar. 1994): 20. For a bleak portrait of the Hispanic family—one that seems excessively pessimistic, in my view—see Stavans, *The Hispanic Condition,* p. 112.

21. Joan W. Moore, *Mexican Americans* (Englewood Cliffs, N.J.: Prentice-Hall, 1970), p. 9.

22. Anthony Quinn, *The Original Sin: A Self-Portrait* (Boston: Little, Brown and Company, 1972), pp. 45–46.

23. James Diego Vigil, *Barrio Gangs: Street Life and Identity in Southern California* (Austin: University of Texas Press, 1988), p. 90.

24. See Albert L. Pulido, "Mexican American Catholicism in the Southwest: The Transformation of a Popular Religion," *Perspectives in Mexican American Studies* 4 (1993): 93–108.

25. For two excellent discussions of the role of Catholicism in Hispanic communities today, see L. H. Gann and Peter J. Duignan, *The Hispanics in the United States: A History*

(Boulder, Colo.: Westview Press, 1986), chap. 14; and Thomas Weyr, *Hispanic U.S.A.: Breaking the Melting Pot* (New York: Harper and Row, 1988), chap. 8.

26. Roberto R. Bacalski-Martínez, "Aspects of Mexican American Cultural Heritage," in *The Chicanos: As We See Ourselves,* ed. Arnulfo D. Trejo (Tucson: University of Arizona Press, 1979), p. 19.

27. Shorris, *Latinos,* p. 105. See also Stavans, *The Hispanic Condition,* p. 111.

28. Carla Trujillo, ed., *Chicana Lesbians: The Girls Our Mothers Warned Us About* (Berkeley: Third Woman Press, 1991), p. ix.

29. Irene I. Blea, *La Chicana and the Intersection of Race, Class, and Gender* (New York: Praeger, 1992), p. 134.

30. For a brief study of MELA, see Mary Pardo, "Mexican American Women Grassroots Community Activists: 'Mothers of East Los Angeles,'" *Frontiers* 11, no. 1 (1990): 1–7.

31. María Linda Apodaca, "A Double Edge Sword: Hispanas and Liberal Feminism," *Critica* 1 (Fall 1986): 96–114.

32. Sylvia Alicia Gonzales, *Hispanic American Voluntary Organizations* (Westport, Conn.: Greenwood Press, 1985), p. 62.

33. For Chicano efforts to find a literary past, see *Recovering the U.S. Hispanic Literary Heritage,* ed. Ramón Gutiérrez and Genaro Padilla (Houston: Arte Público Press, 1993), and *Reconstructing a Chicano/a Literary Heritage: Hispanic Colonial Literature of the Southwest,* ed. María Herrera-Sobek (Tucson: University of Arizona Press, 1993).

34. Genaro M. Padilla, *My History, Not Yours: The Formation of Mexican American Autobiography* (Madison: University of Wisconsin Press, 1993), p. 5.

35. Nicolás Kanellos, "Literature," in *The Hispanic Almanac: From Columbus to Corporate America,* ed. Nicolás Kanellos (Detroit: Visible Ink Press, 1994), p. 390.

36. Ibid., p. 392.

37. Frank N. Magill, ed., *Masterpieces of Latino Literature* (New York: Harper Collins, 1994), p. 41.

38. See Teresa McKenna, *Migrant Song: Politics and Process in Contemporary Chicano Literature* (Austin: University of Texas Press, 1997), p. 21.

39. According to *Hispanic* 10 (Nov. 1997), p. 12, sixteen Hispanics have won this coveted award since its inception in 1981. Mexican-origin winners include former MALDEF president Joaquín Avila, COPS founder Ernie Cortés, Jr., performance artist Guillermo Gómez-Peña, historian Ramón Gutiérrez, artist Amalia Mesa-Bains, and FLOC director Baldemar Velásquez.

40. Ray González, ed., *Mirrors beneath the Earth: Short Fiction by Chicano Writers* (Willimantic, Conn.: Curbstone Press, 1992), p. 1.

41. However, there are exceptions: "...Gary Soto couldn't write his way out of a paper bag," avers Harold Bloom, among the most outspoken critics of ethnic literature, in *Newsweek,* 10 Oct. 1994, p. 75.

42. Ed Morales, "Shadowing Valdez," *American Theatre* 9 (Nov. 1992): 14.

43. A relatively complete list of these films is found in Gary D. Keller, "Film," in *The Hispanic Almanac,* pp. 497–559.

44. Geoffrey Fox, *Hispanic Nation: Culture, Politics, and the Construction of Identity* (Tucson: University of Arizona, 1996), p. 213.

45. For the underclass controversy, see the selections in *In the Barrios: Latinos and the Underclass Debate,* ed. Joan Moore and Raquel Pinderhughes (New York: Russell Sage, 1993).

46. Carlos G. Vélez-Ibáñez, *Border Visions: Mexican Cultures of the Southwest United States* (Tucson: University of Arizona Press, 1996), pp. 189–90.

47. Refugio I. Rochín and Mónica D. Castillo, *Immigration and Colonia Formation in Rural California,* CLPP Working Paper, vol. 2 (Berkeley: Institute for the Study of Social Change, University of California, Berkeley, 1995), p. 14.

48. Quoted in *Mexican Voices/American Dreams,* ed. Marilyn P. Davis (New York: Henry Holt, 1990), p. 262.

49. Juan L. Gonzales, Jr., *Racial and Ethnic Families in America* (Dubuque, Ia.: Kendall/ Hunt, 1992), p. 180, gives an exogamy rate of 18 percent for the Mexican-origin population in the United States.

SELECT BIBLIOGRAPHY
OF WORKS AFTER 1965

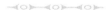

BOOKS

Achor, Shirley. *Mexican Americans in a Dallas Barrio*. Tucson: University of Arizona Press, 1978.

Acosta-Belén, Edna, and Barbara R. Sjostrom, eds. *The Hispanic Experience in the United States: Contemporary Issues and Perspectives*. New York: Praeger, 1988.

Acuña, Rodolfo. *Anything but Mexican: Chicanos in Contemporary Los Angeles*. New York: Verso, 1996.

———. *Occupied America: A History of Chicanos*. 3d ed. New York: Harper and Row, 1988.

Alarcón, Norma, Ana Castillo, and Cherríe Moraga, eds. *Third Woman: The Sexuality of Latinas*. Berkeley: Third Woman Press, 1989.

Alford, Harold J. *The Proud Peoples: The Heritage and Culture of Spanish-Speaking Peoples in the United States*. New York: David McKay Company, 1972.

Allsup, Carl. *The American G.I. Forum: Origins and Evolution*. Austin: Center for Mexican American Studies, University of Texas, 1982.

Almaguer, Tomás. *Racial Fault Lines: The Historical Origins of White Supremacy in California*. Berkeley: University of California Press, 1994.

Alonso, Armando. *Tejano Legacy: Rancheros and Settlers in South Texas, 1734–1900*. Albuquerque: University of New Mexico Press, 1998.

Alvarez, Robert R., Jr. *Familia: Migration and Adaptation in Baja and Alta California, 1800–1975*. Berkeley: University of California Press, 1987.

Anzaldúa, Gloria. *Borderlands/La Frontera: The New Mestiza*. San Francisco: Spinsters/Aunt Lute Book Company, 1987.

Balderrama, Francisco E. *In Defense of La Raza: The Los Angeles Mexican Consulate and the Mexican Community, 1929 to 1936*. Tucson: University of Arizona Press, 1982.

Balderrama, Francisco E., and Raymond Rodríguez. *Decade of Betrayal: Mexican Repatriation in the 1930s*. Albuquerque: University of New Mexico Press, 1995.

Bannon, John Francis. *The Spanish Borderlands Frontier, 1513–1821*. New York: Holt, Rinehart and Winston, 1970.

Barger, W. K., and Ernesto M. Reza. *The Farm Labor Movement in the Midwest: Social Change and Adaptation among Migrant Farmworkers*. Austin: University of Texas Press, 1994.

Barrera, Mario. *Beyond Aztlán: Ethnic Autonomy in Comparative Perspective*. Notre Dame: University of Notre Dame Press, 1988.

———. *Race and Class in the Southwest: A Theory of Racial Inequality*. Notre Dame: University of Notre Dame Press, 1979.

Bean, Frank, and Marta Tienda. *The Hispanic Population of the United States*. New York: Russell Sage, 1987.

Blackwelder, Julia Kirk. *Women of the Depression: Caste and Culture in San Antonio, 1929–1939*. College Station: Texas A&M University Press, 1984.

Boyle, Susan Calafate. *Los Capitalistas: Hispano Merchants on the Santa Fe Trail.* Albuquerque: University of New Mexico Press, 1997.

Burma, John H., comp. *Mexican Americans in the United States: A Reader.* Cambridge, Mass.: Schenkman Publishing Company, 1970.

Camarillo, Albert. *Chicanos in a Changing Society: From Mexican Pueblos to American Barrios in Santa Barbara and Southern California, 1848–1930.* Cambridge: Harvard University Press, 1979.

———. *Chicanos in California: A History of Mexican Americans in California.* San Francisco: Boyd and Fraser Publishing, 1984.

Campa, Arthur L. *Hispanic Culture in the Southwest.* Norman: University of Oklahoma Press, 1979.

Cardoso, Lawrence A. *Mexican Emigration to the United States, 1897–1931.* Tucson: University of Arizona Press, 1971.

Carlson, Alvar W. *Spanish-American Homeland: Four Centuries in New Mexico's Río Arriba.* Baltimore: Johns Hopkins University Press, 1990.

Castillo, Pedro, and Alberto Camarillo, eds. *Furia y Muerte: Los Bandidos Mexicanos.* Aztlán Publications, no. 4. Chicano Studies Center, University of California, Los Angeles, 1973.

Castillo-Speed, Lillian, ed. *Women's Voices from the Borderlands.* New York: Simon and Schuster, 1995.

Chávez, Fray Angélico. *My Penitente Land: Reflections on Spanish New Mexico.* Albuquerque: University of New Mexico Press, 1974.

Chávez, John R. *The Lost Land: The Chicano Image of the Southwest.* Albuquerque: University of New Mexico Press, 1984.

Chávez, Leo. *Shadowed Lives: Undocumented Immigrants in American Society.* Fort Worth, Tex.: Harcourt Brace Jovanovich, 1992.

Chávez, Linda. *Out of the Barrio: Toward a New Politics of Hispanic Assimilation.* New York: BasicBooks, 1991.

Chávez, Lydia. *The Color Bind: The Battle to End Affirmative Action.* Berkeley: University of California Press, 1998.

Cockcroft, James D. *Outlaws in the Promised Land: Mexican Immigrant Workers and America's Future.* New York: Grove Press, 1986.

Connor, Walker, ed. *Mexican-Americans in Comparative Perspective.* Washington, D.C.: The Urban Institute Press, 1985.

Cotera, Martha. *Diosa y Hembra: The History and Heritage of Chicanas in the U.S.* Austin, Tex.: Information Systems Development, 1976.

———. *Profile on the Mexican American Woman.* Austin, Tex.: National Educational Laboratory Publishers, 1976.

Craig, Richard. *The Bracero Program: Interest Groups and Foreign Policy.* Austin: University of Texas Press, 1971.

Craver, Rebecca McDowell. *The Impact of Intimacy: Mexican-Anglo Intermarriage in New Mexico, 1821–1846.* El Paso: Texas Western Press, 1982.

Cruz, Gilbert R. *Let There Be Towns: Spanish Municipal Origins in the American Southwest, 1610–1810.* College Station: Texas A&M University Press, 1988.

Cruz, Gilbert R., and Marta Cruz. *A Century of Service: The History of the Catholic Church in the Lower Rio Grande Valley.* Harlingen, Tex.: United Printers and Publishers, 1979.

Daniel, Cletus E. *Bitter Harvest: A History of California Farmworkers, 1870–1941.* Ithaca: Cornell University Press, 1981.

Davidson, R. Theodore. *Chicano Prisoners: The Key to San Quentin.* New York: Holt, Rinehart and Winston, 1974.

Davis, Marilyn, ed. *Mexican Voices, Mexican Dreams: An Oral History of Mexican Immigration to the United States.* New York: Henry Holt and Company, 1990.

de la Garza, Rodolfo, and Harley L. Browning. *Mexican Immigrants and Mexican Americans:*

An Evolving Relation. Austin: Center for Mexican American Studies, University of Texas, 1986.

de la Garza, Rodolfo, Z. Anthony Kruszewski, and Tomás A. Arciniega, comps. *Chicanos and Native Americans: The Territorial Minorities.* Englewood Cliffs, N.J.: Prentice-Hall, 1973.

de la Torre, Adela, and Beatríz M. Pesquera, eds. *Building with Our Hands: New Directions in Chicana Studies.* Berkeley: University of California Press, 1993.

De León, Arnoldo. *Ethnicity in the Sunbelt: A History of Mexican-Americans in Houston.* Houston: Mexican American Studies Program, University of Houston, 1989.

———. *Mexican-Americans in Texas: A Brief History.* Arlington Heights, Ill.: Harlan Davidson, 1993.

———. *The Tejano Community, 1836–1900.* Albuquerque: University of New Mexico Press, 1982.

———. *They Called Them Greasers: Anglo Attitudes toward Mexicans in Texas, 1821–1900.* Austin: University of Texas Press, 1983.

de Varona, Frank, ed. *Hispanic Presence in the United States: Historical Beginnings.* Washington, D.C.: National Hispanic Quincentennial Commission, 1993.

Del Castillo, Adelaida R., ed. *Between Borders: Essays on Mexican/Chicana History.* Encino, Calif: Floricanto Press, 1990.

Deutsch, Sarah. *No Separate Refuge: Culture, Class, and Gender on an Anglo-Hispanic Frontier in the American Southwest, 1880–1940.* New York: Oxford University Press, 1987.

Dolan, Jay, and Allan Figueroa Deck, eds. *Hispanic Catholic Culture in the U.S.: Issues and Concerns.* Notre Dame: University of Notre Dame Press, 1994.

Dolan, Jay, and Gilberto M. Hinojosa, eds. *Mexican Americans and the Catholic Church, 1900–1965.* Notre Dame: University of Notre Dame Press, 1994.

Dunne, John Gregory. *Delano.* Rev. ed. New York: Farrar, Straus and Giroux, 1971.

Durán, Livie Isauro, and H. Russell Bernard, eds. *Introduction to Chicano Studies: A Reader.* New York: Macmillan, 1973.

Foley, Douglas E., Clarice Mora, Donald E. Post, and Ignacio Lozano. *From Peones to Políticos: Ethnic Relations in a South Texas Town, 1900–1977.* Austin: Center for Mexican American Studies, University of Texas, 1977.

Foley, Neil. *The White Scourge: Mexicans, Blacks, and Poor Whites in Texas Cotton Culture.* Berkeley: University of California Press, 1997.

Fontana, Bernard. *Entrada: The Legacy of Spain and Mexico in the United States.* Tucson: Southwest Parks and Monuments Association, 1994.

Forbes, Jack D. *Aztecas del Norte: The Chicanos of Aztlán.* Greenwich, Conn.: Fawcett Publications, 1973.

Forrest, Suzanne. *The Preservation of the Village: New Mexico's Hispanics and the New Deal.* Albuquerque: University of New Mexico Press, 1989.

Fox, Geoffrey. *Hispanic Nation: Culture, Politics, and the Constructing of Identity.* Tucson: University of Arizona Press, 1996.

Fregoso, Rosa Linda. *The Bronze Screen: Chicana and Chicano Film Culture.* Minneapolis: University of Minnesota Press, 1993.

Galarza, Ernesto. *Barrio Boy.* Notre Dame: University of Notre Dame Press, 1971.

———. *Merchants of Labor: The Mexican Bracero Story.* Charlotte, N.C.: McNally and Loftin, 1964.

Gallegos, Bernardo P. *Literacy, Education, and Society in New Mexico, 1693–1821.* Albuquerque: University of New Mexico Press, 1992.

Gann, L. H., and Peter J. Duignan. *The Hispanics in the United States: A History.* Boulder, Colo.: Westview Press, 1986.

García, F. Chris, and Rudolph O. de la Garza. *The Chicano Political Experience: Three Perspectives.* North Scituate, Mass.: Duxbury Press, 1977.

García, Ignacio M. *Chicanismo: The Forging of a Militant Ethos.* Tucson: University of Arizona Press, 1997.

———. *United We Win: The Rise and Fall of the Raza Unida Party.* Tucson: Mexican American Studies and Resource Center, University of Arizona, 1989.

García, John A., Theresa Córdova, and Juan García, eds. *The Chicano Struggle: An Analysis of Past and Present Efforts.* Binghamton, N.Y.: Bilingual Press/Editorial Bilingüe, 1984.

García, Juan R. *Mexicans in the Midwest, 1900–1932.* Tucson: University of Arizona Press, 1996.

———. *Operation Wetback: The Mass Deportation of Mexican Undocumented Workers in 1954.* Westport, Conn.: Greenwood Press, 1980.

García, Juan R., Julia Curry Rodríguez, and Clara Lomas, eds. *In Times of Challenge: Chicanos and Chicanas in American Society.* Houston: Mexican American Studies Program, University of Houston, 1988.

García, Mario T. *Desert Immigrants: The Mexicans of El Paso, 1880–1920.* New Haven: Yale University Press, 1981.

———. *Mexican Americans: Leadership, Ideology, and Identity, 1930–1960.* New Haven: Yale University Press, 1989.

———, ed. *Memories of Chicano History: The Life and Narrative of Bert Corona.* Berkeley: University of California Press, 1994.

García, Richard A. *Rise of the Mexican American Middle Class: San Antonio, 1929–1941.* College Station: Texas A&M University Press, 1991.

Getz, Lynne Marie. *Schools of Their Own: The Education of Hispanos in New Mexico, 1850–1940.* Albuquerque: University of New Mexico Press, 1997.

Gómez-Quiñones, Juan. *Chicano Politics: Reality and Promise, 1940–1990.* Albuquerque: University of New Mexico Press, 1990.

———. *Mexican American Labor, 1790–1990.* Albuquerque: University of New Mexico Press, 1994.

———. *Roots of Chicano Politics, 1600–1940.* Albuquerque: University of New Mexico Press, 1994.

Gonzales, Manuel G. *The Hispanic Elite of the Southwest.* El Paso: Texas Western Press, 1989.

Gonzales, Sylvia Alicia. *Hispanic American Voluntary Organizations.* Westport, Conn.: Greenwood Press, 1985.

González, Gilbert G. *Chicano Education in the Era of Segregation.* Philadelphia: Balch Institute Press, 1990.

———. *Labor and Community: Mexican Citrus Worker Villages in a Southern California County, 1890–1950.* Urbana: University of Illinois Press, 1994.

González, Nancie L. *The Spanish-Americans of New Mexico: A Heritage of Pride.* Albuquerque: University of New Mexico Press, 1969.

Grebler, Leo, Joan W. Moore, and Ralph C. Guzmán. *The Mexican-American People: The Nation's Second Largest Minority.* New York: Free Press, 1970.

Griswold del Castillo, Richard. *La Familia: Chicano Families in the Urban Southwest, 1848 to the Present.* Notre Dame: Notre Dame University Press, 1984.

———. *The Los Angeles Barrio, 1850–1890: A Social History.* Berkeley: University of California Press, 1979.

———. *The Treaty of Guadalupe Hidalgo: A Legacy of Conflict.* Norman: University of Oklahoma Press, 1990.

Griswold del Castillo, Richard, and Arnoldo De León. *North to Aztlán: A History of Mexican Americans in the United States.* New York: Twayne Publishers, 1996.

Griswold del Castillo, Richard, and Richard A. García. *César Chávez: A Triumph of Spirit.* Norman: University of Oklahoma Press, 1995.

Griswold del Castillo, Richard, and Manuel Hidalgo, eds. *Chicano Social and Political History in the XIX Century.* Encino, Calif.: Floricanto Press, 1992.

Guerin-Gonzales, Camille. *Mexican Workers and American Dreams: Immigration, Repatriation, and California Farm Labor, 1900–1939.* New Brunswick, N.J.: Rutgers University Press, 1994.

Gutiérrez, David G., ed. *Between Two Worlds: Mexican Immigrants in the United States.* Wilmington, Del.: Scholarly Resources, 1996.

———. *Walls and Mirrors: Mexican Americans, Mexican Immigrants, and the Politics of Ethnicity.* Berkeley: University of California Press, 1995.

Gutiérrez, Ramón A. *When Jesus Came, the Corn Mothers Went Away: Marriage, Sexuality, and Power in New Mexico, 1500–1846.* Stanford: Stanford University Press, 1991.

Gutiérrez-Jones, Carl. *Rethinking the Borderlands: Between Chicano Culture and Legal Discourse.* Berkeley: University of California Press, 1994.

Haas, Lisbeth. *Conquests and Historical Identities in California, 1769–1936.* Berkeley: University of California Press, 1995.

Hadley-García, George. *Hispanic Hollywood: The Latins in Motion Pictures.* New York: Carol Publishing, 1990.

Hall, Thomas D. *Social Change in the Southwest, 1350–1880.* Lawrence: University Press of Kansas, 1989.

Hernández, José Amaro. *Mutual Aid for Survival: The Case of the Mexican American.* Malabar, Fla.: Robert E. Krieger, 1983.

Hernández, Luis F. *Aztlán: The Southwest and Its People.* Rochelle Park, N.J.: Hayden Book Company, 1975.

Herrera-Sobek, María. *The Mexican Corrido: A Feminist Analysis.* Bloomington: Indiana University Press, 1990.

———. *Northward Bound: The Mexican Immigrant Experience in Ballad and Song.* Bloomington: Indiana University Press, 1993.

———, ed. *Reconstructing a Chicano/a Literary Heritage: Hispanic Colonial Literature of the Southwest.* Tucson: University of Arizona Press, 1998.

Heyck, Denis Lynn Daly, ed. *Barrios and Borderlands: Cultures of Latinos and Latinas in the United States.* London: Routledge, 1994.

Hinojosa, Gilberto Miguel. *A Borderlands Town in Transition: Laredo, 1755–1870.* College Station: Texas A&M University Press, 1983.

Hoffman, Abraham. *Unwanted Mexican-Americans in the Great Depression: Repatriation Pressures, 1929–1939.* Tucson: University of Arizona Press, 1974.

Hondagneu-Sotelo, Pierrette. *Gendered Transitions: Mexican Experiences of Immigration.* Berkeley: University of California Press, 1994.

Jiménez, Alfredo, ed. *Handbook of Hispanic Cultures in the United States.* Houston: Arte Público Press and Instituto de Cooperación Iberoamericana, 1994.

Jiménez, Carlos M. *The Mexican American Heritage.* Berkeley: TQS Publications, 1993.

John, Elizabeth A. H. *Storms Brewed in Other Men's Worlds: The Confrontation of Indians, Spanish, and French in the Southwest, 1540–1795.* College Station: Texas A&M University Press, 1975.

Jones, Oakah L., Jr. *Los Paisanos: Spanish Settlers on the Northern Frontier.* Norman: University of Oklahoma Press, 1979.

Kanellos, Nicolás. *A History of Hispanic Theatre in the United States: Origins to 1940.* Austin: University of Texas Press, 1990.

———, ed. *The Hispanic-American Almanac: A Reference Work on Hispanics in the United States.* Detroit: Gale Research, 1993.

Keefe, Susan E., and Amado M. Padilla. *Chicano Ethnicity.* Albuquerque: University of New Mexico Press, 1987.

Langley, Lester D. *MexAmerica.* New York: Crown, 1988.

Larralde, Carlos. *Mexican-Americans: Movements and Leaders.* Los Alamitos, Calif.: Hwong Publishing, 1976.

Leonard, Karen Isaksen. *Making Ethnic Choices: California's Punjabi Mexican Americans.* Philadelphia: Temple University Press, 1992.

Levy, Jacques E. *César Chávez: Autobiography of La Causa.* New York: W. W. Norton, 1975.

Limón, José. *Mexican Ballads, Chicano Poems: History and Influence in Mexican-American Social Poetry.* Berkeley: University of California Press, 1992.

Loza, Steven. *Barrio Rhythm: Mexican American Music in Los Angeles.* Urbana: University of Illinois Press, 1993.

Machado, Manuel A., Jr. *Listen, Chicano! An Informal History of the Mexican American.* Chicago: Nelson Hall, 1978.

Maciel, David R., and María Herrera-Sobek, eds. *Culture across Borders: Mexican Immigration and Popular Culture.* Tucson: University of Arizona Press, 1998.

Maciel, David R., and Isidro D. Ortiz, eds. *Chicanas/Chicanos at the Crossroads: Social, Economic, and Political Change.* Tucson: University of Arizona Press, 1996.

Madsen, William. *The Mexican-Americans of South Texas.* 2d ed. New York: Holt, Rinehart and Winston, 1973.

Marín, Marguerita V. *Social Protest in an Urban Barrio: A Study of the Chicano Movement, 1966–1974.* Lanham, Md.: University Press of America, 1991.

Márquez, Benjamin. *LULAC: The Evolution of a Mexican American Political Organization.* Austin: University of Texas Press, 1993.

———. *Power and Politics in a Chicano Barrio: A Study of Mobilization Efforts and Community Power in El Paso.* Lanham, Md.: University Press of America, 1985.

Martin, Patricia Preciado. *Songs My Mother Sang to Me: An Oral History of Mexican American Women.* Tucson: University of Arizona Press, 1992.

Martínez, Elizabeth Sutherland, and Enriqueta Longeaux y Vásquez. *Viva La Raza! The Struggle of the Mexican-American People.* Garden City, N.Y.: Doubleday, 1974.

Martínez, Oscar J. *Border Boom Town: Ciudad Juárez Since 1848.* Austin: University of Texas Press, 1978.

———. *Troublesome Border.* Tucson: University of Arizona Press, 1988.

Martínez, Rubén. *The Other Side: Notes from the New L.A., Mexico City, and Beyond.* New York: Vintage Books, 1993.

Massey, Douglas, Rafael Alarcón, Jorge Durand, and Humberto González. *Return to Aztlán: The Social Process of International Migration from Western Mexico.* Berkeley: University of California Press, 1987.

Matovina, Timothy M. *Tejano Religion and Ethnicity: San Antonio, 1821–1860.* Austin: University of Texas Press, 1995.

Mazón, Mauricio. *The Zoot-Suit Riots: The Psychology of Symbolic Annihilation.* Austin: University of Texas Press, 1984.

McKenna, Teresa, and Flora Ida Ortiz, eds. *The Broken Web: The Educational Experience of Hispanic American Women.* Claremont and Berkeley: The Tomás Rivera Center and Floricanto Press, 1988.

McWilliams, Carey. *North from Mexico: The Spanish-Speaking People of the United States.* Rev. ed. Westport, Conn: Greenwood Press/Praeger, 1990.

Meier, Matt S. *Mexican American Biographies: A Historical Dictionary, 1836–1987.* Westport, Conn.: Greenwood Press, 1988.

Meier, Matt S., and Feliciano Rivera. *The Chicanos: A History of the Mexican American.* 2d ed. New York: Hill and Wang, 1993.

Meinig, Donald W. *Southwest: Three Peoples in Geographical Change, 1600–1970.* New York: Oxford University Press, 1971.

Melville, Margarita B., ed. *Mexicanas at Work in the United States.* Houston: Mexican American Studies Program, University of Houston, 1988.

———, ed. *Twice a Minority: Mexican American Women.* St. Louis, Mo.: C. V. Mosby, 1980.

Menchaca, Martha. *Mexican Outsiders: A Community History of Marginalization and Discrimination in California.* Austin: University of Texas Press, 1995.

Mindiola, Tatcho, Jr., and Emilio Zamora, eds. *Chicano Discourse: Selected Conference Proceedings of the National Association for Chicano Studies.* Houston: Mexican American Studies Program, University of Houston, 1992.

Miranda, M. L. *A History of Hispanics in Southern Nevada.* Reno: University of Nevada Press, 1997.

Mirandé, Alfredo. *The Chicano Experience: An Alternative Perspective.* Notre Dame: University of Notre Dame Press, 1985.

———. *Hombres y Machos: Masculinity and Latino Culture.* Boulder, Colo.: Westview Press, 1997.

Mirandé, Alfredo, and Evangelina Enríquez. *La Chicana: The Mexican-American Woman.* Chicago: University of Chicago Press, 1979.

Monroy, Douglas. *Thrown among Strangers: The Making of Mexican Culture in Frontier California.* Berkeley: University of California Press, 1990.

Montejano, David. *Anglos and Mexicans in the Making of Texas, 1836–1986.* Austin: University of Texas Press, 1987.

Moore, Joan W. *Homeboys: Gangs, Drugs, and Prison in the Barrios of Los Angeles.* Philadelphia: Temple University Press, 1978.

Moore, Joan W., with Harry Pachón. *Mexican Americans.* 2d ed. Englewood Cliffs, N.J.: Prentice-Hall, 1976.

Moore, Joan W., and Raquel Pinderhughes, eds. *In the Barrios: Latinos and the Underclass Debate.* New York: Russell Sage, 1993.

Mora, Magdalena, and Adelaida R. del Castillo, eds. *Mexican Women in the United States: Struggles Past and Present.* Los Angeles: Chicano Studies Research Center, University of California, Los Angeles, 1980.

Morales, Armando. *Ando Sangrando (I Am Bleeding): A Study of Mexican American-Police Conflict.* La Puente, Calif.: Perspectiva Publications, 1972.

Morín, Raúl. *Among the Valiant: Mexican Americans in WWII and Korea.* Alhambra, Calif.: Borden Publishing Company, 1966.

Muñoz, Carlos, Jr. *Youth, Identity, Power: The Chicano Movement.* New York: Verso, 1989.

Navarro, Armando. *Mexican American Youth Organization: Avant-Garde of the Chicano Movement in Texas.* Austin: University of Texas Press, 1995.

Noriega, Chon, ed. *Chicanos and Film: Representation and Resistance.* Minneapolis, University of Minnesota Press, 1992.

Nostrand, Richard L. *The Hispano Homeland.* Norman: University of Oklahoma Press, 1992.

Officer, James E. *Hispanic Arizona, 1536–1856.* Tucson: University of Arizona Press, 1987.

Ortiz, Roxanne Dunbar. *Roots of Resistance: Land Tenure in New Mexico, 1680–1980.* Los Angeles: Chicano Studies Center and American Indian Center, University of California, 1980.

Padilla, Félix M. *Latino Ethnic Consciousness: The Case of Mexican Americans and Puerto Ricans in Chicago.* Notre Dame: University of Notre Dame Press, 1985.

Paredes, Américo. *Folklore and Culture on the Texas-Mexican Border.* Ed. by Richard Bauman. Austin: Center for Mexican American Studies, University of Texas, 1993.

Pastor, Robert A., and Jorge G. Castañeda. *Limits to Friendship: The United States and Mexico.* New York: Vintage, 1993.

Peña, Devon. *The Terror of the Machine: Technology, Work, Gender, and Ecology on the U.S.-Mexico Border.* Austin: Center for Mexican American Studies, University of Texas, 1997.

Peña, Manuel H. *The Texas-Mexican Conjunto: History of a Working-Class Music.* Austin: University of Texas Press, 1985.

Pérez, Emma. *Writing Chicanas into History: Theories of Representation and Difference.* Bloomington: Indiana University Press, 1999.

Perrigo, Lynn I. *Hispanos: Historic Leaders in New Mexico.* Santa Fe: Sunstone Press, 1985.

Pitt, Leonard. *The Decline of the Californios: A Social History of the Spanish-Speaking Californians, 1846–1900.* Berkeley: University of California Press, 1966.

Portes, Alejandro, and Robert L. Bach. *Latin Journey: Cuban and Mexican Immigrants in the United States.* Berkeley: University of California Press, 1985.

Portes, Alejandro, and Rubén G. Rumbaut. *Immigrant America: A Portrait.* Berkeley: University of California Press, 1990.

Poyo, Gerald E., and Gilberto M. Hinojosa, eds. *Tejano Origins in Eighteenth-Century San Antonio.* Austin: University of Texas Press, 1991.

Quinn, Anthony. *One Man Tango.* New York: HarperCollins, 1995.

———. *The Original Sin: A Self-Portrait.* Boston: Little, Brown and Company, 1972.

Ramírez, Ricardo. *Faith Expressions of Hispanics in the Southwest.* San Antonio: Mexican American Cultural Center, 1990.

Rebolledo, Tey Diana, ed. *Nuestras Mujeres: Hispanas of New Mexico, Their Images and Their Lives, 1582–1992.* Albuquerque: El Norte Publications/Academia, 1992.

Reisler, Mark. *By the Sweat of Their Brow: Mexican Immigrant Labor in the United States, 1900–1940.* Westport, Conn.: Greenwood Press, 1976.

Riding, Alan. *Distant Neighbors: A Portrait of the Mexicans.* New York: Alfred A. Knopf, 1984.

Ríos-Bustamante, Antonio. *Mexican Los Angeles: A Narrative and Pictorial History.* Encino, Calif.: Floricanto Press, 1992.

———. *Regions of La Raza: Changing Interpretations of Mexican American Regional History and Culture.* Encino, Calif.: Floricanto Press, 1992.

Ríos-Bustamante, Antonio, and Pedro Castillo. *An Illustrated History of Mexican Los Angeles, 1781–1985.* Los Angeles: Chicano Studies Research Center, University of California, 1986.

Rocard, Marcienne. *The Children of the Sun: Mexican-Americans in the Literature of the United States.* Trans. by Edward G. Brown, Jr. Tucson: University of Arizona Press, 1989.

Rochín, Refugio I. *Economic Perspectives of the Hispanic Community.* San Antonio: Tomás Rivera Center, 1988.

Rodríguez, Luis J. *Always Running, La Vida Loca: Gang Days in L.A.* Willimantic, Conn.: Curbstone Press, 1993.

Romero, Mary, and Cordelia Candelaria, eds. *Community Empowerment and Chicano Scholarship.* Los Angeles: National Association for Chicano Studies, 1992.

Romo, Ricardo. *History of a Barrio: East Los Angeles.* Austin: University of Texas Press, 1983.

Romo, Ricardo, and Raymund Paredes, eds. *New Directions in Chicano Scholarship.* Santa Barbara: Center for Chicano Studies, University of California, Santa Barbara, 1984.

Rosaldo, Renato, Robert A. Calvert, and Gustav L. Seligmann, comps. *Chicano: The Evolution of a People.* 2d ed. Malabar, Fla.: Robert E. Krieger, 1982.

Rosenbaum, Robert J. *Mexicano Resistance in the Southwest: "The Sacred Right of Self-Preservation."* Austin: University of Texas Press, 1981.

Rosenus, Alan. *General M. G. Vallejo and the Advent of the Americans.* Albuquerque: University of New Mexico Press, 1995.

Ruiz, Vicki L. *Cannery Women/Cannery Lives: Mexican Women, Unionization, and the California Food Processing Industry, 1930–1950.* Albuquerque: University of New Mexico Press, 1987.

———. *From Out of the Shadows: Mexican Women in Twentieth-Century America.* New York: Oxford University Press, 1998.

Ruiz, Vicki L., and Susan Tiano, eds. *Women on the U.S./Mexican Border: Responses to Change.* London: Allen and Unwin, 1987.

Salas, Elizabeth. *Soldaderas in the Mexican Military: Myth and History.* Austin: University of Texas Press, 1990.

Saldívar, José David. *Border Matters: Remapping American Cultural Studies.* Berkeley: University of California Press, 1997.

Saldívar, Ramón. *Chicano Narrative: The Dialectics of Difference.* Madison: University of Wisconsin Press, 1990.

Samora, Julián. *Los Mojados: The Wetback Story.* Notre Dame: University of Notre Dame Press, 1971.

———, ed. *La Raza: Forgotten Americans.* Notre Dame: University of Notre Dame Press, 1966.

Samora, Julián, and Patricia Vandel Simon. *A History of the Mexican-American People.* 2d ed. Notre Dame: University of Notre Dame Press, 1993.

Sánchez, George J. *Becoming Mexican American: Ethnicity, Culture and Identity in Chicano Los Angeles, 1900–1945.* New York: Oxford University Press, 1993.

Sánchez, Rosaura. *Telling Identities: The Californio Testimonios.* Minneapolis: University of Minnesota Press, 1995.

Sánchez, Rosaura, and Rosa Martínez Cruz, eds. *Essays on la Mujer.* Los Angeles: Chicano Studies Center, University of California, Los Angeles, 1977.

San Miguel, Guadalupe, Jr. *"Let All of Them Take Heed": Mexican Americans and the Campaign for Educational Equality in Texas, 1910–1981.* Austin: University of Texas Press, 1987.

Servín, Manuel P., ed. *An Awakened Minority: The Mexican Americans.* 2d ed. Beverly Hills, Calif.: Glencoe Press, 1974.

———, ed. *The Mexican Americans: An Awakening Minority.* Beverly Hills, Calif.: Glencoe Press, 1970.

Sheridan, Thomas E. *Los Tucsonenses: The Mexican Community in Tucson, 1854–1941.* Tucson: University of Arizona Press, 1986.

Shorris, Earl. *Latinos: A Biography of the People.* New York: W.W. Norton, 1992.

Simmons, Ozzie G. *Anglo-Americans and Mexican Americans in South Texas.* New York: Arno Press, 1974.

Skerry, Peter. *Mexican Americans: The Ambivalent Minority.* New York: The Free Press, 1993.

Smith, Michael M. *The Mexicans in Oklahoma.* Norman: University of Oklahoma Press, 1980.

Stavans, Ilan. *The Hispanic Condition: Reflections on Culture and Identity in America.* New York: HarperCollins, 1995.

Steiner, Stan. *La Raza: The Mexican Americans.* New York: Harper and Row, 1969.

Stoddard, Ellwyn R. *Mexican Americans.* New York: Random House, 1973.

Stoddard, Ellwyn R., Richard L. Nostrand, and Jonathan P. West, eds. *Borderlands Sourcebook.* Norman: University of Oklahoma Press, 1983.

Strachuitz, Chris, with James Nicolopulos, comp. *Lydia Mendoza: A Family Autobiography.* Houston: Arte Público Press, 1993.

Suárez-Orozco, Carola, and Marcelo Suárez-Orozco. *Transformations: Migration, Family Life, and Achievement Motivation among Latino Adolescents.* Stanford: Stanford University Press, 1995.

Swadesh, Frances León. *Los Primeros Pobladores: Hispanic Americans of the Ute Frontier.* Notre Dame: University of Notre Dame Press, 1974.

Taylor, Ronald B. *Chávez and the Farm Workers.* Boston: Beacon Press, 1975.

Tijerina, Andrés. *Tejanos and Texas under the Mexican Flag, 1821–1836.* College Station: Texas A&M University Press, 1994.

Trejo, Arnulfo D., ed. *The Chicanos: As We See Ourselves.* Tucson: University of Arizona Press, 1979.

Trujillo, Charley, ed. *Soldados: Chicanos in Viet Nam.* San Jose, Calif.: Chusma House Publications, 1990.

Valdés, Dennis Nodín. *Al Norte: Agricultural Workers in the Great Lakes Region, 1917–1970.* Austin: University of Texas Press, 1991.

―――. *El Pueblo Mexicano en Detroit y Michigan: A Social History.* Detroit: Wayne State University Press, 1982.

Valdés, Guadalupe. *Con Respeto: Bridging the Distances between Culturally Diverse Families and Schools—An Ethnographic Portrait.* Williston, Vt.: Teachers College Press, 1996.

Valdez, Armando, Albert Camarillo, and Tomás Almaguer, eds. *The State of Chicano Research in Family, Labor and Migration Studies.* Stanford: Stanford Center for Chicano Research, 1983.

Vargas, Zaragoza. *Proletarians of the North: A History of Mexican Industrial Workers in Detroit and the Midwest, 1917–1933.* Berkeley: University of California Press, 1993.

Vélez-Ibáñez, Carlos G. *Border Visions: Mexican Cultures of the Southwest United States.* Tucson: University of Arizona Press, 1996.

Vigil, James Diego. *Barrio Gangs: Street Life and Identity in Southern California.* Austin: University of Texas Press, 1988.

―――. *From Indians to Chicanos: A Sociocultural History.* St. Louis, Mo.: C. V. Mosby, 1980.

Vigil, Maurilio E. *Hispanics in American Politics: The Search for Political Power.* Lanham, Md.: University Press of America, 1987.

―――. *The Hispanics of New Mexico: Essays on History and Culture.* Bristol, Ind.: Wyndham Hall Press, 1985.

―――. *Los Patrones: Profiles of Hispanic Political Leaders in New Mexico History.* Washington, D.C.: University Press of America, 1980.

Vigil, Ralph H., Frances W. Kaye, and John R. Wunder, eds. *Spain and the Plains: Myths and Realities of Spanish Exploration and Settlement on the Great Plains.* Niwot, Colo.: University Press of Colorado, 1994.

Weber, David J. *Foreigners in Their Native Land: Historical Roots of the Mexican Americans.* Albuquerque: University of New Mexico Press, 1973.

―――. *The Mexican Frontier, 1821–1846: The American Southwest under Mexico.* Albuquerque: University of New Mexico Press, 1982.

―――. *The Spanish Frontier in North America.* New Haven: Yale University Press, 1992.

―――, ed. *Myth and History of the Hispanic Southwest: Essays by David J. Weber.* Albuquerque: University of New Mexico Press, 1988.

Weber, Devra. *Dark Sweat, White Gold: California Farm Workers, Cotton, and the New Deal.* Berkeley: University of California Press, 1994.

Weyr, Thomas. *Hispanic U.S.A.: Breaking the Melting Pot.* New York: Harper and Row, 1988.

Williams, Norma. *The Mexican American Family: Tradition and Change.* Dix Hills, N.Y.: General Hall, 1990.

Ybarra Lea, and Alex Saragoza. *Nuestras Raíces: The Mexican Community of the Central San Joaquin Valley.* Fresno: La Raza T.E.A.C.H. Project, California State University, 1980.

Zamora, Emilio. *The World of the Mexican Worker in Texas.* College Station: Texas A&M University Press, 1993.

Zavella, Patricia. *Women's Work and Chicano Families: Cannery Workers of the Santa Clara Valley.* Ithaca: Cornell University Press, 1987.

ARTICLES

Aguirre, Yjinio F. "Echoes of the Conquistadores: Stock Raising in Spanish-Mexican Times." *Journal of Arizona History* 16 (Autumn 1975): 267–86.

Albrecht, Elizabeth. "Estevan Ochoa: Mexican-American Businessman." *Arizoniana* 4 (Summer 1963): 35–40.

Alfaro, Juan. "The Spirit of the First Franciscan Missionaries in Texas." *U.S. Catholic Historian* 9 (Spring 1990): 49–66.

Allsup, Carl. "Education Is Our Freedom: The American G.I. Forum and the Mexican American School Segregation in Texas, 1948–1957." *Aztlán* 8 (Spring, Summer, Fall 1977): 29–49.

Almaguer, Tomás. "Historical Notes on Chicano Oppression: The Dialectics of Racial and Class Domination in North America." *Aztlán* 5 (Spring and Fall 1974): 27–56.

———. "Interpreting Chicano History: The World-System Approach to Nineteenth-Century California." *Review* 4 (Winter 1981): 459–508.

Almaráz, Felix D., Jr. "Franciscan Evangelization in Spanish Frontier Texas: Apex of Social Contact, Conflict, and Confluence, 1751–1761." *Colonial Latin American Historical Review* 2 (Summer 1993): 253–87.

———. "Harmony, Discord, and Compromise in Spanish Colonial Texas: The Río San Antonio Experience, 1691–1741." *New Mexico Historical Review* 67 (Oct. 1992): 329–56.

———. "An Uninviting Wilderness: The Plains of West Texas, 1534–1821." *Great Plains Quarterly* 12 (Summer 1992): 169–80.

Año Nuevo de Kerr, Louise. "Chicano Settlement in Chicago: A Brief History." *Journal of Ethnic Studies* 2 (Winter 1975): 22–32.

Aragón, Janie Louise. "The People of Santa Fe in the 1790s." *Aztlán* 7 (Fall 1976): 391–417.

Arbelaez, María Soledad. "The Sonoran Missions and Indian Raids of the Eighteenth Century." *Journal of the Southwest* 33 (Autumn 1991): 366–86.

Arroyo, Luis L. "Chicano Participation in Organized Labor: The CIO in Los Angeles, 1938–1950. An Extended Research Note." *Aztlán* 6 (Summer 1975): 227–303.

Bannon, John Francis. "The Mission As a Frontier Institution: Sixty Years of Interest and Research." *Western Historical Quarterly* 10 (July 1979): 3–22.

Barr, Alwyn. "Occupational and Geographic Mobility in San Antonio, 1870–1900." *Southwestern Historical Quarterly* 51 (Sept. 1970): 396–403.

Barrera, Mario. "La Raza Unida Party and the Chicano Student Movement." *Social Science Journal* 19 (1982): 101–19.

Baxter, John O. "Salvador Armijo: Citizen of Albuquerque, 1823–1879." *New Mexico Historical Review* 53 (July 1978): 219–37.

Bean, Frank, and Benjamin Bradshaw. "Intermarriage between Persons of Spanish and Non-Spanish Surname: Changes from the Mid-Nineteenth to the Mid-Twentieth Century." *Social Science Quarterly* 51 (Sept. 1970): 389–95.

Betten, Neil, and Raymond A. Mohl. "From Discrimination to Repatriation: Mexican Life in Gary, Indiana, during the Great Depression." *Pacific Historical Review* 42 (Aug. 1973): 370–88.

Brack, Gene M. "Mexican Opinion, American Racism, and the War of 1846." *Western Historical Quarterly* 1 (Apr. 1970): 61–74.

Bustamante, Adrian. "'The Matter Was Never Resolved': The Casta System in Colonial New Mexico, 1693–1823." *New Mexico Historical Review* 66 (Apr. 1991): 143–64.

Bustamante, Jorge. "The Historical Context of the Undocumented Immigration from Mexico to the United States." *Aztlán* 3 (Fall 1972): 257–82.

Camarillo, Albert. "Chicano Urban History: A Study of Compton's Barrio, 1936–1970." *Aztlán* 3 (Fall 1972): 257–82.

———. "Perspectives on Mexican-American Urban Life and Culture." *Journal of American Ethnic History* 5 (Spring 1986): 72–79.

Campa, Arthur. "Immigrant Latinos and Resident Mexican Americans in Garden City, Kansas: Ethnicity and Ethnic Relations." *Urban Anthropology* 19 (Winter 1990): 345–661.

Campbell, Leon G. "The First Californios: Presidial Society in Spanish California, 1769–1822." *Journal of the West* 11 (Oct. 1972): 582–95.

———. "The Spanish Presidio in Alta California during the Mission Period, 1769–1784." *Journal of the West* 16 (Oct. 1977): 63–77.

Cárdenas, Gilbert. "Los Desarraigados: Chicanos in the Midwestern Region of the United States." *Aztlán* 7 (Summer 1976): 153–86.

Castañeda, Antonia I. "Engendering the History of Alta California, 1769–1848: Gender, Sexuality, and the Family." *California History* 76 (Summer and Fall 1997): 230–59.

———. "Gender, Race, and Culture: Spanish-Mexican Women in the Historiography of Frontier California." *Frontiers* 11, no. 1 (1990): 8–30.

Chacón, Ramón D. "The Chicano Immigrant Press in Los Angeles: The Case of *El Heraldo de México*, 1916–1920." *Journalism History* 4 (Summer 1977): 48–50, 62–64.

———. "Labor Unrest and Industrialized Agriculture in California: The Case of the 1933 San Joaquin Valley Cotton Strike." *Social Science Quarterly* 65 (June 1984): 336–53.

Chávez, John A. "Aztlán, Cíbola, and Frontier New Spain." *Campo Libre* 1 (Summer 1981): 193–211.

Chávez, Leo R. "Settlers and Sojourners: The Case of Mexicans in the United States." *Human Organization* 47 (Summer 1988): 95–108.

Christian, Carole E. "Joining the American Mainstream: Texas's Mexican Americans during World War I." *Southwestern Historical Quarterly* 92 (Apr. 1989): 559–95.

Clark, Harry. "Their Pride, Their Manners, and Their Voices: Sources of the Traditional Portrait of the Early Californians." *California Historical Quarterly* 53 (Spring 1974): 71–82.

Cortés, Carlos E. "Mexican Americans in Twentieth-Century California." *Masterkey* 60 (Summer/Fall 1986): 36–48.

Cortés, Enrique. "Mexican Colonies during the Porfiriato." *Aztlán* 10 (Summer-Fall 1979): 1–14.

Corwin, Arthur F. "Mexican-American History: An Assessment." *Pacific Historical Review* 42 (Aug. 1973): 269–308.

Cuéllo, José. "Beyond the 'Borderlands' is the North of Colonial Mexico: A Latin Americanist Perspective to the Study of the Mexican North and the United States Southwest." *Proceedings of the Pacific Coast Council on Latin American Studies* 9 (1982): 1–24.

———. "The Persistence of Indian Slavery and Encomienda in the Northeast of Colonial Mexico, 1577–1723." *Journal of Social History* 21 (Summer 1988): 683–700.

De la Teja, Jesús Francisco. "Indians, Soldiers, and Canary Islanders: The Making of a Texas Frontier Community." *Locus* 3 (Fall 1990): 81–96.

De León, Arnoldo. "Accomodacionistas: Defensores del Barrio." *Caracol* 3 (Dec. 1976): 16–17.

———. "Tejanos and the Texas War for Independence: Historiography's Judgment." *New Mexico Historical Review* 61 (Apr. 1986): 137–46.

De León, Arnoldo, and Kenneth L. Stewart. "Lost Dreams and Found Fortunes: Mexican and Anglo Immigrants in South Texas." *Western Historical Quarterly* 14 (July 1983): 291–310.

———. "A Tale of Three Cities: A Comparative Analysis of the Socio-Economic Condition of Mexican-Americans in Los Angeles, Tucson, and San Antonio, 1850–1900." *Journal of the West* 24 (Apr. 1985): 664–74.

Delgado, Edmundo. "A Spanish Ranker in New Mexico: Captain Manuel Delgado of Santa Fe, 1738–1815." *New Mexico Historical Review* 66 (Jan. 1991): 1–13.

Downs, Fane. "Governor Antonio Martínez and the Defense of Texas from Foreign Invasion, 1817–1822." *Texas Military History* 7 (Spring 1968): 27–43.

Durán, Tobias. "Francisco Chávez, Thomas B. Catron, and Organized Political Violence in Santa Fe in the 1890's." *New Mexico Historical Review* 59 (July 1984): 291–310.

Duron, Clementina. "Mexican Women and Labor Conflict in Los Angeles: The ILGWU Dressmakers' Strike of 1933." *Aztlán* 15 (1984): 145–61.

Dysart, Jane. "Mexican Women in San Antonio, 1850–1860: The Assimilation Process." *Western Historical Quarterly* 7 (Oct. 1976): 365–75.

Ellis, Bruce. "Fraud without Scandal: The Roque Lovato Grant and Gaspar Ortiz y Alarid." *New Mexico Historical Review* 57 (Jan. 1982): 43–62.

Escobar, Corinne. "Here to Stay: The Mexican Identity of Moapa Valley, Nevada." *Nevada Historical Society Quarterly* 36 (Summer 1993): 71–89.

Escobar, Edward J. "The Dialectics of Repression: The Los Angeles Police Department and the Chicano Movement, 1968–1971." *Journal of American History* 79 (Mar. 1993): 1483–1514.

———. "The Forging of a Community: The Latino Experience in Northwest Indiana." *Latino Studies Journal* 2 (Jan. 1991): 38–57.

Espinosa, J. Manuel, and W. Charles Bennett, Jr. "Don Diego de Vargas: Portrait of a Seventeenth-Century Conquistador." *New Mexico Historical Review* 64 (July 1989): 305–17.

Estrada, Daniél, and Richard Santillán. "Chicanos in the Northwest and the Midwest United States: A History of Cultural and Political Commonality." *Perspectives in Mexican American Studies* 6 (1997): 195–228.

Foley, Douglas E. "The Legacy of the *Partido Raza Unida* in South Texas: A Class Analysis." *Ethnic Affairs* 2 (Spring 1988): 47–73.

Foote, Cheryl. "Spanish-Indian Trade along New Mexico's Frontier in the Eighteenth Century." *Journal of the West* 24 (Apr. 1985): 25–30.

Forbes, Jack D. "Hispano-Mexican Pioneers of the San Francisco Bay Region: An Analysis of Racial Origins." *Aztlán* 14 (Spring 1983): 175–89.

Fregoso, Rosa Linda. "*Seguín*: The Same Side of the Alamo." *Bilingual Review/La Revista Bilingue* 10 (May-Dec. 1983): 146–52.

Galarza, Ernesto. "Mexicans in the Southwest: A Culture in Process." *Campo Libre* 1 (Winter 1981): 87–117.

Gamboa, Erasmo. "Braceros in the Pacific Northwest: Laborers in the Domestic Front, 1942–1947." *Pacific Historical Review* 61 (Aug. 1987): 378–98.

———. "Chicanos in the Northwest: An Historical Perspective." *El Grito* 6 (Summer 1973): 57–70.

———. "Mexican Immigration into Washington State: A History, 1940–1950." *Pacific Northwest Quarterly* 72 (July 1981): 121–31.

García, Alma M. "The Development of Chicana Feminist Discourse, 1970–1980." *Gender and Society* 3 (June 1989): 217–38.

García, F. Chris. "Manitos and Chicanos in Nuevo Mexico Politics." *Aztlán* 5 (Spring and Fall 1974): 177–88.

García, Gilberto. "Beyond the Adelita Image: Women Scholars in the National Association for Chicano Studies, 1972–1992." *Perspectives in Mexican American Studies* 5 (1995): 35–61.

García, Ignacio M. "Constructing the Chicano Movement: Synthesis of a Militant Ethos." *Perspectives in Mexican American Studies* 6 (1997): 1–19.

García, Juan R. "History of Chicanos in Chicago Heights." *Aztlán* 7 (Summer 1976): 291–306.

———. "Midwest Mexicanos in the 1920s: Issues, Questions, and Direction." *Social Science Journal* 19 (Apr. 1982): 89–99.

García, Mario T. "Americanization and the Mexican Immigrant, 1880–1930." *Journal of Ethnic Studies* 6 (Summer 1978): 19–34.

———. "Americans All: The Mexican American Generation and the Politics of Wartime Los Angeles, 1941–45." *Social Science Quarterly* 65 (June 1984): 278–89.

———. "The Californios of San Diego and the Politics of Accommodation." *Aztlán* 6 (Spring 1975): 69–85.

————. "The Chicana in American History: The Mexican Women of El Paso, 1880–1920." *Pacific Historical Review* 49 (May 1980): 285–314.

————. "A Chicano Perspective on San Diego History." *Journal of San Diego History* 18 (Fall 1971): 14–21.

————. "La Frontera: The Border as Symbol and Reality in Mexican-American Thought." *Mexican Studies/Estudios Mexicanos* 1 (Summer 1985): 195–225.

————. "Merchants and Dons: San Diego's Attempt at Modernization, 1850–1860." *Journal of San Diego History* 21 (Winter 1975): 52–80.

García, Richard A. "César Chávez: A Personal and Historical Testimony." *Pacific Historical Review* 63 (May 1994): 225–33.

————. "The Chicano Movement and the Mexican American Community, 1972–1978: An Interpretive Essay." *Socialist Review* (July-Oct. 1978): 117–36.

————. "Class, Consciousness, and Ideology—The Mexican Community of San Antonio, Texas: 1930–1940." *Aztlán* 9 (Spring, Summer, Fall 1978): 23–69.

————. "Dolores Huerta: Woman, Organizer, Symbol." *California History* 72 (Spring 1993): 56–71.

Gómez, Arthur. "Royalist in Transition: Facundo Melgares, the Last Spanish Governor of New Mexico, 1818–1822." *New Mexico Historical Review* 68 (Oct. 1993): 371–87.

Gómez-Quiñones, Juan. "The First Steps: Chicano Labor Conflict and Organizing, 1900–1920." *Aztlán* 3 (Spring 1972): 25–31.

Gómez-Quiñones, Juan, and Luis L. Arroyo. "On the State of Chicano History." *Western Historical Quarterly* 7 (Apr. 1976): 155–86.

Gonzales, Manuel G. "Carlos I. Velasco." *Journal of Arizona History* 25 (Autumn 1984): 265–84.

————. "Dr. Mariano Samaniego, Citizen of the El Paso Valley." *Password* 35 (Winter 1990): 159–70.

————. "Mariano G. Samaniego." *Journal of Arizona History* 31 (Summer 1990): 141–60.

Gonzales, Phillip B. "The Hispano Homeland Debate: New Lessons." *Perspectives in Mexican American Studies* 6 (1997): 123–41.

González, Gilbert G. "A Critique of the Internal Colony Model." *Latin American Perspectives* 1 (Spring 1974): 154–61.

————. "Labor and Community: The Camps of Mexican Citrus Pickers in Southern California." *Western Historical Quarterly* 22 (Aug. 1991): 289–312.

————. "The Mexican Citrus Picker Union, the Mexican Consulate, and the Orange County Strike of 1936." *Labor History* 35 (Winter 1994): 48–65.

————. "Racism, Education and the Mexican Community in Los Angeles, 1920–1930." *Societas* 4 (Autumn 1974): 287–301.

————. "Segregation of Mexican Children in a Southern California City: The Legacy of Expansionism and the American Southwest." *Western Historical Review* 16 (Jan. 1985): 55–76.

————. "Women, Work, and Community in the Mexican *Colonias* of the Southern California Citrus Belt." *California History* 74 (Spring 1995): 58–67.

González, Michael J. "'The Child of the Wilderness Weeps for the Father of Our Country': The Indian and the Politics of Church and State in Provincial California." *California History* 76 (Summer and Fall 1997): 147–72.

Greenleaf, Richard E. "The Inquisition in Eighteenth-Century New Mexico." *New Mexico Historical Review* 60 (Jan. 1985): 29–60.

Griswold del Castillo, Richard. "The 'Mexican Problem': A Critical View of the Alliance of Academics and Politicians during the Debate over Mexican Immigration in the 1920's." *The Borderlands Journal* 4 (Spring 1981): 251–72.

————. "Quantitative History in the Southwest: A Survey and Critique." *Western Historical Quarterly* (Oct. 1984): 407–26.

———. "*Tucsonenses and Angelenos*: A Socio-Economic Study of Two Mexican-American Barrios, 1860–1880." *Journal of the West* 18 (Jan. 1979): 58–65.

Guest, Francis F. "An Examination of the Thesis of S.F. Cook on the Forced Conversion of Indians in the California Missions." *Southern California Quarterly* 41 (Spring 1979): 1–77.

———. "An Inquiry into the Role of Discipline in California Mission Life." *Southern California Quarterly* 71 (Spring 1989): 1–68.

Gutíerrez, David G. "*Sin Fronteras?*: Chicanos, Mexican Americans, and the Emergence of the Contemporary Mexican Immigration Debate, 1968–1978." *Journal of American Ethnic History* 10 (Summer 1991): 5–37.

Gutíerrez, Ramón A. "Honor Ideology, Marriage Negotiation, and Class-Gender Domination in New Mexico, 1690–1848." *Latin American Perspectives* 12 (Winter 1985): 81–104.

Hall, G. Emlen. "Giant before the Surveyor-General: The Land Career of Donaciano Vigil." *Journal of the West* 19 (July 1980): 64–73.

———. "Juan Estevan Pino, 'Se Los Coma': New Mexico Land Speculation in the 1820s." *New Mexico Historical Review* 57 (Jan. 1982): 27–42.

———. "San Miguel del Bado and the Loss of the Common Lands of New Mexico Community Land Grants." *New Mexico Historical Review* 66 (Oct. 1991): 413–32.

Hall, G. Emlen, and David J. Weber. "Mexican Liberals and the Pueblo Indians, 1821–1829." *New Mexico Historical Review* 59 (Jan. 1984): 5–32.

Heizer, Robert. "Impact of Colonization on the Native California Societies." *Journal of San Diego History* 24 (Winter 1978): 121–39.

Hernández, Frances. "The Secret Jews of the Southwest." *Outlook* 63 (Fall 1992): 12–13, 30.

———. "The Secret Legacy of Christopher Columbus in the Southwest." *Password* 35 (Summer 1990): 55–70.

Hernández, Salomé. "No Settlement without Women: Three Spanish California Settlement Schemes, 1790–1800." *Southern California Quarterly* 72 (Fall 1990): 203–34.

Hinojosa, Gilberto Miguel. "Friars and Indians: Towards a Perspective of Cultural Interaction in the San Antonio Mission." *U.S. Catholic Historian* 9 (Spring 1990): 7–25.

Hughes, Charles. "The Decline of the Californios: The Case of San Diego, 1846–1856." *Journal of San Diego History* 21 (Summer 1975): 1–31.

Hurtado, Albert L. "Sexuality in California's Franciscan Missions: Cultural Perceptions and Sad Realities." *California History* 71 (Fall 1992): 370–85.

Jackson, Robert H. "Epidemic Disease and Population Decline in the Baja California Missions, 1697–1834." *Southern California Quarterly* 63 (Winter 1981): 308–46.

Jiménez, Andrés E. "The Political Formation of a Mexican Working Class in the Arizona Copper Industry, 1870–1917." *Review* 4 (Winter 1981): 536–69.

John, Elizabeth A. H. "Bernardo de Gálvez on the Apache Frontier: A Cautionary Note for Gringo Historians." *Journal of Arizona History* 29 (Winter 1988): 427–30.

———. "Crusading in the Hispanic Borderlands: An Essay Review." *Journal of the Southwest* 30 (Summer 1988): 190–99.

———. "Nurturing the Peace: Spanish and Comanche Cooperation in the Early Nineteenth Century." *New Mexico Historical Review* 59 (Oct. 1984): 345–69.

Kearney, Michael. "From the Invisible Hand to Visible Feet: Anthropological Studies of Migration and Development." *Annual Review of Anthropology* 15 (1986): 331–61.

Kelsey, Harry. "European Impact on the California Indian." *The Americas* 41 (Apr. 1985): 494–511.

———. "Finding the Way Home: Spanish Exploration of the Round-Trip Route across the Pacific Ocean." *Western Historical Quarterly* 17 (Apr. 1986): 145–64.

Kessell, John L. "Friars versus Bureaucrats: The Mission as a Threatened Institution on the

Arizona-Sonora Frontier, 1767–1842." *Western Historical Quarterly* 5 (Apr. 1974): 151–59.

Kiser, George. "Mexican American Labor before World War II." *Journal of Mexican American History* 2 (Spring 1972): 122–42.

Lamb, Blaine P. "The Convenient Villain: The Early Cinema Views the Mexican American." *Journal of the West* 12 (Apr. 1973): 75–81.

Langum, David J. "From Condemnation to Praise: Shifting Perspectives on Hispanic California." *California Historical Society Quarterly* 61 (Winter 1983): 282–90.

Larralde, Carlos. "J. T. Canales and the Texas Rangers." *The Journal of South Texas* 10 (1997): 38–68.

Larson, Robert. "The White Caps of New Mexico: A Study of Ethnic Militancy in the Southwest." *Pacific Historical Review* 44 (May 1975): 171–85.

Leal, Luis. "Américo Paredes and Modern Mexican American Scholarship." *Ethnic Affairs* 1 (Fall 1987): 1–11.

Lecompte, Janet. "Coronado and the Conquest." *New Mexico Historical Review* 64 (July 1989): 279–304.

———. "The Independent Women of Hispanic New Mexico, 1821–1846." *Western Historical Quarterly* 12 (Jan. 1981): 17–35.

———. "La Tules and the Americans." *Arizona and the West* 20 (Autumn 1978): 215–30.

———. "Manuel Armijo and the Americans." *Journal of the West* 19 (July 1980): 51–63.

Ledesma, Irene. "Texas Newspapers and Chicana Workers' Activism, 1919–1974." *Western Historical Quarterly* 26 (Autumn 1995): 309–31.

Limón, José. "El Primer Congreso Mexicanista de 1911: A Precursor to Contemporary Chicanismo." *Aztlán* 5 (Spring and Fall 1974): 85–117.

López, Manuel. "Patterns of Interethnic Residential Segregation in the Urban Southwest, 1960 and 1970." *Social Science Quarterly* 62 (Mar. 1981): 50–62.

López, Ronald. "The El Monte Berry Strike of 1933." *Aztlán* 1 (Spring 1970): 101–14.

Lotchin, Roger W., and David J. Weber. "The New Chicano Urban History: Two Perspectives." *The History Teacher* 16 (Feb. 1983): 219–47.

Machado, Manuel A., Jr. "Mexican Labor in the United States: The View from Mexican Cantinas." *Journal of the West* 25 (Apr. 1986): 59–64.

Madrid-Barela, Arturo. "In Search of the Authentic Pachuco." *Aztlán* 4 (Spring 1973): 31–60.

Magnaghi, Russell M. "Plains Indians in New Mexico: The Genízaro Experience." *Great Plains Quarterly* 10 (Spring 1990): 86–95.

Marín, Christine. "Mexican Americans on the Home Front: Community Organizations in Arizona during World War II." *Perspectives in Mexican American Studies* 4 (1993): 75–92.

———. "Rodolfo 'Corky' Gonzales: The Mexican-American Movement Spokesman, 1962–1972." *Journal of the West* 14 (Oct. 1975): 107–120.

Márquez, Benjamín. "The Politics of Race and Assimilation: The League of United Latin American Citizens, 1929–40." *Western Political Quarterly* 42 (June 1989): 355–75.

———. "The Politics of Race and Class: The League of United Latin American Citizens in the Post–World War II Period." *Social Science Quarterly* 68 (Mar. 1987): 85–101.

Martínez, Arthur D. "Los de Dodge City, Kansas: A Mexican-American Community in the Heartland of the United States." *Journal of the West* 24 (Apr. 1985): 88–95.

Martínez, Oscar J. "Chicanos and the Border Cities: An Interpretive Essay." *Pacific Historical Review* 46 (Feb. 1977): 85–106.

Mason, William Marvin. "Indian-Mexican Cultural Exchange in the Los Angeles Area, 1781–1834." *Aztlán* 15 (Spring 1984): 123–44.

McBride, James D. "Liga Protectora Latina: An Arizona Mexican-American Benevolent Society." *Journal of the West* 14 (Oct. 1975): 82–90.

McLemore, S. Dale. "The Origins of Mexican American Subordination in Texas." *Social Science Quarterly* 53 (Mar. 1973): 656–70.

Medeiros, Francine. "*La Opinión*, A Mexican Exile Newspaper: A Content Analysis of Its First Years, 1926–1929." *Aztlán* 11 (Spring 1980): 668–75.

Meier, Matt S. "Esteban Ochoa, Enterpriser." *Journal of the West* 25 (Jan. 1986): 15–21.

———. "'King Tiger': Reies López Tijerina." *Journal of the West* 27 (Apr. 1988): 60–68.

Meighan, Clement W. "Indians and California Missions." *Southern California Quarterly* 69 (Fall 1987): 187–201.

Mellinger, Phil. "'The Men Have Become Organizers': Labor Conflict and Unionization in the Mexican Mining Communities of Arizona, 1900–1915." *Western Historical Quarterly* 23 (Aug. 1992): 323–47.

Melville, Margarita B. "Mexican Women Adapt to Migration." *International Migration Review* 12 (1978): 225–35.

Meyer, Doris L. "Early Mexican-American Responses to Negative Stereotyping." *New Mexico Historical Review* 53 (Jan. 1978): 75–91.

Meyer, Edward H. "The Evolution of Culture and Tradition in Utah's Mexican-American Community." *Utah Historical Quarterly* 49 (Spring 1981): 133–44.

Miller, Darlis A. "Cross-Cultural Marriages in the Southwest: The New Mexico Experience, 1846–1900." *New Mexico Historical Review* 57 (Oct. 1982): 335–59.

———. "Hispanos and the Civil War in New Mexico: A Reconsideration." *New Mexico Historical Review* 54 (Apr. 1979): 105–23.

Miller, Thomas L. "Mexican-Texans in the Texas Revolution." *Journal of Mexican American History* 3 (1973): 105–30.

Miranda, Gloria E. "Gente de Razón Marriage Patterns in Spanish and Mexican California: A Case Study of Santa Barbara and Los Angeles." *Southern California Quarterly* 63 (Spring 1981): 1–21.

———. "Hispano-American Childrearing Practices in Pre-American Santa Barbara." *Southern California Quarterly* 65 (Winter 1983): 307–20.

———. "Racial and Cultural Dimensions in Gente de Razon Status in Spanish and Mexican California." *Southern California Quarterly* 70 (Fall 1988): 265–78.

Mohl, Raymond A. "*The Saturday Evening Post* and the 'Mexican Invasion.'" *Journal of Mexican American History* 3 (1973): 131–36.

Monroy, Douglas. "Anarquismo y Comunismo: Mexican Radicalism and the Communist Party in Los Angeles during the 1930s." *Labor History* 24 (Winter 1983): 34–59.

———. "The Creation and Re-creation of Californio Society." *California History* 76 (Summer and Fall 1997): 173–95.

———. "Like Swallows at the Old Mission: Mexicans and the Racial Politics of Growth in Los Angeles in the Interwar Period." *Western Historical Quarterly* 14 (Oct. 1983): 435–58.

Montoya, María E. "The Roots of Economic and Ethnic Divisions in Northern New Mexico: The Case of the Civilian Conservation Corps." *Western Historical Quarterly* 26 (Spring 1995): 15–34.

Moorhead, Max L. "The Spanish Deportation of Hostile Apaches: The Policy and the Practice." *Arizona and the West* 17 (Autumn 1975): 205–20.

Morrissey, Marietta. "Ethnic Stratification and the Study of the Chicanos." *Journal of Ethnic Studies* 10 (Winter 1983): 71–99.

Muñoz, Carlos, Jr. "The Politics of Protest and Chicano Liberation: A Case Study of Repression and Cooption." *Aztlán* 5 (Spring and Fall 1974): 119–42.

Muñoz, Carlos, Jr., and Mario Barrera. "La Raza Unida Party and the Chicano Student Movement in California." *Social Science Journal* 19 (Apr. 1982): 101–19.

Myres, Sandra L. "Mexican Americans and Westering Anglos: A Feminine Perspective." *New Mexico Historical Review* 57 (Oct. 1982): 317–33.

Navarro, Armando. "The Evolution of Chicano Politics." *Aztlán* 5 (Spring and Fall 1974): 57–84.

———. "The Post Mortem Politics of the Chicano Movement: 1975–1996." *Perspectives in Mexican American Studies* 6 (1997): 52–79.

Nelson-Cisneros, Victor B. "UCAPAWA and Chicanos in California: The Farm Worker Period, 1937–1940." *Aztlán* 7 (Fall 1976): 453–77.

———. "UCAPAWA Organizing Activities in Texas, 1935–50." *Aztlán* 9 (Spring, Summer, Fall 1978): 71–84.

Nixon-Méndez, Nina L. "Los Fundadores Urbanos (Urban Pioneers): The Hispanics of Dallas, 1850–1940." *Journal of the West* 32 (Oct. 1993): 76–82.

———. "Mexican-American Voluntary Associations in Omaha, Nebraska." *Journal of the West* 28 (July 1989): 73–85.

Nostrand, Richard L. "The Century of Hispano Expansion." *New Mexico Historical Review* 62 (Oct. 1987): 361–86.

Nuttall, Donald A. "Gaspar de Portolá: Disenchanted Conquistador of Spanish Upper California." *Southern California Quarterly* 53 (Sept. 1971): 185–98.

Officer, James. "Historical Factors in the Interethnic Relations in the Community of Tucson." *Arizoniana* 1 (Fall 1960): 12–16.

Officer, James, and Henry F. Dobyns. "Teodoro Ramírez, Early Citizen of Tucson." *Journal of Arizona History* 25 (Autumn 1984): 221–44.

Oppenheimer, Robert. "Acculturation or Assimilation: Mexican Immigrants in Kansas, 1900 to World War II." *Western Historical Quarterly* 16 (Oct. 1985): 429–48.

Pardo, Mary. "Mexican American Women Grassroots Community Activists: 'Mothers of East Los Angeles.'" *Frontiers* 11, no. 1 (1990): 1–7.

Paredes, Raymund A. "The Origins of Anti-Mexican Sentiment in the United States." *The New Scholar* 6 (1977): 139–65.

Peña, Manuel. "From Ranchero to Jaitón: Ethnicity and Class in Texas-Mexican Music (Two Styles in the Form of a Pair)." *Ethnomusicology* 29 (Winter 1985): 29–55.

Phillips, George Harwood. "Indians and the Breakdown of the Spanish Mission System in California." *Ethnohistory* 21 (Fall 1974): 291–302.

———. "Indians in Los Angeles, 1781–1875: Economic Integration, Social Disintegration." *Pacific Historical Review* 49 (Aug. 1980): 427–51.

Pichardo, Nelson A. "The Establishment and Development of Chicano Voluntary Associations in California, 1910–1930." *Aztlán* 19 (Fall 1988–1990): 93–155.

Powell, Philip Wayne. "Genesis of the Frontier Presidio in North America." *Western Historical Quarterly* 13 (Apr. 1982): 124–41.

Poyo, Gerald E., and Gilberto M. Hinojosa. "Spanish Texas and Borderlands Historiography in Transition: Implications for United States History." *Journal of American History* 75 (Sept. 1988): 393–416.

Pulido, Alberto L. "Are You an Emissary of Jesus Christ?: Justice, the Catholic Church, and the Chicano Movement." *Explorations in Ethnic Studies* 14 (Jan. 1991): 17–34.

———. "Mexican American Catholicism in the Southwest: The Transformation of a Popular Religion." *Perspectives in Mexican American Studies* 4 (1993): 93–108.

Quintana, Frances León. "Land, Water, and Pueblo-Hispanic Relations in Northern New Mexico." *Journal of the Southwest* 32 (Autumn 1990): 288–99.

Reisler, Mark. "Always the Laborer, Never the Citizen: Anglo Perceptions of the Mexican Immigrant during the 1920s." *Pacific Historical Review* 45 (May 1976): 231–54.

Remy, Caroline. "Hispanic-Mexican San Antonio: 1836–1861." *Southwestern Historical Quarterly* 71 (Apr. 1969): 564–70.

Richards, Susan V. "From Traders to Traitors? The Armijo Brothers through the Nineteenth Century." *New Mexico Historical Review* 69 (July 1994): 215–28.

Riley, Carroll L. "Early Spanish-Indian Communication in the Greater Southwest." *New Mexico Historical Review* 46 (Oct. 1971): 285–314.

Ríos-Bustamante, Antonio. "The Barrioization of Nineteenth-Century Mexican Californians: From Landowners to Laborers." *Masterkey* 60 (Summer/Fall 1986): 26–35.

————. "New Mexico in the Eighteenth Century: Life, Labor and Trade in the Villa de San Felipe de Albuquerque, 1706–1790." *Aztlán* 7 (Fall 1976): 357–90.

Rivera, George, Jr. "Social Change in the Barrio: The Chicano Movement in South Texas." *Aztlán* 3 (Fall 1972): 205–14.

Robinson, Cecil. "Flag of Illusion: The Texas Revolution Viewed as a Conflict of Cultures." *American West* 5 (May 1968): 10–17.

Robinson, Robin. "Accommodation to Domination: Demise of the Tejano Elite in the Lower Rio Grande." *The Journal of South Texas* 10 (1997): 69–87.

Romero, Mary, and Eric Margolis. "Tending the Beets: Campesinas and the Great Western Sugar Company." *Revista Mujeres* 2 (June 1985): 17–27.

Romo, Ricardo. "Responses to Mexican Immigration, 1910–1930." *Aztlán* 6 (Summer 1975): 173–91.

————. "The Urbanization of Southwestern Chicanos in the Early 20th Century." *The New Scholar* 6 (1977): 183–208.

————. "Work and Restlessness: Occupational and Spatial Mobility among Mexicans in Los Angeles, 1918–1928." *Pacific Historical Review* 46 (May 1977): 157–80.

Rosales, Francisco A. "Mexicanos in Indiana Harbor during the 1920s: From Prosperity to Depression." *Revista Chicano Requeña* 4 (1976): 88–98.

————. "Mexicans in Houston: The Struggle to Survive, 1908–1975." *Houston Review* 3 (Summer 1981): 224–48.

————. "Mexicans, Interethnic Violence, and Crime in the Chicago Area during the 1920s and 1930s: The Struggle to Achieve Ethnic Consciousness." *Perspectives in Mexican American Studies* 2 (1989): 59–97.

————. "The Regional Origins of Mexicano Immigrants to Chicago during the 1920s." *Aztlán* (Summer 1976): 187–202.

————. "Shifting Self-Perceptions and Ethnic Consciousness among Mexicans in Houston, 1908–1946." *Aztlán* 16 (1985): 71–94.

Rosales, Francisco A., and Daniel T. Simon. "Mexican Immigrant Experience in the Urban Midwest: East Chicago, Indiana, 1919–1945." *Indiana Magazine of History* 77 (Dec. 1981): 333–57.

Rose, Margaret. "Traditional and Nontraditional Patterns of Female Activism in the United Farm Workers of America, 1962–1980." *Frontiers* 11, no. 1 (1990): 26–32.

Rosen, Gerald. "The Development of the Chicano Movement in Los Angeles from 1967–1969." *Aztlán* 4 (Spring 1973): 155–83.

Rouse, Roger. "Mexican Migration and the Social Space of Postmodernism." *Diaspora* 1 (Spring 1991): 8–23.

Ruiz, Ramón Eduardo, and Mario T. García. "Conquest and Annexation." *New Scholar* 7 (1978): 237–54.

Ruiz, Vicki L. "California's Early Pioneers: Spanish/Mexican Women." *Social Science Review* 29 (Fall 1989): 24–30.

————. "A Promise Fulfilled: Mexican Cannery Workers in Southern California." *Pacific Historian* 30 (Summer 1986): 50–61.

Sánchez, Federico A. "Rancho Life in Alta California." *Masterkey* 60 (Summer/Fall 1986): 15–25.

Sandos, James A. "Junípero Serra's Canonization and the Historical Record." *American Historical Review* 93 (Dec. 1988): 1253–69.

————. "The Plan of San Diego: War and Diplomacy on the Texas Border, 1915–1916."

Arizona and the West 14 (Spring 1972): 5–24.

Sandoval, David A. "Gnats, Goods, and Greasers: Mexican Merchants on the Santa Fe Trail." *Journal of the West* 28 (Apr. 1989): 22–31.

San Miguel, Guadalupe, Jr. "Culture and Education in the American Southwest: Towards an Explanation of Chicano School Attendance, 1850–1940." *Journal of American Ethnic History* 7 (Spring 1988): 5–21.

Saragoza, Alex M. "The Significance of Recent Chicano-Related Historical Writings: An Appraisal." *Ethnic Affairs* 1 (Fall 1987): 24–62.

Schilz, Thomas Frank, and Donald E. Worcester. "Spread of Firearms among the Indian Tribes on the Northern Frontier of New Spain." *American Indian Quarterly* 11 (Winter 1987): 1–10.

Schlesinger, Andrew. "Las Gorras Blancas, 1889–1891." *Journal of Mexican American History* 1 (1971): 87–143.

Segura, Denise A., and Beatríz M. Pesquera. "Beyond Indifference and Antipathy: The Chicana Movement and Chicana Feminist Discourse." *Aztlán* 19 (Fall 1988–1990): 69–92.

Sepúlveda, Ciro H. "The Origins of Urban Colonias in the Midwest, 1910–1930." *Revista Chicano Riqueña* 4 (1976): 99–109.

Servín, Manuel Patricio. "California's Hispanic Heritage: A View into the Spanish Myth." *Journal of San Diego History* 19 (Winter 1973): 1–9.

———. "The Mexican-American Awakens—An Interpretation." *Journal of the West* 14 (Oct. 1975): 121–30.

———. "The Secularization of the California Missions: A Reappraisal." *Southern California Quarterly* 47 (June 1965): 133–49.

Servín, Manuel P., and Robert L. Spude. "Historical Conditions of Early Mexican Labor in the United States: Arizona—A Neglected Story." *Journal of Mexican American History* 5 (1975): 43–56.

Sheridan, Thomas E. "Peacock in the Parlor: Frontier Tucson's Mexican Elite." *Journal of Arizona History* 25 (Autumn 1984): 245–64.

Simmons, Marc. "Spanish Attempts to Open a New Mexico-Sonora Road." *Arizona and the West* 17 (Spring 1975): 5–20.

———. "Tlascalans in the Spanish Borderlands." *New Mexico Historical Review* 39 (Apr. 1964): 101–10.

Slatta, Richard W. "Chicanos in the Pacific Northwest: An Historical Overview of Oregon's Chicanos." *Aztlán* 6 (Fall 1975): 327–40.

Smith, Michael M. "The Aztlan Migrations of the Nahuatl Chronicles: Myth or History?" *Ethnohistory* 31 (1984): 153–86.

———. "Beyond the Borderlands: Mexican Labor in the Central Plains, 1900–1930." *Great Plains Quarterly* 1 (Fall 1981): 239–51.

———. "Mexicans in Kansas City: The First Generation, 1900–1920." *Perspectives in Mexican American Studies* 2 (1989): 29–57.

Sosa Riddell, Adaliza. "Chicanas and El Movimiento." *Aztlán* 5 (Spring and Fall 1974): 155–66.

Stoller, Marianne L. "Grants of Desperation, Lands of Speculation: Mexican Period Land Grants in Colorado." *Journal of the West* 19 (July 1980): 22–39.

Timmons, W. H. "The El Paso Area in the Mexican Period, 1821–1848." *Southwestern Historical Quarterly* 84 (July 1980): 1–28.

Tirado, Miguel David. "Mexican American Community Political Organization." *Aztlán* 1 (Spring 1970): 53–78.

Tjarks, Alicia V. "Comparative Demographic Analysis of Texas, 1777–1793." *Southwestern Historical Quarterly* 77 (Jan. 1974): 291–338.

———. "Demographic, Ethnic and Occupational Structure of New Mexico, 1790: The Census Report of 1790." *The Americas* 35 (July 1978): 45–88.

Torres, Lorenzo. "Short History of Chicano Workers." *Southwest Economy and Society* 3 (Winter 1977/1978): 4–17.

Treviño, Roberto R. "*Prensa y patria*: The Spanish-Language Press and the Biculturation of the Tejano Middle Class, 1920–1940." *Western Historical Quarterly* 22 (Nov. 1991): 451–72.

Trujillo, Larry. "Race, Class, Labor, and Community: A Local History of Capitalist Development." *Review* 4 (Winter 1981): 571–96.

Trulio, Beverly. "Anglo-American Attitudes toward New Mexican Women." *Journal of the West* 12 (Apr. 1973): 229–39.

Tyler, Daniel. "Anglo-American Penetration of the Southwest: The View from New Mexico." *Southwestern Historical Quarterly* 75 (Jan. 1972): 325–38.

———. "Gringo Views of Governor Manuel Armijo." *New Mexico Historical Review* 45 (Jan. 1970): 23–36.

———. "Mexican Indian Policy in New Mexico." *New Mexico Historical Review* 55 (Apr. 1980): 101–20.

Urrutia, Liliana. "An Offspring of Discontent: The Asociación Nacional México-Americana, 1949–1954." *Aztlán* 15 (Spring 1984): 177–84.

Valdés, Dennis Nodín. "Betabeleros: The Formation of an Agricultural Proletariat in the Midwest, 1877–1930." *Labor History* 30 (Fall 1989): 536–62.

———. "Machine Politics in California Agriculture, 1945–1990s." *Pacific Historical Review* 63 (May 1994): 203–24.

———. "Perspiring Capitalists: Latinos and the Henry Ford Service School, 1918–1928." *Aztlán* 12 (Autumn 1981): 227–40.

———. "Settlers, Sojourners, and Proletarians: Social Formation in the Great Plains Sugar Beet Industry, 1890–1940." *Great Plains Quarterly* 10 (Spring 1990): 110–23.

Vargas, Zaragoza. "Life and Community in the 'Wonderful City of the Magic Motor': Mexican Immigrants in 1920s Detroit." *Michigan Historical Review* 15 (Spring 1989): 47–68.

———. "Tejana Radical: Emma Tenayuca and the San Antonio Labor Movement during the Great Depression." *Pacific Historical Review* 66 (Nov. 1997): 553–80.

Vigil, Maurilio. "The Ethnic Organization as an Instrument of Political and Social Change: MALDEF, A Case Study." *Journal of Ethnic Studies* 18 (Spring 1990): 15–31.

Vigil, Ralph H. "Bartolomé de las Casas, Judge Alonso de Zorita, and the Franciscans: A Collaborative Effort for the Spiritual Conquest of the Borderlands." *The Americas* 38 (July 1981): 45–57.

———. "John Francis Bannon and the Historiography of the Spanish Borderlands: Retrospect and Prospect." *Journal of the Southwest* 29 (Winter 1987): 331–63.

——— "The New Borderlands History: A Critique." *New Mexico Historical Review* 48 (July 1973): 189–200.

———. "Spanish Exploration and the Great Plains in the Age of Discovery: Myth and Reality." *Great Plains Quarterly* 10 (Winter 1990): 3–17.

Weber, David J. "Here Rests Juan Espinoza: Toward a Clearer Look at the Image of the 'Indolent' Californios." *Western Historical Quarterly* 10 (Jan. 1979): 61–68.

———. "The Spanish Legacy in North America and the Historical Imagination." *Western Historical Quarterly* 23 (Feb. 1992): 5–24.

———. "Turner, the Boltonians, and the Borderlands." *American Historical Review* 91 (Feb. 1986): 66–81.

Weber, Devra Anne. "The Organization of Mexican Agricultural Workers: The Imperial Valley and Los Angeles, 1928–1934, An Oral History Approach." *Aztlán* 3 (Fall 1972): 307–47.

Wells, Miriam J. "Power Brokers and Ethnicity: The Rise of a Chicano Movement." *Aztlán* 17 (Spring 1986): 47–77.

Westphall, Victor. "Fraud and the Implications of Fraud in the Land Grants of New Mexico."

New Mexico Historical Review 69 (July 1974): 189–218.

Wollenberg, Charles. "Race and Class in Rural California: The El Monte Berry Strike of 1933." *California Historical Quarterly* 51 (Summer 1972): 155–64.

———. "Working on El Traque: The Pacific Electric Strike of 1903." *Pacific Historical Review* 42 (Aug. 1973): 358–69.

Worcester, Donald E. "The Significance of the Spanish Borderlands to the United States." *Western Historical Quarterly* 7 (Jan. 1976): 279–93.

Zamora, Emilio. "Chicano Socialist Labor Activity in Texas, 1900–1920." *Aztlán* 6 (Summer 1975): 221–36.

Zavella, Patricia. "'Abnormal Intimacy': The Varying Work Networks of Chicana Cannery Workers." *Feminist Studies* 11 (Fall 1985): 541–57.

DOCTORAL DISSERTATIONS

Abney-Guardado, Armando. "Chicano Intermarriage in the United States: A Sociological Analysis." University of Notre Dame, 1983.

Achor, Shirley Coolidge. "Of Thorns and Roses: Variations in Cultural Adaptations among Mexican Americans in an Urban Texas Barrio." Southern Methodist University, 1974.

Acuña, Rudolph Francis. "The Times of Ignacio Pesqueira: Sonora, Mexico, 1856–1876." University of Southern California, 1968.

Albro, Ward Sloan, III. "Ricardo Flores Magón and the Liberal Party: An Inquiry into the Origins of the Mexican Revolution of 1910." University of Arizona, 1967.

Allsup, Vernon Carl. "The American GI Forum: A History of a Mexican-American Organization." University of Texas, Austin, 1976.

Almaguer, Tomás. "Class, Race and Capitalist Development: The Social Transformation of a Southern California County, 1848–1903." University of California, Berkeley, 1979.

Alonso, Armando C. "*Tejano* Rancheros and Changes in Land Tenure, Hidalgo County, Texas, 1848–1900." Indiana University, 1994.

Alvarado, Rudolph Valier. "A History of Teatro in Lubbock Texas." Texas Tech University, 1995.

Ambrecht, Biliana María Cicin-Sain. "Politicization as a Legacy of the War on Poverty: A Study of Advisory Council Members in a Mexican-American Community." University of California, Los Angeles, 1973.

Apodaca, María Linda. "They Kept the Home Fires Burning: Mexican-American Women and Social Change." University of California, Irvine, 1994.

Archibald, Robert Reid. "The Economic Development of the Hispanic California Missions." University of New Mexico, 1975.

Arroyo, Luis L. "Industrial Unionism and the Los Angeles Furniture Industry, 1918–1945." University of California, Los Angeles, 1979.

Badillo, David A. "From South of the Border: Latino Experiences in Urban America." City University of New York, 1988.

Baker, Susan González. "Many Rivers to Cross: Mexican Immigrants, Women Workers, and the Structure of Labor Markets in the Urban Southwest." University of Texas, Austin, 1989.

Bakewell, Elizabeth Avery. "Picturing the Self: Mexican Identity and Artistic Representation, Post–1968." Brown University, 1991.

Balderrama, Francisco Enrique. "En Defensa de la Raza: The Los Angeles Mexican Consulate and Colonia Mexicana during the Great Depression." University of California, Los Angeles, 1978.

Barker, E. Shannon. "Los Tejanos de San Antonio: Mexican Immigrant Family Acculturation, 1880–1929." George Washington University, 1996.

Barton-Cayton, Amy Elizabeth. "A Woman's Resistance Is Never Done: The Case of Women Farm Workers in California." University of California, Santa Cruz, 1988.

Berge, Dennis. "Mexican Response to United States Expansion: 1841–1848." University of California, Berkeley, 1965.

Blevins, Audie Lee. "Rural to Urban Migration of Poor Anglos, Mexican Americans, and Negroes." University of Texas, Austin, 1970.

Borrego, John Gerald. "Capitalist Accumulation and Revolutionary Accumulation: The Context for Chicano Struggle." University of California, Berkeley, 1978.

Bouvier, Virginia Mayo. "Women, Conquest, and the Production of History: Hispanic California, 1542–1840." University of California, Berkeley, 1995.

Briegel, Kaye Lynn. "Alianza Hispano-Americana, 1894–1965: A Mexican American Fraternal Insurance Society." University of Southern California, 1974.

Brown, Jerald Barry. "The United Farm Workers Grape Strike and Boycott, 1965–1970: An Evaluation of the Culture of Poverty Theory." Cornell University, 1972.

Brune, Betty Jean. "Mexican-American and Anglo-American Attitudes toward Women: An Investigation of Traditionalism, Biculturalism, and Ethnicity." University of Texas, Austin, 1989.

Bustamante, Adrian H. "Los Hispanos: Ethnicity and Social Change in New Mexico." University of New Mexico, 1982.

Bustamante, Jorge Agustín. "Mexican Immigration and the Social Relations of Capitalism." University of Notre Dame, 1975.

Cabrera-Mereb, Claudine. "The Biocultural Profile of a Population at Risk in the U.S.-Mexican Border." University of Arizona, 1992.

Cadena, Gilbert Ramón. "Chicanos and the Catholic Church: Liberation Theology as a Form of Empowerment." University of California, Riverside, 1987.

Calderón, Roberto Ramón. "Mexican Politics in the American Era, 1846–1900: Laredo, Texas." University of California, Los Angeles, 1993.

Camarillo, Albert M. "The Making of a Chicano Community: A History of the Chicanos in Santa Barbara, California, 1850–1930." University of California, Los Angeles, 1975.

Cameron, Jack William. "The History of Mexican Public Education in Los Angeles, 1910–1930." University of Southern California, 1976.

Campa, Arthur León, Jr. "Ivory Towers and Ethnic Revival: Chicanos in Academe." University of Colorado, 1980.

Campbell, Howard L. "Bracero Migration and the Mexican Economy, 1951–1964." American University, 1972.

Cárdenas, Gilberto. "A Theoretical Approach to the Sociology of Mexican Labor Migration." University of Notre Dame, 1977.

Cárdenas de Dwyer, Carlota. "Chicano Literature, 1965–1975: The Flowering of the Southwest." State University of New York, Stony Brook, 1976.

Cardoso, Lawrence Anthony. "Mexican Emigration to the United States, 1900 to 1930: An Analysis of Socio-Economic Factors." University of Connecticut, 1974.

Casper, Ellen. "A Social History of Farm Labor in California with Special Emphasis on the United Farm Workers Union and California Rural Legal Assistance." New School for Social Research, 1984.

Cassidy, Joseph Eugene. "Life and Times of Pablo de la Guerra, 1819–1874." University of California, Santa Barbara, 1977.

Castañeda, Antonia I. "Presidarias y Pobladoras: The Journey North and Life in Frontier California, 1770–1821." Stanford University, 1990.

Castillo, Pedro. "The Making of a Mexican Barrio, 1890–1920." University of California, Santa Barbara, 1978.

Castillo Crimm, Ana Caroline. "Success in Adversity: The Mexican Americans of Victoria County, Texas, 1800–1880." University of Texas, Austin, 1994.

Chacón Gómez, Fernando. "The Intended and Actual Effects of Article VIII of the Treaty of Guadalupe Hidalgo: Mexican Treaty Rights under International and Domestic Law." University of Michigan, Ann Arbor, 1966.

Chandler, Charles Ray. "The Mexican-American Protest Movement in Texas." Tulane University, 1968.

Chávez, Ernesto. "Creating Aztlán: The Chicano Movement in Los Angeles, 1966–1978." University of California, Los Angeles, 1994.

Chavira, Alicia. "Women, Migration, and Health: Conditions and Strategies of a Mexican Migrant Population in the Midwest." University of California, Los Angeles, 1987.

Churchill, Charles Bradford. "Adventurers and Prophets: American Autobiographies in Mexican California, 1828–1847." University of California, Santa Barbara, 1989.

Ciuccio, Victor A. "Political Change in a Mexican-American Industrial Community." Pennsylvania State University, 1975.

Contréras, Raoul. "The Ideology of the Political Movement for Chicano Studies." University of California, Los Angeles, 1993.

Córdova, G. B. "Missionization and Hispanicization of Santo Tomás Apostal de Abiquiu, 1750–1770." University of New Mexico, 1979.

Craig, Richard B. "Interest Groups and the Foreign Policy Process: A Case Study of the Bracero Program." University of Missouri, Columbia, 1970.

Crampton, Helen Mickelsen. "Acculturation of the Mexican-American in Salt Lake County, Utah." University of Utah, 1967.

Crisp, James Ernest. "Anglo-Texan Attitudes toward the Mexican, 1821–1845." Yale University, 1976.

Cruz, Gilbert Ralph. "Spanish Town Patterns in the Borderlands: Municipal Origins in Texas and the Southwest, 1610–1810." St. Louis University, 1974.

Cuádraz, Gloria Holguin. "Meritocracy (Un)Challenged: The Making of a Chicano and Chicana Professoriate and Professional Class." University of California, Berkeley, 1993.

Davalos, Karen May. "Ethnic Identity among Mexican and Mexican-American Women in Chicago, 1920–1991." Yale University, 1993.

De Borhegyi-Forrest, Suzanne Sims. "The Preservation of the Village: The Origins and Implementation of New Mexico's Hispanic New Deal." University of Wyoming, 1986.

De la Teja, Jesús Francisco. "Land and Society in 18th Century San Antonio de Béxar: A Community on New Spain's Northern Frontier." University of Texas, Austin, 1988.

De la Torre, Adela. "Campesinos and the State: Control of the California Harvest Labor Market, 1950–1970." University of California, Berkeley, 1982.

De León, Arnoldo. "White Racial Attitudes toward Mexicanos in Texas, 1821–1900." Texas Christian University, 1974.

Deutsch, Sarah Jane. "Culture, Class, and Gender: Chicanas and Chicanos in Colorado and New Mexico, 1900–1940." Yale University, 1985.

Dickens, Edwin Larry. "The Political Role of the Mexican Americans in San Antonio." Texas Tech University, 1969.

Dieppa, Ismael. "The Zoot-Suit Riots Revisited: The Role of Private Philanthropy in Youth Problems of Mexican-Americans." University of Southern California, 1973.

Dimas, Pete Rey. "Progress and a Mexican-American Community's Struggle for Existence: Phoenix's Golden Gate Barrio." Arizona State University, 1991.

Domínguez, Majel Dean. "A Comparison of Mexican Americans and Non-Hispanic Whites in Higher Education in the Southwest." Arizona State University, 1979.

Donato, Rubén. "In Struggle: Mexican-Americans in the Pajaro Valley Schools, 1900–1979." Stanford University, 1987.

Downs, Fane. "The History of Mexicans in Texas, 1820–1845." Texas Tech University, 1970.

Dunbar, Roxanne Amanda. "Land Tenure in Northern New Mexico: An Historical Perspective." University of California, Los Angeles, 1974.

Erenburg, Mark Edward. "A Study of the Potential Relocation of Texas-Mexican Migratory Farm Workers to Wisconsin." University of Wisconsin, Madison, 1969.

Escobar, Edward Joseph. "Chicano Protest and the Law: Law Enforcement Responses to Mexican Activism in Los Angeles, 1850–1936." University of California, Riverside, 1983.

Espinoza, Dionne Elaine. "Pedogogies of Nationalism and Gender: Cultural Resistance in Selected Representational Practices of Chicana/o Movement Activists, 1967–1972." Cornell University, 1996.

Fineberg, Richard A. "Green Card Workers in Farm Labor Disputes: A Study of Post-Bracero Mexican National Farm Workers in the San Joaquin Valley." Claremont Graduate School, 1971.

Fireman, Janet Ruth. "Spain's Royal Corps of Engineers in the Western Borderlands, 1764–1815." University of New Mexico, 1972.

Flores, Estevan T. "Post-Bracero Undocumented Mexican Immigration to the United States and Political Recomposition." University of Texas, Austin, 1982.

Flores, Lisa Angela. "Shifting Visions: Intersections of Rhetorical and Chicana Feminist Theory in the Analysis of Mass Media." University of Georgia, 1994.

Flores, Yvette Gisele. "The Impact of Acculturation on the Chicano Family: An Analysis of Selected Variables." University of California, Berkeley, 1982.

Foley, Neil Francis. "The New South in the Southwest: Anglos, Blacks, and Mexicans in Central Texas, 1880–1930." University of Michigan, Ann Arbor, 1990.

Frank, Ross Harold. "From Settler to Citizen: Economic Development and Cultural Change in Late Colonial New Mexico, 1750–1820." University of California, Berkeley, 1992.

Fricke, Carl Henry, III. "Mexican Braceros in California Agriculture." University of California, Los Angeles, 1970.

Frisbie, William Parker. "Militancy among Mexican Americans: A Study of High School Students." University of North Carolina, 1972.

Gallegos, Bernardo P. "Literacy, Schooling, and Society in Colonial New Mexico: 1692–1821." University of New Mexico, 1988.

Gamboa, Erasmo. "Under the Thumb of Agriculture: Bracero and Mexican American Workers in the Pacific Northwest, 1940–1950." University of Washington, 1984.

García, Jorge. "Forjando Ciudad: The Development of a Chicano Political Community in East Los Angeles." University of California, Riverside, 1986.

García, Juan Ramón. "Operation Wetback: 1954." University of Notre Dame, 1977.

García, Mario T. "Obreros: The Mexican Workers of El Paso, 1900–1920." University of California, San Diego, 1975.

García, Richard Amado. "The Making of the Mexican-American Mind, San Antonio, Texas, 1929–1941: A Social and Intellectual History of an Ethnic Community." University of California, Irvine, 1980.

García y Griego, Larry Manuel. "The Bracero Policy Experiment: U.S.-Mexican Responses to Mexican Labor Migration, 1942–1955." University of California, Los Angeles, 1988.

Garcilazo, Jeffrey Marcos. "'Traqueros': Mexican Railroad Workers in the United States, 1870 to 1930." University of California, Santa Barbara, 1995.

Garner, Van Hastings. "Cultural Contact and Conflict in Late 17th Century New Mexico." University of California, Santa Barbara, 1972.

Garr, Daniel J. "Hispanic Colonial Settlement in California: Planning and Urban Development on the Frontier, 1769–1850." Cornell University, 1971.

Garza, Hisauro Alvarado. "Nationalism, Consciousness, and Social Change: Chicano Intellectuals in the United States." University of California, Berkeley, 1984.

Goldstein, Marcy. "Americanization and Mexicanization: The Mexican Elite and Mexican-Americans in the Gadsden Purchase Lands, 1853–1880." Case Western Reserve University, 1977.

BIBLIOGRAPHY ◄o►◄o►◄o►◄o►◄o►◄o►◄o►◄o►◄o►◄o►◄o►

306

Gómez-Quiñones, Juan. "Social Change and Intellectual Discontent: The Growth of Mexican Nationalism, 1890–1911." University of California, Los Angeles, 1972.

Gonzales, Juan L., Jr. "Social Mobility among Mexican-American Agricultural Workers in Northern California." University of California, Berkeley, 1980.

Gonzales, Phillip B. "A Perfect Furor of Indignation: The Racial Attitude Controversy of 1933." University of California, Berkeley, 1985.

González, Alfredo Guerra. "Mexicano/Chicano Gangs in Los Angeles: A Sociohistorical Case Study." University of California, Berkeley, 1981.

González, Deena J. "The Spanish-American Women of Santa Fe: Patterns of Their Resistance and Accommodation, 1820–1880." University of California, Berkeley, 1986.

González, Gilbert G. "The System of Public Education and Its Function within the Chicano Communities, 1920–1930." University of California, Los Angeles, 1974.

González, Michael J. "Searching for the Feathered Serpent: Exploring the Origins of Mexican Culture in Los Angeles, 1830–1850." University of California, Berkeley, 1993.

González, Rosalinda M. "Capital Accumulation and Mexican Immigration to the United States: A Comparative Historical Study of the Political Economy of International Labor Migrations." University of California, Irvine, 1981.

Griswold del Castillo, Richard. "La Raza Hispano Americana: The Emergence of an Urban Culture among the Spanish Speaking of Los Angeles." University of California, Los Angeles, 1974.

Guerin-Gonzales, Camille. "Cycles of Immigration and Repatriation: Mexican Farm Workers in California Industrial Agriculture, 1900–1940." University of California, Riverside, 1985.

Guerrero, Andrés Gonzales, Jr. "The Significance of Nuestra Señora de Guadalupe and La Raza Cósmica in the Development of a Chicano Theology of Liberation." Harvard University, 1984.

Gutiérrez, Armando George. "The Socialization of Militancy: Chicanos in a South Texas Town." University of Texas, Austin, 1974.

Gutiérrez, David G. "Ethnicity, Ideology, and Political Development: Mexican Immigration as a Political Issue in the Chicano Community, 1910–1977." Stanford University, 1988.

Gutiérrez, José Angel. "Toward a Theory of Community Organization in a Mexican American Community in South Texas." University of Texas, Austin, 1977.

Gutiérrez, Ramón. "Marriage, Sex, and the Family: Social Change in Colonial New Mexico, 1660–1846." University of Wisconsin, Madison, 1980.

Guzmán, Ralph Cortez. "The Political Socialization of the Mexican American People." University of California, Los Angeles, 1970.

Haas, Mary Lisbeth. "The Barrios of Santa Ana: Community, Class, and Organization." University of California, Irvine, 1985.

Hackel, Steven W. "Indian-Spanish Relations in Colonial California: Mission San Carlos Borromeo, 1770–1834." Cornell University, 1994.

Hansberger, Bernd. "Mining and Colonisation on the Northwest Frontier of New Spain: Aspects of the Economical and Social History of Sonora, 1640–1767." University of Vienna, 1990.

Haverluk, Terence William. "Mex-America: The Maintenance and Expansion of an American Cultural Region." University of Minnesota, 1993.

Hayes-Bautista, David E. "Latino Health Indicators and the Underclass Model: From Paradox to New Policy Models." University of California, Los Angeles, 1990.

Hernández, José A. "The Political Development of Mutual Aid Societies in the Mexican American Community: Ideals and Principles." University of California, Riverside, 1979.

Hernández, Philip Anthony. "The Other North Americans: The American Image of Mexico and Mexicans, 1550–1850." University of California, Berkeley, 1974.

Hernández-Fujigaki, Jorge. "Mexican Steelworkers and the United Steelworkers of America in the Midwest: The Inland Steel Experience (1836–1976)." University of Chicago, 1991.

Hernández Tovar, Inez. "Sara Estela Ramírez: The Early Twentieth Century Texas Mexican Poet." University of Houston, 1984.

Heyman, Josiah. "The Working People of the United States–Mexico Border in the Region of Northeastern Sonora, 1886–1936." City University of New York, 1988.

Hinojosa, Gilbert Miguel. "Settlers and Sojourners in the 'Chaparral': A Demographic Study of Borderlands in Transition." University of Texas, Austin, 1979.

Hoffman, Abraham. "The Repatriation of Mexican Nationals from the United States during the Great Depression." University of California, Los Angeles, 1970.

Hribar, Paul Anthony. "The Social Fasts of César Chávez: A Critical Study of Nonverbal Communication, Nonviolence, and Public Opinion." University of Southern California, 1978.

Huaco-Nuzum, Carmen Juana. "Mestiza Subjectivity: Representation and Spectatorship in Mexican and Hollywood Films." University of California, Santa Cruz, 1993.

Huginnie, Andrea Yvette. "'Strikitos': Race, Class, and Work in the Arizona Copper Industry, 1870–1920." Yale University, 1991.

Hurtado, Albert L. "Ranchos, Gold Mines and Rancherias: A Socioeconomic History of Indians and Whites in Northern California, 1821–1860." University of California, Santa Barbara, 1981.

Hurtado, Juan. "An Attitudinal Study of Social Distance between the Mexican American and the Church." United States International University, 1975.

Jones, Lamar Babington. "Mexican-American Labor Problems in Texas." University of Texas, Austin, 1965.

Jungmeyer, Robert L. "The Bracero Program, 1942–1951: Mexican Contract Labor in the United States." University of Missouri, Columbia, 1988.

Kane, Tim D. "The Effect of Labor Market Change upon the Employment of Low Income Mexican Americans: The San Antonio Experience." University of Texas, Austin, 1972.

Keefe, Susan Elaine. "Women in Power: Anglo and Mexican-American Female Leaders in Two Southern California Communities." University of California, Santa Barbara, 1974.

Kenner, Charles L. "A History of New Mexican–Plains Indian Relations." Texas Tech University, 1966.

Kenneson, Susan Reyner. "Through the Looking-Glass: A History of Anglo-American Attitudes toward the Spanish-Americans and Indians of New Mexico." Yale University, 1978.

Kerr, Louise Año Nuevo de. "The Chicano Experience in Chicago: 1920–1970." University of Illinois, Chicago Circle, 1976.

Kirstein, Peter Neil. "Anglo over Bracero: A History of the Mexican Worker in the United States from Roosevelt to Nixon." St. Louis University, 1973.

Kiser, George C. "The Bracero Program: A Case Study of Its Development, Termination, and Political Aftermath." University of Massachusetts, 1974.

Kurtz, Donald V. "Politics, Ethnicity, Integration: Mexican-Americans in the War on Poverty." University of California, Davis, 1970.

Laird, Judith Fincher. "Argentine, Kansas: The Evolution of a Mexican- American Community, 1905–1940." University of Kansas, 1975.

Landolt, Robert G. "The Mexican-American Workers of San Antonio, Texas." University of Texas, Austin, 1965.

Lane, John Hart, Jr. "Voluntary Associations among Mexican Americans in San Antonio, Texas: Organization and Leadership Characteristics." University of Texas, Austin, 1968.

Larralde, Carlos Montalvo. "Chicano Jews in South Texas." University of California, Los Angeles, 1978.

BIBLIOGRAPHY ◄o►◄o►◄o►◄o►◄o►◄o►◄o►◄o►◄o►◄o►◄o►

308

Leal, Ray Robert. "The 1966–1967 South Texas Farm Workers Strike." Indiana University, 1983.

Ledesma, Irene. "Unlikely Strikers: Mexican-American Women in Strike Activity in Texas, 1919–1974." Ohio State University, 1992.

Loza, Stephen Joseph. "The Musical Life of the Mexican/Chicano People in Los Angeles, 1945–1985: A Study in Maintenance, Change, and Adaptation." University of California, Los Angeles, 1985.

Lugo, Alejandro. "Fragmented Lives, Assembled Goods: A Study in Maquilas, Culture, and History at the Mexican Borderlands." Stanford University, 1995.

Luján, Joe Roy. "Dennis Chavez and the Roosevelt Era, 1933–1945." University of New Mexico, 1987.

Maciel, David. "Ignacio Ramírez, ideologo del liberalismo social en Mexico." University of California, Santa Barbara, 1978.

Maldonado, Carlos Saldívar. "'The Longest Running Death in History': A History of Colegio Cesar Chavez, 1973–1983." University of Oregon, 1986.

Mantovina, Timothy Matthew. "San Antonio Tejanos, 1821–1860: A Study of Religion and Ethnicity." Catholic University of America, 1993.

Marín, Eugene Acosta. "The Mexican-American Community and Leadership of the Dominant Society in Arizona: A Study of Their Mutual Attitudes and Perceptions." United States International University, 1973.

Marín, Marguerite. "Protest in an Urban Barrio: A Study of the Chicano Movement." University of California, Santa Barbara, 1980.

Mariscal, Jorge O. "The Economics of International Migration: Mexican Undocumented Migrants in the U.S." New York University, 1986.

Márquez, Benjamin. "Power and Politics in a Chicano Barrio." University of Wisconsin, Madison, 1983.

Martínez, Camilo Amado, Jr. "The Mexican and Mexican-American Laborers in the Lower Rio Grande Valley of Texas, 1870–1930." Texas A&M University, 1987.

Martínez, Fredda Gregg. "Familism in Acculturated Mexican Americans: Patterns, Changes, and Perceived Impact on Adjustment to U.S. Society." Northern Arizona University, 1992.

Martínez, María Zuñiga de. "Los Ancianos: A Study of the Attitudes of Mexican Americans Regarding Support of the Elderly." Brandeis University, 1979.

Martínez, Oscar J. "Border Boom Town: Ciudad Juárez since 1880." University of California, Los Angeles, 1975.

Martínez, Rubén Orlando. "A Conceptual Approach to Chicano Labor History." University of California, Riverside, 1984.

Martínez Saldaña, Jesús. "At the Periphery of Democracy: The Binational Politics of Mexican Immigrants in Silicon Valley." University of California, Berkeley, 1993.

Mata, Alberto Guardiola. "The Drug Street Scene: An Ethnographic Study of Mexican Youth in South Chicago." University of Notre Dame, 1978.

Matthiasson, Carolyn W. "Acculturation of Mexican-Americans in a Midwestern City." Cornell University, 1968.

McClain, Johnny Mac. "Contract Labor as a Factor in the United States–Mexican Relations, 1942–1947." University of Texas, Austin, 1970.

McKay, R. Reynolds. "Texas Mexican Repatriation during the Great Depression." University of Oklahoma, 1982.

McReynolds, James Michael. "Family Life in a Borderland Community: Nacogdoches, Texas, 1779–1861." Texas Tech University, 1978.

Mellinger, Philip. "The Beginnings of Modern Industrial Unionism in the Southwest: Labor Trouble among Unskilled Copper Workers, 1903–1917." University of Chicago, 1978.

Menchaca, Martha. "Chicano-Mexican Conflict and Cohesion in San Pablo, California." Stanford University, 1987.

Minge, Ward Alan. "Frontier Problems in New Mexico Preceding the Mexican War, 1840–1846." University of New Mexico, 1965.

Miranda, Gloria Elizarraras. "Family Patterns in the Social Order in Hispanic Santa Barbara, 1784–1848." University of Southern California, 1979.

Miranda, Porfirio J. "Perceptions of Locus of Control among Multi-Generation Chicano/Mexican Families." University of California, Los Angeles, 1978.

Mitchell, Robert Joseph. "Peace in the Fields: A Study of the Passage and Subsequent History of the California Agricultural Labor Relations Act of 1975." University of California, Riverside, 1980.

Monroy, Douglas Guy. "Mexicanos in Los Angeles: An Ethnic Group in Relation to Class Forces, 1930–1941." University of California, Los Angeles, 1978.

Montejano, David. "A Journey through Mexican Texas, 1900–1930: The Making of a Segregated Society." Yale University, 1982.

Montgomery, Charles H. "History As Culture: The Making of Spanish Heritage in New Mexico, 1883–1940." Cornell University, 1995.

Montoya, María Elaine. "Dispossessed People: Settler Resistance on the Maxwell Land Grant, 1860–1901." Yale University, 1993.

Monzón, Mauricio. "Social Upheaval in World War II: Zoot-Suiters and Servicemen in Los Angeles, 1943." University of California, Los Angeles, 1976.

Mora, Joshua Al. "Man's Inhumanity to Man: Justice and Injustice in Three Mexican-American Playwrights." Texas Tech University, 1994.

Morales, Armando. "A Study of Mexican-American Perceptions of Law Enforcement Policies and Practices in East Los Angeles." University of Southern California, 1972.

Moreno, Daniel Thomas. "Social Equality and Industrialization: A Case Study of Colorado Beet Sugar Industry." University of California, Irvine, 1981.

Mosqueda, Lawrence Joseph. "Chicanos, Catholicism, and Political Ideology." University of Washington, 1979.

Muñoz, Carlos. "The Politics of Chicano Urban Protest: A Model of Political Analysis." Claremont Graduate School, 1972.

Murillo, Christopher Louis. "The Detroit Mexican 'Colonia' from 1920 to 1932: Implications for Social and Educational Policy." Michigan State University, 1981.

Navarro, Armando. "El Partido de La Raza Unida in Crystal City: A Peaceful Revolution." University of California, Riverside, 1974.

Neri, Michael. "Hispanic Catholicism in Transitional California: The Life of José González Rubio." Graduate Theological Union, Berkeley, 1974.

Nostrand, Richard Lee. "The Hispanic-American Borderland: A Regional Historical Geography." University of California, Los Angeles, 1968.

O'Brien, William Patrick. "Independence, Missouri's Trade with Mexico, 1827–1860: A Study in International Consensus and Cooperation." University of Colorado, 1994.

Orozco, Cynthia E. "The Origins of the League of United Latin American Citizens (LULAC) and the Mexican American Civil Rights Movement in Texas with an Analysis of Women's Political Participation in a Gendered Context, 1910–1929." University of California, Los Angeles, 1992.

Pagán, Eduardo Obregón. "Sleepy Lagoon: The Politics of Youth and Race in Wartime Los Angeles, 1940–1945." Princeton University, 1996.

Palmer, Susan L. "Building Ethnic Communities in a Small City: Roumanians and Mexicans in Aurora, Illinois, 1900–1940." Northern Illinois University, 1986.

Pardo, Mary Santoli. "Identity and Resistance: Mexican American Women and Grassroots Activism in Two Los Angeles Communities." University of California, Los Angeles, 1990.

Paredes, Raymund Arthur. "The Image of the Mexican in American Literature." University of Texas, Austin, 1973.

Peña, Devon G. "The Class Politics of Abstract Labor: Organizational Form and Industrial Relations in the Mexican Maquiladoras." University of Texas, Austin, 1983.

Peña, Manuel Heriberto. "The Emergence of Texas-Mexican Conjunto Music, 1935–1960: An Interpretive History." University of Texas, Austin, 1987.

Pesquera, Beatríz Margarita. "Work and Family: A Comparative Analysis of Professional, Clerical and Blue-Collar Chicana Workers." University of California, Berkeley, 1985.

Prichard, Nancy Lee. "Paradise Found? Opportunities for Mexican, Irish, Italian and Chinese Born Individuals in the Jerome Copper Mining District, 1890–1910." University of Colorado, 1992.

Privett, Stephan A., S.J. "Robert E. Lucey: Evangelization and Cathesis among Hispanic Catholics." Catholic University of America, 1985.

Pubols, Helen Louise. "The Casa De La Guerra: Family and Community in Nineteenth Century Santa Barbara." University of California, Santa Barbara, 1991.

Pulido, Alberto López. "Race Relations within the American Catholic Church: An Historical and Sociological Analysis of Mexican-American Catholics." University of Notre Dame, 1989.

Pycior, Julie Leininger. "La Raza Organizes: Mexican American Life in San Antonio, 1915–1930: As Reflected in Mutualista Activities." University of Notre Dame, 1979.

Quiñones, Naomi Helena. "Hijas de la Malinche (Malinche's Daughters): The Development of Social Agency among Mexican American Women and the Emergence of First Wave Chicana Cultural Production." Claremont Graduate School, 1996.

Radding, Cynthia. "Ethnicity and the Emerging Peasant Class of Northwestern New Spain, 1760–1840." University of California, San Diego, 1990.

Ramírez, Elizabeth Cantú. "A History of Mexican American Professional Theatre in Texas: 1875–1935." University of Texas, Austin, 1982.

Ramírez, Nora Ethel. "The Vaquero and Ranching in the Southwestern United States, 1600–1970." Indiana University, 1979.

Ramos, Juan. "Spanish-Speaking Leadership in Two Southwestern Cities: A Descriptive Study." Brandeis University, 1968.

Reccow, Louis. "The Orange County Citrus Strikes of 1935–1936: The Forgotten People in Revolt." University of Southern California, 1971.

Reich, Alice Higman. "The Cultural Production of Ethnicity: Chicanos in the University." University of Colorado, 1977.

Reisler, Mark. "Passing through Our Egypt: Mexican Labor in the United States, 1900–1940." Cornell University, 1973.

Remy, Martha Caroline Mitchell. "Protestant Churches and Mexican-Americans in South Texas." University of Texas, Austin, 1970.

Rentería, Tamis Hoover. "The Culture of Mexican-American Professionals Today: Legacy of the Chicano Movement." Stanford University, 1992.

Riddell, Adaljiza Sosa. "Who Cares Who Governs? An Historical Analysis of Local Governing Elites in Mexicali, Mexico." University of California, Riverside, 1974.

Riley, John Denny. "Santos Benvides: His Influence on the Lower Rio Grande, 1823–1891." Texas Christian University, 1976.

Ríos-Bustamante, Antonio. "Los Angeles, Pueblo and Region, 1781–1850: Continuity and Adaptation on the North Mexican Periphery." University of California, Los Angeles, 1985.

Rivera, Fred George. "El Barrio: A Sociological Study of Acculturation in a Mexican American Community." State University of New York, Buffalo, 1971.

Roberts, Donovan O. "Theory and Practice in the Life and Thought of César E. Chávez: Implications for a Social Ethic." Boston University, 1979.

Rocha, Rodolfo. "The Influence of the Mexican Revolution on the Mexico-Texas Border, 1910–1916." Texas Tech University, 1981.

Rodríguez, Julia Curry. "Reconceptualizing Undocumented Labor Immigration: The Causes, Impact and Consequences in Mexican Women's Lives." University of Texas, Austin, 1988.

Romero, Yolanda García. "The Mexican American Frontier Experience in Twentieth Century Northwest Texas." Texas Tech University, 1993.

Romo, Ricardo. "Mexican Workers in the City: Los Angeles, 1915–1930." University of California, Los Angeles, 1975.

Rosales, Francisco A. "Mexican Immigration to the Urban Midwest during the 1920s." Indiana University, 1978.

Rosales, Rodolfo. "The Rise of Chicano Middle Class Politics in San Antonio, 1951–1985." University of Michigan, Ann Arbor, 1991.

Rose, Margaret. "Women in the United Farm Workers: A Case Study of Chicana and Mexicana Participation in a Labor Union." University of California, Los Angeles, 1988.

Rosen, Gerald Paul. "Political Activity and the Chicano Movement: A Study of the Political Ideology of Activists in the Chicano Movement." University of California, Los Angeles, 1972.

Rosenbaum, Robert J. "Mexicano versus Americano: A Study of Hispanic-American Resistance to Anglo-Americano Control in New Mexico Territory, 1870–1900." University of Texas, Austin, 1972.

Rouse, Roger. "Mexican Migration to the United States: Family Relations in the Development of a Transnational Migrant Circuit." Stanford University, 1989.

Rubalcava, Luis Alberto. "Assimilation among Urban Chicanos: A Structural and Cultural Analysis." University of Michigan, Ann Arbor, 1980.

Ruiz, Vicki. "UCAPAWA, Chicanos and the Chicano Food Processing Industry, 1937–1950." Stanford University, 1982.

Rynearson, Ann M. "Hiding within the Melting Pot: Mexican Americans in St. Louis." Washington University, 1980.

Salinas, Susan Mary. "The Effect of Domestic Values on Marriage between Anglos and Hispanics." University of Texas, Arlington, 1986.

San Miguel, Guadalupe, Jr. "Endless Pursuits: The Chicano Educational Experience in Corpus Christi, Texas, 1880–1960." Stanford University, 1979.

Sánchez, Federico Alberto. "Antonio F. Coronel, a Californio and a Ranchero." University of Southern California, 1983.

Sánchez, George J. "Becoming Mexican American: Ethnicity and Acculturation in Chicano Los Angeles, 1900–1943." Stanford University, 1989.

Sánchez, Joseph Patrick. "The Catalonian Volunteers and the Defense of Northern New Spain, 1767–1803." University of New Mexico, 1974.

Sandos, James A. "The United States and the Mexican Revolution, 1915–1917: The Impact of Culture Conflict in the Tamaulipas-Texas Frontier upon the Emergence of Revolutionary Government in Mexico." University of California, Berkeley, 1978.

Sandoval, David Alex. "Trade and the 'Manito' Society in New Mexico, 1821–1848." University of Utah, 1978.

Santillán, Richard Anthony. "The Politics of Cultural Nationalism: El Partido De La Raza Unida in Southern California: 1969–1978." Claremont Graduate School, 1978.

Saragoza, Alexander M. "The Formation of a Mexican Elite: Industrialization of Monterrey, Nuevo Leon, 1880–1920." University of California, San Diego, 1978.

Scott, Robin Fitzgerald. "The Mexican American in the Los Angeles Area, 1910–1950: From Acquiescence to Activity." University of Southern California, 1971.

Sedeno, Michael Victor. "Chicanismo in Selected Poetry from the Chicano Movement, 1969–1972: A Rhetorical Study." University of Southern California, 1980.

Sego, Eugene B. "Six Tlaxcalan Colonies on New Spain's Northern Frontier: A Comparison of Success and Failure." Indiana University, 1990.

Segura, Denise Anne. "Chicanas and Mexican Immigrant Women in the Labor Market: A Study of Occupational Mobility and Stratification." University of California, Berkeley, 1986.

Sepúlveda, Ciro. "La Colonia del Harbor: A History of Mexicanos in East Chicago, Indiana, 1919–1932." University of Notre Dame, 1976.

Shaw, Jimmy Lee. "Gramsci's Theory of Hegemony and the United Farm Workers: An Empirical Case Study." University of Kansas, 1983.

Shockley, John Staples. "Crystal City, Texas: Mexican-Americans and Political Change." University of Wisconsin, Madison, 1972.

Sierra, Christine Marie. "The Political Transformation of a Minority Organization: The Council of La Raza, 1965–1980." Stanford University, 1983.

Simmons, Marc Steven. "Spanish Government in New Mexico at the End of the Colonial Period." University of New Mexico, 1965.

Smith, Walter E. "Mexican Resistance to Schooled Ethnicity: Ethnic Student Power in South Texas, 1930–1970." University of Texas, Austin, 1978.

Solache, Saúl. "Urban Growth Patterns and Mexican Immigration to the United States, 1790 to 1970." University of California, Los Angeles, 1981.

Soldatenko, María Angelina. "The Everyday Lives of Latina Garment Workers in Los Angeles: The Convergence of Gender, Race, Class, and Immigration." University of California, Los Angeles, 1992.

Sosa, Luis Roberto. "An Analysis of Chicano Organizations and Their Leaders." University of California, Berkeley, 1982.

Soto, Antonio Robert. "The Chicano and the Church in Northern California, 1848–1978: A Study of an Ethnic Minority within the Roman Catholic Church." University of California, Berkeley, 1978.

Street, Richard Steven. "'We Are Not Slaves': A History of California Farmworkers, 1769–1869—The Formative Years." University of Wisconsin, Madison, 1995.

Sunseri, Alvin R. "New Mexico in the Aftermath of the Anglo-American Conquest, 1846–1861." Louisiana State University, 1973.

Swadesh, Frances León. "Hispanic Americans of the Ute Frontier from the Chama Valley to the San Juan Basin, 1694–1960." University of Colorado, 1966.

Taylor, Jacqueline Jo Ann. "Ethnic Identity and Upward Mobility of Mexican Americans in Tucson." University of Arizona, 1973.

Tijerina, Andrés A. "Tejanos and Texas: The Native Mexicans of Texas, 1820–1850." University of Texas, Austin, 1977.

Tirado, Miguel David. "The Mexican American's Participation in Voluntary Political Associations." Claremont Graduate School, 1970.

Titscomb, Mary Ruth. "Americanization and Mexicans in the Southwest: A History of Phoenix's Friendly House, 1920–1983." University of California, Santa Barbara, 1984.

Treviño, Roberto R. "La fe: Catholicism and Mexican Americans in Houston, 1911–1972." Stanford University, 1993.

Trujillo, Armando J. "Community Empowerment and Bilingual/Bicultural Education: A Study of the Movimiento in a South Texas Community." University of Texas, Austin, 1993.

Trujillo, Larry Dean. "The Quest for Chicano Community Control: A Case Study." University of California, Berkeley, 1978.

Turpen, Twila Faye. "Cohesion, Inequality, and Interethnic Conflict in Territorial New Mexico." University of New Mexico, 1987.

Tyler, Daniel. "New Mexico in the 1820's: The First Administration of Manuel Armijo." University of New Mexico, 1970.

Van Handel, Robert Michael. "The Jesuit and Franciscan Missions in Baja California." University of California, Santa Barbara, 1991.

Van Ness, John R. "Hispanos in Northern New Mexico: The Development of Corporate Community and Multicommunity." University of Pennsylvania, 1979.

Vargas, Zaragoza. "Mexican Auto Workers at Ford Motor Company, 1918–1933." University of Michigan, Ann Arbor, 1984.

Vega, Manuel de Jesús. "El Teatro Campesino Chicano y la vanguardia teatral: 1965–1975." Middlebury College, 1983.

Veloz, Josefina Estrada. "Chicana Identity: Gender and Ethnicity." New Mexico State University, 1981.

Villar, María de Lourdes. "From Sojourners to Settlers: The Experience of Mexican Undocumented Migrants in Chicago." Indiana University, 1989.

Walker, Randi Jones. "Protestantism in the Sangre de Cristos: Factors in the Growth and Decline of the Hispanic Protestant Churches in New Mexico and Southern Colorado, 1850–1920." Claremont Graduate School, 1983.

Walsh, Jane MacLaren. "Myth and Imagination in the American Story: The Coronado Expedition, 1540–1542." Catholic University of America, 1993.

Weber, David Stafford. "Anglo Views of Mexican Immigrants: Popular Perceptions and Neighborhood Realities in Chicago, 1900–1940." Ohio State University, 1982.

Weber, Devra Anne. "The Struggle for Stability and Control in the Cotton Fields of California: Class Relations in Agriculture, 1919–1942." University of California, Los Angeles, 1986.

Webster, Michael G. "Texan Manifest Destiny and the Mexican Border Conflict." Indiana University, 1972.

Williams, Brett. "The Trip Takes Us: Chicano Migrants on the Prairie." University of Illinois, Urbana-Champaign, 1975.

Wilson, Tamar Diana. "Vamos Para Buscar La Vida: A Comparison of Patterns of Outmigration from a Rancho in Jalisco and Immigration to a Mexicali Squatter Settlement." University of California, Los Angeles, 1992.

Winn, Charles Carr. "Mexican Americans in the Texas Labor Movement." Texas Christian University, 1972.

Yáñez-Cávez, Aníbal, "Development and Crisis: Geographical Industrialization in Coahuila and Mexico-U.S. Economic Integration." University of California, Berkeley, 1994.

Ybarra, Leonarda. "Conjugal Role Relationships in the Chicano Family." University of California, Berkeley, 1972.

Zamora, Emilio. "Mexican Labor Activity in South Texas, 1900–1929." University of Texas, Austin, 1983.

Zarrugh, Laura Hoffman. "Gente de mi Tierra: Mexican Village Migrants in a California Community." University of California, Berkeley, 1973.

Zavella, Patricia. "Women, Work and Family in the Chicano Community: Cannery Workers in the Santa Clara Valley." University of California, Berkeley, 1982.

Zinn, Maxine Baca. "Marital Roles, Marital Power and Ethnicity: A Study of Changing Families." University of Oregon, 1978.

INDEX

◄(O)► ◄(O)► ◄(O)►

MANUEL G. GONZALES is a professor of History at Diablo Valley College. A specialist in both Modern Europe and the American Southwest, he has been teaching the history of Mexicans in the United States for the past twenty-five years. Dr. Gonzales has been a visiting professor of Chicano history in the Ethnic Studies department at the University of California, Berkeley. His publications include *Andrea Costa and the Rise of Socialism in the Romagna* and *The Hispanic Elite of the Southwest.*

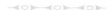